The Ultimate EU Career Development Book Edition 2.0

For the full range of our books on EU careers and institutions, visit **www.johnharperpublishing.co.uk**

The Ultimate EU Career Development Book

Edition 2.0

by

Jan De Sutter

JOHN HARPER PUBLISHING

The Ultimate EU Career Development Book 2.0
ISBN: 978-1-8380898-6-3

Published by John Harper Publishing, London
www.johnharperpublishing.co.uk

Typeset mainly in 9 & 10/11pt Palatino.
Printed and bound in the UK by Severn, Gloucester

TABLE OF CONTENTS

ABOUT THE AUTHOR

After a career in IT, defence systems and people management, Jan De Sutter joined the European Economic and Social Committee in 2000, where he was Head of Unit of the budget and finance department. While at the EESC Jan served on EPSO Selection Boards and was president of a Selection Board for IT specialists. Since 2013 Jan has worked as an independent entrepreneur and coach, focusing on personalised coaching and preparation for the EPSO Assessment Centre and other aspects of career development in the EU administration. He is happy to share his knowledge and experience in this book – and in person through individual face-to-face coaching or classroom training. Jan's full biography can be found on LinkedIn at https://be.linkedin.com/in/jandesutter

ACKNOWLEDGEMENTS

Of course, a book with this ambition cannot be put together by just one man. I consulted many of my former colleagues, most of them now high-ranking EU officials, with a vast experience in the EU realm. All of them preferred to stay anonymous but, when reading this book, they will recognise their contribution, and I thank them for that.

I also wish to address a special word of gratitude to my publisher, John Harper, for believing in this project and for all the editorial work. A special mention to for James Scott-Faulkner, the webmaster of John Harper Publishing who did a good job in debugging and deploying the app accompanying this book.

It is customary – but no less true – to add that the final responsibility on all issues of fact, interpretation and balance is mine alone. When it comes to the challenges of personal development tackled in this book, there is rarely a definitive 'right' or 'wrong' approach: each individual is different, and each situation has its nuances. I will warmly welcome any feedback that reflects on such nuances.

Jan De Sutter
Brussels
November 2021
jandesutter9@gmail.com

INTRODUCTION

According to Universum[1], in 2020 the EU was the number one 'attractive employer' in Belgium for law students, and number two for students in humanities, liberal arts and education. For business students, the EU still occupies an honourable eighth place. Not surprisingly, more than 50,000 candidates present themselves for the European Personnel Selection Office (EPSO) competitions every year, but only around 2% are recruited. The quality of the output of the selection process determines the quality of recruited officials, who often spend their whole careers in the EU institutions. People who work for the EU are amongst Europe's finest – and they are proud of it.

The EU is a unique mix of politics, diplomacy and administration, directly impacting the lives of millions of Europeans and with a significant influence on the rest of the world. Broadly speaking, the 'EU system' can be seen as three overlaid layers as depicted below:

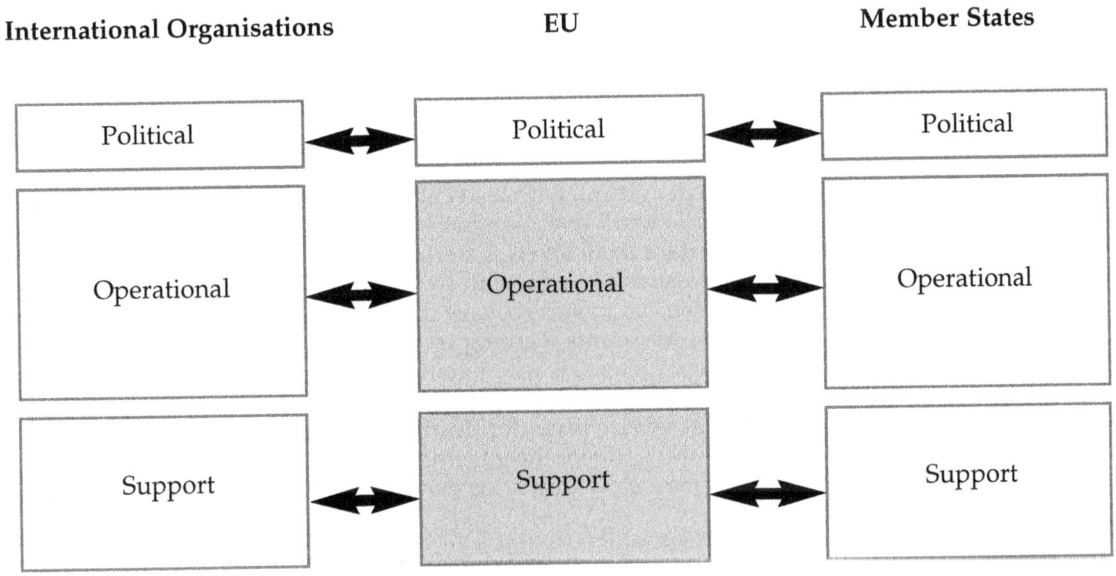

Strategic decisions are negotiated, and positions are taken by the 'Political' layer. This level is reinforced by the 'Operational' layer. In turn, the 'Support' layer manages the financial, human, and material resources needed by the entire system.

Each layer interacts with its counterparts in the same layer of the Member States and international organisations (UN, OECD, NGOs, World Bank, …) or non-EU countries or associations (US, China, Russia, EFTA, African Union, …).

This is not a book about politics. In this book, I am only going to talk about the 'EU administration' – represented by the greyed areas in the diagram – and the people working for this administration.

Who is this book for?

This book is for all EU staff, at all levels, permanent, temporary or contract agents – and indeed anyone with ambitions to work in the European administration.

1 https://www.universumglobal.com/rankings/company/european-commission/

As a former EU official, having served on EPSO selection boards and with decades of front-line experience in management roles in both the public and private sector, I currently work as a coach and trainer with EU staff and EPSO competition candidates. In this capacity, I meet broadly four categories of people:

- People who never worked with or for the EU and want to make a career change to working for the 'EU system.' Already working in the private or public sector, most of them are experienced professionals – lawyers, economists, engineers, etc. – who are dreaming of an EU career but don't know where to start.
- Blue Book or Schuman trainees, who have already had a taste of working in the EU and want to become an EU official.
- Temporary Agents and Contract Agents, who want to land a permanent position with better career prospects or more challenging and interesting work.
- Permanent officials who are seeking faster career progress or are wanting to grow into a middle or senior management position.

This book is for all of them.

What is this book about?

The EU is changing its management culture, with a so-called 'competency-based' approach to creating a more effective and dynamic work environment to the fore. Continuously developing your 'general competencies' is important at all levels. External candidates for the EPSO competitions will need them to pass the Assessment Centre with flying colours. Temporary and contract agents will need the general competencies to survive and thrive in the EU environment, and to do well in the internal competitions. Assistants wanting to become Administrators will have to formally demonstrate their general competencies when going through the 'certification' process. Candidates for a middle or senior management position will have to undergo an Assessment Centre with an independent, external service provider. And finally, every EU agent or official is subject to the annual appraisal procedure, where the general competencies play a major role. Not doing well in the annual appraisal may slow down, or even stop, your progress on the career ladder of the EU administration.

In Part I, I first explain why the EU administration is a very special work environment and give you an overview of the wide variety of working relationships one can have with this unique employer. In Part II, the biggest section of the book, I describe what the competency-based approach is about, after which I explain in detail each of the general competencies and how to improve them. Then, in Part III I cover some of the special challenges that working for the EU in the 2020s is posing: digital persuasion, teleworking, and working in a multicultural environment.

This book is also intended as a reference manual for all things related to the general competencies as defined by the EU administration. That is why you will find in the Part IV Annexes a comprehensive overview of the eight general competencies, a glossary of terms, and finally an extensive list of books and other resources that can be helpful for your personal development.

This EU Career Development book is itself part of a wider series, 'The Ultimate EU Test Book' created to help and support candidates in their preparation for EPSO competitions. The series covers the entire competition process, from filling out the application form, the pre-selection tests, the talent screener, the intermediate test, up to the Assessment Centre.

Is working for the EU for me?

This is a bit of a top-level question, but it is very relevant and important to your longer-term career prospects and job satisfaction that you make sure that you are sitting in the right position and that you are doing the type of job that fits your personality.

Let's look at a few ideas. Are you more of an organiser type or an analytical type? This is an over-simplification and a quite blunt way of approaching your personality type. However, many people are more inclined to be an organiser type, whether they are more agile and like fast moving things or instead an analytical or 'PhD-type,' who would rather go deep into a given file.

In the case of jobs that require a lot of analysis, maybe in legal affairs or as a translator or lawyer-linguist, analytical types get more satisfaction and stay longer in these jobs than organisers. At the same time, even these jobs have lot of organisational issues to handle, such as managing stakeholder contacts, research projects or on-site visits. Therefore, just because a unit or DG deals with a given topic, don't make up your mind too soon whether a particular job is the right fit for you.

The other thing to consider is whether you prefer a flat organisation or a hierarchical organisation. If you have the liberty to choose between two different jobs or decide on the type of employer whom you'd like to work for, smaller institutions, such as the European Data Protection Supervisor or the Committee of the Regions may be a better fit as there is less hierarchy in these organisations than at the European Commission.

Another point to consider is whether you should plan for the long term or the short term. If there is a career opportunity that you are interested in, you should ask yourself how well it would fit your CV. Would it help in building the consistent, coherent profile that you would like to have? Or would it instead be a good opportunity in the short term – for example, because it pays well – but not the perfect fit when it comes to your overall profile and the impression it would give to a potential future employer.

PART I: THE EU CAREER PATHWAYS

1. Working for the EU

'Wanderer, your footsteps are the path, and nothing else; wanderer, there is no path, the path is made by walking.' – Antonio Machado[1]

The European Union (EU) is a highly populated, culturally diverse coalition of 27 member states embracing the majority of countries west of Russia. In February 2020, after Brexit, the population was around 445 million people, some 5.8% of the world total. The EU aims to enable all EU citizens to study, live, shop, work, and retire in any EU country and enjoy products and services from all over Europe. To do this, the EU safeguards the free movement of goods, services, capital and people in a single internal market.

'United in diversity,' the European Union's motto, first came into use in 2000. It signposts how Europeans have come together to work for peace and prosperity while at the same time being enriched by the member states' many different cultures, traditions, and languages.

The European Union has seven core institutions: the European Parliament, the European Council, the Council of the European Union (often called the Council of Ministers, or simple Council), the European Commission, the Court of Justice of the European Union, the European Central Bank, and the European Court of Auditors. There are also several additional bodies which advise the EU or operate in a specific area. In terms of employment opportunities (both permanent and temporary contracts), the European Commission is by far the largest employer, followed by the Parliament and the Council of the European Union. The decentralised EU agencies, of which there are now several dozen dispersed around the member states have also become a major source of employment, much of it on a contract basis. Most, but not all, EU recruitment is carried out by the various institutions themselves following selection procedures organised by the European Personnel Selection Office (EPSO).

One of the EU's founding principles is multilingualism. However, the EU does not have a common language policy as such. This is the responsibility of member states, and the EU administration only plays a supporting role in this field, based on the principle of subsidiarity. The EU is home to 24 official languages and some 150 regional or minority languages. Important documents, such as legislation, are translated into every official language[2]. Due to the high number of official languages, most of the institutions use only a handful of procedural languages: English, French, and German. The European Parliament accepts all official languages as working languages. The European Court of Justice uses only French as a working language.

While all bureaucracies have their similarities, the environment of the EU administration has many aspects that are unique to it as a multi-national project with no predetermined limits or end goals. Working for the EU is something special. Working for the EU is not just a job; it is a life experience!

1 Antonio Machado (1875–1939), was a Spanish poet and one of the leading figures of the Spanish literary movement known as the Generation of '98.

2 https://europa.eu/european-union/abouteuropa/language-policy_en

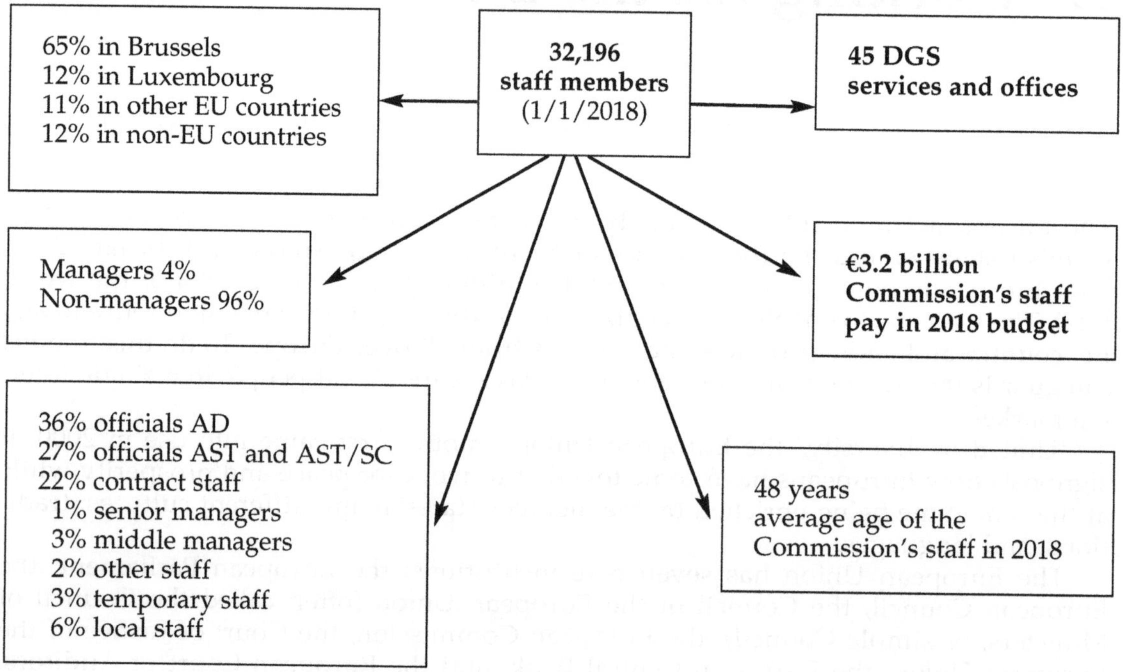

Figure 1.1: Commission Staff in Brief (source: European Court of Auditors)

The EU workforce

At the start of 2020, the total number of people employed by the 'EU system' was some 60,000. To put this number in perspective, the French Ministry of Justice has a head-count of around 80,000. Comparisons between developed countries relating to the public sector employment are tricky because of national differences with regard to the scope of each country's public sector[3]. In the UK, the number of public servants per 1000 inhabitants is 80. Norway has about twice as many public servants and, perhaps surprisingly, Italy has fewer than the UK with around 55. In the EU administration, the number of public employees per 1000 inhabitants is only 7.4. So, in comparison with national administrations, the EU is not such a big bureaucracy after all. Of course, for the most part the EU administration is not delivering direct services so beyond a certain point the debate about whether there are 'too many' or 'too few' EU civil servants can become meaningless.

The largest institution, the European Commission, has about 32,000 employees. An overview of how the Commission workforce was composed in 2018 is given in Fig. 1.1.

3 https://www.europeandatajournalism.eu/eng/News/Data-news/Public-employees-comparisons-between-European-countries-are-deceptive

There are many categories of jobs in the EU institutions and ever-increasing numbers of staff are employed on a wide variety of time-limited contracts. However, as Fig 1.1. illustrates, the majority of staff in the core institutions like the Commission are permanent officials. These are divided into the Administrator (AD) and Assistant (AST) 'function groups', as they are called in the EU jargon. Administrators and Assistants have separate career ladders. Entry level for Administrators is AD5 and for many Assistants it is AST3. There is a further category referred to as AST-SC, or simply SC, for Secretaries/Clerks.

Gender equality

Fig. 1.2 on the next page presents the gender balance at the Commission (officials and temporary staff only) by grade, grouped to reflect pay level (i.e., AST5 and AD5 together, AST1 and SC2 together).

As can be seen, the AST and AST/SC function groups remain predominantly female due to the high rates of female applicants for the relevant competitions. On the other hand, for the higher pay grades, there is still an historical dominance of male officials.

On 30 September 2020, the College of Commissioners adopted conclusions aimed at strengthening gender equality within the Commission. It was proposed to designate a Head of Unit as 'Deputy Director' in each DG. The College asked Directors-General to draw up a list designating a Head of Unit who would deputise for each post of Director. This list should, in principle, include at least 55% women. The Deputy Director is only intended to replace the Director when the Director is not there so, formally speaking, the role is not an additional level that is added to the hierarchy. However, in practice the Deputy Director will need to have a privileged relationship with the Director, for reasons of continuity of the service. This means that he or she will become a de facto 'shadow' Director, thus adding an extra layer in the hierarchy after all.

The College also decided to create a function of Deputy Head of Unit within each unit. Directors-General will have to ensure that these positions are carried out in a gender-balanced manner by the end of 2022.

Furthermore, the College decided that four of the permanent members of the Consultative Committee on Appointments (CCA) will give opinions on any requests for publication of senior management posts and on the appropriateness of conducting CCA interviews and with which candidates, and that the pre-selection phase of candidates remains subject to review until the opinion of that body is delivered.

If the objective of these measures is commendable, concerns have been expressed about the de facto multiplication of hierarchical levels. This move by the College can also be seen as a desire to centralise the appointment procedures in the hands of the political level of the Commission. It is also argued that achieving equality between men and women cannot be achieved solely in terms of access to positions of responsibility, but also by reference to precariousness or even the occupation of posts at the bottom of the pay scale.

4 https://eur-lex.europa.eu/legal-content/EN/TXT/?uri=CELEX%3A01962R0031-20210101

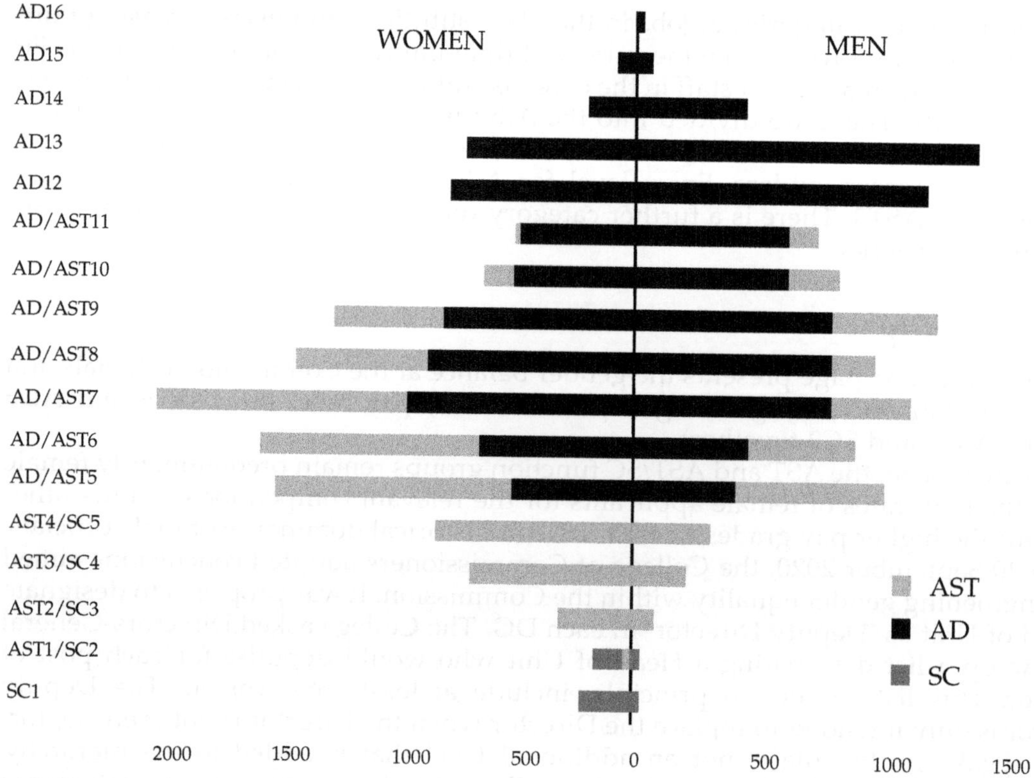

Figure 1.2: 2019 gender balance at the Commission (source: European Court of Auditors)

National diversity

The EU workforce also reflects the motto 'United in Diversity' as it is composed of staff from all over the EU. Article 27 of the Staff Regulations[4] requires that EU institutions recruit staff on the broadest possible geographical basis. It provides a legal basis for each institution to adopt appropriate measures where a significant imbalance between nationalities of officials, which is not justified by objective criteria, is observed. Fig. 1.3 gives an overview of the distribution of Commission staff per country of origin in 2020.

Staff from the EU's five largest member states by size of population – in descending order, Germany, France, Italy, Spain and Poland – were also (other than Belgians) the five largest national groups in the Commission. However, all five countries are under-represented relative to their share of the total EU population. The biggest discrepancy is in the case of Germany, which accounted for 18.6% of the population of the EU in 2020, according to Eurostat but, as the table shows, only 6.5% of Commission staff are of German nationality. Belgium, with the highest percentage of all, is obviously a special case because most Commission staff work in Belgium, and this reflects local recruitment.

Table 1.1: Commission staff by nationality at 1 January 2021, with percentage of total

TOTAL	32,281	100%
Belgium	4791	14.9
Italy	4141	12.8
France	3246	10.1
Spain	2560	7.9
Germany	2104	6.5
Non-EU or UK nationalities	1963	6.1
Poland	1517	4.7
Greece	1447	4.5
Romania	1433	4.4
Portugal	786	2.4
Hungary	781	2.4
Bulgaria	752	2.3
United Kingdom	613	1.9
Netherlands	611	1.9
Ireland	552	1.7
Finland	537	1.7
Czechia	533	1.7
Sweden	518	1.6
Austria	479	1.5
Lithuania	452	1.4
Slovakia	440	1.4
Croatia	374	1.2
Denmark	357	1.1
Slovenia	330	1.0
Latvia	279	0.9
Estonia	269	0.8
Malta	170	0.5
Cyprus	139	0.4
Luxembourg	107	0.3

Recruitment since the 2004 enlargement has been heavily skewed to the newer member states. In good measure the EPSO selection system encourages this as it is (generally speaking) 'nationality blind.' EU salaries are particularly attractive to those from the ex-communist bloc, ergo the most applicants, including many of the most talented who see few opportunities in their own countries. We now have a situation where (to caricature a bit) if you meet someone senior it is likely to be a man from Western Europe, if someone junior a woman from Eastern Europe. Inevitably in 20 years' time this newer recruitment will fill the senior positions. Western European countries offer better job prospects at home, so produce fewer candidates (especially Germany and France). Poland is a special case as consistently it is under-represented in EPSO competitions and I have never been able to think of a reason for this other than the intensity of Euroscepticism in the country and also the existence of well-trodden routes for talented young Poles to get work in Western Europe and beyond. Only 4.7 per cent of Commission staff are of Polish nationality, whereas Poland has 8.5 per cent of the EU population.

You can find more information on cultural diversity in the EU administration in Chapter 13 of this book.

Career options

Working for the EU, you can pursue many different career options, depending on your background. For example, if you're a lawyer, economist, engineer, or linguist by training, you should think about roles where the maximum will be made of your skills and previous work experience. This chapter will only give a brief overview of the various employment opportunities in the EU public administration. If you want to know more about the different types of employment, I can only recommend the book 'Working for the EU – How to Get In' by Johannes de Berlaymont [5].

Statutory and non-statutory staff

When talking about the EU workforce, there is first a distinction to be made between so-called 'statutory' and 'non-statutory' staff.

Statutory staff are bound by the 'Staff Regulations'. This is the case for permanent officials, temporary agents, contract agents, local staff, special advisers and accredited parliamentary assistants. The Staff Regulations are the official 'labour code' setting out the rules of their employment, obligations, rights, pension, salary, and any other matter concerning the relationship with the EU administration. The reason for the Staff Regulations' existence is the independence these 'agents' or 'servants' enjoy from any governmental or other entity: they are not bound by any EU member state's labour laws given their only affiliation is to the EU institution or body that employs them.

Permanent officials

The most sought after but also the most difficult to get are the so-called 'permanent positions.' Within the EU civil service, three types of permanent contracts that can be awarded: Administrators (AD), Assistants (AST), and Secretary/Clerks (AST/SC).

If you are employed as an Administrator, you will generally be involved in drafting policies, implementing EU law, analysis, or advisory work. An Administrator career ranges from grades AD5 to AD16, with AD5 being the entry-level grade for university graduates. Selection and recruitment may also be offered at higher grades AD6 or AD7 in more specialist roles, where the applicant will have to demonstrate several years' relevant experience.

Management positions are usually filled by officials of the European institutions. However, in certain circumstances, temporary positions can be opened to external applicants.

Middle managers are the line managers of the Commission. They play a key role in the effective delivery of the Commission's political priorities. They can be appointed to grades AD9 to AD14. Middle management includes Heads of Unit, Heads of

5 https://www.johnharperpublishing.co.uk/working-for-the-eu-how-to-get-in/

Department, and Heads of Task Force. Middle managers must possess the necessary skills to motivate and manage teams, expertise in specific policies or activities, and – where appropriate – relevant professional and management experience.

Senior managers include Directors-General, Deputy Directors-General, Directors, and Principal Advisers. Directors-General are the top-level EU civil servants who report directly to the Commissioner responsible for the policy area covered by their Directorate-General (DG). Directors report to Directors-General and are accountable for the management of financial and human resources within their Directorates. Senior managers are selected based on a variety of high-level qualifications. They must have management experience and be able to demonstrate leadership skills. They are also required to demonstrate high standards of efficiency, ability and integrity. Directors-General are appointed to grade AD15 or AD16, while Directors are appointed to grade AD14 or AD15.

Assistants are typically engaged in an executive or technical role in administration, finance, communication, research, or policy development and implementation. An Assistant career ranges from grades AST1 to AST11, with staff entering at grades AST1 to AST3. As a minimum, an AST1 candidate must have completed secondary education and have previous relevant experience or have a pertinent vocational qualification. It is worth saying that AST jobs should not be underrated. Because of the way the EU administration is arranged in silos, with Administrators and Assistants having separate career ladders, it is actually Assistants who often play pivotal roles in the daily functioning of the institutions. Assistants can be managers with wide responsibilities in areas including staff management, budget implementation and political coordination.

If you are employed as a Secretary/Clerk, you will be involved in office management or providing administrative support. A Secretary/Clerk career ranges from grade AST/SC1 to AST/SC6. New staff enter at grades AST/SC1 or AST/SC2. As a minimum, an AST/SC1 candidate must have post-secondary education of at least one year attested by a diploma directly related to the nature of the duties, or secondary education attested by a certificate giving access to post-secondary education followed by at least 3 years' professional experience directly related to the nature of the duties, or professional training of at least 1 year, followed by a minimum of 3 years' professional experience. Both the training and experience must be directly related to the nature of the duties.

Temporary agents

Temporary agents can be hired to do essentially the same kind of work as permanent officials but for a limited time. Although the rules on the length of initial contracts and subsequent contract extensions vary, as a rule temporary agents may be hired for a maximum period of six years. Temporary agents may be employed within one of the following categories:

- For non-standard (highly specialised jobs) or temporary tasks.
- To make up for staff shortages in cases where EPSO competition reserve lists have been exhausted.

- For Commissioners' private offices ('cabinets'). Temporary agents in this category work in the private office of a European Commissioner during their term in office.
- For specific requirements in the scientific sector. Temporary agents in this category work in one of the various research centres set up by the EU to promote research and to manage European framework programmes for research and development.

CAST Permanent

CAST is variously interpreted as standing for Contract Agents for Specific Tasks or Contract Agents Selection Tool. 'CAST Permanent' means that there is no deadline to apply to a CAST profile. It is an open-ended selection method where candidates keep their successful results for a pre-determined period. Contract agents are recruited to do manual or administrative support service tasks or provide additional capacity in specialised fields where an insufficient number of officials with the required skills are available. There has been a steady growth in the numbers recruited via CAST selections.

Contract agents are employed for a fixed maximum period of 6 years, often with a shorter initial but renewable contract of 6 to 12 months, depending on the type of job. In some agencies, offices, representations and delegations the contract can lead to an indefinite contract.

Contract staff positions are available for a wide range of jobs, requiring different levels of qualifications. They are divided into four function groups:

I. Manual and administrative support service tasks

II. Clerical or secretarial tasks, office management, and other equivalent tasks

III. Executive tasks, drafting, accountancy, and other equivalent technical tasks

IV. Administrative, advisory, linguistic, and equivalent technical tasks

Local agents in EU delegations

Abroad, the EU is represented through more than 140 diplomatic representations, also known as EU delegations, which have a similar function to that of an embassy. As diplomatic missions, the EU delegations operate under the Vienna Convention on Diplomatic Relations and each is managed by a Head of Delegation who is accredited to the local authorities with the rank of ambassador. Besides EU staff (permanent, temporary, or contract agents), the EU delegations also employ local agents.

Parliamentary assistants

Members of the European Parliament (MEPs) can hire their own staff, within a budget set by Parliament. They can choose different kinds of assistants:

- 'Accredited assistants' are managed administratively directly by Parliament's administration, under the same employment conditions as temporary EU staff. MEPs can recruit a maximum of three accredited assistants (under certain conditions four).

- 'Local assistants' are based in their member states. They are managed administratively by qualified paying agents to ensure that tax and social security requirements are adequately met.

Traineeships

Each year, around 1,900 young people are offered the chance to increase their professional skills, develop their personal qualities, and enhance their EU knowledge through the EU trainee programmes. Most of the EU institutions organise traineeships for young university graduates, each lasting usually between 3 and 5 months.

Twice a year, the Commission offers the so-called Blue Book[6] traineeships, 5-month paid internships in EU Directorates, institutions and agencies, which have signed a service level agreement with DG EAC/the Commission. EU citizens and non-EU citizens can apply, and successful trainees receive a monthly allowance. Applicants must be graduates and must have an excellent knowledge of two EU languages (non-EU citizens must only have one). Subsequent career opportunities may vary between these different entities.

The European Parliament offers two types of traineeships[7]: traineeships in the Secretariat (Schuman traineeships) and traineeships with Members of the European Parliament. The Schuman traineeships are paid and can be undertaken at one of the European Parliament's official places of work – Brussels, Luxembourg and Strasbourg – or in its Liaison Offices in the member states. Members of the European Parliament may offer paid traineeships at their offices in the European Parliament in Brussels (or Strasbourg) based on an agreement with the European Parliament.

Junior Professionals in Delegation

The EU has delegation offices around the world. Traineeships of up to 18 months are offered in the EU delegations to give talented and promising university postgraduates the opportunity to gain first-hand experience in the delegation's work and a deeper insight into their role in the implementation of EU external relations policies.

Seconded National Experts

Seconded National Experts (SNEs) are national or international civil servants who are working temporarily for the Commission under the rules applicable to such experts[8]. SNEs have a dual role: to bring to the Commission their experience of the issues they are used to dealing with where they normally work, and to take back to their home administration the knowledge of Community issues they acquire during their secondment.

The initial period of secondment may not be shorter than six months or more than two years. It may be renewed once or more, up to a total period not exceeding four

6 https://traineeships.ec.europa.eu

7 https://www.europarl.europa.eu/at-your-service/en/work-with-us/traineeships

8 https://ec.europa.eu/jrc/sites/jrcsh/files/c%282008%296866.pdf

years. Exceptionally, at the DG's request and where the interests of the service warrant it, the Director-General of HR and Security may authorise one or more extensions of the secondment for a maximum of two more years at the end of the four-year period.

Interim staff

The EU administration employ staff on short-term contracts through temping agencies. Posts are rarely longer than six months in duration.

Interim consultants

Some EU departments employ consultants directly through tendering procedures.

Freelance linguists

A freelance career is available to translators and interpreters in the European Commission, the European Parliament, and the Court of Justice.

EU experts

Experts are employed by the European Commission to evaluate tenders and project proposals, monitor projects and design policies and programmes.

Special advisers

A 'special adviser' is a person who, because of their unique qualifications and notwithstanding that they may be employed elsewhere in some other capacity, is engaged to assist one of the institutions of the Union either regularly or for a specified period and who is paid from the total appropriations for the purpose under the section of the budget relating to the institution in which they serve.

Special advisers are selected based on their expertise and qualifications. There are two types:

- Non-institutional special advisers provide direct assistance to the President, the Vice-Presidents and the Commissioners.
- Institutional special advisers assist institutional bodies of the Commission.

Special advisers work on a short-term basis for a limited number of days per year, and these days may be paid or not. Each special adviser must sign a document declaring that there is no conflict of interest between their duties as an adviser to the European Commission and their other activities.

How much do EU officials earn?

The media often portray EU officials as 'fat cats'. The term was, it is said, first used in the 1920s in the United States to describe rich political donors, but today refers more generally to people considered to be making more money than they deserve, by implication at everyone else's expense.

Indeed, the top EU jobs are well paid, especially by public service standards, hovering around the 25,000 EUR per month mark with extra perks. However, for most EU employees their salaries and other benefits are significantly lower and depend on multiple factors such as contract duration, seniority, family situation, the location of the post, and whether you are an "expat," working in another country than your country of origin.

Overall, the EU salaries are by no means low compared to most EU countries' average pay levels and come with additional allowances and other benefits. When comparing EU administration salaries with those of the poorer member states (East and South of Europe) these salaries can be called royal, and this is of course an important reason why the EU administration is very attractive for people from these countries. However, this attractiveness is less obvious in comparison with the richer member states (West and North), explaining the geographical imbalance in people interested in an EU career.

Caveat: averages can be misleading

According to British Prime Minister Benjamin Disraeli, there are three kinds of lies: lies, damned lies, and statistics. Averages are misleading when used to compare different groups, apply group behaviour to an individual scenario, or when there are numerous outliers in the data. The root causes of these problems appear to be over-simplification and rationalisations — what people want to believe.

Another element to consider is the difference between private sector and public sector salaries. The EU salaries are, in general, better than the member states' public sector wages, but can be lower than in the private sector, especially when talking about experienced specialist or managerial positions. On the other hand, job security is better, and so are the health care and pension schemes.

For people who are contemplating an EU job, and even fresh recruits, it is often hard to understand what the final salary will look like. Here's a brief overview of how your salary will be calculated.

Basic salary

Everything starts with the so-called 'basic salary'. This is based on the type of contract, the grade, and the step (i.e., seniority in the grade; one step equals 2 years) of the official. The basic salary grid for permanent and temporary officials is given in Article 66 of the Staff Regulations. Basic salaries are adjusted annually in line with inflation and purchasing power in the EU countries (Article 65 and Annex XI).

To reflect the higher or lower cost of living in the place of employment compared with Brussels, the basic salary is weighted by applying a coefficient. This may have a considerable impact on the net sum received as this coefficient varies widely.[9]

On 1 July 2020, for Administrators and Assistants, the grid was as in Table 1.2.

Table 1.2: Basic monthly salary for Administrators and Assistants, 1 July 2020

Grade	Step 1	Step 2	Step 3	Step 4	Step 5
AD 16	19 127,29	19 931,05	20 768,57	20 768,57	20 768,57
AD 15	16 905,33	17 615,72	18 355,95	18 866,64	19 127,29
AD14	14 941,46	15 569,34	16 223,58	16 674,95	16 905,33
AD13	13 205,78	13 760,70	14 338,93	14 737,88	14 941,46
AD12	11 671,70	12 162,15	12 673,23	13 025,81	13 205,78
AD11/AST 11	10 315,83	10 749,30	11 201,00	11 512,64	11 671,70
AD10/AST 10	9 117,48	9 500,59	9 899,84	10 175,25	10 315,83
AD9/AST 9	8 058,32	8 396,94	8 749,80	8 993,22	9 117,48
AD8/AST 8	7 122,21	7 421,49	7 733,35	7 948,51	8 058,32
AD7/AST 7	6 294,84	6 559,36	6 834,99	7 025,15	7 122,21
AD6/AST 6	5 563,58	5 797,38	6 040,98	6 209,06	6 294,84
AD5/AST 5	4 917,29	5 123,92	5 339,22	5 487,78	5 563,58
AST4	4 346,06	4 528,68	4 718,98	4 850,27	4 917,29
AST3	3 841,17	4 002,60	4 170,80	4 286,82	4 346,06
AST2	3 394,97	3 537,62	3 686,28	3 788,84	3 841,17
AST 1	3 000,59	3 126,66	3 258,05	3 348,71	3 394,97

Secretaries and clerks (AST/SC) fulfilling various secretarial and clerical duties had the grid shown in Table 1.3.

9 For example, in 2021 the coefficient for Copenhagen was 131.3 while for Sofia a mere 59.1 was applied.

Table 1.3: Basic monthly salary for Secretaries and Clerks, 1 July 2020

Grade	Step 1	Step 2	Step 3	Step 4	Step 5
AST/SC 6	4 878,26	5 083,26	5 296,86	5 444,21	5 519,44
AST/SC 5	4 311,57	4 492,75	4 682,20	4 811,78	4 878,26
AST/SC 4	3 810,72	3 970,83	4 137,70	4 252,82	4 311,57
AST/SC 3	3 368,02	3 509,55	3 657,05	3 758,77	3 810,72
AST/SC 2	2 976,76	3 101,86	3 232,22	3 322,13	3 368,02
AST/SC 1	2 630,97	2 741,53	2 856,74	2 936,19	2 976,76

Salaries of contract agents mostly depend on which function group and grade they are in, as seen in Table 1.4.

Table 1.4: Basic monthly salary for Contract Agents, 1 July 2020

	Grade	Step 1	Step 2	Step 3	Step 4	Step 5	Step 6	Step 7
FG IV	18	6 593,66	6 730,78	6 870,74	7 013,62	7 159,49	7 308,37	7 460,34
	17	5 827,65	5 948,83	6 072,54	6 198,83	6 327,74	6 459,32	6 593,66
	16	5 150,62	5 257,72	5 367,07	5 478,68	5 592,63	5 708,93	5 827,65
	15	4 552,24	4 646,91	4 743,55	4 842,20	4 942,90	5 045,68	5 150,62
	14	4 023,40	4 107,07	4 192,48	4 279,67	4 368,69	4 459,50	4 552,24
	13	3 555,98	3 629,93	3 705,41	3 782,48	3 861,13	3 941,43	4 023,40
FG III	12	4 552,18	4 646,84	4 743,48	4 842,11	4 942,80	5 045,58	5 150,51
	11	4 023,37	4 107,02	4 192,42	4 279,60	4 368,60	4 459,44	4 552,18
	10	3 555,97	3 629,91	3 705,39	3 782,45	3 861,10	3 941,40	4 023,37
	9	3 142,88	3 208,23	3 274,95	3 343,06	3 412,58	3 483,53	3 555,97
	8	2 777,78	2 835,54	2 894,51	2 954,69	3 016,15	3 078,86	3 142,88
FG II	7	3 142,81	3 208,18	3 274,90	3 343,00	3 412,56	3 483,53	3 555,98
	6	2 777,65	2 835,41	2 894,39	2 954,59	3 016,04	3 078,77	3 142,81
	5	2 454,90	2 505,95	2 558,08	2 611,30	2 665,59	2 721,04	2 777,65
	4	2 169,66	2 214,79	2 260,86	2 307,89	2 355,88	2 404,89	2 454,90
FG I	3	2 672,85	2 728,32	2 784,96	2 842,75	2 901,74	2 961,96	3 023,45
	2	2 362,91	2 411,95	2 462,01	2 513,11	2 565,27	2 618,52	2 672,85
	1	2 088,92	2 132,29	2 176,53	2 221,70	2 267,81	2 314,88	2 362,91

The contracts of accredited parliamentary assistants are for a fixed period and specify the grade in which the assistant is classified. There are no steps.

Table 1.5: Basic monthly salary for Parliamentary Assistants, 1 July 2020

Grade	Basic salary
1	1 900,13
2	2 213,65
3	2 400,04
4	2 602,16

Grade	Basic salary
5	2 821,28
6	3 058,88
7	3 316,47
8	3 595,78
9	3 898,57

Grade	Basic salary
10	4 226,86
11	4 582,80
12	4 968,73
13	5 387,14
14	5 840,80

Grade	Basic salary
15	6332,66
16	6865,95
17	7444,14
18	8070,99
19	8750,68

Allowances and benefits

In addition to the basic salary, Agents may receive various allowances depending on their personal circumstances (values below are indicative).

- Head of household allowance. Basic amount of €176.01, plus 2% of basic salary.
- Dependent child allowance. Per month and per dependent child: €384.60.
- Education allowances:

o Pre-school allowance €93.95 per month and per child.

o Education allowance up to a maximum of €260.95 per month for each dependent child, which can be doubled in some cases.

- Expatriation allowance (equal to 16% of the total of the basic salary) or a foreign-residence allowance (equal to 4% of the total basic salary), depending on nationality and time spent in the place of employment.
- Installation allowance. Between one third of basic salary and two full basic salaries, depending on contract duration and personal circumstances.
- Daily subsistence allowance. Fixed amounts of €40.43 per day or €32.59 per day, depending on whether the Agent is entitled to the household allowance or not.
- Removal and travel expenses. Agents with contract duration of at least twelve months are entitled to reimbursement of removal expenses up to the amount of a quotation approved in advance. On taking up duties, Agents are entitled to reimbursement of travel expenses from the place of recruitment to the place of employment. Similar allowances such as resettlement allowance may be granted upon end of service.

Deductions

Salaries and allowances of EU officials are exempt from any national taxation in all EU Member States, but subject to a European tax (deducted at source) for the benefit of the European Communities.

- Social security contributions (% of basic salary)
  - Pension (10.1%)
  - Health insurance (1.70%)
  - Accident cover (0.10%)
  - Unemployment insurance (0.81%)
- Income tax, levied progressively at a rate of between 8% and 45% of the taxable portion of the salary.
- Special levy (6%) calculated on the part of the remuneration exceeding the minimum remuneration.

The final salary is calculated by adding the relevant allowances and by deducting social security contributions and other taxes.

If all this seems complicated, you can make a rough estimate of your salary with eutraining's salary calculator at https://eutraining.eu/salary-calculator#

Teleworking

EU officials work 40 hours per week. Flexitime was introduced in 2007 as part of the institutions' modernisation. These flexible working arrangements gave employees more freedom in the organisation of their working time by making use of information technology, and the development of the EU's IT infrastructure has made the transition to 'work anywhere, anytime' possible since 2017-2018. At least in theory, since the 2004 reform, the EU administration focuses on results-based management and objective-driven performance, which do not necessarily require staff to be physically present in the office. But in practice, this turnaround only came in 2020, with Covid-19.

Before 2020 teleworking was looked upon with much suspicion by the average manager in the Commission. And it was not a right but a favour that could only be granted if compatible with work. There were two kinds of telework: structural and occasional, and you needed the permission of your manager for both. Structural telework was recurrent – for example, every Wednesday. Occasional telework was ad hoc – for example 'I won't come to the office next Monday because I have something urgent to finish' (though obviously not 'because I expect a private Amazon delivery'). In conclusion, teleworking was an uncomfortable fit with the office culture.

When Covid-19 hit, a relative mastery of the technical dimension of telework had to be acquired quickly, and this went amazingly well. The managers had to adapt, of course, and generally speaking, staff were happy. But the major discovery was a general lack of knowledge of what modes of work have to be adopted. The adoption of teleworking has been a sort of progress, but it has also favoured the fragmentation of the civil service and invaded the private sphere with professional activities. It has not helped in giving a proper welcome to new colleagues, nor in assisting links with external stakeholders. Nevertheless, the prevailing consensus is that teleworking will stay a structural part of the 'new normal' of working for the EU.

Even though the details of the future teleworking policy are not known at this point, it is clear that not everybody will spend 100% of their working time at the office. The Commission has already seized the opportunity to approve a new 'master plan' for its buildings. In January 2021, the EU Commissioner for Budget and Administration, Johannes Hahn proposed to reduce the Commission's office space by 200,000 m^2, by a target date of 2030. The core idea is that the Commission should 'eat its own dog food' from its Green Deal environmental policy. The result of this drastic reduction will be that most EU staff won't have a fixed workspace anymore but instead will be working in 'collaborative spaces,' 'open spaces,' or 'hot desks.' For example, in the first quarter of 2021, DG-HR[10], DG-DIGIT[11], and DG-SCIC[12] moved to a building called 'The One[13],' rue de la Loi, 107. This building has workplaces for less than 70% of the people who are working there. Everybody has a locker on a specific floor, but people have to reserve their workspace beforehand. This new concept will be rolled out gradually because the existing buildings have to be transformed and renovated to make the open space possible.

Of course, teleworking only works if the home office can be used as a fully-fledged workplace, and the Commission supports its staff to convert the home environment into a proper working environment. Since the end of 2020 there has been financial compensation to cater for an ergonomic office chair and a decent computer screen (to avoid having to work on a small laptop screen the whole day). In the near future, Commission officials will dispose of a 'homeworking package,' comprising an office chair, computer screen, docking station, keyboard and mouse, identical to the equipment that is used in the Commission premises. Telephones already disappeared before Covid-19 and were replaced by a Skype for Business account (now Microsoft Teams).

There are, of course, some outstanding issues. For example, some staff are asking for the opportunity to work from abroad (typically their home country). This is a delicate matter indeed. Obviously, it doesn't really matter where you are when teleworking, but the thing is that expats receive a 16% allowance, and nobody wants to create the perception that EU officials can spend most of their working time alongside a pool on the Spanish costas. The outcome will probably be that there will be a quota on the number of days one can work away from the official posting. To be seen.

You can find more information on teleworking in the EU administration in Chapter 12 of this book.

10 Human Resources

11 Digital transformation

12 Interpretation (for its former French name Service Commun Interprétation–Conférences)

13 https://www.smakarchitects.eu/projects/the-one

Selection and recruitment

An overview of the selection and recruitment procedures for the main types of staff is given in Fig. 1.3.

Permanent positions as an official (or 'fonctionnaire') in the EU administration are mainly accessible through open competitions or 'concours' managed centrally by the European Personnel Selection Office, EPSO[14]. The EPSO open competitions are an indirect way of recruitment; laureates (i.e., those who pass all the qualifying tests) are placed on a so-called 'reserve list' from which the respective EU institutions can source their vacant positions, provided the vacancy cannot be filled by means of internal mobility or from another institution (Article 29 of the Staff Regulations). Reserve lists are only valid for a limited time. EPSO selection procedures may take more than one year between the publication of the Notice of Competition and the availability of the reserve list.

Figure 1.3:
Overview of selection and recruitment procedures

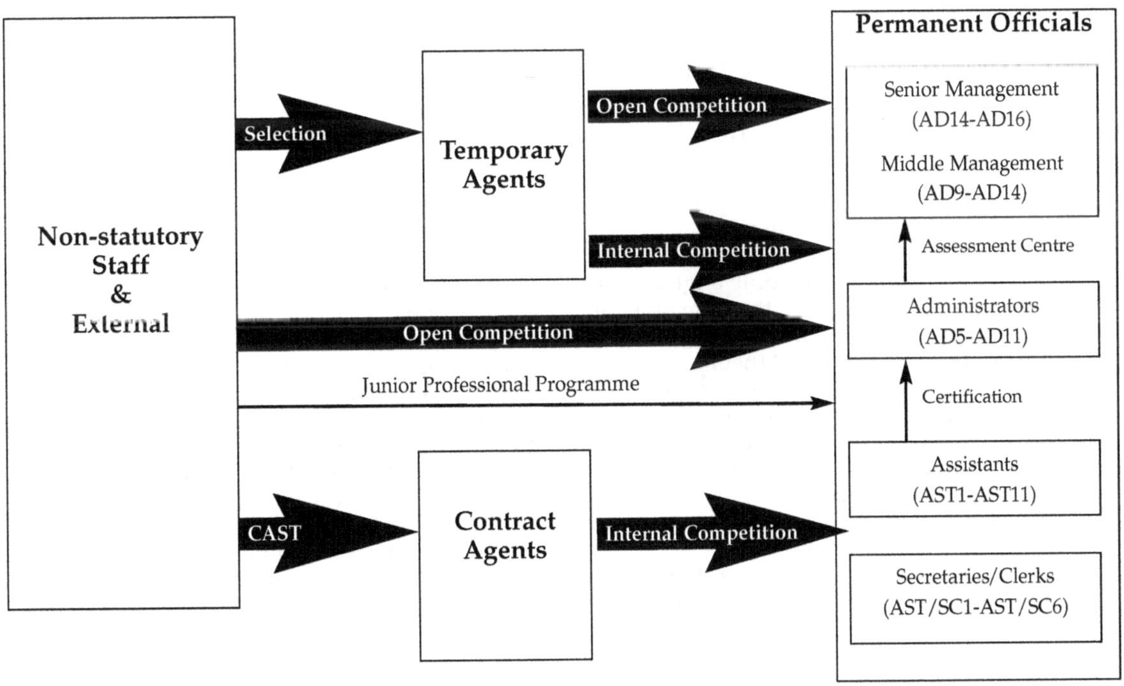

14 https://epso.europa.eu/

The two key elements of EPSO competitions are reasoning-type tests (numerical, verbal and abstract reasoning), which are computer-based and Assessment Centres, where selected candidates are brought together to engage in exercises that test their 'general' and 'specific' competencies. (During the Covid pandemic, EPSO has conducted the Assessment Centre testing, with modifications, online.) The general or core competencies are analysis and problem solving, communicating, delivering quality and results, learning and development, prioritising and organising, resilience, working with others and leadership. These general competencies, which remain the underpinning to your entire career, are the main subject of this book.

EPSO open competitions are very selective. Only a limited number of the initial candidates end up on the reserve list. For the more popular 'generalist' competitions, this can be as low as 0.5%, though the success rate can be significantly higher for some more specialised competitions.

Permanent officials can always participate in the open competitions with a view to faster promotion to a higher rank, or to pass from AST to AD. Assistants, as of grade AST 5, can be proposed by their manager to take part in an annual 'certification exercise' to become Administrators. This certification exercise includes training at the European School of Administration and an Assessment Centre organised by EPSO. Finally, the transition to a middle or senior management position also requires an assessment, conducted by an external service provider.

Against the background of the 2016 Talent Management Strategy and the Commission report on geographical balance[15], and as part of the response to improving its attractiveness, and modernising and diversifying selection and recruitment, the Commission decided to develop the Junior Professionals Programme (JPP). The JPP aims at better retaining and developing new resources from the Commission's known

The 'electron hole' theory

Having studied electronic engineering – a very long time ago – the selection and recruitment processes in the EU makes me think of the 'electron hole' theory.

In physics, an electron hole (often simply called a hole) is the lack of an electron at a position where one could exist in an atom or atomic lattice. Since in a normal atom or crystal lattice the negative charge of the electrons is balanced by the positive charge of the atomic nuclei, the absence of an electron leaves a net positive charge at the hole's location. Holes can move through the lattice as electrons can, and act similarly to positively charged particles. They play an important role in the operation of semiconductor devices such as diodes, transistors and integrated circuits. If an electron is excited into a higher state it leaves a hole in its old state.

In my experience as a coach for EPSO competitions, a substantial proportion of people who make it to the Assessment Centre stage are already working for the EU in some capacity, and they participate in the EPSO competitions either to become a permanent official or to have a faster promotion. This means that when they are recruited to fill a vacant position, they leave a new vacant position (a 'hole') behind. So, the 'net' number of new people recruited for the EU is far below the number of people on the reserve lists.

This is not only a problem of in-breeding but also a major source of bureaucratic overhead and efficiency loss in the human resources management of the EU administration.

15 COM(2018)377

talent pool (Blue Books, contract agents, etc...). During the selection process, the candidates have to demonstrate why the Commission should offer them an AD5 position, which is their added value for the institution. The final test consists of a structured presentation, on a subject related to the European Union institutions, and an interview. In 2018, the College mandated DG HR to launch the pilot project and to organise two calls for expression of interest per year until 2020 for the recruitment of 50 junior professionals per year.

This short-cutting of the 'regular' EPSO competitions has sparked protests among existing Commission staff and trade unions amid broader concerns that well-connected people are being given preferential treatment. Nevertheless, the overall results of the consultations and the data collected since the launch of the programme, confirmed that the pilot has been largely successful. And a consensus emerged in the focus group of stakeholders that the programme should be continued. As a consequence, DG HR recommended the establishment of the programme on a permanent basis, and the continuation of the programme as a pilot, pending adoption of a Commission decision on JPP. This decision will be adopted after consultation with Commission services and the staff representation.

Following the 2013 Staff Regulation reform, EPSO and EU institutions now regularly announce internal competitions in which only existing Administrators, Assistants and temporary agents (but not contract agents) can take part. The goal is to help in the career mobility of those who may be eligible for higher positions or temporary agents who wish to obtain a permanent employment contract. These exams follow the same rules as any other set by EPSO and the Staff Regulations.

Temporary agents are hired directly by the institutions or agencies, usually though an ad hoc selection procedure, with or without the support of EPSO. If you are interested in a temporary position, you should consult the website of the institution or agency you want to work for, or you could use the handy tool[16] provided by eutraining.eu.

Contract staff are recruited from a pool of applicants (kept in a database) following a selection procedure[17] known as CAST Permanent, usually organised by EPSO. The selection procedure may include CV sifting, reasoning tests, and/or competency tests that may be written, oral, or other practical tests in the field. The CAST selection procedure has no Assessment Centre and there is no predefined number of successful candidates. It is important to remember that you are always applying for a profile and not for a specific job position.

The conditions for employment of local agents in an EU delegation are governed by the European External Action Service (EEAS), but the delegation does the recruitment. Those who wish to become a local agent in one of the EU delegations should check the information on the EU delegation's website in their country.

If you want to work as an accredited assistant to one of the 705 Members of the European Parliament, you can check the European Parliament's website[18] for more information. You can also consult the individual websites of Political Groups[19] for information about their recruitment procedures.

16 https://eutraining.eu/eu_jobs#

17 https://epso.europa.eu/content/Cast-Permanent_en

18 https://www.europarl.europa.eu/meps/en/home

19 https://www.europarl.europa.eu/about-parliament/en/organisation-and-rules/organisation

The selection procedures for traineeships are run individually by the EU institutions and agencies themselves. You can check the traineeship[20] page of EPSO for the outstanding opportunities and conditions of employment. For more information on a traineeship in an EU delegation, see the Junior Professionals in Delegation programme[21] .

If you are interested in working as a Seconded National Expert, the vacancies are published by the Permanent Representations of the member states to the EU. SNEs must have worked for their employer on a permanent or contract basis for at least 12 months before their secondment and will remain in the service of that employer throughout secondment. The SNE's employer undertakes to pay their salary and maintain their administrative status (permanent official or contract staff member) throughout the secondment period.

If you are interested in temporary work you can contact a temping agency like Daoust, Randstad, or Adecco to find out more about short-term opportunities at the EU institutions in Brussels and Luxembourg.

For more information on how to work for the institutions as an external contractor or consultant, consult the EU tenders and contracts website[22].

To become a freelance translator for the European Commission, consult the notices of call for tenders[23]. To become a freelance translator for the Court of Justice, consult the contract notices[24]. To become a freelance interpreter at the European Commission, the European Parliament or the European Court of Justice, see Interpreting for Europe[25].

Finally, if you want to become an expert at the European Commission, you can register to be added to a database of experts[26].

Is my age important?

The honest answer to this is 'it depends'.

First of all, you should know that there is no age limit in the admission criteria in any of the competitions (including CAST) organised by EPSO, or the selection of temporary agents and it would even be illegal for them to use your age as a parameter to score you. However, there is an implicit lower limit in the diploma – and professional experience – requirements (unless you are a child prodigy of course) and another more explicit upper limit at the pensionable age for EU officials; even though you could participate in a competition, you will never be hired when you have already reached the pensionable age.

In terms of how your age could influence your scores in the EPSO Assessment Centre there is a distinction to be made between those competitions that do not require any previous professional experience, and those that have a minimum professional experience requirement. A typical example of the first category would be the AD5 gen-

20 https://epso.europa.eu/job-opportunities/traineeships_en

21 https://eeas.europa.eu/headquarters/headquarters-homepage/2463/junior-professional-in-delegation-jpd_en

22 https://etendering.ted.europa.eu/cft/cft-search.html

23 https://ec.europa.eu/info/funding-tenders_en

24 https://curia.europa.eu/jcms/jcms/Jo2_10741/direction-generale-de-la-traduction-collaborateurs-free-lance

25 https://europa.eu/interpretation/index_en.html

26 https://ec.europa.eu/info/jobs-european-commission/experts/become-expert-european-commission_en

eralist, so-called graduate competitions, as opposed to the 'specialist' competitions for the second category.

For those competitions where no professional experience is required, it is the intention to recruit people who are still young enough to be 'malleable' into good all-round EU officials. So, in theory, the younger you are, the better. However, it should be clear that people fresh from education and without much real-life work experience will find it harder to demonstrate their 'general competencies' in the Assessment Centre. Since the exercises are typically simulating a work environment, they will have more difficulties in understanding what is expected in terms of behaviour at work. The effect of all this is that the average age at recruitment of AD5 generalists (in the Commission) is around 34.

For the specialist competitions (which have come to dominate) there is a completely different picture. Usually, the pre-selection of specialists is done with a so-called Talent Screener. The main parameter in the Talent Screener is the duration of your (relevant) experience, which means that only very experienced people are invited to the Assessment Centre. Usually, it is not enough to have the minimum required experience; other candidates with (much) more experience than you will make it. This is of course a major source of frustration for younger professionals. Once in the Assessment Centre, the experience factor kicks in again, resulting in older candidates on the Reserve List. I have no statistics about this, but my guess is that the average age of successful specialists must be around 45, certainly much older than for generalists anyway. For the institutions, this has the tremendous advantage that specialists can be 'operational from day one'. The drawback is of course that older people are less inclined to follow the whims of management and politicians; they are more difficult to handle. For the candidates, the drawback is that they are typically landing in a (much) lower hierarchical position than they had in their previous job, and this may affect how motivated they feel.

The 2020 Court of Auditors' report

EPSO's competition-based selection process has been running in its current form since 2012. The language regime under which competitions operated has been challenged in court, and the EU administration has begun to question the effectiveness of the selection procedure. In this context, EPSO's management board launched an interinstitutional reflection group on the selection process in the second half of 2019. In 2020, the European Court of Auditors (ECA) provided further analysis, conclusions and recommendations of relevance for a possible significant update of the selection process. The objective of the audit was to assess whether the EPSO selection process has enabled the EU institutions to meet their recruitment needs for all types of staff. The audit focused on EPSO's activities in 2012-2018. ECA reviewed EPSO's management information, interviewed staff from EPSO and the human resources services in some EU institutions, reviewed a sample of open competitions to analyse their costs and duration, and carried out a survey of managers in some EU institutions.

ECA found that the selection process is broadly effective for large-scale competitions, for the following reasons: the planning is suited to these competitions, EPSO

Figure 1.4: EPSO in numbers
(source: European Court of Auditors)

manages to attract a high number of candidates and promotes the 'EU Careers' brand mainly in Brussels. Despite a number of weaknesses in the selection process, the overall quality of the successful candidates is high. In years yielding the highest number of successful candidates, the cost of competitions is low, and holding regular competitions for candidates with generalist profiles has helped to ensure an adequate supply of potential recruits.

ECA also found that the selection process is not adapted to small-scale, targeted competitions, which are those most suited to the current recruitment needs of the EU administration: the planning of these competitions is not reliable and takes place too early to be accurate. EPSO does not consistently target its communications towards attracting suitable candidates to specialist competitions; candidates with strong specialist profiles risk being eliminated early in the selection process; the cost of competitions is higher than the institutions' own alternative selection procedures when only a small number of specialists are needed; and specialist competitions are less suitable to fill urgent recruitment needs than the institutions' own procedures.

Appraisal

Article 43 of the Staff Regulations stipulates:

> 'The ability, efficiency and conduct in the service of each official shall be the subject of an annual report as provided for by the appointing authority of each institution in accordance with Article 110. That report shall state whether or not the performance level of the official has been satisfactory. The appointing authority of each institution shall lay down provisions conferring the right to lodge an appeal within the reporting procedure, which has to be exercised before the lodging of a complaint as referred to in Article 90(2).

As of grade AST 5, the report may also contain an opinion as to whether the official, on the basis of his performance, has the potential to carry out an administrator's function.

The report shall be communicated to the official. He shall be entitled to make any comments thereon which he considers relevant.'

Article 44 (first paragraph) continues:

'An official who has been at one step in his grade for two years shall automatically advance to the next step in that grade, unless his performance has been evaluated as unsatisfactory pursuant to the last annual report referred to in Article 43. An official shall advance to the next step in his grade after no later than four years, unless the procedure laid down in Article 51(1) is applied.'

In its 'Special Report N° 10/2012'[27] the European Court of Auditors made the observation that the appraisal and promotion system in place until 2011 did not sufficiently distinguish between good performers who developed their skills and poor performers who did not. The new system introduced in 2012 aims to make a clearer distinction and not to promote those whose performance is below average.

In the new appraisal system, the Commission uses the same framework of eight 'general competencies' as EPSO. In other words, you had better take the development of your general competencies seriously, because not only will it influence your career progress, but also there are potentially severe consequences in case of incompetence.

Article 51, first paragraph:

'The appointing authority of each institution shall define procedures to identify, deal with and remedy cases of incompetence in a timely and appropriate fashion.

When adopting internal provisions, the appointing authority of each institution shall respect the following requirements:

(a) an official who, on the basis of three consecutive unsatisfactory annual reports as referred to in Article 43, still shows no progress in his professional competence shall be downgraded by one grade. If the following two annual reports still show unsatisfactory performance, the official shall be dismissed.

(b) any proposal to downgrade or dismiss an official shall set out the reasons on which it is based and shall be communicated to the official concerned. The proposal from the appointing authority shall be referred to the Joint Advisory Committee provided for in Article 9(6).'

Promotion

In virtually all organisations, promotions are a hot topic. A promotion is a way for an employer to express their appreciation for the good work, and the loyalty, of the pro-

27 http://www.eca.europa.eu/en/Pages/NewsItem.aspx?nid=1944

moted employee. The problem with promotions, especially in bigger organisations, is that it is very difficult, if not impossible, to find a system that is found to be 'fair' by everybody. If the promotion system is 'automatic' – based on seniority – the risk exists that underperformers are also promoted, and that this will make the high-performers unhappy. If, on the contrary, promotion is only based on (perceived) merit, some high-performers may be left behind because they stayed unnoticed by the management, and underperformers who manage to hide their failures – or are the bosses' favourites – can get a promotion.

Another tricky thing connected to promotions is the 'Peter Principle' (a management concept first developed by Laurence J. Peter): 'everybody is promoted to his level of incompetence.' A nasty corollary of this principle is that in the highest ranks of the organisation you will only find 'incompetent,' so unproductive people. Even though there is some truth in Peter's ideas, I do not entirely agree because he ignores the fact that people can change (they 'grow') throughout their career, by developing their competencies. So, if a person is promoted based on potential (and not on seniority or merit) the risk of people ending up at the final stage (of incompetence) is seriously diminished.

Anyone coming in from the private sector will be familiar with career paths that range from being fired for being ineffective or just in the wrong place at the wrong time, all the way to giddy fast tracking that takes people to the highest positions at breath-taking speed. The EU administration, being a civil service, is not like that. In fact, it is almost impossible to get fired once you are in, and on the other hand you simply can't come in as a 34-year-old AD5 and at 40 be a Director.

In the EU administration, the promotion system is based on a mixture of seniority and merit, and to a certain extent on potential. It is governed by the Staff Regulations:

(Article 45, first paragraph):

> 'Promotion shall be by decision of the appointing authority in the light of Article 6(2). Unless the procedure laid down in Articles 4 and 29(1) is applied, officials may only be promoted if they occupy a post which corresponds to one of the types of posts set out in Annex I, Section A, for the next higher grade. Promotion shall be effected by appointment of the official to the next higher grade in the function group to which he belongs. Promotion shall be exclusively by selection from among officials who have completed a minimum of two years in their grade after consideration of the comparative merits of the officials eligible for promotion. When considering comparative merits, the appointing authority shall in particular take account of the reports on the officials, the use of languages in the execution of their duties other than the language for which they have produced evidence of thorough knowledge in accordance with point (f) of Article 28 and the level of responsibilities exercised by them.'

Even though the concepts of merit and potential are prominently there, seniority is also taken into consideration. The Staff Regulations provide for the mathematical calculation of the number of promotion possibilities each year. The Appointing Authority (AA) may deviate from this, but the five-year average must comply with these calculations.

Say, for example, that for a given grade the average promotion rate is 33%. This effectively means that – on average – people who are currently in that grade are to be promoted after three years. This does not prevent the AA from promoting individual people already after two years (which is the minimum) or only after five, or six years, or never. In 2005, staff had to wait on average 5.6 years for a promotion. Based on all grades and categories, the average wait is now 3.4 years. That was the promise made in the 2004 reform: although starting salary levels were reduced, faster promotions would ensure at least equivalent 'career earnings'. That promise has been kept.

I think it will be clear by now that your general competencies play a major role in the promotion process. In some institutions (like the Commission), however, there is no formal score given in the appraisal report; the report only gives a qualitative description of the performance over the past year, not points. It has to be said that the EU trade unions are not very happy with this situation, because it leaves an enormous discretionary power in the hands of the Appointing Authority. Formally speaking, the AA can promote whomever they want, provided that the person is 'promotable' (after 2 years in the same grade) and that the budget of the institution allows it through the *'establishment plan'*. Likewise, a person can be put on hold forever if he or she is unlucky enough to be on the 'blacklist' of the AA. (Officially, these lists do not exist, at least not on paper, but the memory of an administration can be very long...) No wonder that the trade unions are watching the yearly promotion procedures with a very critical eye.

Retirement

It may appear a bit premature to talk about retirement at the stage when you have not even been recruited, but especially for those who have already built a career and are not 'first-jobbers' in any sense, this may be an important issue to consider before making the decision to work for the EU.

It is impossible to predict the future, especially when this is 20, 30 years from now. Our society is changing rapidly, and the EU administration is no exception to that. Two reforms (2004 and 2013) of the Staff Regulations prove this point. Hence, it is only possible to describe the situation as of today, without making any assumptions for the future.

EU officials in service before 1 January 2014 retire at 65 and EU officials recruited after 1 January 2014 retire at 66. However, it is possible to take early retirement with a reduced pension from the age of 58, or to work up until the age of 67 or, exceptionally, until the age of 70.

Pensions are paid as a percentage of the final basic salary. Officials accumulate 1.8% pension rights every year and are entitled to a maximum pension of 70% of their final basic salary. Whilst working at the EU, your contribution to the pension scheme will correspond to 10.3% of your basic salary.

As mentioned before, the average age of entry for AD5 (entry-level) staff in the Commission is 34 years old, and of course this means that some are starting at significantly older ages than this. Your age at entry, therefore, will determine how 'complete' a career you have in terms of pension rights. Most importantly, of course, your final grade and step at the moment of your retirement will determine your final basic salary and therefore pension entitlements.

Staff can apply to transfer pension rights they already have from a previous job or as a self-employed person. Similarly, you can also transfer the pension rights you gain while working at the EU into another pension fund.

It is important to note that the transfer of pension rights is not mandatory; within 2 years from your appointment, you can decide to do this or not. Very often, especially when you have been working in the private sector before, or if you have been self- employed, this transfer is not interesting, because the accumulated amount is converted into an 'equivalent' number of years of contribution and this figure can be very disappointing. Under these circumstances it can be beneficial to aim for a 'mixed' pension; one part being paid on the basis of your previous career and the other part by the EU.

Motivation of EU staff

In 2009, Wouter Vandenabeele (Public Management Institute, Catholic University of Leuven) and visiting scholar Carolyn Ban (Graduate School of Public and International Affairs, University of Pittsburgh) presented an illuminating paper on motivation and values of European Commission staff. The data used for this paper were gathered through a web-based survey to all employees of the European Commission as part of their annual satisfaction survey. As Table 1.6 shows, employees of the EC (including permanent officials, temporary staff and contract agents, and seconded national experts) reported a range of entry motivations. (As respondents could choose up to three responses, the responses total well over 100 percent.)

Broadly speaking, motivations for entry can be seen as more altruistic or more instrumental. A response such as 'I am committed to building Europe' would be classified as highly altruistic, while responses such as 'the remuneration and benefits are good'," or 'for personal or family reasons' are more instrumental. Some responses are

Entry Motivation	Percentage
Build Europe	39,5
Shape European Policy	11,4
Specific Policy Area	8,9
Work in an International Organisation	59,7
Work is Challenging and Interesting	33,2
Career Enhancement	31,7
Natural Progression	9,9
Salary/Benefits	50
Personal/Family	19,8

Table 1.6 (Source http://aei.pitt.edu/33022/1/Ban._Carolyn.pdf)

Entry Motivation	To 29	30-39	40-49	50-59	60+
Build Europe	36	38	39	41	51
Shape European Policy	12	12	11	11	12
Specific Policy Area	11	9	9	9	14
Work in an International Organisation	53	62	62	56	48
Work is Challenging and Interesting	33	32	34	33	32
Career Enhancement	45	34	30	29	27
Natural Progression	21	14	8	5	8
Salary/Benefits	45	48	51	56	48
Personal/Family	11	20	21	22	24

Table 1.7 (Source http://aei.pitt.edu/33022/1/Ban._Carolyn.pdf)

difficult to categorise in this way. While the desire for interesting and challenging work is not specifically altruistic, it can be considered an *intrinsic motivation* (i.e. driven by a desire for satisfaction or a sense of achievement), unlike a focus on salary and benefits, which is an *extrinsic motivation*. Similarly, almost two-thirds of those responding to the survey cited the desire to work in an international organisation as one of their reasons for entering, a finding that is hardly surprising, since someone who did not find such a work environment appealing would not have been likely to self-select (i.e., to apply), and since the *concours*, which is highly competitive, clearly favours individuals who already have international experience and will thus adapt easily to the EC's work environment. But without context, this response is difficult to categorise as either altruistic or instrumental.

Entry Motivation	AD	AST
Build Europe	46	35
Shape European Policy	19	4
Specific Policy Area	13	3
Work in an International Organisation	58	63
Work is Challenging and Interesting	37	27
Career Enhancement	25	36
Natural Progression	14	5
Salary/Benefits	48	58
Personal/Family	14	26

Table 1.8 (Source http://aei.pitt.edu/33022/1/Ban._Carolyn.pdf)

If we combine the first three responses, we see that almost 60 percent of respondents gave as one of their choices a more altruistic reason for entering, while 42 percent saw working for the EC as a way of advancing their career, or as a natural progression from their studies, and half identified the salary and benefits as one of the attractions. Finally, about 20 percent came for personal or family reasons. In sum, more people identified either altruistic motives or the desire to work in an international environment than salary or benefits. It is clear that, for many of those working within the EC, these values contributed to their desire to work within the European institutions.

Age and length of service both have some effect on entry motivation too. It is not uncommon to hear within the Commission that the younger generation is just not as idealistic as the old-timers. Some quite senior people are relatively recent arrivals as a result of enlargement, so length of service should be the better measure of whether the 'old guard' holds different values, but the measure used by the Commission uses categories that are not ideal for this analysis, as they end at 'more than 15 years of service'. Therefore we have only included here the analysis by age, which breaks out those older than 60 (Table 1.7).

First, an examination of the number saying that they entered because they wanted to participate in building Europe finds a moderate difference by years of service, but a much sharper difference by age, especially among the oldest group; among those over 60 still working, over half identify building Europe as a reason for joining. On the other hand, those who are younger and recently hired are more likely to say that career enhancement was a motive for joining the European Commission. Of course, one needs to be aware of the questionable accuracy of recall data, especially over a long period of time, but, taken together, this is moderate support for the hypothesis that entry motivation of new staff has changed over time. But we should be careful about interpreting it in this way because in virtually every study of motivation, there is a generational effect, with older employees identifying with more idealistic values. Whether this is a natural function of aging or a generational effect is not clear, but the findings in the Commission are in line with previous research in national governments. It is also interesting to note that salary and benefits were not ranked higher by younger or newer staff, who were much more likely than older staff to value working in an international environment.

One pattern that emerges reflects the changing nature of the EU itself. Far from a political experiment, it has become an established organisation, the importance of which is well understood. And this has led to an increasing number of academic programs focusing specifically on EU law, politics and policy, and economics. These programs spread rapidly in the new member states, attracting a significant number of students even before accession and providing a natural feeder group ready to apply for positions in the European institutions. In addition, the new member states of central and Eastern Europe had large staffs within their governments working specifically on the complex negotiations necessary for admission. So, the younger entrants are more likely to specify that they see working within the Commission as a natural progression, either from their studies or from their working within their government.

Reported reasons for entry also vary by function group. This is quite logical, as those in Assistant or secretarial positions (AST) will, in reality, have much less direct impact on policy than Administrators (AD), who report a higher interest in building Europe, although it is important to note that over one-third of AST do see building Europe as part of the reason for working in the EC. AST, predictably, don't see their roles as shaping policy or working in a specific policy area but, on the other hand, place a higher value on the tangible rewards of salary and benefits.

Women also report more instrumental reasons for joining, but this is entirely a function of their organisational role, i.e., of the fact that far more women are in AST positions, where they have little direct policy responsibility.

Staff policy

As can be understood from the above, the current human resources management mechanisms are complex, time-consuming, and expensive. There is a general feeling that HR management in the EU administration is inefficient, and that the needs of the EU institutions and agencies are not satisfied in a sufficient way. In 2019, this problem was picked up by the new Commission President, Ursula von der Leyen, and clearly expressed in her 'Mission Letter'[28] to Johannes Hahn, the Commissioner for Budget and Administration, which included the following:

- 'I want you to develop a new human resources strategy to continue the modernisation of the Commission. This should seek to create the right conditions for our skilled and motivated workforce to thrive and deliver on our priorities. The need to attract, develop and retain highly qualified staff from across all Member States will be crucial to achieving this.
- We will work closely together on my commitment to gender equality at all levels of Commission management by the end of our mandate, as well as on ensuring the Commission is a diverse and inclusive place to work.
- I want you to implement the full digitalisation of the Commission and ensure that staff have the digital skills they need.
- You should also ensure that the Commission has the right infrastructure to face up to ever evolving physical and digital security threats. This will include putting in place a genuine security culture and raising awareness on threats and the need to handle sensitive information appropriately. '

The level of the sponsorship of this undertaking can only underline its importance. The Commission seeks to enable staff to achieve their full potential and be rewarded appropriately while ensuring that the right people are in the right job at the right time, in the interest of the organisation. Even though the Commission employs only part of the total EU staff, the impact of this initiative on the other institutions cannot be underestimated; one can expect initiatives from the other institutions and agencies to align their policies with those of the Commission over the coming years.

28 Since this letter dates from 1/12/2019, the last bullet point in von der Leyen's letter turned out to be almost prophetic because then, the coronavirus just seemed a remote and insignificant threat. We know better now.

The case for change

On 16 March 2020 – right at the beginning of the pandemic – the new Director-General for Human Resources and Security of the Commission, Gertrud Ingestad, took office. She immediately started the preparatory work for a complete overhaul of the Commission's HR strategy. Her 'case for change' is based on the following ideas:

- The world is changing, and the speed of change is accelerating.
- The Commission needs to lead by example and implement internally the policies that are promoted at European level.
- The challenges are increasing, but the resources are shrinking (2014 reform, Long-term EU Budget 2021-2027).
- The Commission's HR services need to be improved.
- The Commission needs to offer attractive career opportunities to recruit the best talent in Europe.
- The 'new normal' after the pandemic will be different from the 'old normal'.
- In the extensive consultation process for this strategy, staff and managers asked for:
  - More empowerment, faster decision-making.
  - More and fairer career opportunities.
  - Greater flexibility in working arrangements.
  - Increased application of common values, including trust, transparency, fairness, empowerment, accountability, collaboration, care, agility, delivering value, learning, innovation, and risk acceptance.

At the time of writing of this book, the Commission was still in the planning stage for these reforms, but the main lines of action are clear:

- Gender equality, diversity, and inclusion.
- Recruiting from all backgrounds.
- Improving the geographical balance.
- Faster and better recruitment. Simplified and shortened EPSO competitions, development of a head-hunting service and creation of a single inter-institutional competence database.
- Simplification of the selection process for temporary and contract agents.
- More career opportunities inside the organisation. Regular internal competitions, extending the maximum duration of contracts, and establishing the Junior Professional Programme on a lasting basis.

PART II:
THE COMPETENCIES

2. Why being smart isn't enough

In the previous chapter, I gave an overview of the wide range of job opportunities in the EU administration. In this chapter, I will discuss the 'competency framework' used by the EU institutions and explain a methodology for how to develop the various competencies throughout your career. But first, let's take a step backwards and have a look at how the EU recruits its staff.

Selection and recruitment

The 'mother of all EU competitions' could well describe the open competitions organised by EPSO. The selection tests vary from one competition to another, but the stages within each competition are similar:

- Pre-selection: competitions that attract more than 1,000 applicants begin with a pre-selection stage composed of computer-based psychometric tests, known as CBTs. Candidates sit the tests in test centres in the EU Member States and sometimes worldwide. (For smaller competitions, the CBTs are done in the Assessment Centre, but in that case candidates only have to reach a pass mark, and the scores are not taken into account in the overall results.)
- Admission: The EPSO Selection Board checks that the candidates that had the best scores in the pre-selection tests also fulfil the eligibility criteria set out in the Notice of Competition and invites the best-performing applicants to the next phase. In practice, the verification of the diploma requirements is only at the very end if and when the Selection Board proposes adding your name on the reserve list.
- Talent screener: For specialist competitions, the Selection Board assesses the applications and selects the candidates whose qualifications best satisfy the criteria set out in the Notice of Competition. This selection is made solely based on the responses to specific questions in the 'talent screener' tab of the online application form in EPSO's IT tool.
- Intermediate test: In some competitions, there is an intermediate phase where candidates have to sit further tests. These tests are usually delivered in test centres in the EU Member States and can, for example, include an e-tray exercise or a translation test.
- Assessment Centre: If candidates' scores in the previous stages are among the best, and they meet the eligibility criteria set out in the Notice of Competition, they are invited to the Assessment Centre. Assessment Centres are designed to evaluate the pre-defined competencies by observing participants' behaviour. They consist of several different simulation exercises in a job-relevant context where behaviour is compared to the competency profile. Candidates may be tested on two types of competencies: field-specific com-

petencies and general competencies. Field-specific competencies are the applied knowledge and skills needed to meet the specific job profile for that particular competition. General competencies are abilities that all officials need to have a successful career within the European institutions.

- Reserve list. The names of the candidates who perform best at the Assessment Centre are put on a reserve list. Institutions can then access their CVs and contact the laureates they think are the most suitable to meet their recruitment needs.

When we look more closely at the various tests, we can see that there are broadly three categories of tests:

- Psychometric tests that measure the candidate's 'general intelligence' – multiple choice questionnaires (MCQs) for abstract, numerical, and verbal reasoning. In some (rare) competitions there is also a situational judgement test (also computer-based).
- Assessment of the 'field-specific competencies' – talent screener, interview 'in the field', and sometimes written tests in the field.
- Assessment of the 'general competencies' – e-tray exercise (computer-based), case study (computer-based), general competency-based interview (GCBI), situational competency-based interview (SCBI), and sometimes an oral presentation, or a role-play exercise.

Remote proctoring

In 2020, due to the Covid-19 outbreak and to conclude the competitions within a reasonable period, EPSO decided to organise remote online testing for the Assessment Centre tests. Remote online testing allows candidates to sit the tests at home, in the office, or in an EPSO accredited test centre throughout Europe and worldwide. The testing takes place via online videoconferencing, using Skype for Business, now Microsoft teams, but the main underlying ideas remained intact.

In June 2021, EPSO announced the introduction of remotely proctored computer-based tests. We all are aware of how the invigilation process works in the offline method of conducting an exam; experienced invigilators are hired to physically monitor the test-taking candidates and then assigned to their respective centres where they are responsible for maintaining a cheat-proof, strict test-taking environment. In the case of remote proctoring, the basics of the invigilation process are same, it's just that it is automated. Remote proctoring allows a proctor to monitor an ongoing online exam with the feasibility of AI integrated technology.

The remote proctoring system not only allows greater flexibility and cost-effectiveness, but it is also particularly relevant in the context of the current global situation, where attendance at test centres may present significant challenges due to public health measures such as travel restrictions and lockdowns in multiple countries, also entailing closure of test centres.

EPSO will inform the candidates via the competition's relevant page on their website if this option is available for a specific test event. If this option is offered, but you do not choose the remote proctoring option, you have the possibility to book a test in one of EPSO's accredited test centres worldwide. It is your responsibility to check if any travel or other restrictions apply or are likely to apply at the selected test centre, bearing in mind the pandemic situation.

This means that candidates are systematically tested or assessed, along three 'dimensions,' as depicted in Figure 2.1.

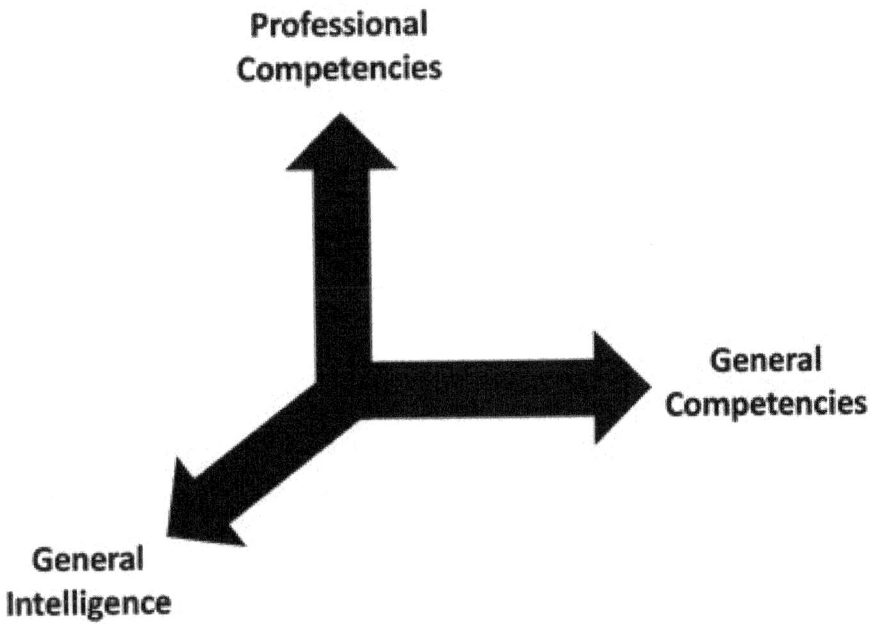

Figure 2.1:
Competencies and intelligence

General intelligence

The definition of 'general intelligence' is somewhat controversial amongst psychologists, but by far the most widely used in practical settings is the psychometric approach, trying to capture the complex concept into a single score known as the Intelligence Quotient, or IQ. The IQ is supposed to be constant in time, and it is influenced by environmental and genetic factors, the relative importance of which has been the subject of much research and debate. A person's IQ is derived from the results of standardised tests and is said to be stable over time.

The IQ score bell curve

Standardised IQ tests are designed so that their scores have a 'bell curve' distribution in the general population with an average of 100. This curve has a peak in the middle where most people score and elongated ends where only a few people score. In statistics this is called a 'normal distribution'.

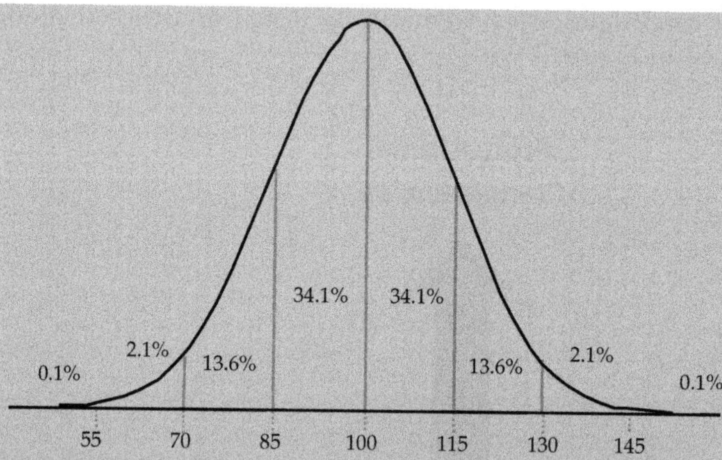

An IQ of 115 or more can be considered a high IQ score or level; it is one standard deviation above the average. Only some 15% of the population have an IQ level of 115 or above. Around 2% of the population has an IQ greater than 130, which is 'gifted' intelligence. This is an IQ of 2 standard deviations from the average IQ. Merely one person in thousand has an IQ that is 3 standard deviations away from the average. At the age of 21, Nikola Tesla[1] earned his first PhD. He ultimately held four PhD degrees (Philosophy, Physics, Electrical Engineering, and Mechanical engineering). His exact IQ score is unknown, because there were no tests at the time he lived, but it is estimated to have been around 200, which is exceptionally high.

For recruitment and job selection purposes more specific verbal, numerical and abstract reasoning tests are preferred.

In the EPSO open competitions, the general intelligence tests (the computer-based tests, CBTs) are mainly used as a pre-selection mechanism; only the candidates with the highest scores make it to the next stage (intermediate test or Assessment Centre). A notable exception is those selection procedures where the CBTs are done during the Assessment Centre phase; the candidates in that case only have to demonstrate that they are 'smart enough' by simply obtaining a pass mark (usually 50%) for the CBTs. Most of the other selection procedures used by the EU administration also have general intelligence tests. Notably, the internal competitions, CAST, JPP, and even the Assessment Centres for senior and middle management have CBTs.

Unlike your IQ score, your scores for the CBTs can be dramatically improved through practice. This can be decisive when participating in a competition or selection procedure. You can practise using 'The Ultimate EU Test Book' (with separate Assistant and Administrator editions) published by the same publisher as this book[2]. An alternative (or, better still, complementary) method simulating exam conditions online can be found on eutraining.eu[3] They have test packs adapted for the various types of competitions.

1 Nikola Tesla (1856 – 1943) was a Serbian-American inventor best known for his contributions to the modern alternating current (AC) electricity supply system. The name Tesla is now used by a famous American company that designs, manufactures, and sells electric cars.

2 https://www.johnharperpublishing.co.uk/books/

3 https://eutraining.eu/products/administrator#preselection-phase

Professional competencies

Professional competencies are skills, knowledge and attributes that are valued by other professionals that are connected to your profession. Professional competencies may also be referred to as 'technical competencies.' More specifically, professional competencies are those 'hard skills' (knowledge and know-how) that are necessary to do a particular job.

Professional competencies are frequently assessed based on the candidate's (formal) education and their (proven) experience in the field through an in-depth interview taken by other – preferably more experienced – professionals in that field. Professional competencies may also be assessed through other, more hands-on exercises such as writing a report, translating a text, or using office automation tools.

Most EPSO competitions involve assessing your professional competencies as part of the selection process. A notable exception here are the AD5 'generalist' competitions. Since this is an entry-level competition there is only a university degree required and no professional experience. Instead, in this competition, the candidates get a 'motivational interview,' mainly testing their knowledge of the EU. One could say that for generalists, knowledge of the EU is the equivalent to the technical knowledge of specialists. All other types of selection procedures (temporary agent, CAST, certification, middle management…) also have some kind of professional competency testing.

For the open competitions, the 'duties' and 'selection criteria' can typically be found in annexes I and II of the Notice of Competition. For the other types of competitions or selection procedures you will find this information in the 'vacancy notice' or 'call for expression of interest'. It is clear that you must carefully read this information and duly prepare for the tests that are provided for the professional competencies.

General competencies

Being an intelligent and seasoned professional is not enough to pass the EPSO selection procedures, or to build a successful career in the EU. You must also possess a series of 'general competencies'. These are the interpersonal and behavioural skills that will enable you to work well with other people in the organisation. For the EU administration one could call these your 'bureaucratic skills'.

General competencies are 'soft skills.' Soft skills help us do our jobs. They allow us to effectively and efficiently use our technical skills and knowledge. They improve the way we interact with other people. They enable us to get our work done on time, and to meet the expectations of our fellow workers, managers, and external contacts. They influence how we feel about our jobs, our motivation, and how others perceive us. General competencies are behaviours to be demonstrated by all staff members, no matter which function they have and in all the institutions of the EU. General competencies are also called 'core competencies.'

It is sometimes said that hard skills are what you need to get a job and soft skills are what you need to keep it. Translated to the EU context, you might say that you need the professional competencies to become a temporary or contract agent, and the general competencies to become a permanent official.

Competency frameworks

Competency frameworks are used in many government and private organisations, including the EU administration.

A competency framework is a model that broadly describes performance excellence within an organisation. Such a framework usually includes a number of competencies that are applied to multiple occupational roles within the organisation. Each competency defines, in generic terms, excellence in working behaviour; this definition then establishes the benchmark against which staff are assessed. A competency framework is a means by which an organisation communicates which behaviours are required, valued, recognised and rewarded with respect to specific occupational roles. It ensures that staff, in general, have a common understanding of the organisation's values and expected excellent performance behaviours. Competencies listed in the competency framework enable staff to have a clear understanding of the behaviours to be displayed and the levels of performance expected in order to achieve organisational results. They provide the individual with an indication of the behaviours and actions that will be valued, recognised and rewarded. A competency framework helps recruiters to select employees more effectively. And as well as for recruitment and selection purposes, competency frameworks are also used in career development, performance management and HR planning.

The competency framework used by the European Personnel Selection Office is the result of a comprehensive job analysis undertaken in 2009 for all entry grades of EU officials across the institutions. All officials recruited at the entry grades between 2004 and 2007 were interviewed and, in parallel, line managers and senior stakeholders were questioned. The outcome of the job analysis was the development of the competency framework. The emphasis was on identifying those competencies common to all European institutions and therefore suitable for use in open competitions. As a result, the EU institutions are looking for employees who demonstrate the following general competencies:

- Analysis and Problem Solving
- Communicating
- Delivering Quality and Results
- Learning and Development
- Prioritising and Organising
- Resilience
- Working with Others
- Leadership

In 2014, EPSO organised a stakeholders' survey, the results of which were unequivocal: all eight competencies are important and there is no need to add additional ones.

You may have noticed that I listed the general competencies (except leadership) in alphabetical order. That is because, in the selection process, they are all equally important. The leadership competency was put at the end of this list because it is only assessed for Administrator competitions, regardless of whether it is for generalists, specialists, or linguists.

The Commission uses the same framework of eight competencies in the new staff appraisal process introduced from 2012. The other institutions and bodies of the EU have somewhat different appraisal processes, but the underlying ideas are largely similar.

This framework does not include competencies commonly found in private sector organisations like 'client focus,' or 'negotiating' because, in essence, the (lower tiers of) the EU is an administration and not a commercial or political organisation.

For middle and senior managers in the EU, the competency frameworks look different:

As you can see, here too the competencies are focused on administration and not on diplomacy or politics. One could say that the competencies that are expected from

Middle Managers	Senior Managers
Information Management	
Integrating	Developing Vision Conceptualising
Task Management	
Managing the organisation Steering	Managing the organisation Organising
People Management	
Motivating Guiding People	Inspiring Directing Teams Building Teams
Interpersonal Management	
Influencing	Influencing
Personal Management	
Coping	Achieving Objectives

Table 2.1:

Competency framework for senior and middle managers

the managers of the EU administration are essentially the same as those of the other staff, but with a much stronger focus on the managerial and leadership dimension of the general competencies. Middle and senior managers are 'super administrators' and not politicians.

A rough 'mapping' of the management competencies and the general competencies may look as depicted in Table 2.2.

Management Competencies	EPSO Competencies
Integrating Developing Vision Conceptualising	Analysis and Problem Solving Communicating Learning and Development
Managing the organisation Steering Organising	Leadership Working with Others Prioritising and Organising
Motivating Guiding People Inspiring Directing Teams Building Teams	Leadership Working with others Prioritising and Organising
Influencing	Leadership Communicating Working with Others
Coping Achieving Objectives	Leadership Delivering Quality and Results Resilience

Table 2.2: Mapping competencies

In practice, the appointment of middle and senior managers is heavily influenced by political considerations (nationality, gender, and personal history). Nevertheless, the results of the mandatory Assessment Centre, run by an external service provider, have to be made available to the Consultative Committee on Appointments (CCA) before it carries out the selection interviews.

Since this book is not about politics, I will further build on the idea that all EU officials, including middle and senior managers, have to develop at least the eight general competencies as laid out in the EPSO competency framework.

EPSO's eight general competencies

Below is an overview of the eight general competencies in the EPSO framework. A more detailed description of each of these competencies, and how to improve them, will be given in chapters 3 to 10.

Analysis and problem solving

Analysis and problem solving is at the centre of what most people do at work; any job will bring problems to be solved, every day, and you are expected to come up with solutions. Employers want people who take personal responsibility for making sure targets are met, who can see that there might be a better way of doing things, and who are prepared to explore and implement change. They want people who don't give up when things go wrong but who will seek a way around problems.

In more concrete and practical terms, EU staff are expected to:

- Solve daily problems autonomously.
- Refer all questions that cannot be answered to the appropriate person.
- Recognise problems that need to be addressed.
- Act promptly to solve or report problems.
- Recommend possible solutions when raising a problem.
- Work in teams to solve problems and exchange information.
- Make decisions only after getting all facts from all stakeholders.
- Think out-of-the-box.
- Use good judgment in making decisions.
- Consult with their supervisor for matters outside the scope of their authority.

Communicating

Communication is very important to any organisation's success. Effective communication leads to an improvement in overall organisational performance. Good communication also increases job satisfaction; employees feel empowered if bosses or managers are really listening to employees and respond. Because of this, communication is key to personal success.

In today's multimedia world, there are more ways than ever before to communicate: email, text messaging, voicemails, blogs, tweets, videoconferences, and social media. But one thing hasn't changed: there are effective and ineffective ways to express yourself. All professionals need to know how to communicate if they want their message to come across.

In more concrete and practical terms, EU staff are expected to:

- Communicate clearly when speaking or writing.

- Listen carefully and ask questions when needed to clarify requests.
- Use appropriate communication tools for the situation.
- Speak clearly and respectfully to others.
- Maintain the confidentiality of information.
- Provide others with information in a clear and timely fashion.
- Write documents with no typos or formatting errors.
- Check spelling on all documents before sending them out.
- Report all accidents or incidents.
- Be open and honest in all communication.
- Keep their supervisor informed of problems as they develop.

Delivering quality and results

Delivering quality and results means not only doing your work well but also delivering on your promises – to everyone, including yourself. Delivering quality and results is about meeting expectations, being a true professional, not some sub-standard amateur that happens to have the technical skills that fit the job description. Meeting expectations is about taking personal responsibility and initiative, within a set environment and following the given rules and procedures. Meeting expectations is also working to your full potential, beyond your strict job description, going the 'extra mile', and surprising your bosses and those you deal with by producing better than anticipated results.

In more concrete and practical terms, EU staff are expected to:

- Meet and exceed the expectations of the people around them.
- Do their work in an enthusiastic and effective manner.
- Work in a professional manner and complete tasks by the deadlines.
- Perform job tasks in a satisfactory manner.
- Demonstrate a willingness to accept extra work.
- Propose new services or improved ways of working.
- Familiarise themselves with the office procedures, rules and regulations.
- Observe administration policies.
- Keep organised, neat, and accurate records.
- Keep all documentation updated as needed.
- Keep up with the knowledge and know-how related to their position.
- Attend job related professional development activities.
- Attend job related social activities.

- Meet production standards for their position.
- Prepare for the meetings they attend.
- Refrain from conducting personal business in working hours.
- Go the 'extra mile'.
- Be courteous to the public at all times.
- Listen to external stakeholders carefully in order to determine their needs.

Learning and development

Learning and developing doesn't end when you finish school. Learning and developing is one of the most important parts of our lives and our work. Yet, despite having attended many years of education, many of us have no idea how to approach our pursuit of knowledge or the development of our skills for either personal or professional reasons.

Learning and developing brings about changes in the way we act, think and/or feel about ourselves, about other people, and about the world around us. These changes may be permanent or temporary depending on our own perceptions of the importance and relevance of the knowledge gained.

In more concrete and practical terms, EU staff are expected to:

- Take active steps to permanently improve their knowledge and development.
- Develop new skills on their own initiative.
- Work actively on developing strengths and overcoming weaknesses.
- Improve knowledge and skills out of personal interest and natural curiosity.
- Actively seek feedback from others to improve their own performance.
- Pool knowledge and expertise.
- Be aware of the wider context and of their own contribution.
- Learn other languages.
- Actively mentor or coach others.

Prioritising and organising

In the workplace some activities are more important than others, and some are more urgent than others. With the exception of planned meetings, there will be no fixed portions of your time during a working day. Your supervisor will likely only give you so much information about when they expect you to deliver your work by – if they even do that.

Prioritising and organising is the behaviour of taking conscious control over the amount of time you spend on specific activities. It is about goal setting, effective scheduling, prioritising and choosing what to do and what not to do, delegating tasks, analysing and reviewing your spent time, organising your workspace, keeping your concentration and focus on your work, and motivating yourself. You have to manage your time to increase your effectiveness, your efficiency, your productivity, and in the end to meet the expectations of people around you.

In more concrete and practical terms, EU staff are expected to:

- Set specific goals and priorities for completing tasks.
- Monitor progress and change plans if needed.
- Complete all work tasks by their deadlines.
- Keep organised, neat, and accurate records.
- Work at a rate that is similar to their fellow workers.
- Maintain a to-do list to stay on top of deadlines.
- Prioritise tasks and properly plan work.
- Delegate assignments to subordinates when appropriate.
- Avoid procrastination.
- Attend scheduled meetings and arrive for these meetings on time.
- Observe time reporting rules and regulations.
- Plan and account for the use of overtime.
- Observe scheduled work and meal breaks.
- Call their supervisor if they must be late or absent.
- Avoid tardiness and report to work on time.
- Use sick leave only for their own personal sickness.
- Request leave in advance at times that do not hinder office operation.

Resilience

Being resilient is adapting well in the face of adversity, trauma, tragedy, threats or significant sources of stress. Resilience – the ability to effectively cope with losing, failing, and not getting what you want – is an important quality for anyone to cultivate to achieve success and well-being. To live and to work is to risk failure, and resilience helps people to bounce back from the unavoidable adversities and obstructions that risk involves.

Resilience is sometimes confused with perseverance, but there is a difference. In short, perseverance keeps you going when you are convinced that you are on the right track, but you are just not getting enough traction to get to your destination. Being resilient enables you to start all over again when the wheels come off.

Another related idea is grit. Grit is a personal characteristic based on person's passion for a particular long-term objective, coupled with a powerful motivation to achieve that objective. This insistence of effort promotes the overcoming of obstacles or challenges and serves as a driving force in achievement realisation.

In more concrete and practical terms, EU staff are expected to:

- Be mentally and physically in top condition.
- Continuously work on self-improvement.
- Manage their workload effectively and efficiently.
- Remain calm under pressure.
- Prepare for busier periods to come.
- Handle failures and interpret setbacks professionally, not personally.
- Be able to control emotions, behaviour and desires.
- Work with the management, not against it.
- Consider failures and setbacks as learning opportunities.
- Embrace change.
- Be self-motivating.
- Be optimistic.

Working with others

Working in teams involves the ability to effectively interact, cooperate, work with and manage conflicts with other people in order to complete tasks and achieve shared goals. This includes working with just one other individual or working in small or large groups of people – for example fellow workers, managers, stakeholders and contractors.

Effectively working with others involves understanding and working within the group's culture, rules and values; joint planning and decision-making; negotiating and compromising; expressing one's opinions and ideas and respecting those of others, including people of divergent backgrounds; and being flexible in terms of roles, including knowing when to take a leadership role and knowing when to look for a team approach.

In more concrete and practical terms, EU staff are expected to:

- Work in teams.
- Treat others with respect.
- Encourage and appreciate individual contributions.
- Share information and knowledge with others.
- Share ideas with other workers.
- Be courteous to fellow employees.
- Assist others when their own work has been completed.
- Encourage others to express their views.
- Take account of different opinions.
- Be able to listen to what others are saying.

- Accept input from others regarding ideas for improvement.
- Make an effort to understand other people.
- Be sensitive to the feelings of other people.
- Refrain from gossiping with other workers.
- Refrain from interfering with co-workers' productivity.
- Assist others when asked to do so.
- Be assertive.
- Be clear about what they feel, what they need and how it can be achieved.
- Balance personal goals and team goals.
- Attend job related social activities.

Leadership

Managing consists of supervising a group of people or a set of entities to achieve a goal. *Leading* refers to influencing, motivating, and enabling others to contribute to organisational success. Leaders are those that others look to for direction, inspiration and advice, and to keep others going when the going gets tough. Influence and inspiration, not power and control, distinguish leaders from managers.

In more concrete and practical terms, EU staff with leadership responsibilities are expected to:

- Explain their vision and ideas clearly and succinctly.
- Strike a good balance between detail and the need for clarity.
- Set specific goals and priorities for completing assignments.
- Design realistic work methods, procedures and timetables for achieving project goals.
- Plan and assign the work of subordinates effectively and fairly.
- Set realistic but challenging goals.
- Provide resources, guidance and training for subordinates to do their jobs.
- Work in an enthusiastic and effective manner.
- Work in a way that inspires confidence and trust among subordinates.
- Adapt their communication to the audience.
- Distinguish between 'need to know' and 'nice to know.'
- Speak with conviction and authority.
- Listen to, synthesise, and integrate others' ideas.
- Display openness and transparency in sharing information with others.
- Be prepared to deliver tough messages when necessary.

- Recommend corrective action or discipline when appropriate.
- Counsel workers privately behind closed doors.
- Inspire and help others develop skills and competencies.
- Show a high degree of self-awareness.
- Ask others for feedback on their own performance.
- Give others feedback on their performance.
- Communicate performance expectations clearly.
- Be 'real' in everything they do or say.
- Lead and motivate others by example.
- Inspire others to perform at their best.
- Show drive and determination to succeed.
- Delegate work to develop skills and knowledge.
- Be visible and accessible to fellow workers.

Anchors and indicators

General competencies are further divided into 'behavioural anchors' and 'indicators.'

Behavioural anchors are specific, easy-to-apply examples of behaviours that demonstrate the competency. With every anchor, there are a number of **positive and negative indicators**, or specific associated behaviour. Indicators – or observable behaviour – can be associated with multiple anchors, as is shown in Fig. 2.2.

In fact, a behavioural anchor is something that is used, for example, to define the level someone has reached on a particular competency from 1 to 10. In this sense it is very similar to an indicator, but indicators tend to be simple 'positive' and 'negative' poles, whereas the anchors define all points in between. For instance, 'team working' would be a behavioural anchor for the working with others competency, which is further translated into positive indicators such as 'listens to others' or 'waits for another to finish speaking before voicing their own contribution'. This behaviour is also considered as part of the communicating and even leadership competencies.
This means that competencies are interrelated or overlapping. Certain anchors or indicators are the hallmark of a given competency but can have a clear relationship with some other competencies as well.

In Annex 1, you will find an extensive overview of anchors and indicators for the eight competencies. Even though these are not exactly the ones that are used by EPSO, this overview is very comprehensive, and it will give you a good idea of what these competencies are about. In the next eight chapters, these competencies will be further discussed in a narrative way.

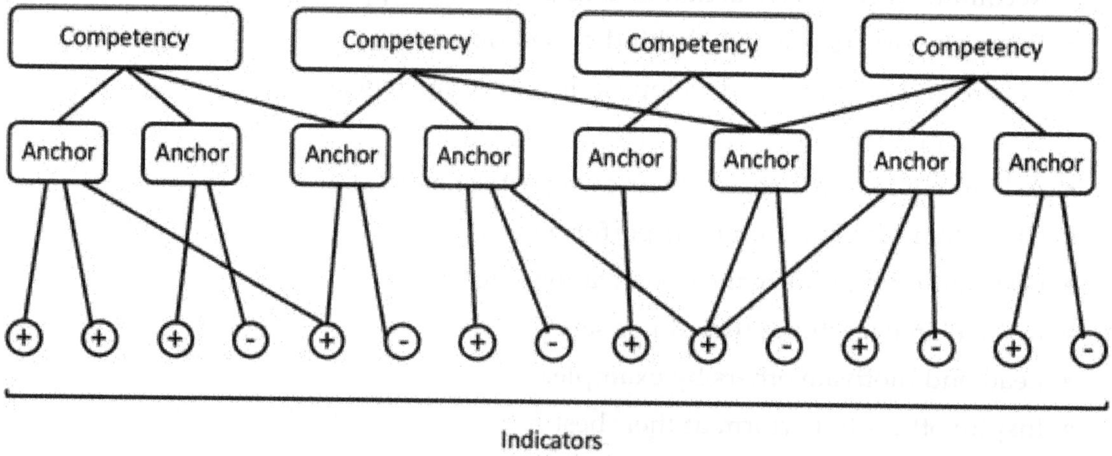

Figure 2.2:
Anchors and Indicators

The competency passport

People who have gone through an Assessment Centre in an EPSO competition will receive a 'competency passport', which consists of an overview of their general competencies in a graphical format, along with a textual description of their strong points and the opportunities for improvement. This competency passport is inserted into the personnel file.

Personal development

As can be understood form the above, the importance of personal development – developing your 'general competencies' – cannot be underestimated. And that is what this book is all about. In the rest of this chapter, I will touch on a methodology you can apply for your own personal development.

Merriam-Webster defines a *methodology* as 'a set of methods, rules, or ideas that are important in a science or art: a particular procedure or set of procedures'. A methodology does not set out to provide solutions – it is, therefore, not the same as a method. Instead, a methodology offers the theoretical underpinning to understand which method, set of methods, or so-called 'best practices' can be applied to a specific case, for example to obtain a specific result. In this book, I suggest you follow the GROW model to improve your performance at work.

The GROW model

This book has been written from a coach's point of view. Coaches use models, and the model I am going to use is the GROW model, so before explaining in more detail about the methodology I suggest you follow, it will be useful to say a bit more about what the GROW model.

The GROW model is a simple, yet powerful method for goal setting and problem solving. It was developed in the United Kingdom, mainly by Sir John Whitmore[4] and is used extensively in corporate coaching. The principle behind the GROW process is rooted in the Inner Game theory[5] developed by Timothy Gallwey[6]. Both methods start from the observation that many individuals are struggling to achieve their goals because they are not learning from experience, and are not aware of the available knowledge that could help them:

> 'In every human endeavour there are two arenas of engagement: the outer and the inner. The outer game is played on an external arena to overcome external obstacles to reach an external goal. The inner game takes place within the mind of the player and is played against such obstacles as fear, self-doubt, lapses in focus, and limiting concepts or assumptions. The inner game is played to overcome the self-imposed obstacles that prevent an individual or team from accessing their full potential.'

The power of the GROW model lies in the fact that it leads to a clear result in four simple steps. Because it is the person being coached who formulates the problem – and generates the ideas – the solution sticks better and leads to lasting results.

The GROW model is a four-step sequence of questions. The acronym stands for:

GOAL – What do you want?

REALITY – What is happening now?

OPTIONS – What could you do?

WAY FORWARD – What will you do?

(Note: some authors refer to 'Obstacles' for the 'O', and to 'Will' for the 'W', but the underlying ideas of the model remain unchanged.)

A useful metaphor for the GROW model is planning a journey. You start with the map: where do you want to go (Goal) and where are you now (Reality)? Then you look at the possible routes (Options). Finally, you pick one route and plan the journey, taking into account all the conditions and obstacles (Way forward).

The GROW model provides a framework for having an effective conversation for achieving any goal or addressing any kind of problem or challenge. But GROW is a model, not the truth! It is of little value without the context of awareness and respon-

4 Sir John Whitmore (†2017) was Chairman of Performance Consultants International, the foremost provider of coaching and leadership development and performance improvement in the workplace globally.

5 www.theinnergame.com

6 Timothy Gallwey is a respected American tennis player and coach, who has written a series of books in which he has set forth a new methodology for coaching known as 'The Inner Game'.

sibility. *Awareness* increases input, interest, learning and recall. *Responsibility* is generated by offering choice, which leads to self-esteem, confidence and self-motivation.

GROW is flexible in terms of the sequence of the steps. The dialogue usually starts with Goal questions and then explores the present with Reality questions. After this, you can move freely between the four elements, as needed. The goal may change along the way. New insights and awareness may require a return to the Reality section, followed by more Options and actions (Will) related to them.

Setting goals

When setting a goal, in the G part of GROW, there are certain parameters, which will make the goal stronger and more achievable.

You may already be familiar with SMART goals. SMART is a mnemonic for the 5 steps of specific, measurable, attainable, relevant, and time-framed goals. It is a simple tool mostly used by businesses and organisations to go beyond the realm of fuzzy goal setting into an actionable plan for results, but it can also be used for individual goal setting:

Specific:

Goals should be simply written and clearly define what you are going to do. This is your vision of the future.

Measurable:

Goals should be measurable so that you have tangible evidence that you have accomplished the goal. Usually, the entire goal statement is a measure on its own, but there are frequently several short-term or smaller measurements built into the goal.

Attainable:

Goals should be attainable; they should stretch you slightly so you feel challenged but defined well enough so that you can achieve them. You can meet almost any goal when you plan your steps wisely and establish a timeframe that allows you to carry out those steps. As you carry out the steps, you can achieve goals that may have seemed impossible when you started. On the other hand, if a goal is impossible to achieve, you may not even try to accomplish it. Attainable goals motivate you – impossible goals demotivate you.

Relevant:

In the context of your performance development, your goals should be linked to a competency and a specific anchor, within the list of your current priorities.

Time-framed:

Goals should be linked to a timeframe that creates a practical sense of urgency, or results in tension between the current reality and the vision of the goal. Without such tension, the goal is unlikely to produce a relevant outcome.

Different levels of goals

When setting yourself goals you should distinguish between final goals and performance goals. A *final goal* may be something like 'I want to run the 20 kilometres of Brussels'; a *performance goal* helps you to achieve your final goals, for example 'I will go jogging for half an hour every morning.'

It is important to recognise that there are different levels of goals, and that we have to attend to each level in our journey.

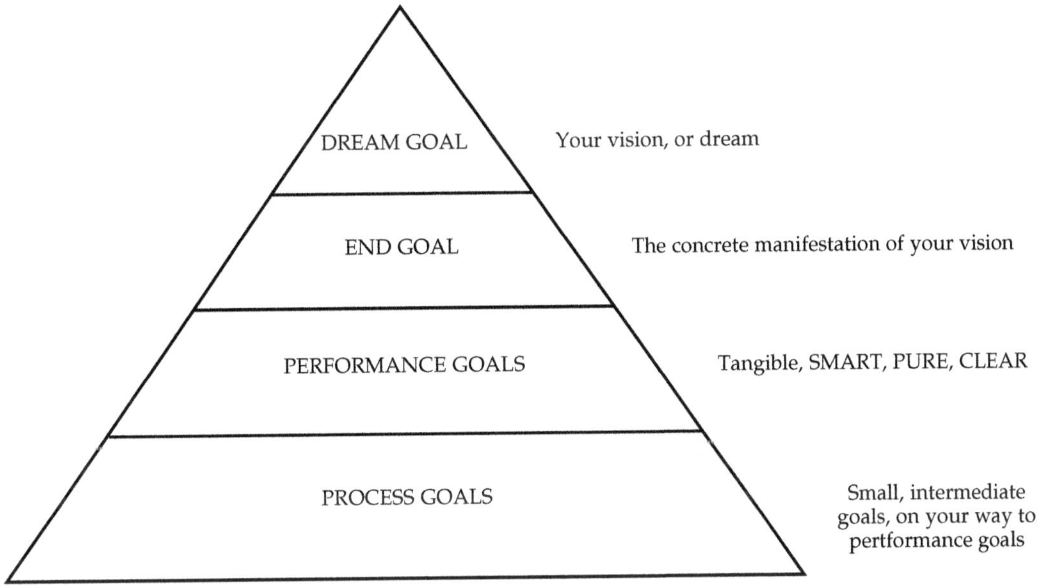

Figure 2.3: Different levels of goals

Methodology

Developing your general competencies starts with awareness and ends with responsibility. If you are not aware that you have a problem with a given competency you will never be inclined to develop it[7]. To build this awareness, the first thing you could do is use the online self-assessment app that accompanies this book. You may find it difficult to do this on your own, because the human mind has a tendency for 'blind spots' when it comes to its own behaviour. You may need external feedback provided by a professional coach or trainer, or at least someone who knows you very well and is willing to discuss it with you in an open and honest manner. Of course, your EPSO competency passport (if you have one) and the feedback from your superiors will come in handy as well.

7 There is a French expression that goes: 'quand on connaît le nom de sa maladie on est à moitié guéri.' You might say: when you've worked out what's wrong with you, you are half-way to being cured.

A brief guide to SMART goal setting

- Develop several goals. A list of five to seven items gives you several things to work on over a period of time.
- State goals as declarations of intention, not items on a wish list. Use clear, specific language. Start your goal statement with 'To' followed by a verb.
- Attach a date to each goal. State what you intend to accomplish and by when. A good list should include some short-term and some long-term goals. You may want a few goals for the year, and some for two or three-month intervals.
- Be specific. Sometimes a more general goal can become the long-term aim, and you can identify some more specific goals to take you there.
- Share your goals with someone who cares if you reach them. Sharing your intentions with your parents, your best friend, or your supervisor will help ensure success.
- Write down your goals and put them where you will see them. The more often you read your list, the more results you will get.
- Review and revise your list. Experiment with different ways of stating your goals. Goal setting improves with practice.

Example:
'To run the '20 km of Brussels' in May 20XX and complete the race in under 1,5 hours to beat my personal best time.'

If your total self-assessment score using the app for a given competency is below 50, you really have an important (and urgent) issue. This is definitely a 'priority 1' competency to work on. If your score is between 50 and 70 there is the possibility for improvement, so it is important, but maybe not so urgent. I would make this your 'priority 2'. If your score is between 70 and 90, then basically all is fine since you meet and exceed the expectations. So, improving on this competency may not be considered as very important; however, since you are already good (aware and responsible) it will probably be easy for you to improve with some fine-tuning of your behaviour through some 'quick wins'. This is your 'priority 3.' Finally, if your score is higher than 90, well, there's not much you can – or should – do; you are exceptionally good at this, so don't bother.

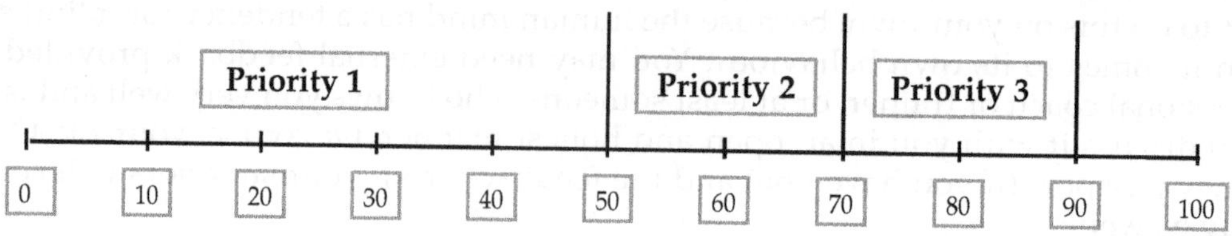

Figure 2.4: Priority setting

Note that I have here been using the ideas behind the **Eisenhower matrix** to help you define your priorities. I refer you to chapter 7 on prioritising and organising for a better understanding of this concept.

Once you have identified the areas where there is room for improvement – and not before – you can start to think about your options. These may be simple things like reading some books on the topic or taking part in some formal training in your domain of activity. But sometimes more drastic options have to be considered: if you are really not good at what you do for a living, and training doesn't help, maybe it's time to go for another challenge and change jobs.

Once you have listed – and carefully considered – your options, it's time to decide and commit to what you will actually do. Step out of your comfort zone. Start with the 'low hanging fruit' to build confidence. Set yourself SMART operational goals and use an 'agile' and iterative approach. Ask for help. Be patient.

Based on your priorities, the understanding of your Goals, your Reality, and the available Options you can then design your own personal development plan (Will or Way Forward).

It is possible to improve every single competency, but there is no point in trying to improve everything at once; this won't work. Once you have a rough idea about your strengths and development areas, make a plan and first try to improve in those areas where your performance is worst. The best approach is to identify your weakest points first, improve and consolidate your development, and then start the process all over again.

Proceed in small, achievable steps. Identify 'quick wins' (process goals) that will make you gain confidence once achieved, before tackling your performance goals. Personal development takes time, a lot of time, and it is too easy to get discouraged when the distant goals are not reached from the first attempt.

And remember: YOU are responsible for your own development, not your boss, your colleagues, your coach, or your mentor. And neither is the HR department.

Online toolkit

This book comes with an online self-assessment and 360-degree feedback toolkit, which can be used independently. The tool is based on the GROW model. The output is an actionable development plan, taking into account your priorities in a personalised way.

The toolkit can be found at:

http://www.johnharperpublishing.co.uk/the-ultimate-eu-career-development-toolkit/

Once registered as a user you can use it for as long as you want, for free.

The foundation of the toolkit is a set of questionnaires, very much like Annex 1 of this book, but the online format makes it user-friendlier, and some extra features are added to make it even more actionable. Not only can you make a self-assessment by

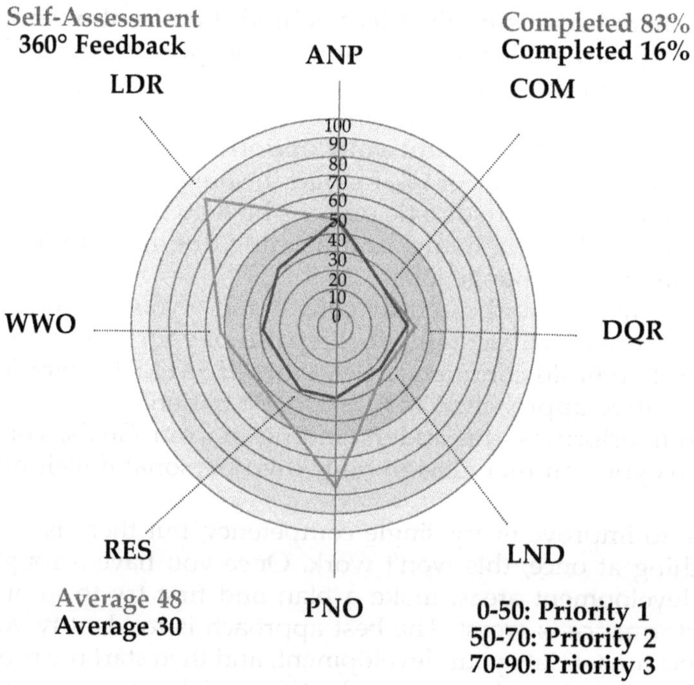

Competency	Self-Assessment	360° Feedback
ANP - Analysis and Problem Solving	47	47
COM - Communicating	25	25
DQR - Delivering Quality and Results	34	30
LND - Learning and Development	26	24
PNO - Prioritising and Organising	76	28
RES - Resilience	44	29
WWO - Working with Others	52	29
LDR - Leadership	87	33

10	Extremely Weak
20	Very Weak
30	Weak
40	Fair
50	Satisfactory
60	Good
70	Strong
80	Very Strong
90	Excellent
100	Outstanding

Figure 2.5: Competency passport

completing these questionnaires, but you can if you want also ask others – friends, colleagues, coaches, and supervisors – to do so. In this way you can build a Johari window[8], and gain a better understanding of your own 'blind spots'. This will effectively increase your self-awareness and allow you for a better self-development.

The intermediate result of the self-assessment, and the 360-degree assessment, is presented in multiple formats: a competency passport (a bit like the example in Fig. 2.5), a Johari window, and an Eisenhower matrix[9]. This concludes the 'Reality' step in the GROW cycle.

Then comes the time for setting your goals. Ideally, your goals are linked to the Priority 1 items in the Eisenhower matrix. The tool also encourages you to set SMART goals, at different levels of development (process, performance, end, dream).

The next step is to think about your options. Options are the things you could do to improve this or that competency, without thinking too much about the feasibility (I suggest you use the 'brainstorming' technique for this part).

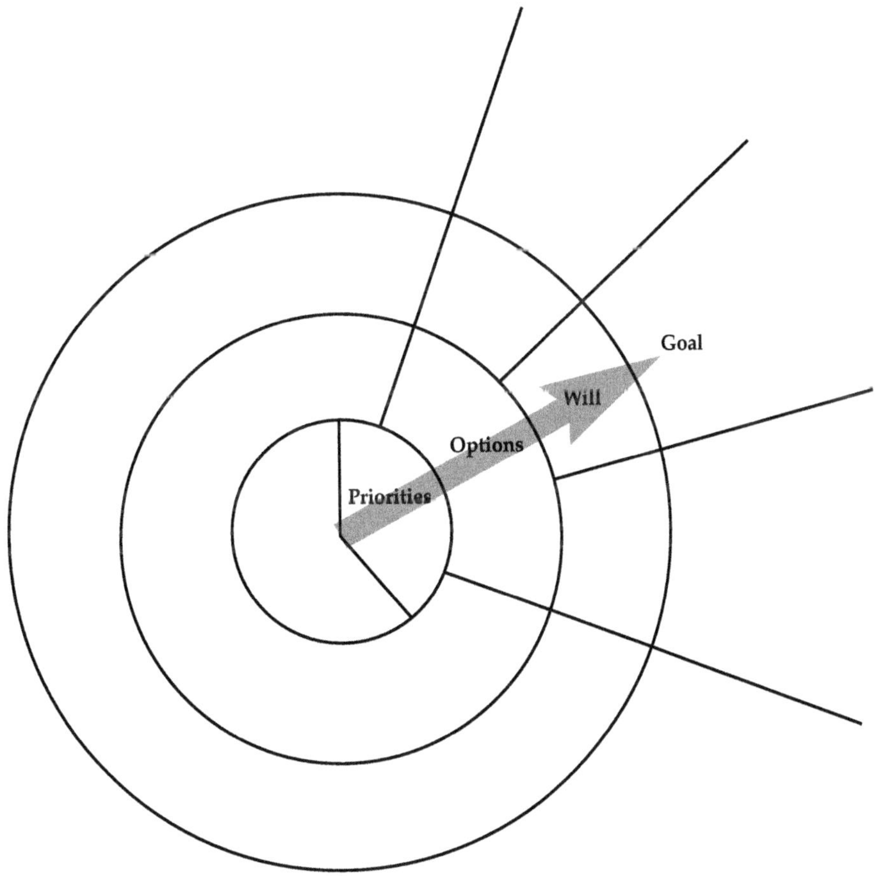

Figure 2.6: GROWing a Competency

8 The Johari window is a technique that helps people better understand their relationship with themselves and others.

9 The Eisenhower Matrix helps you decide on and prioritise tasks by urgency and importance.

Finally, comes the 'Way Forward' – or 'Will' – part of the GROW cycle. Here you make a (realistic) selection of the options, attach timing to them, and commit to the actions you will effectively undertake to achieve your goals.

The idea is to use the online tool (and the book) in an iterative way, building your development in small cycles, as is illustrated in Fig. 2.7.

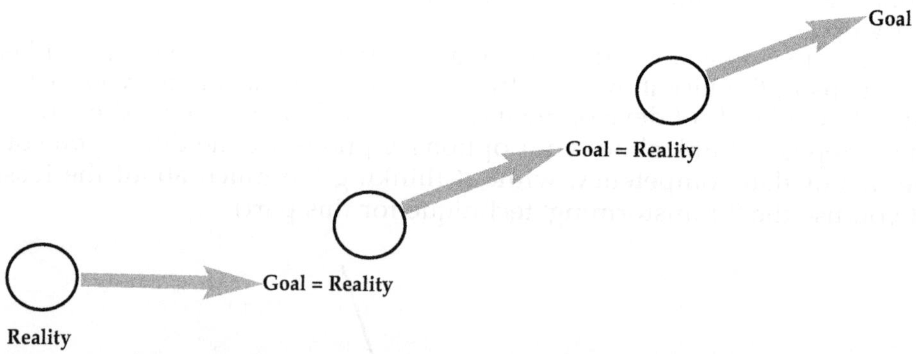

Figure 2.7: GROW cycles

3. Analysis and problem solving

Competency definition: 'Identify the critical facts in complex issues and develop creative and practical solutions'.

'Most people spend more time and energy going around problems than in trying to solve them.' – Henry Ford[1]

Problems are at the centre of what most people deal with at work every day; a fundamental part of working life is finding ways to solve them. So being a confident problem solver is really important to your success. Much of that confidence comes from having a good process when approaching a problem.

Some problems are clearly more difficult or complex than others. Unfortunately there is no single, universal way in which all problems can be resolved. There is a universal methodology though, the steps of which are outlined below:

- Identification
- Analysing
- Generating possible solutions
- Making a decision
- Implementation
- Feedback

A somewhat simplified mnemonic for this is IDEAL:

- **I**dentify the problem
- **D**efine the problem
- **E**xamine the options
- **A**ct on a plan
- **L**ook at the consequences.

This methodology is applicable to virtually any kind of problem, including the ones that are regularly encountered in the EU institutions, such as defining a new policy, drafting a new regulation, or in the day to day business when preparing a new IT project, setting up a new evaluation system etc.

We will go over the different steps in more detail in the following pages.

The most prominent difference between an issue and a problem is the solution. When you have an issue, you generally can easily come up with the solution. A problem, on the other hand, is not something that you can solve without serious consideration, and possibly even a certain amount of guesswork.

1 Henry Ford (1863–1947) was an American industrialist, the founder of the Ford Motor Company, and pioneer of the development of the assembly line technique of mass production.

How physicians, engineers and scientists approach problems differently

Physicians, scientists and engineers are trained to have different approaches to problem solving. These three types of problem solvers can be seen as archetypes representing the training methods each field is known for. Of course, any individual would use a mix of these problem-solving methods based on their knowledge and experience, but they may never have received formal training in methods other than the ones they are knowledgeable in.

The physician. Medical doctors are trained to think about differences and categories. A patient's presenting signs and symptoms are processed, and then historical information is used to determine the most common diagnosis associated with the collected evidence. This is a categorical approach to problem solving, based on probabilities. This is a very efficient approach when a patient has a problem that has been encountered before. However, when the patient has something not seen before, this is a very inefficient way of treating the problem, as the MD moves to less and less common solutions.

The scientist. In contrast to the physician, the scientist is trained to look at a problem in the abstract and use testable assumptions (models) to isolate all the component parts of a problem and solve them (individually, if possible) in a logical way. Breaking down the problem into its component parts can determine the independent root causes. Then, using those root causes, the scientist can arrive at a solution to the overall problem. Solving problems in this way is more resource- and time-intensive than the physician's method, but if the right hypotheses are posed, this system can handle a broader range of problems and generate new data that are applicable to other problems.

The engineer. One way to think of the engineer's method is as a hybrid of the scientist's and physician's methods. The scientist starts with a new set of hypotheses for each problem, and the physician starts with a set of solutions that can be applied. The engineer is trained to take a known solution and then use that as a starting point to find a solution that applies to the problem. A very simple example can illustrate this. The most common way to find the area of a triangle is to multiply the base and height and to divide the result by two. This rule has been proven by mathematicians, and applies to all types of triangles (right, equilateral, isosceles, obtuse, and acute). So, if an engineer has to calculate the surface of a triangle, he will simply apply this rule, and not try to re-invent the theory behind it.

Problem identification

'A problem well put is half solved.' – John Dewey

Problem identification involves detecting and recognising that there is a problem, and identifying the nature of the problem – in other words, *defining* the problem. Identifying a very clearly defined and specific problem is the first critical step to successful problem solving.

A problem occurs when there is a difference between what 'should be' and what 'is' – a difference between the ideal and the actual situation. A problem is directly or indirectly related to a desired outcome or standard of behaviour.

Is it an issue or a problem?

Size often dictates the difference between an issue and a problem. An issue is smaller, and it doesn't present such a degree of difficulty that you have to seek out the advice of others in order to figure out the impact of the issue. A problem is larger in scale; it requires the advice and guidance of those around you in order to solve it.

An issue is something that might only cause you some frustration. On the other hand, a problem can impact people and situations around you, even if they are not directly related to the problem. For instance, forgetting your lunch is an issue, but losing your job is a problem.

At an organisational level, an issue is something that can be handled behind closed doors, impacting no one but the people of highest authority in the situation. A problem involves information that must be available, because there will be cause to involve other employees, other organisations, or citizens, in the solution to the problem.

When confronted with a problem, the natural tendency is to propose possible solutions. Consequently, thinking and discussion focus on the merits of the proposed *solution(s)*, rather than an in-depth discussion of the possible *causes* of the problem itself. Inexperienced problem solvers will soon find out that a great solution isn't worth much, if the problem it resolves was misidentified.

Very often, finding or identifying a problem is more important than the solution. For example, Galileo recognised the problem of needing to know the speed of light, but did not come up with a solution. It took ages of advances in mathematics and science to solve this problem. But Galileo still received credit for identifying the problem.

Sometimes problem identification may be nothing more than the art of asking the right questions at the right time (this is actually the best kept secret of coaching).

Problem analysis

'If I had an hour to solve a problem I'd spend 55 minutes thinking about the problem and 5 minutes thinking about solutions.' – Albert Einstein

Following the problem identification, problem analysis involves gaining more information about the problem and increasing understanding. This phase is all about fact finding and analysis, building a more comprehensive picture of both the goal(s) and the barrier(s). This stage may not be necessary for simple problems – or issues – but it is essential for more complex problems. The following things need to be done in problem analysis:

- Identifying the stakeholders
- Understanding the root causes
- Identifying the constraints

Identifying the stakeholders

A *stakeholder* is anyone who is affected by the problem and its resolution. The following questions can be helpful in identifying the stakeholders:

- Who are the main users?

- Are there any other internal or external users whose needs must be addressed?
- Who are the beneficiaries or customers?
- Who else is affected?
- Is there anyone else who cares?
- Who will evaluate and approve the solution when it is delivered and deployed?
- Who will monitor and provide feedback?

Stakeholder analysis is a process of systematically gathering and analysing qualitative information to determine whose interests should be taken into account when developing and/or implementing a policy or program. An interesting read can be found on the website of WHO[2].

Understanding the root causes

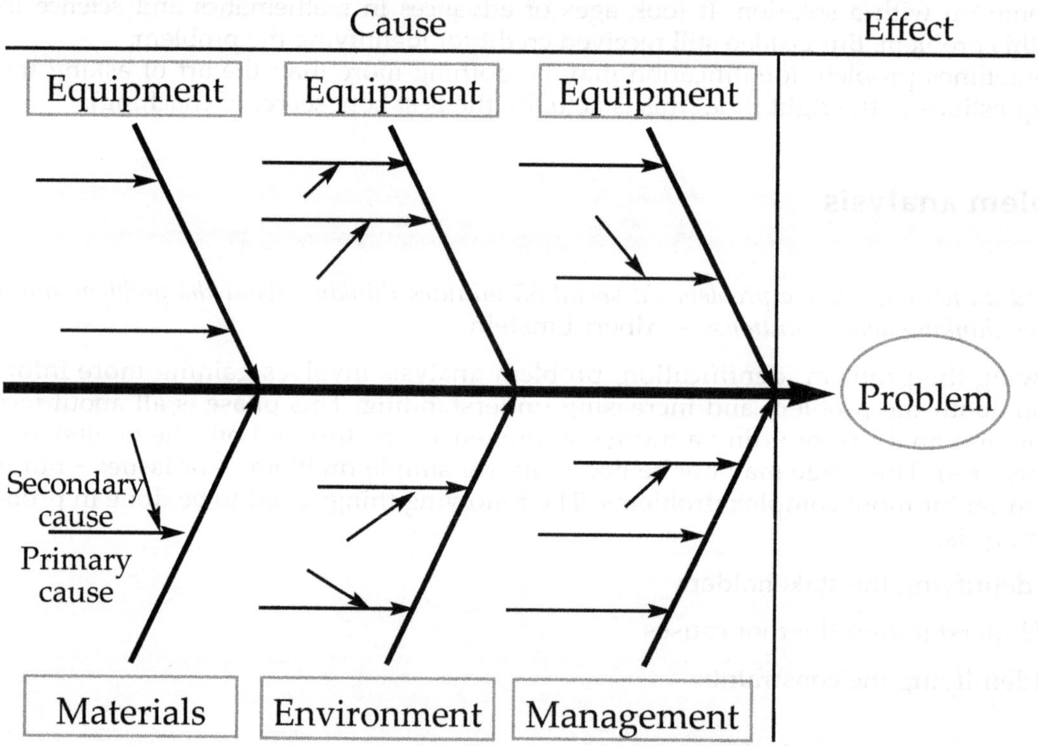

Figure 3.1: A fishbone diagram (Wikipedia)

2 http://www.who.int/workforcealliance/knowledge/toolkit/33.pdf

A root cause analysis is a systematic way of uncovering the 'roots' – or underlying causes of an identified problem, or the symptom of a problem. The fishbone (or Ishikawa[3]) diagram identifies the possible causes for an effect or problem. It can be used to structure a brainstorming session. It immediately sorts ideas into useful categories (see Figure 3.1).

'5 *Whys*' is an iterative question-asking technique used to explore the cause-and-effect relationships underlying a particular problem by repeating the question 'Why?' The '5' in the name derives from an empirical observation on the number of iterations typically required to solve a problem.

Not all the root causes are equally important. That is why another way of looking at the root causes is the Pareto[4] diagram (Figure 3.2).

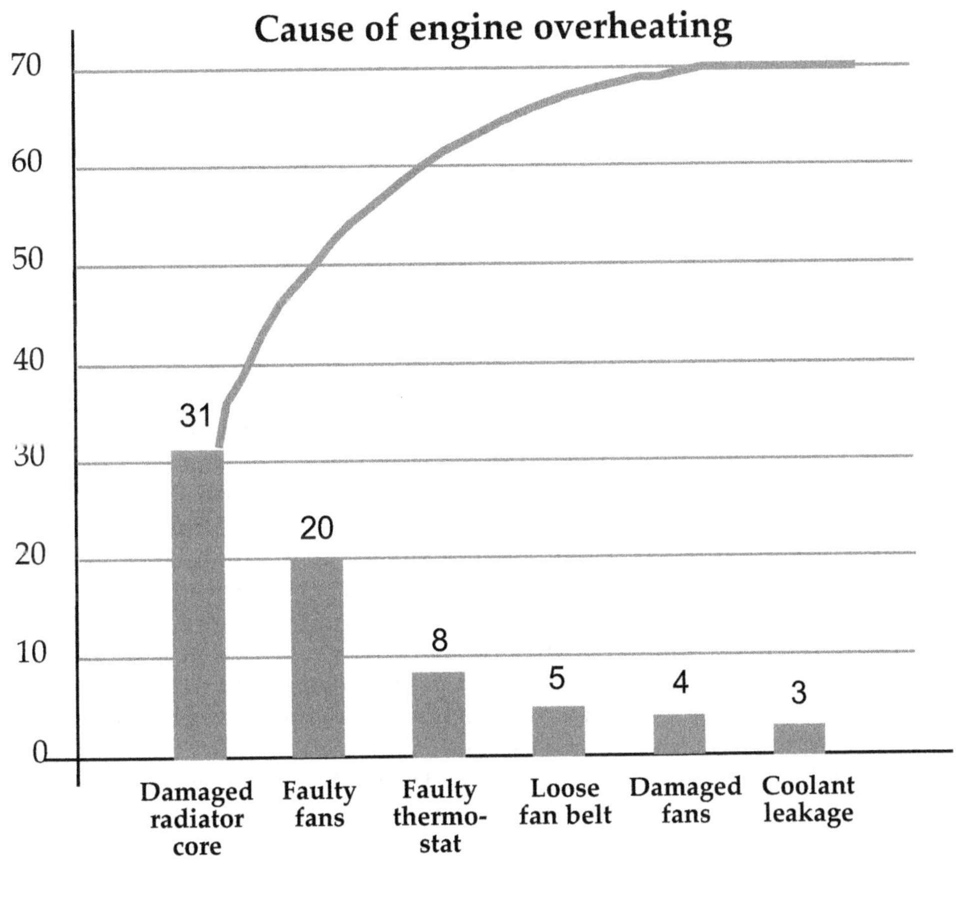

Figure 3.2: A Pareto diagram (Wikipedia)

3 Kaoru Ishikawa (1915–1989) was a Japanese organisational theorist, and professor at the Faculty of Engineering at the University of Tokyo.

4 Vilfredo Pareto (1848–1923) was an Italian engineer, sociologist, economist, political scientist, and philosopher.

This technique helps to identify the top portion of causes that need to be addressed to resolve the majority of problems. In essence, the problem-solver estimates the benefit delivered by each action, then selects a number of the most effective actions that deliver a total benefit reasonably close to the maximum possible one.

Although Pareto charts can be easily graphed in various project management applications, not everyone has access to software of this type. Fortunately, these analysis tools can also be created in Microsoft Excel.

Identifying the constraints

Constraints are restrictions on the degree of freedom we have in providing a solution. Constraints have the potential to restrict our ability to deliver a solution as we imagine it. Therefore, each constraint must be carefully considered as part of the problem solving process, and some constraints may even cause us to reconsider the entire approach we initially conceived. Below is a non-exhaustive list of some possible constraints:

- What are the financial or budgetary constraints?
- Do internal or external political issues affect potential solutions?
- Are there environmental or regulatory constraints?
- Are there legal constraints?
- Is the schedule defined, are there deadlines?
- What (human) resources are available?

Kurt Lewin's **Force Field Analysis** is a powerful strategic tool used to understand what's needed for change in both corporate and personal environments. Lewin states: 'An issue is held in balance by the interaction of two opposing sets of forces – those seeking to promote change (driving forces) and those attempting to maintain the status quo (restraining forces)'. What he postulates is that whenever driving forces are stronger than restraining forces, the status quo or equilibrium will change.

This is an interesting idea, especially if we apply it to understanding how people move in response to change and why they resist change. There will always be driving forces that make change attractive to people, and restraining forces that work to keep things as they are; successful change is achieved by either strengthening the driving forces or weakening the restraining forces.

The force field analysis integrates with Lewin's **three-stage theory of change**[5] as you work towards unfreezing the existing equilibrium, moving towards the desired change, and then freezing the change at the new level so that a new equilibrium exists that resists further change.

This point is of particular importance in the EU context, as it differs considerably from a typical private sector situation. For example, an independent publisher can publish what he wants about the EU, he can work with whatever authors, printers, etc. that he chooses without any tendering process. An independent publisher can initiate a project without doing an impact assessment or getting a sign-off from anyone else. He doesn't have to make versions available in multiple languages, can set his own

5 http://www.change-management-coach.com/kurt_lewin.html

deadlines, budget etc. The range of options for most staff in the EU are much more circumscribed and even a director-general cannot just decide to do his own thing.

Generating possible solutions

'Be passionate about solving the problem, not proving your solution.' – Nathan Furr

During this stage you generate a range of potential solutions, but with little or no attempt to evaluate them at this point. In a group situation this stage is often carried out as a brainstorming session, letting each person in the group express their views on possible courses of action. Different people will have different expertise in different areas and it is useful, therefore, to hear the views of everyone.

During brainstorming, defer judgement on whether solutions are achievable, practical, or reasonable. This is the time for creative thinking, not critical thinking. Creative thinking is like putting your foot on the accelerator of a car. Critical thinking is putting your foot on the brake. There is a time for each but not at the same time, or otherwise the engine will stall.

I invite you to have a look at the TED talk by Tom Wujec[6]: 'Got a wicked problem? First tell me how you make toast.'[7] His books are worthwhile reading too.

Making a decision

Following on from the previous stage it is now time to look at each potential solution and carefully analyse it on its merits. Some solutions may have to be eliminated, due to the constraints that were previously identified.

Determine the criteria you are going to use to evaluate the pros and cons of the potential solutions. Agree upon both the criteria and the weighting. Determine whether you will evaluate ideas primarily on the basis of cost, timeframe, and interference with existing operations, or on any other considerations.

For each criterion, assess its importance relative to the other criteria. If the criteria are weighted equally, your evaluation will simply be based on how each potential solution measures up to all the criteria alike. If the criteria deserve different weightings, assign a unique weighting to each.

Since the world around us is constantly changing, solutions don't last as long as people typically think. Also realise that many 'good enough' solutions – or 'quick fixes' – meant for a few months end up in place for a few years, long past their intended lifespan and appropriateness. Reach agreement on the likely lifespan of the alternative solutions before evaluating them.

Finally, you make a decision on which course of action to take. Decisions can be made through either an intuitive or reasoned process. Intuition is a combination of your past experience and your personal values. It is worth taking your intuition into

6 Tom Wujec (1959) is the author and editor of several books, and a pioneer in the emerging practice of business visualisation.

7 https://www.ted.com/talks/tom_wujec_got_a_wicked_problem_first_tell_me_how_you_make_toast?language=en

account, especially for simple problems, but complicated decisions tend to require a more formal approach, involving reasoning.

There are a number of reasons that can prevent effective decision-making. These can include (among others):

- Not enough information.
- Too much information.
- Too many stakeholders.
- Emotional attachments, or the lack thereof.
- Incomplete problem definition, analysis or invalid proposed solutions.
- Too many, or contradictory constraints.
- Lack of experience or knowledge of the problem domain.
- (Political) taboos or inability to think outside the box.

The dangers of groupthink

The term *groupthink* was first described in 1972 by social psychologist Irving Janis[8]. It is a phenomenon that occurs when a group makes incorrect decisions because group pressures lead to a deterioration of 'mental efficiency, reality testing, and moral judgment'[9]. Groups affected by groupthink ignore alternatives and tend to take irrational actions that dehumanise other groups. A group is especially vulnerable to groupthink when its members are similar in background, when the group is insulated from outside opinions, and when there are no clear rules for decision-making.

Janis documented eight symptoms of groupthink:

- *Illusion of invulnerability* – Creates excessive optimism that encourages taking extreme risks.
- *Collective rationalisation* – Members discount warnings and do not reconsider their assumptions.
- *Belief in inherent morality* – Members believe in the rightness of their cause and therefore ignore the ethical or moral consequences of their decisions.
- *Stereotyped views of out-groups* – Negative attitudes to those seen as the 'enemy' make effective responses to different opinions seem unnecessary.
- *Direct pressure on dissenters* – Members are under pressure not to express arguments against any of the group's views.
- *Self-censorship* – Doubts and deviations from the perceived group consensus are not expressed.

8 Irving Lester Janis (1918–1990) was a research psychologist at Yale University and a professor emeritus at the University of California at Berkeley.

9 'Victims of Groupthink: A psychological Study of foreign-policy decisions and fiascoes' (1972) by Irving Janis.

- *Illusion of unanimity* – The majority view and judgments are assumed to be unanimous.
- *Self-appointed 'mind guards'* – Members protect the group and the leader from information that is problematic or contradictory to the group's cohesiveness, view, and/or decisions.

Clearly, the EU institutions are not immune to the hazards of groupthink, and – in fact – most of these symptoms can be frequently observed. One deep-seated example of groupthink in the institutions is the idea that the only reason people don't like the EU is because they are ignorant and it is just a matter of educating them. This reflects the perspective of the institutions, embedded in the founding treaties themselves, that the EU and indeed further integration are by definition a 'good thing' – and it makes genuine engagement with those outside that consensus uncomfortable and at times impossible.

Adopting some of the following measures may prevent groupthink:

- The leader should assign the role of critical evaluator to each member.
- The leader should avoid stating preferences and expectations at the outset.
- Each member of the group should routinely discuss the group's deliberations with a trusted associate and report back to the group on the associate's reactions.
- One or more experts should be invited to each meeting on a staggered basis. The outside experts should be encouraged to challenge the views of the members.
- At least one articulate and knowledgeable member should be given the role of devil's advocate (to question assumptions and plans).
- The leader should make sure that a sizeable block of time is set aside to survey warning signals from rivals; leader and group construct alternative scenarios of rivals' intentions.

Implementation

'An idea that is developed and put into action is more important than an idea that exists only as an idea.' – Edward de Bono[10]

Implementation means acting on the chosen solution. During implementation new problems may arise, especially if identification or analysis of the original problem was not carried out properly. If this happens one should go back to the previous stages. I will expand on some possible implementation strategies below.

10 Edward de Bono (1933-2021) was a Maltese physician, psychologist, author, inventor and consultant.

Seeking feedback

The final stage of problem solving is verifying that the implemented solution has been successful. This can be achieved by monitoring and gaining feedback from the stakeholders for any changes that have occurred. It is good practice to keep a record of outcomes and any additional problems that occurred. This is a very important stage, because in this you verify if the stakeholders' expectations were met, and to what extent – in other words this is the 'delivering quality' part of the delivering quality and results competency.

Implementation strategies

In large and complex projects, various implementation strategies can be applied. These can be roughly divided into three categories: waterfall, iterative, and agile.

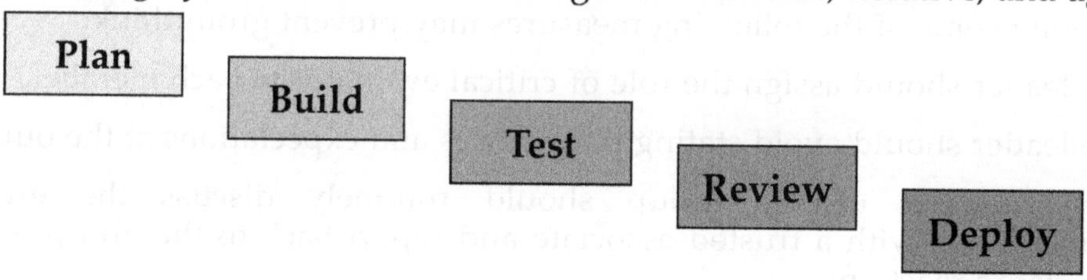

Figure. 3.3: The waterfall approach

The more traditional **waterfall approach** is a linear approach in which each stage of the problem-solving project has to be finished before the next one can begin. There is also typically a milestone between the stages; for example, the problem definition must be reviewed and approved by the stakeholders before the analysis and solution generation can begin. Figure 3.3 describes the distinctive phases of this approach. In this figure the horizontal axis is time, and the vertical axis describes the functional dependencies between the phases. For example, you must have a plan before you can start building; the system has to be built before you can test it; you can only review once you have tested; and finally, you can only deploy if it has been reviewed (and accepted).

One of the positive things about this approach is that all agree – in writing – very early in the project on what will be delivered. This makes planning, budgeting and allocating resources more straightforward. Progress is easily measured, as the full scope of the work and the milestones are known in advance. A major potential drawback of the pure waterfall approach, however, is the risk that the stakeholders will be dissatisfied with the implemented solution, once delivered. As all deliverables are based exclusively upon documented requirements, a stakeholder may not entirely understand what solution will be delivered until the project is almost finished. By that time, changes can be difficult (and costly) to implement.

In the **iterative approach**, the problem is split up into a few, more or less independent chunks, and these chunks are then executed separately and consecutively, sometimes even by different teams. In public administrations this technique is frequently used to stay within the constraints of the (annual) budget.

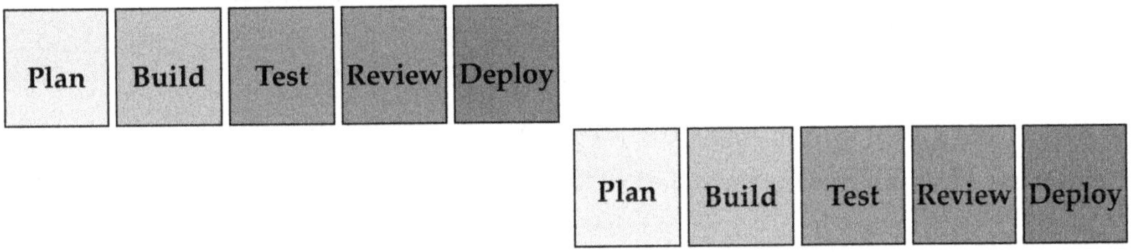

Figure 3.4: The iterative approach

One issue with this approach is linked to the difficulty of making accurate estimates of the time and resources needed to complete the work and meet the expectations of the stakeholders. With this approach we implicitly 'fix' the time (e.g. the budget year) and the resources (money, people, etc) but because of the many uncertainties it is impossible to guarantee that the deliverables will effectively meet the expectations of all the stakeholders.

Agile is also an iterative approach, but with a much finer granularity, both in terms of timing and deliverables, along with the possibility of adjusting the overall planning on-the-fly. This approach emphasises the rapid delivery of partial solutions, and every partial solution is 'time-boxed'. Each time box has a defined duration with an agreed list of deliverables, planned at the start of the time box. Deliverables are prioritised by business value as determined by the stakeholders. If all planned work for the time box cannot be completed, work is reprioritised and this information is used for future planning. Agile relies on a very high level of stakeholder involvement throughout the project.

The main advantage of the agile approach is easy to see: the stakeholders have frequent and early opportunities to see the work being delivered, and to make decisions and changes throughout the project. However, the very high degree of stakeholder involvement may present problems for some of them, because they simply may not have the time or the interest for this type of participation.

Teamwork

'Coming together is a beginning, staying together is progress, and working together is success.' – Henry Ford

In organisations, the individual competency of analysis and problem solving is closely related to the competency of working with others.

A team is a small group of people who regularly meet – in person or perhaps online – to discuss shared agendas, causes, or interests. Each team is unique and draws on the backgrounds and abilities of its members. Depending on the situation, teams can have a different name: task force, work group, study group, commission, committee, or such like. In the EU administration, teamwork is frequently used alongside – and across – the hierarchical organisation.Members of a team can exchange information, personal experiences and the results of individual endeavours and set up physical meetings, online conferences, or any other form of collaborative work. You need three types of people in any team effort:

- *Deciders* - They hold the authority and are the 'bosses'.
- *Doers* - The implementers get the job done.
- *Experts* - They bring the knowledge, expertise and/or charisma to the table.

In order to have really productive problem solving meetings, the best behaviour of all participants is as follows:

Maximize	Minimize
Listening	Criticising
Appreciating	Impatience
Seeking usefuness	Being judgmental
Clarifying	Boredom
Accepting	Rejecting

Table 3.1

Why should we have teams to solve problems?

Firstly, when you are working in a team there is a higher chance that most of the things you are uncertain about will come to the surface and the answers will arise naturally.

Secondly, it is often quite hard to grasp every detail of a problem when you are alone.

Thirdly, through their cooperative but also competitive nature, teams promote both critical thinking and creativity in the form of new questions and explanations within discussions and debates.

Finally, when you are alone, the temptation to procrastinate is much larger than when in an interactive environment. Although taking breaks is important, dipping in and out of your work mood can only make you waste time, and contribute to the build-up of frustration due to being inefficient.

'Too many cooks spoil the broth' is an expression meaning that a team becomes inefficient if too many people are involved, as it becomes more difficult to coordinate, communicate with all members and maintain the necessary discipline. In workplace situations the ideal size of a team tends to be around three to four people, but sometimes more are needed, for example if a variety of specific technical expertise is required.

Critical thinking

'It is the mark of an educated mind to be able to entertain a thought without accepting it.' – Aristotle

Critical thinking is the process we use to reflect on, assess, and judge the assumptions underlying our own and others' ideas and efforts. The Socratic method[11] is at the heart of critical thinking. It is a method of disciplined questioning that can be used to pursue thought in many directions and for many purposes, including: to explore complex ideas, to get to the truth of things, to open up issues and problems, to challenge assumptions, to analyse concepts, to distinguish what we know from what we don't know, and to follow out the logical implications of thought or to control the discussion. The key to distinguishing Socratic questioning from questioning per se is that Socratic questioning is systematic, disciplined, deep and usually focuses on fundamental concepts, principles, theories, issues or problems.

According to authors Richard Paul and Linda Elder there are nine types of Socratic questions:

- Questions of clarification
- Questions that probe purpose
- Questions that probe assumptions
- Questions that probe information, reasons, evidence, and causes
- Questions about viewpoints or perspectives
- Questions that probe implications and consequences
- Questions about the question
- Questions that probe concepts
- Questions that probe inferences and interpretations

You can find out more about this method in their book 'The Thinker's Guide to the Art of Socratic Questioning.'[12]

Creative thinking

'The significant problems we face cannot be solved at the same level of thinking we were at when we created them.' — Albert Einstein

Creative thinking uses very different approaches from critical thinking; it involves a much more relaxed, open, and playful approach. *Thinking outside the box* is a

11 Named after the classical Greek philosopher Socrates.

12 'The Thinker's Guide to the Art of Socratic Questioning' (2007) by Richard Paul and Linda Elder.

metaphor that means to think differently, unconventionally, or from a new perspective; it refers to creative thinking.

When thinking creatively we are looking for many possible solutions, rather than just one. We allow ourselves to make wild and crazy suggestions, make mistakes, and we do not judge ideas early in the process. We allow ourselves to doodle, daydream or play with a theory or a suggestion.

Creative thinking is more about attitude and self-confidence than it is about talent. Creativity is often disorderly, unstructured, and unpredictable. Strong emotional self-control is needed to allow creative thinking states to arise, as it is important to be able to cope with risk, confusion, disorder and the feeling that you are not progressing.

In hindsight, every great idea seems obvious. But how can you be the person who comes up with those ideas? In his book 'Thinkertoys'[13], Michael Michalko unveils the secrets of creative genius and brings creative techniques within everyone's reach. This book presents dozens of field-tested, immediately usable tools for generating ideas and stimulating creativity, and provides an understanding of many creativity techniques that can be applied to problems, opportunities, or situations. The principles and methodologies include a variety of options developed by Michalko, and the strategies are easily adapted to specific needs or industries.

Lateral thinking

'Everyone has the right to doubt everything as often as he pleases and the duty to do it at least once. No way of looking at things is too sacred to be reconsidered. No way of doing things is beyond improvement.' – Edward de Bono

The late Dr Edward de Bono coined the term *lateral thinking* in his book called 'The Use of Lateral Thinking'[14]. De Bono is widely regarded as one of the leading experts in the fields of creativity and lateral thinking. He was the first person to propose that the human brain is a self-organising system. It was from this understanding that he developed his thinking tools and creativity methods that have helped people and organisations transform their thinking by avoiding the normal thought-blocks that inhibit their everyday thinking.

According to De Bono, lateral thinking deliberately distances itself from standard perceptions of creativity as either 'vertical' logic (the classic method for problem solving: working out the solution step-by-step from the given data) or 'horizontal' imagination (having many ideas but being unconcerned with the detailed implementation of them).

De Bono defines four types of thinking tools:

- Idea-generating tools intended to break current thinking patterns – routine patterns, the status quo.

13 'Thinkertoys – A Handbook of Creative Thinking Techniques' (2006) by Michael Michalko.

14 'The Use of Lateral Thinking' (1967) by Edward de Bono.

Left brain or right brain?

Maybe you think you are 'right-brained': creative, artistic, an open-minded thinker. Or perhaps you are more of a 'left-brained' person: a critical thinker, analytical, good at tasks that require attention to detail, and more logically minded.

It is true that some brain functions occur in one or the other side of the brain; language tends to be on the left, attention more on the right. But in reality people don't tend to have a stronger left- or right-sided brain network.

Researchers from the University of Utah looked for something called 'lateralisation,' which is the idea that certain mental processes occur mainly in either the right or left hemisphere of the brain. They divided the brain into 7,000 regions, to see if any brain connections between regions were left-lateralised or right-lateralised, and found no patterns where the whole left-brain network is more connected or the whole right-brain network is more connected in some people. The conclusion was that being 'right-brained' or 'left-brained' is more a figure of speech than anything else. Our personality seems to be determined more connection by connection, than by the side of our brain we are using for any particular behaviour.

- Focus tools intended to broaden where to search for new ideas.
- Harvest tools intended to ensure more value is received from idea generating output.
- Treatment tools that promote consideration of real-world constraints, resources, and support.

One famous technique that was promoted by de Bono is his 'Six Thinking Hats'; you can read more about this in the chapter on working with others.

Strategic thinking

Strategic thinking is a mental process that is applied by an individual in the context of achieving success in a game or other endeavour. General André Beaufre[15] wrote in 1963 that strategic thinking 'is a mental process, at once abstract and rational, which must be capable of synthesising both psychological and material data.' The work of Henry Mintzberg[16] and other authors, points towards the conclusion that the critical strategic question is not the conventional 'What?' but 'Why?' or 'How?' So strategic thinking is closely related to the leadership competency.

Strategic thinking is the ability to come up with effective plans in line with an organisation's objectives within a particular economic or political situation. Strategic thinking helps managers review policy issues, perform long term planning, set goals and determine priorities, and identify potential risks and opportunities. Clearly, within the EU institutions, strategic thinking is important.

15 André Beaufre (1902–1975) was a French general and military strategist, well known as an exponent of an independent French nuclear force. He was also chief of staff at SHAPE, the NATO headquarters in Europe.

16 Henry Mintzberg (1939) is a renowned academic and author on business and management.

Strategic thinking involves developing an entire set of critical skills:

- Strategic thinkers have the ability to use both the logical and the creative capabilities of their brain.
- They have the ability to balance their tremendous amount of creativity with a sense of realism and honesty about what is achievable in the longer term.
- They have the ability to develop a clearly defined and focused vision for the organisation, and a personal vision.
- They have the ability to clearly define their objectives and develop a strategic action plan with each objective broken down into tasks and each task having a list of needed resources and a specific timeline.
- They have the ability to design flexibility into their plans by creating some benchmarks in their thinking to review progress.
- They are remarkably aware and perceptive. They will listen, hear and understand what is said and will read and observe whatever they can so that they have very helpful and strategic information to guide them.
- They are committed lifelong learners and learn from each of their experiences. They use their experiences to enable them to think better on strategic issues.
- They are committed to and seek advice from others. They may use a coach, a mentor, a peer advisory group or some other group that they can confide in and offer up ideas for feedback.
- They have the ability to be non-judgmental and they do not allow themselves to be held back or restricted by judging their own thinking or the thinking of others when ideas are initially being developed and shared.
- They have the ability to be patient and not rush to conclusions and judgments. Great ideas and thoughts require time to develop into great successes in the future to reach their vision.

You can also have a look at Michael Porter's[17] TED Talk[18] 'Why businesses can be good at solving social problems'. This is what strategic thinking is about.

17 Michael Porter (1947) is an economist, researcher, author, advisor, speaker and teacher at Harvard Business School.

18 http://www.ted.com/talks/michael_porter_why_business_can_be_good_at_solving_social_problems?language=en#t-864545

Developing your analysis and problem solving skills

At its essence, thinking analytically involves breaking things down into their parts quickly and applying gut-level judgement to decisions. If you have a large project, you are going to have to break it down into smaller components.

First, you need to look at the big picture, and ask what purpose it serves and who it benefits. Second, you need to prioritize the steps you have to take and decide in what order. Third, you might have to delegate several parts of the project to get it done on time. Fourth, you will have to manage the progress and results of the project.

If you have a technical problem to solve, your first step would be to determine the cause of the problem. Then, you must fix the error. After that, you want to take precautionary measures to ensure it never happens again. All these things require questioning, researching and analytical problem solving techniques. Without strong analytical thinking skills, you might come up with the wrong answers that could be damaging your workplace reputation.

Please refer to Annex 1 for further development of this competency, or check out the easy-to-use app at:

http://www.johnharperpublishing.co.uk/the-ultimate-eu-career-development-toolkit/

4. Communicating

Competency definition: 'Communicates clearly and precisely both orally and in writing.'

"Rhetoric is the art of ruling the minds of men." – Plato

Why do we communicate?

According to Chris Anderson[1], the curator of TED, 'your number one task as a speaker is to transfer into your listener's mind an extraordinary gift, a strange and beautiful object that we call an idea.' More specifically, public speakers usually have one of the following desired results in mind: to *inform, convince, inspire,* or *entertain*. And of course, you also want your audience to remember your message once the event is over.

Informing

The main goal of informative communication is to pass information to the audience. It requires a context that will allow the audience to take the information on board and make it usable.

I used the word *information* informally here because it is only part of something that is called the 'DIKW pyramid.' The DIKW pyramid refers to a model representing structured and or functional relationships between Data, Information, Knowledge and Wisdom. The original idea comes from the American organisational theorist Russell Ackoff, published in 1989:

- *Data* is conceived of as symbols or signs, representing stimuli or signals, that is 'of no use until...in a usable (that is, relevant) form'. In books, printed characters are data. In computers, bits and bytes are data.

- *Information* is knowledge by description and is different from pure data in that it has a meaning. Information is deduced from data in the process of answering questions like Who? What? Where? and When? making the data useful for decision or action.

- *Knowledge* is information that has been processed, organised, or structured in some way or else is being applied or put into action.

- Ackoff refers to *Understanding* as an appreciation of why? and Wisdom as 'evaluated understanding.' He suggested 'understanding' to be a discrete layer between Knowledge and Wisdom.

1 https://www.youtube.com/watch?v=-FOCpMAww28

The second word that needs some further clarification is context. Context matters. I like the example by Daniel Pink in his book *A Whole New Mind:*

> Suppose that one night you and your spouse are preparing dinner. Suppose too that midway through the preparations, your spouse discovers that you forgot to buy the dinner's most important ingredient. Suppose then that your spouse grabs the car keys, curls a lip, glares at you, and hisses, 'I'm going to the store.' Nearly everyone with an intact brain would understand two things about the words your spouse just uttered. First, your spouse is heading to Safeway[2]. Second, your spouse is pissed.
>
> This has to do with how our brain works. To oversimplify just a bit, the left hemisphere handles what is said; the right hemisphere focuses on how it's said. However tempting it is to talk of right and left hemispheres in isolation, they are actually two half-brains, designed to work together as a smooth, single integrated whole in one entire, complete brain.

The way you deliver your message, from the words you use to how you use them, relies on the situational context. *Situational context* refers to the reason why you're speaking or writing. For example, you wouldn't read a eulogy at a wedding, would you? The *environmental context* refers to the physical space and time in which you speak. Think of the environmental context as the time and venue of the event. The audience will connect with you in different ways, depending on the environmental context.

Informative speaking or writing is used in educational settings, colleges, universities and seminars. It is also used in hierarchical environments, where the lower tiers of the food chain keep the higher ranks up to date with an evolving situation. As is frequently the case in the EU administration.

Convincing

Another type of communication is where the speaker or writer aims to *convince* the audience to accept their perspective. The speech or written text is arranged in such a way as to cause the audience to agree with the expressed opinion.

In The *Dynamics of Persuasion,* Richard Perloff[3] defines persuasion as 'a symbolic process in which communicators try to convince other people to change their attitudes or behaviour regarding an issue through the transmission of a message in an atmosphere of free choice.'

The critical elements of this definition of persuasion are:

- It involves a deliberate attempt to influence others
- People are not coerced; they are instead free to choose through self-persuasion
- Persuasive messages are transmitted in a variety of ways, including verbally and non-verbally via television, radio, internet, or face-to-face
- Persuasion is symbolic, utilizing words, images, sounds, etc.

2 Replace as appropriate by any grocery store
3 https://richardperloff.com/

Persuasion is *not* coercion or manipulation. Coercion uses force to mandate a change of a person's opinions, beliefs, values, or actions. Coercion only lasts while the pressure is applied. Once the pressure is released, the change will disappear. Manipulation is using deception to make a person change. Manipulation leaves out part of the information, such as the arguments opposing change. Manipulation only provides one side of the story.

The art of persuasion has developed into a unique field of communication. Traditional persuasion uses techniques that will move the audience to adopt a new thought, concept, or way of doing things. Unlike informative communication, where the speaker – or writer – is charged with making some information known to an audience, persuasive communication attempts to influence people to think or behave in a particular way.

An example of a convincing speech is a sales pitch. During a sales pitch, the speaker tries to convince the audience to buy their product or service. If the salesperson is successful, the audience will choose to purchase the product or service. However, salespeople understand that just because someone does not buy after the first sales pitch does not mean the pitch failed. Persuasion is often a process. People may need multiple persuasive pitches and a lot of outside information before they are ready to accept a new view.

Inspiring

Whereas a traditional persuasive communication may want to result in listeners buying product X or agreeing with view Y, a motivational speaker seeks to *inspire* people more broadly. Motivational speaking is a highly specialised form of persuasive speaking commonly delivered in business, social or religious contexts.

A motivational public speaker uses stories, illustrations and metaphors to engage the audience and share a lesson or moral that will inspire or have a lasting impact on those who listen. Motivational speakers must have a delivery style that is good enough and content that is strong enough to motivate their audience members to start doing something, stop doing something, or change something. I invite you to have a look at Al Gore's 2016 TED talk[4]. He focuses on the human part in causing climate change and shows how we can overcome and save ourselves from a dramatic end.

Becoming a motivational speaker is not achievable for everyone. That's why the term 'motivational speaker' has become a generic term to describe a professional speaker, a speaker paid to speak in front of an audience. Motivational public speaking has become an industry on its own.

Entertaining

Finally, another objective of public speaking can be to *entertain* the audience. Whereas informative and persuasive speaking is focused on the result of the speech process, entertainment speaking focuses on the theme and occasion. An entertaining speech can be either informative or convincing at its root. Still, the speech's context or theme requires speakers to think about the address primarily for audience enjoyment.

4 https://www.ted.com/talks/al_gore_the_case_for_optimism_on_climate_change

Entertaining speeches can be funny or serious. Entertaining discourses are not designed to give the audience a deep understanding of life but instead function to divert people from their day-to-day lives for a short time. This is not to say that an entertaining speech cannot have real content that is informative or persuasive. Its goal is primarily about the enjoyable aspects of the address and not about its informative or convincing quality.

Two common forms of entertaining speeches are the after-dinner speech and the formal speech. The after-dinner address is a form of speaking where a speaker picks a thoughtful topic and injects some humour to make it entertaining. In a formal speech, the specific context is the driving force of the speech. Common types of formal speeches include introductions, toasts and eulogies. In each of these cases, there are specific events that drive the speech. Stand-up comedy is the most extreme form of entertaining speech. In the context of the EU administration, this form of communication is rather exceptional – but more senior staff, in particular, might well find themselves making a speech to mark a colleague's retirement or other landmark event, and how well and appropriately they do this will certainly be noticed.

Being remembered

In 1946, Edgar Dale introduced the 'Cone of Experience' in a textbook on audio-visual methods in teaching. Dale's concept was intended to provide an intuitive model of the concreteness of various kinds of audio-visual media. Dale included no numbers and did not base his cone on scientific research. He also warned readers not to take the cone too seriously.

In the early 1960s, a pyramid model was developed by the National Training Laboratories[5] Institute. This model was based on the original ideas of Edward Dale. NTL's model was based on experimental research but, unfortunately, the study was lost, and the results were heavily criticised for that reason. An overview of NTL's findings is given on the next page.

Even though this model in its detail may stand on shaky foundations, the general conclusions can be accepted and have important consequences.

The shocking truth is that, when you intend only to speak, your audience will generally remember less than 5% of what you said, which is less than if they had just read your handout text. When showing images or videos during a presentation, the retention rate roughly doubles and if you give a live demo, it triples. Adding some interaction (Q&A for example) or engaging the audience in a group discussion may raise the retention rate to 50%. Letting them participate in a hands-on workshop will further boost the retention rate, and when you let them use the acquired knowledge and know-how immediately, or if they teach someone else, their retention rate will be as high as 90%.

5 https://www.ntl.org/

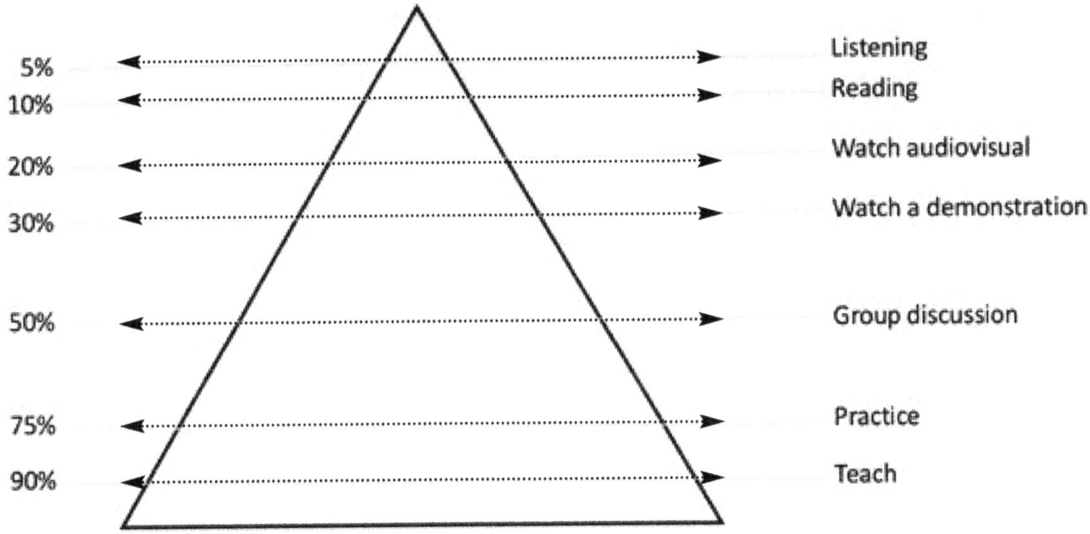

Figure 4.1: Retention rate in the pyramid model

Types of communication

Communication is a complex human behaviour in which auditory and visual patterns learned from others or perceived in the environment are encoded, processed, and modified to transfer information to other people.

There are two basic types of communication: verbal and non-verbal. Verbal communication uses words to convey information and can be oral or written. Communication without spoken or written words is called non-verbal communication. It happens through signs, symbols, colours, body language, tone of voice, or facial expressions.

Verbal communication

In his book *The Voices Within,* Charles Fernyhough argues that thinking is intimately connected to language. Thinking is *dialogic,* he says, meaning that it has the quality of an internal conversation, and it is *linguistic* – verbal or visual. Fernyhough states that language is necessary for thinking and that thinking is defined in terms of its reliance on language. So, thinking is *inner speech*. In 1934, the Soviet psychologist Lev Vygotsky proposed that the inner language we are using is condensed to become a 'note-form' version of the external dialogue from which it derives. In its condensed form, the language that forms inner speech has all of its acoustic properties stripped away, losing the qualities of tone, accent, timbre, and pitch that distinguish spoken language. We are still using language in this kind of thinking, but it may not subjectively seem like spoken language. At other times, our thinking takes the form of another type of inner speech, called *expanded* inner speech. You have a sense of participating in a real internal conversation, with one point of view answering another, just like a dialogue spoken aloud between two people.

Modern languages result from the contributions of many generations of people living in the same territory. Once the basic set of symbols (characters) were established, specific patterns of those characters (words) were assigned to particular objects or concepts. The words were arranged in sequences to describe the temporal or physical relationships between the objects and concepts (sentences). The number of words in the English language in everyday use is well over 200,000. Considering the number of discipline-specific words, this number is at least an order of magnitude larger. And there is an almost infinite number of sentences and stories that can be made up using even a small fraction of the total number of words. Remarkably, the learning of languages and the potentially infinite number of stories (word sequences) that an individual can construct are accomplished using a finite number of neurons in the language-processing areas of our brain. This has everything to do with our superior pattern recognition capabilities.

Non-verbal communication

Most people believe that speech is our main form of communication. However, in evolutionary terms, speech has been part of our communications repertoire only in recent times. Speech probably developed between two million and five hundred thousand years ago, during which our brain tripled in size. Before then, body language and sounds made in our throat were the primary forms of conveying emotions and feelings. And this is still the case today.

The most influential pre-twentieth-century work on body language was Charles Darwin's *The Expression of the Emotions in Man and Animals,* published in 1872. Albert Mehrabian, a pioneer researcher in body language in the 1950s, found that communication's total impact is about 7 percent for the words, 38 percent for the tone of voice, inflection, and other sounds, and 55 percent non-verbal. It was anthropologist Ray Birdwhistell who pioneered the original study of non-verbal communication. He estimated that the average person speaks words for a total of about ten to eleven minutes a day and that the average sentence takes only about 2,5 seconds. Birdwhistell also estimated that we could make and recognize around 250,000 facial expressions. Like Mehrabian, he found that the verbal component of a face-to-face conversation is less than 35 percent and that 65 percent of communication is non-verbal.

When we meet people for the first time, we quickly judge their friendliness, dominance, and potential as a sexual partner – and their eyes are *not* the first place we look. Most researchers now agree that we use words primarily to convey information. In contrast, body language is used for negotiating interpersonal positions and, in some cases, is used as a substitute for verbal messages. Many people find it difficult to accept that humans are, biologically speaking, still animals. We are a species of primate, *Homo Sapiens,* a hairless ape that has learned to walk on two limbs and has a cunning, flexible, and advanced brain. But like any other species, we are still dominated by biological rules that control our actions, reactions, body language and gestures. However, the human animal is rarely aware that its postures, movements, and gestures can tell one story, while its voice may be telling another.

Most of the primary communication signals are the same all over the world. When people are happy, they smile; they frown or scowl when they are sad or angry. Shaking the head from side to side to indicate 'no' is also universal and appears to be a gesture learned in infancy. When a baby has enough milk, it turns its head from side to side to reject its mother's breast. Nevertheless, a lot of our body language is culturally determined.

Written communication

One advantage to written communication is that written messages do not have to be delivered on the spot; instead, they can be edited and revised several times before they are sent so that the content can be moulded to maximum effect. Another advantage is that written communication provides a permanent record that can be saved for later. Since they are permanent, written messages also enable recipients to review the message and provide more appropriate feedback. For these reasons, written forms of communication are often considered more suitable for complex messages and contexts where traceability is key. In the context of misunderstandings or faced with a colleague whose unclear expression or reception of ideas is a constant source of concern, having a written record of what was said/agreed or instructed is very important in a working context. Depending on oral communication, this situation can be detrimental to one or both parties involved (peer colleagues or colleague/manager).

However, there is also a potential downside associated with written communication. Unlike oral communication, the sender of written communication does not generally receive immediate feedback to his or her message. Besides, written messages often take more time to compose because of their content-rich nature and the difficulty that many individuals have in writing such communication.

EU staff have to write many different types of documents. Whatever the type – legislation, a technical report, minutes, a press release or speech – a clear document will be more effective, and more easily and quickly understood. A very good guide to how to write clearly can be found on the Commission's website[6].

Correct grammar, spelling and punctuation are key in written communications. The reader will form an opinion about you, the author, based on both the content and the presentation, and errors are likely to lead them to get a negative impression. Checking for poor writing and spelling mistakes should be regarded as showing respect for your readers since it will take them much longer to understand the messages in your writing if they have to think and re-read text to interpret these. You have to make their life easy.

A *style guide* is a set of standards for the writing and design of documents, either for general use or for a specific publication, organisation, or field. A style guide establishes and enforces style to improve communication. To do that, it ensures consistency within a document and across multiple documents and enforces best practice in usage and in language composition, visual composition, orthography and typography. Non-native speakers often write in a foreign language such as English as if it was their own written language just dressed up in English words. For example, a German colleague writes very long convoluted sentences with lots of commas, parentheses, dashes and

6 https://ec.europa.eu/info/sites/default/files/clear_writing_tips_en.pdf

asides (comments on what he is saying). A sentence can take up a whole paragraph. Perfectly acceptable German style perhaps, but totally frustrating for those of us not used to this kind of writing – and it makes it doubly hard for the message to be understood. Following courses in written English stylistics would benefit many, I feel.

The EU publishes an *Interinstitutional Style Guide*[7] encompassing 23 languages across the European Union. This manual is 'obligatory' for all those employed by the institutions of the EU who are involved in preparing EU documents.

Detailed information on in-house conventions for English spelling, punctuation and usage is in the *English Style Guide*[8] produced by DG Translation. Clear writing guides and style guides for several other official languages are also on the DG Translation's website[9].

Guidance on drafting Community legislation in all official languages is in the *Joint practical Guide*[10].

For advice on writing for the web, see the *Information Providers Guide*[11].

You can find practical tips on how to write effective emails in chapter 10 on digital persuasion.

Information theory

'The fundamental problem of communication is that of reproducing at one point either exactly or approximately a message selected at another point.' – Claude Shannon

Claude Shannon is said to be the 'father of information theory.' In his landmark paper, A *Mathematical Theory of Communication* (1948) he described the chain of transformations in a telecommunication system[12].

Telecommunication systems use a channel (radio waves, copper wires, glass fibres) to bridge the distance between the source and the destination of a message (text, sound, image). First, the original message needs to be 'encoded' into a signal before presenting it to the channel. Signals are pure data. Signals have no meaning on their own and need to be 'decoded' at the receiver side to extract the information/knowledge/wisdom again. Encoding and decoding are 'lossy,' meaning that part of the information is lost in the process. For example, MP3 encoding works by reducing the accuracy of specific sound components that are considered to be beyond most humans' hearing capabilities. On top of that, the signal is distorted while transiting in the channel – a phenomenon called 'noise.' In other words, the received message is never identical to the original message. It has been reduced, altered, and distorted in the process.

7 http://publications.europa.eu/code/en/en-000100.htm

8 https://ec.europa.eu/info/sites/default/files/styleguide_english_dgt_en.pdf

9 http://ec.europa.eu/translation/language_aids

10 https://eur-lex.europa.eu/content/techleg/EN-legislative-drafting-guide.pdf

11 https://wikis.ec.europa.eu/display/WEBGUIDE/01.+Web+writing+overview

12 The prefix 'tele' comes from Greek, meaning "far off, afar, at or to a distance."

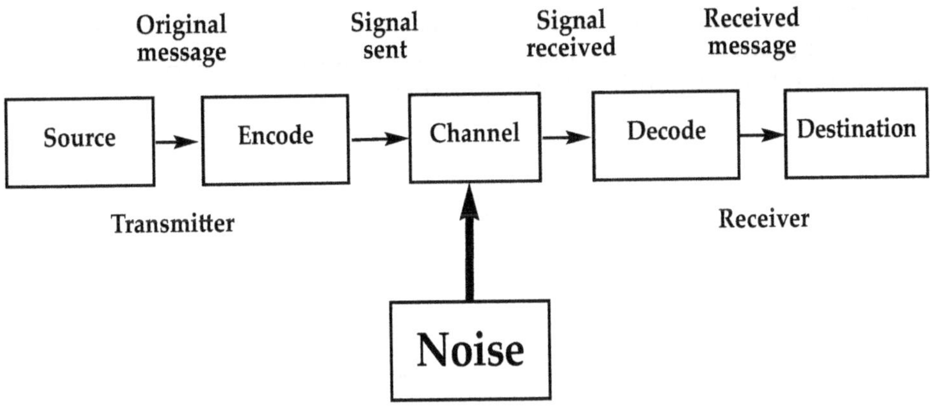

Figure 4.2: Information theory

Communicator

The term *communicator* refers to all of the people in the communication setting. I use it instead of 'transmitter' and 'receiver' because we are not only sending a message when we communicate. We are also receiving messages from others at the same time. When we speak, we observe others' non-verbal behaviour to see if they understand us and assess their emotional state. The information we get from these observations is known as feedback. When speaking, we watch and listen to audience members' responses. When writing, we read and interpret the texts we receive in response, with a delay depending on the channel used (note, memo, email, or text message).

Encoding and decoding

Encoding refers to the process of taking an idea or mental image, associating that image with words, and then speaking or writing those words to carry a message. So, if you wanted to explain to your friend the directions to your new apartment, you would picture in your mind the neighbourhood, streets, and buildings. Then you would select the best words that describe the route so that your friend could find you.

Language and mother tongue make a central part of our mental programming, including encoding and decoding ideas. We actually 'think' in our mother tongue, and you can say that you only have a good command of a foreign language when your mind is capable of skipping the mental translation of your thoughts to the words you speak (or write). There are estimated to be about 150 regional and minority languages in the European Union. These languages may be specific to a region such as Catalan, Basque, Breton, Welsh, Sardinian, or languages spoken by a minority in one Member State but which are official languages in another EU country: Hungarian in Slovakia or German in southern Denmark. The European languages are vastly different. There are even words or concepts that cannot be adequately translated – for example, Finnish has only gender-neutral pronouns and completely lacks grammatical gender. There has also been some recent research into behavioural differences between speakers of verb-based languages as distinct from noun-based ones.

Also of significance nowadays is the increasing number of EU citizens whose first language is neither an EU official language nor a regional language of a Member State. Examples include Russian and Turkish speakers.

Message

The *message* involves those verbal and non-verbal behaviours that are interpreted with meaning by others. The verbal portion of the message refers to the words that we speak. In contrast, the non-verbal portion includes our tone of voice and other non-vocal components such as personal appearance, posture, gestures and body movements, eye behaviour, the way we use space, etc.

For instance, the person who gets up to speak wearing a nice suit will be interpreted more positively than a person giving the same speech wearing sloppy jeans and an untidy T-shirt. Or if a speaker uses a monotone voice, they will not be as effective as the speaker who gives the same speech with a lively and engaging tone of voice. The message can also be intentional or unintentional. When the message is intentional, we have an image in our mind that we wish to communicate to an audience or a person in a conversation. We can successfully deliver the idea with relative accuracy. An unintentional message is sent when the message the other person receives is not the same as the message we wish to share. Therefore, as communicators, we cannot always be sure that the message we want to communicate is interpreted as we intended. That is why we need feedback to stay attuned.

Channel

The *channel* is the medium through which the message travels. In face-to-face communication, the channel involves all of our senses, so the channel is what we see, hear, touch, smell and taste. When we're communicating with someone online, the channel is the computer. When writing a note or a memo, the channel is the paper we're writing our message on. When emailing, the channel is our desktop or laptop. When texting, the channel is the mobile phone. And when streaming a movie on Netflix, the channel is the TV. The channel can have a profound impact on the way a message is interpreted. For example, listening to a recording does not have the same psychological effect as listening to the same speech in person or watching that person on television. The 1960 Kennedy-Nixon debates[13] are a perfect illustration of the importance of the channel in communication.

Noise

The next aspect of the model of communication is noise. Noise refers to anything that interferes with message transmission or reception. There are several different types of noise.

- *Physiological noise* refers to bodily processes and states that interfere with a message. For instance, if a speaker has a headache or is otherwise sick, or if audience members are hot or hungry, these conditions may interfere with message accuracy.

13 https://www.maryferrell.org/pages/Kennedy-Nixon_Debates.html

- *Psychological noise* refers to mental states or emotional states that interfere with message transmission or reception. For example, if someone has just broken up with their partner or is worried about their child in the hospital or thinking about a disturbing email they received just before the speech, this may interfere with communication.
- *Physical noise* is the background noise in a room. Loud music playing at a party, voices of people talking, a lawnmower outside the window, or anything that is overly loud will interfere with communication.
- *Cultural noise* refers to message interference that results from differences in people's worldviews. The more significant the difference in worldview, the more difficult it is to communicate effectively. I will say more on worldviews below.

Context

The context refers to the norms that rule communication. Initially, the context was seen as the physical setting where communication occurred, such as a church, apartment, workplace, restaurant, or a grocery store. People communicate differently in each of these places as unwritten rules (called norms) govern these settings. More recently, the concept of context has evolved and expanded to include the type of relationships we have with others and the rules that govern those relationships. So, you do not speak the same way to your best friend as you do to a small child, your parent, your boss, your doctor, or a police officer. And you may speak to your best friend differently in your apartment than you do in your parents' home, and your communication may also change when you are both out with other friends on the weekend.

Worldview

While the encoding and decoding process may appear to be relatively straightforward, it is much more complicated than it seems. The reason for this is because we all have different *worldviews*. A person's worldview is the overall framework through which they see, think about and interpret the world, and interact with it. It is essential to understand the concept of worldview because it impacts the encoding and decoding process and our ability to be understood by others.

Try this simple experiment. Ask a few people to imagine a dog. 'Dog' is a concrete word that describes an object that can be perceived through the senses. Wait a few seconds and then ask each person what type of dog they were thinking of. Was it a Chihuahua? A greyhound? Golden retriever? Rottweiler? Or some other dog? Most likely, each person you asked had a different image in their mind than you had. This is our worldview at work. Things get even more complicated with abstract words, words that refer to ideas or concepts that are part of immaterial reality like 'peace', 'love', 'immoral', 'justice', 'freedom,' 'success,' and 'honour.' Abstract words can have many different meanings, each of which is grounded in one's worldview.

There are five core components to our worldview.

- *Epistemology* is the way that we acquire knowledge and or what counts as knowledge. Epistemology is linked to public speaking because it governs audience members' preferred learning styles and what they consider credible sources.

- *Ontology* refers to our belief system, how we see the nature of reality, or what we see as true or false. Speechwriters should be careful not to presume that audience members share the same beliefs. If a speaker claims that illness can be relieved with prayer, but several people in the audience are atheists, at best the speaker has lost credibility. At worst, these audience members could be offended.
- *Axiology* represents our value system – what we see as right or wrong, good or bad, and fair or unfair. Our values define the things that we hope for – they do not represent reality. Values can have an impact on multiple levels of the public speaking process. In particular, values impact speaker credibility and effectiveness in persuasion.
- *Cosmology* means the way that we see our relationship to the universe and other people. Cosmology shapes our view of power relationships and may involve our religious or spiritual beliefs. Interestingly, cosmology also plays a role in logistical points such as who is allowed to speak, the order of speakers, the amount of time a speaker has, the seating arrangement on the stage, and who gets the audience's front seats. This aspect can be a point of difficulty in the EU institutions where there are complex protocols as to precedence. For example, in public tripartite discussions involving the presidents of the European Council and European Commission and a non-EU head of state the sitting arrangement would typically be triangular, so no one is dominant. In a notable snub in Ankara in April 2021, the host, Turkish president Erdogan, seated European Council president Charles Michel alongside himself while Commission president Ursula von der Leyen was obliged first to stand and then sit at a distance on a sofa. This awkward moment was widely seen as happening because von der Leyen is a woman.
- *Praxeology* means our preferred method of completing everyday tasks or our approach to solving problems. For example, some speechwriters may begin working on their outlines as soon as they know they will need to give a speech, while others may wait until a few days before their address to begin. Praxeology may also impact a speaker's preference of delivery style, methods of arranging main points, and choice of visual aids and props.

Five canons of rhetoric

Rhetoric aims to study the capacities of writers or speakers needed to inform, persuade, or motivate particular audiences in specific situations.

Aristotle was the first to describe rhetoric as a way to develop and prepare public speeches, but it was only some three hundred years later that the Roman philosopher Cicero laid down 'the five canons[14] of rhetoric': *Invention, Arrangement, Style, Memory, and Delivery.* Today, these rules are still a useful guide for creating powerful speeches or writing clear texts.

14 From the Latin *canonicus*, derived from the Greek *kanonikós*, and meaning 'relating to a rule' or 'regular.'

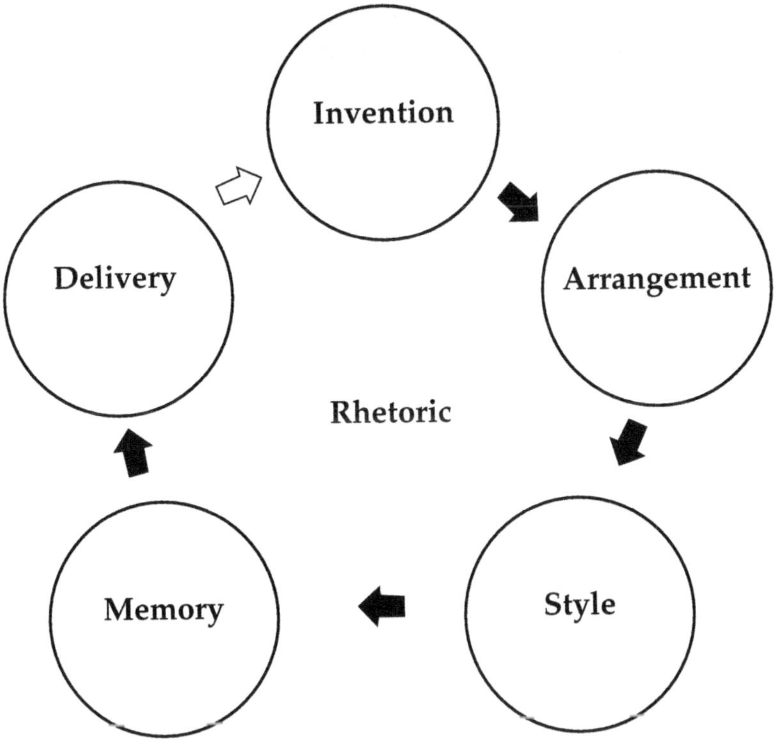

Figure 4.3: Cicero's five canons of rhetoric

Invention (Inventio)

Invention is about discovering the best available means of persuasion for the audience at hand. The audience is at the centre of attention. What are their needs? What do they expect?

Invention is possibly the most difficult phase in crafting a speech as it lays the foundation for all the other phases. During the Invention phase, the goal is to brainstorm ideas on what you're going to say and how you're going to say it to maximise persuasion.

Prompting Action

Here are some action words to help determine what you are asking to your audience:

Accept - agree - begin - believe - change - collaborate - commence - create - defend - desire - differentiate - do - empathise - empower - encourage - engage - establish - examine - facilitate - familiarise - form - implement - include - influence - invest - invigorate - know - learn - like - persuade - plan - promote - pursue - recommend - receive - remember - report - respond - secure - support - simplify - start - try - understand - validate

Part of getting to know your audience is figuring out what kinds of arguments they will find most credible and compelling. Some people need cold hard facts and statistics to be persuaded. Others find the testimony of peers or a reputable authority more convincing.

Different appeals will better persuade different audiences. Using appeal to emotion to convince a room full of scientists that you have discovered a new law of physics probably won't get you very far. A focus on rational, indisputable facts would work much better. Again, it's all about suiting your rhetoric to your audience.

Audiences are receptive to specific ideas at different times, depending on context. Presenting a new technology to create a vaccine for Covid-19 before the outbreak of the pandemic would have had a much smaller impact than if you'd done it after the pandemic started. Another aspect of timing is the duration of your speech. Sometimes a long, well-developed, and nuanced speech is appropriate. At other times, a shorter and more energetic presentation will be more effective.

Arrangement (Dispositio)

Arrangement is the structure of a speech to ensure maximum persuasion. Classical rhetoricians divided a speech into six different parts:

- Introduction (*exordium*)
- Statement of facts (*narratio*)
- Division (*partitio*)
- Proof (*confirmatio*)
- Refutation (*refutatio*)
- Conclusion (*peroratio*)

The *introduction* is crucial for the success of your speech. There are two aspects of an effective introduction: introducing your topic and establishing credibility. It doesn't matter how logical your argument is. If people don't think you're trustworthy or a credible source, they will not listen to you.

The *statement* of facts is the background information needed to get your audience up to speed on your issue's history. The goal is to provide enough information for your audience to understand your argument.

In the *division* part, you provide a transition into your argument with a summary of the arguments you're about to make. Think of the division as your audience's roadmap. You're about to take them on a journey of logic and emotion, so give them an idea of where they're going.

The main body of your speech is the *proof*. In this section, you want to construct logical arguments that your audience can understand and follow. If you're suggesting a course of action, you want to convince people that your solution is the best one for resolving the problem you have just described.

After you've crafted a strong and convincing argument, it is now time to highlight the weaknesses in your argument in the *refutation* part. This might seem surprising but sharing the weaknesses of your arguments will actually make you *more* persuasive. First, it gives you a chance to proactively answer any counter-arguments and resolve the doubts your audience might be holding. Second, a bit of intellectual humility can go a long way to getting the audience to trust and like you, and consequently, be persuaded by what you have to say.

Finally, in *conclusion*, you to sum up your argument as forcefully and as memorably as possible. If you want people to remember what you said, you have to inject some emotion into your conclusion.

Style (Elocutio)

When speaking in public, the focus is usually on *what* you are going to say. But it is also important *how* you present your ideas. It doesn't matter how great your message is, if you don't wrap it up with style, people will probably ignore it in favour of a message packaged nicely.

Two pupils of Aristotle, Theophrastus and Demetrius, developed the so-called 'Five virtues of Style': *Correctness, Clarity, Evidence, Propriety,* and *Ornateness.*

Correctness means speaking or writing following the rules and norms of the language. An effective communicator uses words correctly and follows the rules of grammar and syntax.

It's hard to be persuasive when people can't understand what you're trying to say. Using *clear and simple* language ensures that your message never gets lost between you and your audience.

For classical rhetoricians, the quality of *evidence* was a way to measure how well language reached the audience's emotions. Remember that most people are persuaded more by emotion than by logic.

Propriety is the quality of style concerned with selecting words that fit your speech's subject matter and ensuring they're appropriate for your audience and for the occasion.

Ornateness involves making your speech or text interesting to listen to or read by using figures of speech, comparisons, and metaphors, and manipulating the sound and rhythm of words.

Memory (Memoria)

The three elements of the canon of memory are: *memorising the speech, making the speech memorable,* and *keeping a treasury of rhetorical fodder.*

In ancient times, almost all rhetorical communication was done orally in the public forum. Ancient orators had to memorise their speeches and reading from notes was looked down upon. In modern times, we still lend more confidence to speakers who give their speeches from memory. Or at least appear to[15].

The most obvious way of memorising a speech is to learn it by heart by rote learning and repetition. For longer speeches this is difficult to achieve.

You can add mnemonics, memory aiding devices, to your speech. The principle is to create in the mind an artificial structure that incorporates unfamiliar ideas or, especially, a series of dissociated ideas that by themselves are difficult to remember. For example, when using *loci,* you concentrate on the layout of a building or home that you're familiar with. You then take a mental walk through each room in the building

15 https://www.politico.com/story/2009/03/obamas-safety-net-the-teleprompter-019663

and commit an engaging visual representation of a part of your speech to each room. When you deliver your speech, you mentally walk through your 'memory house' to retrieve the information you're supposed to deliver. The loci memory technique is powerful because it's so flexible.

The second element of this canon entails organising your speech to *help your audience remember what you said*. What good is spending hours memorising a speech if your listeners forget what you have said as soon as they walk out the door? Throughout your speech, stop and give your audience a roadmap of where you're at in your speech. If you've just finished the first part of your speech, say something like, 'We've just covered ABC. We'll now move on to my second point, DEF.' This continual reviewing of where you've been and where you go next will help burn your speech's main points into the minds of your audience. Other tools to make your speech more memorable are figures of speech and repetition.

A third component of the canon of memory involved storing up quotations, facts and anecdotes that could be used at any time for future speeches or even an impromptu speech. A master orator always has a treasury of rhetorical fodder to call upon.

Delivery (Actio)

Like the canon of style, the canon of delivery is concerned with *how* something is said. While the canon of style focuses primarily on what sort of language you use, delivery focuses on the non-verbal part of your communication.

For ancient orators, delivery meant how a speaker used his body language and hand gestures and how he changed his tone of voice during his oration. But while the Greeks admired men for their eloquence, modern audiences tend to be suspicious of a speaker who appears too well-polished.

How you approach your delivery will need to be determined during the invention stage of your speech. Find out the overall demographics and cultural background of your audience. What does your audience fear? What are their desires? What are their needs? This information will help you decide if you should use a more sophisticated and polished delivery or go with a more informal approach.

Patterns of persuasion

Communication involves using patterns (symbols, words, and sounds) to code for objects and events encountered either via direct experience or communication from other people. Communication can create new patterns (stories, paintings, songs, and so on) of 'things' that may (reality) or may not (fiction) exist. But communication is more than just conveying information; it is about convincing others to accept your perspective, to adopt a new thought, concept, or way of doing things, or to share a lesson or moral that will inspire and have a lasting impact on those who listen. Communication is about persuasion, and specific patterns of persuasion have been used throughout the history of mankind.

Ethos, Logos, and Pathos

For Aristotle, the goal of argumentative speaking is to persuade your audience that your ideas are more valid than someone else's. In his *treatise on rhetoric*, dating from the 4th century BC, he divided the act of persuasion into three rhetorical appeals: *Ethos, Logos,* and *Pathos*. They are also referred to as the three artistic proofs or the Rhetorical Triangle.

Ethos is the Greek word for 'character.' According to Aristotle, our perception of a speaker's character influences how acceptable or convincing we find what that person has to say. This projected character is called the speaker's *ethos*. We are more likely to be persuaded by a person who, we think, has personal warmth, consideration of others, a sound mind and erudition. People whose education, experience and previous performance qualify them to speak on a particular issue earn the ethos of authority. But whether or not we know anything about the speaker, the actual text we hear, the way it is spoken, and what it says also conveys an impression of the author's character. This impression is known as *intrinsic* ethos.

Ethos is about your audience's perception of you, and this perception can be formed over many months or years, or perhaps over many past speeches. However, your introduction is probably the single best opportunity for you to establish your ethos with *this* audience on *this* day. For this reason, you should always write your introduction yourself. Don't let an event organiser improvise it. Highlight the essential facts that establish your trustworthiness, authority and reputation. Ethos can also be projected by choosing appropriate language for the audience and topic, choosing the proper vocabulary, making yourself sound fair or unbiased, and using correct grammar and syntax in your slides or handouts.

Institutions, public personalities and publications also project an ethos or credibility. For example, we may well assume that The Economist is a more credible source than our daily newspaper or that BBC News is more reliable than something posted on social media by an influencer. And we usually believe that a person selected for a public position of responsibility is more credible than someone without official sanction.

Logos is the Greek term for 'word,' but the concept of logos goes beyond that and can be better described as 'that by which the inward thought is expressed' and 'the inward thought itself.'[16] The word 'logic' is derived from logos.

With logos, we come to the arguments, the exact reasons the arguer provides to support a position. To use logos would be to cite facts and statistics, make relevant analogies, and quote recognised authorities on a subject. Logos uses premises, propositions upon which an argument is based or from which a conclusion is drawn. Premises can be classified into the following categories:

- Arguments based on definition.
- Analogies or comparisons, citing similar cases.
- Appeals to cause and consequences.
- Opinions of experts or public opinion.

Pathos reaches out to the audience's sense of identity, self-interest and emotions. Appeals to our identity and self-interest exploit common biases. We naturally bend in the direction of what is advantageous to us, what serves our interests, or the interests

16 http://www.perseus.tufts.edu/hopper/text?doc=Perseus:text:1999.04.0058:entry%3Dlo/gos

of the group we belong to. Even when advantage is not an issue, speakers or writers who belong to groups we identify with or create groups we can belong to, often seem more persuasive. We also naturally find more convincing the speaker or writer who flatters us (indirectly) instead of insulting us. Thus, skilful speakers create a positive image in their words, with which their audience can identify.

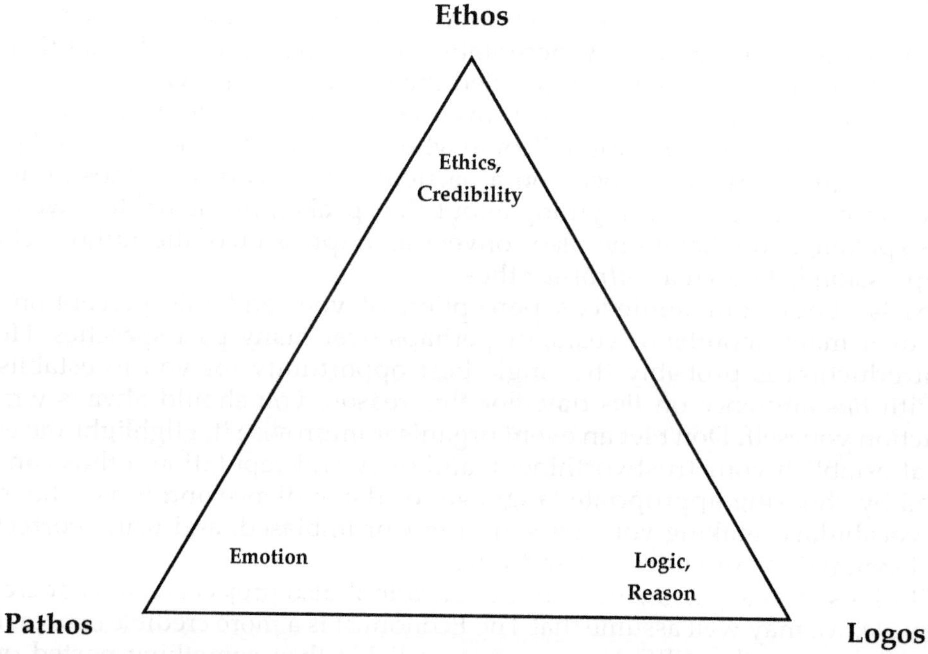

Figure 4.4: The Rhetorical Triangle

The power of metaphors

According to Oxford Dictionaries, a *metaphor* is 'a figure of speech in which a word or phrase is applied to an object or action to which it is not literally applicable'. Metaphors are effective communication because analogy – a process of finding the properties of a thing by comparing it to another thing – is fundamental to thought. 'Human thought processes are largely metaphorical,' write Lakoff and Johnson in their book *Metaphors We Live by*. 'The human conceptual system is metaphorically structured and defined ... Metaphor is as much a part of our functioning as our sense of touch, and as precious.'

We use metaphors all the time. As Lakoff and Johnson point out, we compare:

- Arguments to war (attack your position, claims are indefensible, criticisms were right on target, shoot down ideas)
- Time to money (spending time, wasting time, saving time, investing time, costing time)

- Computers to offices (desktops, files, folders, documents, notepads)
- In our brains, 'love is a journey', 'problems are puzzles', and 'the EU is a family'.

When you give information in the form of a metaphor, you effectively pre-process it for your audience. Your listeners don't have to invest the mental effort of finding an analogy in their memory. When you use a metaphor, you are coming about as close as you can to placing a thought directly into your audience's mind – speaking of effective communication!

In Martin Luther King's famous *I had a Dream* speech[17], about 20 percent of what he said was metaphorical. One of the most explicit metaphors he uses to make his point about the lack of civil rights is a banking metaphor. He suggests that the thousands of marchers have come to Washington to 'cash a check' while he claims that the government has given the people of colour a check which has come back marked 'insufficient funds':

> 'It is obvious today that America has defaulted on this promissory note insofar as her citizens of color are concerned. Instead of honoring this sacred obligation, America has given the Negro people a bad check which has come back marked 'insufficient funds.'

Metaphors are powerful methods of persuasion because they allow you to convey the information and also how your audience should think about that information. *Scientific American* reported a study in which a group of subjects read a passage that said, 'Crime is a beast.' Another group read a quote that said, 'Crime is a virus.' In the following surveys, those who had read the beast passage were more likely to prescribe punishment as a means to control crime, while those who read the virus passage were more likely to prescribe treatment. Thus, a good metaphor goes beyond effective communication to something approaching thought control. So, pick your metaphors carefully and use them responsibly.

Storytelling

People are attuned to relating to and remembering stories. Character-driven stories with emotional content result in a better understanding and recollection of the key ideas and lessons learned. Audiences forget facts, but they remember stories.

Storytelling is one of the most familiar forms of human activity. Recent scientific work explains how stories change our attitudes, beliefs and behaviours. Storytelling evokes a strong neurological response. Research by Professor Paul Zak at Claremont Graduate University indicates that our brains produce the stress hormone *cortisol* during the tense moments in a story, which allows us to focus, while the cute factor releases *oxytocin*. This feel-good chemical promotes connection and empathy. Other neurological research tells us that a happy ending to a story triggers the limbic system, our brain's reward centre, to release *dopamine*, making us feel more hopeful and optimistic.

As social creatures, we depend on others for our survival and happiness. Professor Zak discovered that oxytocin is a key 'it's safe to approach others' signal in the brain. Oxytocin is produced when we are trusted or shown kindness, and it motivates coop-

17 https://www.youtube.com/watch?v=3vDWWy4CMhE

eration with others. It does this by enhancing the sense of empathy, our ability to experience others' emotions. Empathy allows us to understand how others are likely to react to a situation, including those we work with.

These findings on the neurobiology of storytelling are also relevant to workplace settings. When you want to motivate, persuade, or be remembered, start with a story of human struggle and eventual success. Why should someone care about the project you are proposing? How does it change the world or improve their lives? How will people feel when it is complete? These are the components that make information persuasive and memorable.

Storytelling may seem like an old-fashioned tool. But that is precisely what makes it so powerful. Data can persuade people, but by itself it doesn't inspire them to engage and act. To do that, you need to wrap your vision in a story that fires the imagination.

Repetition

We only receive part of a message because we are not listening all the time. So, it is often a good idea to build some redundancy into your message by repeating the same information.

People rate statements that have been repeated as more valid or correct than things they have heard only once. And when we think something is 'truer,' we also tend to be more persuaded by it. Simply said, people are more influenced when they hear statements of opinion and persuasive messages more than once. Especially in verbal arguments that are highly emotional, frequent repetition of key emotionally charged phrases (*pathos*) can be effective.

Psychological studies suggest that moderate repetition has a positive effect on someone's reception of, and agreement with a persuasive argument. Low to moderate levels of repetition within a message tend to create a better agreement with the message, along with greater recall. However, too much repetition has a negative impact and can lead to more vigorous disagreement with the argument being made.

Repetition consists of repeating a word, phrase, sentence, or even a complex idea. It is a rhetorical technique to add emphasis, unity, and power. Therefore, repetition has been an essential part of oral storytelling and can be found in legends, folk tales, and religious texts.

Probably one of the most famous examples of the use of repetition can be found in the *We Shall Fight on the Beaches* speech, delivered by the British Prime Minister Winston Churchill to the House of Commons on 4 June 1940:

> ...We shall not flag or fail. We shall go on to the end. We shall fight in France, we shall fight on the seas and oceans, we shall fight with growing confidence and growing strength in the air, we shall defend our island, whatever the cost may be, we shall fight on the beaches, we shall fight on the landing grounds, we shall fight in the fields and in the streets, we shall fight in the hills. We shall never surrender...

The rule of three

What is the rule of three? What are some examples? How can you use it to be more effective?

I just used the rule of three to introduce ... the rule of three.

The rule of three is a technique frequently used in communication. It states that concepts or ideas presented in a group of three are more attractive, more enjoyable, and more memorable. It makes you appear knowledgeable (ethos) while being catchy and straightforward. Why? Because three is the smallest number that allows us to recognise a pattern.

By repeating something three times or using the alliteration with three words, an ordinary speech becomes emotive (pathos):

> *Friends, Romans, Countrymen* (William Shakespeare in *Julius Caesar*)
>
> *Blood, sweat and tears* (General Patton)
>
> *Our priorities are: Education, Education, Education* (Prime Minister Tony Blair)

If you want your message to be remembered, put it into a list of three:

> *Government of the people, by the people, for the people* (the Gettysburg Address)
>
> *There are three kinds of lies: lies, damned lies, and statistics* (Benjamin Disraeli)
>
> *This is not the end. It is not even the beginning of the end. But it is, perhaps, the end of the beginning* (Winston Churchill)

Organisational patterns

You will remember from earlier in this chapter that the second canon of rhetoric is 'arrangement,' the organisational pattern of a speech to ensure maximum persuasion. Classical rhetoricians divided their speeches into six parts: Introduction, Statement of Facts, Division, Proof, Refutation, and Conclusion. However, more specialised structures, tailored to the type of persuasive speech you want to give, are possible.

In essence, there are three types of persuasive speeches:

- Questions of fact: something is *true, exists, or does not exist.*
- Questions of value: something is *good, bad, beautiful, or worthwhile.*
- Questions of policy: something *should be.*

Questions of fact concern what is or is not true, what does or does not exist, what did or did not happen. Some questions of fact are easily answered but the questions of fact that we deal with in persuasive speeches are usually not. Although these questions also have answers, the answers are not that easy to find and may never be found. These questions concern controversial issues for which different people have different answers. Your job as a speaker persuading an audience on a question of fact is to get them to believe that your answer is as close to the fact as possible.

For example, say you are preparing a persuasive speech on the question of whether there is still a glass ceiling for women in the EU. You might phrase your thesis as 'The EU discriminates against women'. Once you've formulated your thesis, you can generate your major propositions by asking the simple question, 'How do you know this?' or 'Why would you believe this is true (factual)?' The answers to these questions will enable you to develop your major propositions. The bare bones of your speech might then look something like this:

I. *Women occupy fewer managerial positions than men.*

II. *Women earn less than men.*

III. *Women are hired less often than men.*

Once these propositions are identified, you would then begin searching for information to support them so that you can convince your audience that women earn less, that women are hired less often, and that women occupy fewer managerial positions than men. Taking the first proposition, you might develop it something like this:

I. *Women occupy fewer managerial positions than men.*

A. *For publicly traded companies in the EU, only 15% of the non-executive and 9% of the executive board members are women.*

B. *For the top 100 companies in the EU, only 4% have a female president of the board.*

C. *For more than 50% of the EU countries there are no women leading the main political parties.*

And so on.

As you see, this speech focuses entirely on questions of fact; the thesis itself is a question of fact. Generally, a topical organisational pattern will prove most effective. Each of your propositions will be approximately of equal value and importance in supporting your thesis. Also note the use of the rule of three in the previous example.

Questions of value concern what you consider good or bad, moral or immoral, just or unjust. As with questions of fact, you can generate your major propositions by asking a strategic question of your thesis. In this case, 'Why is this good?' or 'Why is this immoral?'

For example, you can take the thesis 'The death penalty is unjustifiable' and ask, 'Why is the death penalty unjustifiable?' The answers to this question will give you the speech's major propositions. The body of your speech might then look something like this:

I. *The judicial system can make mistakes.*

II. *The death penalty constitutes cruel and unusual punishment.*

III. *No one has the moral right to take another's life.*

You would then begin to search for evidence to show that mistakes have been made and you might simply list three or four high profile cases where people were put to death and later, through say DNA evidence, found to have been innocent.

Notice that in this example, the speaker aims to strengthen or change the listener's belief about the death penalty. The speaker is not asking the audience to do anything about it but just to believe that it's not justified. However, you might also use this question of value as a first step toward persuading your audience to take some action. In that case you're into a question of policy.

Questions of policy concern what should be done, what procedures should be adopted, what laws should be changed, in short, what policy should be followed. Questions of policy almost invariably involve questions of values.

Like speeches dealing with questions of fact and values, you can develop your speech on questions of policy by asking a strategic question of your thesis. With policy issues, the questions would be 'Why should the proposed policy be adopted?' or 'Why is the proposed policy desirable?' or 'Why is this policy better than what we have now?'

If you are dealing with a question of fact, or a question of value, the typical organisational pattern is by topic. If you are dealing with a question of policy, a variety of organisational patterns are possible:

- Problem/cause/solution
- Comparative advantage
- Monroe's 'motivated sequence'[18]

If you are using problem/cause/solution then your first point would be the problem, the second main point would be the cause(s) of the problem and the third main point the solution(s) to the cause(s) of the problem.

If you are using comparative advantage then you are comparing two items, topic by topic, to demonstrate the advantages of one of the items over the other item.

If you are using Monroe's motivated sequence, then you have five sections to the speech:

- *Attention*. Get the audience to listen. Make them think, 'I want to hear what you have to say.'
- *Need*. Make the audience feel the need or want so they think 'I agree. I have that need/want.'
- *Satisfaction*. Tell the audience how to fill the need or want, so they think, 'I see your solution will work.'
- *Visualisation*. Get the audience to see the benefits of your solution so they think, 'This a great idea.'
- *Action*. Get the audience to take action, then they will think, "I want it."

Non-verbal patterns of persuasion

A substantial portion of our communication is non-verbal. Non-verbal communication adds, subtracts, and amends our message. Experts have found we respond to thousands of non-verbal cues and types of behaviour every day. From the way we dress, our handshakes, and our hairstyles, non-verbal details reveal who we are and impact how we relate to other people.

The clothing you wear can have an impact beyond the way you look standing in front of the room. It takes less than seven seconds for people to make judgments about your confidence, competence, professional status and warmth (*ethos*).

18 https://www.toolshero.com/toolsheroes/alan-monroe/

Most of us know that we should dress professionally when we are in the spotlight. What we wear goes a long way in shaping other's opinions. But it's not always easy adjusting to what that means. A good rule of thumb is to dress at (or slightly above) the same level as your audience.

If the venue is a recurring conference or setting, go with what people wore last time. If you are presenting at a new venue, ask the event organiser what the usual dress code is. If there is a strong dress code, adhere to it!

It is a scientific fact that people's **body language** gives away their true intentions. Yet most of us don't realise how our physical movements and expressions speak to others or how we can manage our own body language. Here are some common patterns in body language to look out for:

- *Posture.* The way a person stands or sits is their posture. Because body language affects how we feel, standing in a straight posture is a great way to raise your mood and give you more energy because you imitate a confident and alert stance. When sitting down, in a video meeting for example, squaring your shoulders and keeping your head straight makes you look sure of yourself.
- *Head position and movement.* Generally, nodding means agreeing with what is said. A milder nod means appreciation and interest, while nodding rapidly may signal impatience and the need to hurry up. A head shaking from one side to the other means a 'no.'
- *Facial expression.* Hidden feelings of anger, fear, confusion, uncertainty, enthusiasm and joy will be revealed by your facial expression. And sometimes, the words that you speak may be contradicted by your facial expression.
- *Gestures.* Movement of hands and fingers enhances communication. Keeping your movements relaxed, using open arm gestures, and showing the palms of your hands are silent signals of credibility and truthfulness. Individuals with open gestures are perceived more positively and are more persuasive than those with closed gestures, with their hands hidden or held close to the body.

It is said that 'eyes are the windows to the soul'. In oral communication, the speaker and listener should face each other and maintain proper eye contact. Looking at another person can indicate a range of emotions, including hostility, interest and attraction. Stable eye contact is often taken as a sign that a person is telling the truth and is trustworthy (*ethos*). Shifty eyes and an inability to maintain eye contact are frequently seen as indicators that someone is lying or being deceptive. In eastern countries, subordinates or younger people may avoid direct eye contact out of respect or submissiveness, but it will be misunderstood in an international context.

Digital persuasion

The ancient art of persuasion has gone digital. More than just texting, emailing, or blogging, digital persuasion has become a far broader discipline, including digital presentations, webcasts, webinars, and other remote collaboration forms. Digital persuasion has become the new normal. For this reason, I have dedicated a special chapter, chapter 11, to this topic.

5. Delivering quality and results

Competency definition: 'Take personal responsibility and initiative for delivering work to a high standard of quality within set procedures.'

Time now to come to the nub of the matter: the quality of the work we produce. Delivering work of good quality, in a timely manner, is after all what we are paid for. All our behaviour at work, whether it is analysing and solving problems, communicating, prioritising and organising, or any of the other 'core' competencies, should ultimately contribute to the same goal: doing what we are paid to do, in the best possible way.

Does one bad apple spoil the barrel?

Unfortunately, in the EU institutions, there are some people who think differently. They believe that they are paid simply because they are so good. They think that being selected out of thousands and thousands of candidates by EPSO, or their seniority, gives them the right to their salary. The fact that they are 'established' officials – they believe – secures a life-long employment, without the necessity to actually produce results. These people think that they only have rights and no obligations. That is probably why they refer to their professional activity as a 'position' and not as a 'job'. I am happy to say that, in my experience, these 'bad apples' only form a small minority of EU staff; but nevertheless they sometimes spoil the barrel for others, or give the EU institutions a bad reputation.

What is work?

'In 1880, about nine out of 10 workers made and moved things; today, that is down to one out of five. The other four are knowledge people or service workers.' – Peter Drucker[1]

A formal definition of work could be:

'Any activity involving mental or physical effort done in order to achieve a result.'

- A *task* is a unit of work, that is, a set of activities needed to produce some result.
- A *result* is the final consequence of a task that can be expressed qualitatively or quantitatively.
- A *job* is a collection of tasks and responsibilities that an employee is responsible to conduct; jobs have titles.
- A *role* is a set of responsibilities or expected results associated with a job. A job usually includes several roles.
- A *career* is something that someone wants to pursue for the rest of their (working) life.

1 Peter Drucker (1909–2005) was an Austrian-born American management consultant, educator and author.

Usually, the concept of work is related to the concept of being paid; most people work to get a salary or revenue. Intuitively, one would think that higher pay should produce better results, but scientific evidence indicates that the link between compensation, motivation and performance is much more complex; why else would people have hobbies, do sports, or be volunteering – and be highly motivated and well-performing – without any financial compensation?

Behavioural scientists usually divide work into two categories: 'algorithmic' and 'heuristic'. An algorithmic task is one in which you follow a set of pre-established instructions, down a single pathway to one conclusion. That is, there is an algorithm for solving it. A heuristic task is the opposite; because there is no algorithm you have to experiment with possibilities and find a novel solution. During the twentieth century, most work was algorithmic, but today, in much of the Western world algorithmic work is disappearing, as it is offshored to wherever it can be done cheaper.

In the EU institutions, most of the employees are so-called 'white collar' workers whose job entails largely heuristic work. The term white collar used to simply characterise non-manual workers, but now it refers to employees or professionals whose work is knowledge-intensive, non-routine, and mostly unstructured. Historically, in the West, clerical workers wore white shirt collars and manual workers wore blue, hence the denomination.

White-collar work is about the exchange of data, information, knowledge, understanding and wisdom. This is what working as an EU official involves – though some may imagine differently (Figure 5.1)!

The inner game of work

In his book 'The Inner Game of Work'[2] Tim Gallwey defines work in terms of a triangle with the words performance, learning and enjoyment at the points. He stresses that all three of these are important and that, therefore, if enjoyment is decreased, performance is also decreased. This has obvious implications for many traditional work cultures; he says:

> 'When either the learning or the enjoyment side is ignored, performance will suffer in the long run. When it does, management feels threatened and pushes even harder for performance. Learning and enjoyment diminish even further. A cycle ensues that prevents performance from ever reaching its potential.'

In the same book Gallwey also introduces the concept of mobility, which he defines as: 'the ability to move or adapt, change or be changed. It also means the ability to reach one's objectives in a fulfilling manner – to reach goals at the right time and in a way we feel good about. Therefore, mobility is not only change but fulfilment and harmony with one's progress.'

2 'The Inner Game of Work: Overcoming Mental Obstacles for Maximum Performance' (2000) by Timothy Gallwey.

Figure 5.1

What is quality?

'Quality in a service or product is not what you put into it. It is what the client or customer gets out of it.' – Peter Drucker

Joseph Juran[3] defined quality as 'fitness for use' but this is – to say the least – somewhat simplistic. Allow me to use a very practical example to illustrate this.

Say that we are talking about smartphones. We all know that there are hundreds of different models and brands out there, and that there is a constant evolution going on, almost forcing people to buy a new smartphone every two years or so. Unless you were really ripped off, or your smartphone recently broke, you can definitely say that the model you are using today is 'fit for use'; you can use it for what it's intended, that is to communicate with others.

But does that mean that it is of 'good' or 'excellent' quality? Or, inversely, that the 'fitness for use' of an older model has dropped over time? Of course not, because we all have different needs – or call it expectations, and these needs evolve over time. Technology freaks will 'need' the most recent, fancy model to show off to their friends, while elderly people will probably be satisfied with the simplest, cheapest, and even

3 Joseph Moses Juran (1904–2008) was a Romanian-born American engineer and management consultant.

The notion of quality

Defining the notion of quality is not straightforward, at least if one wants to define it in general terms, without the context. For example, when assessing the quality of a translation, you really cannot do so without introducing subjectivity, which is the enemy of fairness. There tends to be an agreed consensus on what quality is NOT (the negatives are more objective: e.g. poor grammar, bad spelling, incorrect terminology, wrong tone, etc.) because the bad can be assessed against an agreed set of common, external standards. What is 'good' however, is often the subjective view of the reader.

For assessment purposes, therefore, once you remove 'the bad', the remainder is, by definition, 'the good' – or at the very least, the tolerable. Take the example of water: what won't kill you is actually perfectly fine. Bottled water may make claims of 'quality' – but tap water won't do you any harm either. Ultimately which one is 'better' is down to personal preference, which is not a valid assessment criterion for an objective yardstick. The trick in assessing quality is to identify all the negatives, quantify them (the more there are, the lower the quality) but don't try to judge the positive – it'll speak for itself through the absence of negatives. Obviously, it's a bit subtler than that: there are usually some commonly agreed positives as well, but this is a generalisation that works in many cases.

out-dated model. In fact, our 'needs' and 'expectations' are to a large extent driven by the market and the outrageous competition between the manufacturers of smartphones. In order to survive, they have to produce – and sell – new models at an ever-increasing pace. Manufacturing costs are dropping constantly, and so are the profit margins. This can only be compensated for by selling higher volumes. The bottom line is that 'fitness for use' is not 'fit for use' as a comprehensive definition of quality; we have to take the expectations of our clients into account.

The ISO[4] definition of quality goes as follows: 'The totality of features and characteristics of a product or service that bear on its ability to satisfy stated or implied needs.'

More directly, one can say that a product or service has good quality when it complies with the requirements specified by the client. A *requirement* is a singular, documented physical and functional need that a particular design, product or process must be able to perform. In the business world, requirements are also called *specifications*.

In the context of office work, quality can be seen as a measure of the degree to which the expectations of your client (your boss, your institution, or the general public) are met. However, 'expectations' are deeper and broader than 'requirements' or 'specifications'. *Expectations* are your client's vision of a future state or action, usually unspoken but nevertheless critical to your success. These expectations are not always clear and obvious. Your Head of Unit may want a piece of work to be 'quick and dirty,' or to be personally 'involved in all the details' or 'not involved at all,' or expect that your work is of 'high quality' without giving any further details as to what that means in practice.

In conclusion, the quality of your work is determined by the person who asked for it, not by society in general. It is not related to cost, and adjectives or descriptors such as 'high' and 'poor' are not applicable as such.

4 ISO – International Organisation for Standardisation.

Bureaucracy

In the definition of delivering quality and results it is also said that the results have to be delivered 'within set procedures'; clearly, what is meant here are the procedures as imposed by the working environment, the EU institutions in our case.

The EU institutions are *bureaucracies* – and there is nothing wrong with that, since a bureaucracy is the administrative system governing virtually every large institution.

Professor Henry Mintzberg[5] labelled a highly bureaucratic organisation as being like a 'machine.' The machine organisation is defined by its standardisation. Work is very formalised, there are many routines and procedures, decision-making is centralised, and tasks are grouped by functional departments. Jobs are clearly defined; there will be a formal planning process with budgets and audits; and procedures are regularly analysed for efficiency.

Bureaucracies have a tight vertical structure. Functional lines go all the way to the top, allowing top managers to maintain centralised control. These organisations can be very efficient, and they rely heavily on economies of scale for their success. However, the formalisation leads to specialisation and, quite often, functional units may have conflicting goals that can even be inconsistent with overall objectives.

The term bureaucracy is French in origin, and combines the French word *bureau* – desk or office – with the Greek word *kratos* – rule or political power. It was coined sometime in the mid-18th century and was a satirical pejorative from the outset.

Bureaucracies have been criticised as being too complex, inefficient, or too inflexible. The dehumanising effects of excessive bureaucracy became a major theme in the work of Franz Kafka[6]. Others have defended the necessity of bureaucracies. The German sociologist Max Weber[7] argued that bureaucracy constitutes the most efficient and rational way in which one can organise human activity, and that systematic processes and organised management levels are necessary to maintain order, maximise efficiency and eliminate favouritism. But Weber also saw unrestricted bureaucracy as a threat to individual freedom.

Ethics and integrity

Civil servants working at the European Commission and other EU institutions must abide by certain rules while in service and after.

These rules are contained in the Staff Regulations and the Code of Good Administrative Behaviour[8], annexed to the Commission's Rules of Procedure. They include potential conflicts of interest, gifts and honours received, external activities while working for the EU and employment after having worked for the EU.

5 Henry Mintzberg (1939) is an internationally renowned academic and author on business and management.

6 Franz Kafka (1883–1924) was an Austrian-Hungarian German language writer, considered to be one of the most influential authors of the 20th century.

7 Max Weber (1864–1920) was a German sociologist, philosopher, jurist, and political economist.

8 https://eur-lex.europa.eu/legal-content/EN/TXT/HTML/?uri=CELEX:02000Q3614-20111116&from=EN

EU staff are obliged to be independent, impartial, objective and loyal. Any personal interest or any interest in any business or organisation that could compromise the respect of these obligations must be declared immediately.

Outside activities covered by these rules, paid or unpaid, must first be approved. Staff members must also inform the institution for which they work if:

- their spouse is employed and where; or
- a personal interest that might impair their independence, or any other conflict of interest, occurs during performance of their duties.

Members of the EU staff may not accept gifts or favours from third parties without obtaining prior permission unless the value of the gift does not exceed €50 and there is no accumulation.

If a member of the EU staff wishes to leave his or her institution and begin a new job within two years, they must inform the Commission to obtain prior authorisation. If that activity is related to work carried out during their last three years in service and might conflict with the legitimate interests of the Commission, the Commission may forbid it or approve it, subject to any necessary conditions.

Senior officials are in principle prohibited, in the 12 months after leaving service, from engaging in lobbying or other advocacy vis-à-vis their former institution on matters for which they were responsible during their last three years in service.

Time management

The competency of delivering quality and results is closely related to the competency of prioritising and organising, better known as *time management*. The modern concept of time management really began with Frederick Taylor's[9] scientific management techniques. His goal was to increase worker productivity (see Table 5.1). To do this, he conducted time and motion studies and began to focus on the best ways for jobs to be performed to maximise the work completed in a given amount of time.

Time management has also been employed as a tool for increasing the productivity of white-collar workers, for whom work output may be hard to measure. In this respect, modern managers in these areas look for ways to monitor worker productivity in terms of time use.

In the specific context of the Commission, new provisions on working time were introduced with the revision of the Staff Regulations in 2014. In a flexible approach to working time, staff can adjust their working hours as long as this is compatible with the Commission's needs.

The Commission adopted a new decision to make *flexitime*[10] the default working arrangement for all staff (with a few exceptions) from 1 June 2014. It also confirmed the increase in working hours, from 37.5 to 40 hours per week, and required that all

9 Frederick Winslow Taylor (1856–1915) was an American mechanical engineer who sought to improve industrial efficiency.

10 Meaning flexible working hours for each individual employee.

Effectiveness	Efficiency	Productivity
Effectiveness is about doing the right task, completing activities and achieving goals.	Efficiency is about doing things in an optimal way, for example doing it the fastest or in the least expensive way.	Productivity is an average measure of efficiency. It can be expressed as the ratio of output to inputs used, i.e. output per unit of input.

Table 5.1

staff members record their daily working hours. Another flexible time management tool is *telework*. Telework practices vary greatly across the EU institutions and even across the Commission's DGs. Furthermore, a considerable number of staff members make use of part-time working, parental leave and family leave.

Obviously, this flexible approach to working time requires a lot of self-discipline and responsibility from EU staff, and good leadership skills from their managers.

Performance management

Performance management is a process by which managers and employees work together to plan, monitor and review an employee's work objectives and overall contribution to the organisation. More than just an annual performance review, performance management is a continuous process of setting objectives, assessing progress and providing on-going feedback to ensure that employees are meeting their objectives and career goals.

One of the cornerstones of performance management is the employee's *job description*. Through their job description an employee will know in general terms what is expected without having to refer to more detailed instructions for a task at hand. Complex positions in the organisation can include many tasks, which are sometimes called functions.

Job descriptions are lists of the general tasks, or functions, and responsibilities of a position. Typically, they also include who the position reports to, and specifications such as the qualifications needed by the person in the job, salary range for the position, etc. It is important to make a job description practical by keeping it dynamic, functional and current. A well-written job description will help the manager avoid hearing a refusal to carry out a relevant assignment because 'it isn't in my job description.' A poor job description will keep employees from trying anything new and from learning how to perform their job more productively. Good job descriptions will help them to grow within their position and make larger a bigger contribution to the organisation.

Expectation management

'Always give people more than what they expect to get.' – Nelson Boswell[11]

Expectation management is very valuable. Managing expectations proactively will increase your chances of success, a great performance review, and ultimately have a positive effect on your career progression.

Obviously, the first thing to do is to make sure you understand exactly what is expected of you. Understanding your job description and learning about the procedures that are to be followed for your particular role or job is clearly a first step in understanding what is expected. People often get into hot water when they assume that somebody else knows what they expect or even what they are talking about. Don't fall into the trap of assuming that someone else has the same understanding of a situation, project, deadline, or task to accomplish. When you have a team to supervise, make sure to share your expectations with them. Giving others a picture of what you think success looks like for the team and each individual will give them a way to move forward. The SMART[12] model can be a useful tool in this respect.

One of the best ways to manage expectations is to make sure you communicate with everyone on a frequent basis. To keep in control of your performance, constant dialogue provides opportunities to measure progress, assess risks, and adjust actions. By keeping your boss in the loop, you also ensure that they are aware of your progress and successes along the way. If you are a manager yourself, share with the people you manage how you expect them to tackle potential issues, so that these can be dealt with in a timely manner and don't become obstacles to your own success.

Finally, *plan for contingencies*. When objectives are set, 'what if?' questions are rarely part of the conversation. Some tasks will be easier than others and some are more dependent on circumstances beyond your control. The landscape can change quickly if a critical assumption does not end up holding true. Assess the risks and identify potential options for addressing the most likely scenarios. That way you will be less likely to be caught by surprise. Speak to your team about the risks they perceive and how you can help them mitigate these risks to achieve their objectives. Also, being honest about a delay is a thousand times better than promising to deliver and then missing your deadline.

Personal responsibility

'The power behind taking responsibility for your actions lies in putting an end to negative thought patterns. You no longer dwell on what went wrong or focus on whom you are going to blame. You don't waste time building roadblocks to your success. Instead, you are set free and can now focus on succeeding.' – Lorii Myers[13]

Personal responsibility is the willingness to both accept the importance of standards for individual behaviour, and to make active personal efforts to live by those standards. But

11 US author of self-help books.

12 Specific, Measurable, Achievable, Realistic and Time-framed (see Chapter 2).

13 'Targeting Success' (2011) by Lorii Myers.

Exceeding expectations

A former colleague who worked at that time in DG TRADE once told me a story about exceeding the expectations of her superiors. She was appointed to be the head of a trade delegation that was sent on a mission to one of Europe's trading partners, in Asia.

Before the mission she had carefully prepared the possible 'landing positions' for the negotiation: a list of possible outcomes, ordered from 'most desirable' through 'acceptable' down to the 'red line' beneath which the outcome should not go. In discussing this list with her Head of Unit, he expressed his doubts about whether even the 'red line' was achievable, and suggested to her to lower the worst, but still acceptable, outcome of the negotiations.

Clearly, the Asian counterparts had done their homework too. They were aware of all the timing constraints (flight plans, travel time, etc.) on the EU delegation, and effectively tried to exploit this information by wasting time, and coming up with a first concrete proposal only towards the end of the meeting – hoping that the EU delegation would quickly give in for the sake of not missing their flight home. (In the chapter on working with others I explain the reasons behind this manoeuvre that is sometimes used in intercultural negotiations.)

As an experienced negotiator, however, she was aware of what was going on, and didn't let herself be put under pressure by this. So, she didn't give in and managed to get the 'most desirable' outcome after all. In doing so, she exceeded by some measure the expectations of her Head of Unit.

personal responsibility also means that when individuals fail to meet expected standards, they do not look around for some factor outside themselves to blame.

Our brain is inclined to flatter and shield our ego from blame when we make mistakes. Despite how difficult it is to counter the mechanisms of our ego defence system we must make the effort. In doing so, you will find that striving to take responsibility for your actions and ownership of your mistakes is worthwhile for many reasons:

- *It allows you to make better decisions.* Self-justifications distort reality. The more you use them, the more you create an alternative universe for yourself. This leads to a decreased ability to make good choices, as the information you're using to do so is distorted. Most dangerously, one self-justification leads to another, setting off a domino effect that sends you more and more off track. Once you justify one decision, you're deeper into it, and you'll make a decision that digs you even further into it ... and so the cycle continues.
- *It keeps little problems from turning into big ones.* If you can own up to a mistake as soon as you make it and do your best to correct it or make it right, you can prevent it from turning into a huge problem that's going to be difficult to solve.
- *It allows you to learn from your mistakes.* You can't learn from your mistakes if you can't acknowledge you've made them! And if you don't learn from your mistakes, you're destined to repeat them. That's a recipe for quickly going nowhere.
- *It engenders the respect of others.* We often hide our mistakes from other people because we worry they will think less of us once they've seen that we've messed up. But, frankly acknowledging your mistakes, apologising

for them, and then earnestly working to make things right almost always has the opposite effect: people will respect you for it.

There are two ways to explain things we get wrong: someone did something because of the *situation*, or, because of *who they are*. We typically use the former explanation for what we do ourselves – 'I forgot we had agreed to discuss this beforehand because I just have so much on my mind right now.' We tend to use the second explanation about others' behaviour: 'He totally forgot we had agreed to discuss this beforehand because he is self-centred and couldn't care less about others.' In the second case we don't evaluate their behaviour, but their personality – they don't do bad stuff, they are bad. The person is stupid, useless, selfish, immature, evil, lazy, etc. We judge them to be failed human beings. This kind of criticism is called a 'global label.' Global labels are rarely accurate, but your brain finds them very satisfying to develop. They allow you to see the other as deliberately hurting you. It is their fault, and you are the victim, so you feel entitled to punish and attack them.

Initiative

'Initiative is doing the right thing without being told.' – Victor Hugo

Initiative is all about taking charge. An initiative is the first in a series of actions. A person with initiative is motivated to do things. If you take the initiative, you are willing to get things done on your own. However, taking the initiative can be risky; if you do something on your own initiative, then there is nobody else you can blame if it goes wrong.

When you show initiative, you do things without being told; you find out what you need to know; you get going when the going gets tough; and you identify and take advantage of opportunities that others pass by. You act, instead of react.

Initiative has become increasingly important in today's workplace. Organisations want employees who can make quick decisions and take action without waiting for someone to tell them what to do.

The good news is that initiative is a skill that you can develop. The first step is to develop your own career plan. Research has shown that people who have a long-term career plan are more likely to take the initiative. The next step is to build your self-confidence. It takes courage to show initiative, especially if you fear that people may disagree with your actions or suggestions. Set yourself small goals so you can achieve some quick wins. Then push yourself to do bigger things. Have another look at the GROW model as introduced in Chapter 2; you will find it to be a good tool to develop your self-confidence.

Unforeseen obstacles

'The greater the obstacle, the more glory in overcoming it.' – Molière

Sometimes, things are not working out as expected, or we have to overcome an unforeseen obstacle. For sure, these are situations of high stress, and we have to deal with them.

Anticipating the various potential outcomes and/or reactions that others may have in a situation is extremely helpful in many ways. Thinking about all the possible actions and reactions of others to a situation makes your planning process more complete. What you ultimately piece together will likely not only have a solid plan 'A', but it may have a plan 'B', 'C', etc. as well.

When you take the time to anticipate, you are less likely to be surprised when and if what you thought *might* happen actually *does* happen. When you are less surprised you are less likely to be destabilised and you will be in better control of your emotions. When you are in control of your emotions you have the upper hand. You never know precisely what's around the corner, but you don't allow that to throw you off your game. Train yourself to anticipate possible challenges, to be prepared.

Of course, not everything can be anticipated, and really unforeseen – or unforeseeable – obstacles can block your way. You will have to find a workaround. You may be forced to 'think outside the box'. This means approaching problems in new, innovative ways; conceptualising problems differently; and understanding your position in relation to any particular situation in a way you have never thought of before. Thinking outside the box, like any skill, is one that can be developed through practice; you may find some ideas on WikiHow[14].

Finally, you should see these unexpected situations as learning opportunities. Being pushed out of your comfort zone creates a learning opportunity, as long as you are not drawn into your panic zone.

Quality management

'It is not necessary to change. Survival is not mandatory.' – W. Edwards Deming

'Kaizen'[15] is a Japanese word which has given its name to a management technique referred to as 'continuous improvement'. When applied to the workplace, it refers to activities that continuously improve all functions and involve all employees, from the top executives to those at entry-level.

Kaizen was first implemented in several Japanese businesses after the Second World War, influenced by the ideas of the American quality guru W. Edwards Deming[16]. It has since spread around the world and been adopted in a wide range of environments, including government and business.

Deming provided a simple, yet highly effective technique that serves as a practical tool to carry out continuous improvement in the workplace. This technique is called the PDCA Cycle or simply Deming Cycle. PDCA is acronym of Plan, Do, Check and Action. The Deming Cycle provides a conceptual as well as practical framework while carrying out Kaizen activities by the employees – see Figure 5.2. Notice the similarities to the GROW model.

14 http://www.wikihow.com/Think-%27Outside-of-the-Box%27

15 'Kaizen: The Key to Japan's Competitive Success' by Masaaki Imai.

16 William Edwards Deming (1900–1993) was an American engineer, statistician and management consultant.

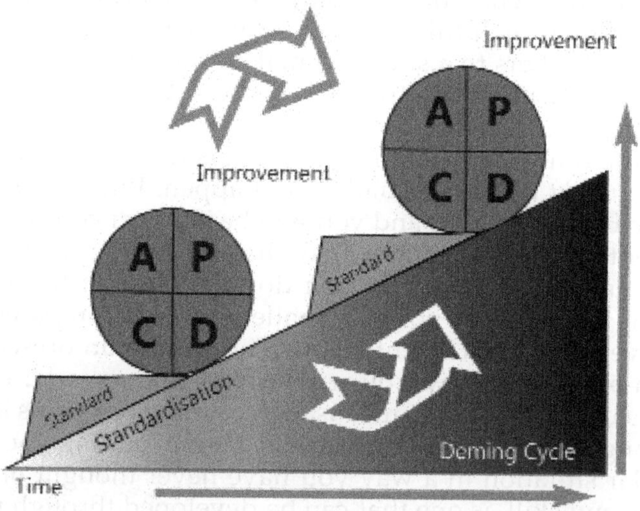

www.totalqualitymanagement.wordpress.com

Figure 5.2: The PDCA or Deming Cycle

Kaizen is continuous improvement that is based on certain guiding principles:

- Good processes bring good results
- Go see for yourself to grasp the current situation
- Speak with data, manage by facts
- Take action to contain and correct root causes of problems
- Work as a team
- Kaizen is everybody's business

One of the most notable features of kaizen is that big results come from many small changes accumulated over time. However, this has been misunderstood to mean that kaizen equals small changes. In fact, kaizen means everyone being involved in making improvements.

In Europe, the concepts of quality management through continuous improvement are promoted by the European Foundation for Quality Management (EFQM), a not-for-profit membership foundation in Brussels, established in 1989 to increase the competitiveness of the European economy. EFQM provides networking, education, and awards, using a framework called the EFQM Excellence Model.

The **Common Assessment Framework (CAF)** is the common European quality management instrument for the public sector. The CAF helps organisations to perform a self-assessment with the involvement of all staff, to develop an improvement plan based on the results of the self-assessment and to implement the improvement actions.

CAF is being used by many public sector administrations, including most of the EU institutions and agencies.

Developing your skills in delivering quality and results

For this competency it is necessary to be fully committed to and immersed in the concept of quality. Quality is the degree to which you meet and exceed the expectations of your 'customers'. It is therefore important to have a good understanding of one's own job description and the wider working environment and to proactively understand and manage the expectations of your colleagues, superiors, and clients.

Please refer to Annex 1 for further development of this competency, or check out the easy-to-use app at:

http://www.johnharperpublishing.co.uk/the-ultimate-eu-career-development-toolkit/

6. Learning and development

Competency definition: 'Develops and improves personal skills and knowledge of the organisation and its environment.'

'At each stage of human existence the adult man is off on his quest of his holy grail, the way of life he seeks by which to live. At his first level he is on a quest for automatic physiological satisfaction. At the second level he seeks a safe mode of living, and this is followed in turn, by a search for heroic status, for power and glory, by a search for ultimate peace; a search for material pleasure, a search for affectionate relations, a search for respect of self, and a search for peace in an incomprehensible world. And, when he finds he will not find that peace, he will be off on his ninth level quest. As he sets off on each quest, he believes he will find the answer to his existence. Yet, much to his surprise and much to his dismay, he finds at every stage that the solution to existence is not the solution he has come to find. Every stage he reaches leaves him disconcerted and perplexed. It is simply that as he solves one set of human problems he finds a new set in their place. The quest he finds is never ending.' – Clare W. Graves[1]

Is there a difference between learning and development?

In her article 'Making the Case for a Developmental Perspective'[2] Susanne Cook-Greuter[3] distinguishes between two directions of human development: horizontal growth and vertical transformation.

Horizontal growth refers to the gaining of new knowledge and skills within a particular stage of development. In doing so, the learner becomes better equipped to perform in their environment.

Vertical transformation is much more subtle. Rather than expanding capability within the same stage of development, the learner promotes their intellect to a higher stage of development.

Horizontal = expansion at same stage (developing new skills, adding information & knowledge, transfer from one area to another)

Up = Transformation, vertical development, new more integrated perspective, higher centre of gravity

Down = temporary or permanent regression due to life circumstances, environment, stress and illness

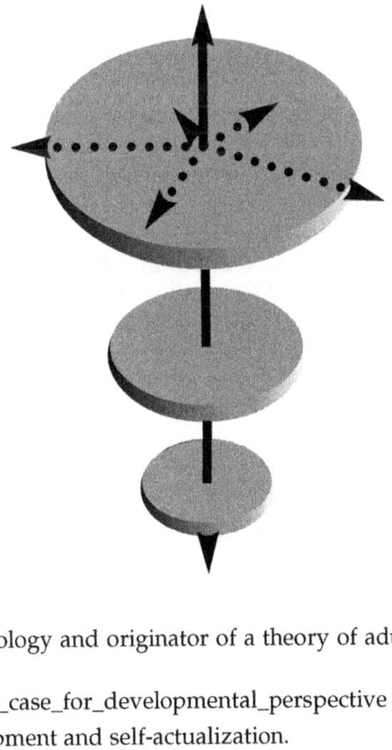

Figure 6.1

1 Clare W. Graves (1914–1986) was an American professor of psychology and originator of a theory of adult human development.

2 https://www.researchgate.net/publication/241580387_Making_the_case_for_developmental_perspective

3 Susanne Cook-Greuter is as a leading expert in mature ego development and self-actualization.

This bidirectional model of development can represent the two sides of the learning and development equation:

- Horizontal growth represents the 'learning' – improving your competence.
- Vertical transformation represents the 'development' – maturing your mind.

In my classroom training and coaching sessions I use a somewhat simpler, less sophisticated, way to explain the difference between learning and development:

- Learning is about hard skills, development about soft skills.
- Learning is about the acquisition of knowledge and know-how, development about changing your behaviour.
- Learning is a process that takes a certain amount of time (and effort), and one can usually demonstrate the effect by passing a test or an exam. Development is an on-going process (you start developing when you are born, and stop when you die), and your behaviour can only be observed, or assessed, but not measured with high precision.

Both learning and development are important, but they occur at different rates. Learning happens via many channels; school, professional training, self-directed and life-long learning, practice, or simply through the exposure to life. Development is much rarer, especially in adults. It refers to how we learn to see the world through new eyes, how we change our interpretations of experience, and how we transform our views of reality. It describes our increasing awareness, and therefore what becomes part of our understanding and behaviour.

Learning and development

In Chapter 8 (Resilience) I use the example of how I taught my daughter to drive a car, in order to explain the notion of the 'comfort zone'. I explain how I passed on knowledge and know-how, and how I gradually increased the challenges so that she would learn how to drive a car. Her learning experience was successfully concluded by the driver's exam.

From that moment on, however, her 'development' started. Mainly by further practice, exposure to various traffic situations, some near misses and a fine, she became more aware of what driving a car is about, and adapted her behaviour accordingly. She has developed 'vertically', and continues to do so.

The Leadership Development Profile

The Leadership Development Profile (LDP) was originally created by Susanne Cooke-Greuter and Bill Torbert[4], and is based on the Leadership Development

4 http://www.williamrtorbert.com/

Framework (LDF) that describes nine sequential changes – or 'action logics' – in how a person interprets events, or makes meaning.

Torbert and Cook-Greuter adapted this instrument for professionals and explored it in managerial populations in the 1980s and 1990s. Harthill5 has continued with improvements and created the Leadership Development Profile (LDP) so that it now provides a unique and highly validated tool for understanding personal and organisational development, and is being used with leading organisations across the world. Only the seven most commonly encountered action logics in the corporate world are referred to in the LDP. These range from the Opportunist, through the Diplomat, Expert and Achiever, to the stages of Individualist, Strategist and Magician (or Alchemist):

- *Opportunist* – focuses on own immediate needs, desires and opportunities. Seeks short-term concrete advantage and what is good for them personally. They often display sarcasm and hostility, resisting feedback and manipulating events to make themselves look good.
- *Diplomat* – seeks approval through socially expected behaviour. Seeks conformity, belonging and pleasant low stress relationships in order to gain approval from others. Diplomats avoid conflict and focus on preserving their status or membership of a group. They will argue to ensure they do not lose face.
- *Expert/Technician* – believes in the 'right way' to do things, seeking to display own skills and expertise in a dogmatic way, following procedures and behaving in ways expected of their role. They admire efficiency, consistency, incremental improvement, quality and perfection, but can get stuck in the details and their need for perfection.
- *Achiever* – seeks effectiveness through logical application of objectives, plans and controls, in order to deliver results and goals that will secure success within the system. They are proactive and use scientific problem solving techniques to assert their views and set high standards for others. Successful managers will have this logic in their psyche.
- *Individualist* – enjoys being appreciated for their own uniqueness, working through diverse relationships, experimenting with own power, developing increased spontaneity and pursuing new ideas. They tend to focus on the interactions between self and system, which means they understand the consequences of specific actions and are able to question assumptions. As a result they can adjust and adapt what they do to fit the context they find themselves in.
- *Strategist* – sees the world as a dynamic of inter-related processes and relationships, playing many roles in these. Sees the big picture and holds long-term perspective. Values integrity, principles and freedom in creating positive change. Strategists understand that reality is a social construction, which is what makes it complex with many interacting elements and factors.

5 http://harthill.co.uk/

They are tolerant of difference, seeing diversity as a resource for finding win-win solutions.

- *Magician/Alchemist* – committed to transformation of self, organisations and society. Seeks common good. Enjoys interplay of purposes, actions and results. Is elusive, chameleon-like and powerful. They have the ability to make meaning by combining practical, ontological, systemic and spiritual practices.

Once an action logic has been assimilated it remains a part of the person's meaning-making capability, even as later and more integrated logics are adopted (just as when a child learns to run it doesn't cease to be able to walk). People may be in transition from one action logic to another or rooted firmly in one central logic. In stressful times adults often revert to behaviour associated with earlier action logics because of unconscious patterns. People may choose to act from earlier action logics if the situation demands it. In contrast, behaviours associated with action logics beyond a person's current logic cannot be reliably drawn on.

In general, every bit of information or topic that can be considered, is viewed and acted upon differently by people at different stages. For example, here is how someone's understanding and response to the concept of 'feedback' changes with increasing development (Table 6.1):

Magician	View feedback (loops) as a natural part of living systems; essential for learning and change; and take it with a grain of salt.
Strategist	Invite feedback for self-actualization; conflict seen as inevitable aspect of viable and multiple relationships.
Individualist	Welcome feedback as necessary for self-knowledge and to uncover hidden aspects of their own behaviour.
Achiever	Accept feedback especially if it helps them to achieve their goals and to improve.
Expert	Take it personally; defend own position; dismiss feedback from those who are not seen as experts in the same field (general manager).
Diplomat	Receive feedback as dissaproval, or as reminder of norms.
Opportunist	React to feedback as an attack or threat.

Table 6.1

It is important to understand that this framework is not a guide to increased happiness (or even wealth). Each action logic has its own merits and difficulties, beauties and shadows. There is no evidence that later stages bring more joy or greater satisfaction from life, only that the nature of what delights and what causes suffering changes. However, the framework does give some very reliable pointers as to the qualities and types of leadership capability an individual may have.

If you are interested to see where you stand you can take an assessment at https://leadershipcircle.com/assessment-tools/, though please note that these tools are not for free.

Hard skills and soft skills

I frequently get asked what exactly the difference is between hard skills and soft skills.

Hard skills are teachable abilities or skills that are easy to quantify. Examples of hard skills include proficiency in a foreign language, a degree or certificate, typing speed, machine operation, computer programming, etc.

Soft skills, on the other hand, are subjective skills that are much harder to quantify. Also known as 'people skills' or 'interpersonal skills,' soft skills concern the way you relate to and interact with other people, to the way you behave. Obviously, the 'core competencies' as described and detailed in this book are soft skills, and, in most cases, your 'professional competencies' are hard skills (even though, for example for press officers, communicating is a hard skill too).

Hard skills are skills where *the rules stay the same* regardless of which organisation, circumstance or people you work with. In contrast, soft skills are skills where *the rules change* depending on the organisational culture, the circumstances and the people you work with. For example, computer programming is a hard skill. The rules for how you can be good at creating a computer program are the same regardless of where you work (provided you know the company's internal standards). Communication skills are soft skills. The rules for how to be effective at communicating change and depend on your audience and on the content you are communicating.

Hard skills can be learned at school, from books, or the internet. There are usually designated levels of proficiency and a direct path to how to excel with each hard skill. For example, accounting is a hard skill. You can take basic accounting and advanced accounting courses. You can then work to get experience and take an exam and be certified as a professional accountant, etc. In contrast, there is no simple path to learn soft skills. Most soft skills have to be learned on the job, by trial and error. There are many books and guides on soft skills (including this one), but they only help to a certain extent, because there aren't any easy step-by-step instructions on how to master a soft skill.

EU careers can roughly be classified into 3 categories:

- Careers that need many hard skills and relatively few soft skills (example: certain AST and AD 'specialists'). This is where you see brilliant people who may not easily work well with others. In the EU institutions however, a minimum level of soft skills is required for all. That is why, even for specialists, all candidates are assessed on their soft skills in the EPSO Assessment Centre.
- Careers that need both hard and soft skills (example: AST and AD 'generalists'). They need to know the rules and procedures of the EU very well, but dealing with their colleagues, the public, and the politicians also requires excellent soft skills.

- Careers that need mostly soft skills and relatively few hard skills (example: senior EU officials and politicians). They don't really need to know that much about the technicalities, just a little more than the public, or the press; they are more dependent on their ability to read public opinion, communicate their messages, persuasion skills, and negotiation skills.

For the EU and for the EU staff alike, life-long learning is definitely a must. The world is changing at a growing pace, so new topics arise and new departments are added to the Commissioners' portfolios all the time. Globalisation and technology shifts only add to this equation.

How we learn

'The genius of our brain's construction is not that it contains a lot of hardwiring, but that it doesn't' – Nicholas Carr

The basic building block of our brain is the neuron or nerve cell. A neuron is a cell that processes and transmits information by electro-chemical signalling. These signals between neurons occur via synapses, specialised connections with other cells. Neurons can connect to each other to form neural networks (Figure 6.2).

It is widely accepted that the synapse plays a role in the construction of memory. The strength of two connected neural pathways is thought to result in the storage of

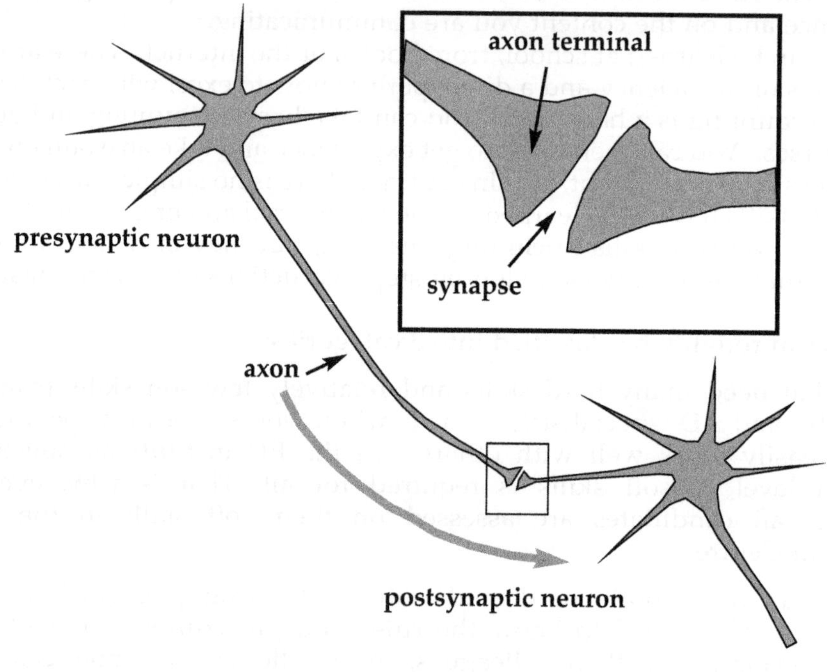

Figure 6.2

information, resulting in memory. There is an interesting video on Youtube[6] that explains in a very lively fashion the way in which this works.

The average human brain has about 100 billion neurons. Each neuron may be connected to up to 10,000 other neurons, passing signals to each other via as many as 1,000 trillion synaptic connections, equivalent by some estimates to a computer with a 1 trillion bit per second processor. Estimates of the human brain's memory capacity vary wildly from 1 to 1,000 terabytes.

Unlike other cells, neurons never divide, and neither do they die off to be replaced by new ones. By the same token, they usually cannot be replaced after being lost, although there are a few exceptions.

At the most basic level, we remember because the connections between our brain's neurons change; each experience primes the brain for the next experience. Memory also represents a change in who we are because it is predictive of who we will become. What we remember from the past has a lot to do with what we can learn in the future. Our behaviour, our habits, our ideologies, our hopes and fears are all influenced by what we remember of our past.

An understanding of memory is an understanding of the role of experience in shaping our lives, a critical tool for effective learning and development.

Scientists divide memory into categories based on how long the memory lasts: the shortest memories lasting only a few milliseconds are called immediate memories, memories lasting about a minute are called working memories, and memories lasting anywhere from an hour to many years are called long-term memories.

Another way to categorise memory is to divide memories about what something is from those about how something is done. Skills like walking, swimming, or riding a bicycle are called non-declarative memories because we perform those activities with no conscious recollection of how we learned the skills. Declarative memories, on the other hand, are memories of facts and events that we can consciously recall and describe verbally.

The end result is that we are good at remembering complex lumps of information while we are not so good at remembering large amounts of simple items of information; it is a lot easier for a person to remember a photograph in great detail than it is to remember a list of telephone numbers. Mnemonic strategies, contextual learning, repetitive rehearsal, and emotional arousal are all good ways to ensure that we remember the things that really matter.

Table 6.2 summarises some other recent brain research findings and their implications for learning.

Recent Brain Research Finding	Implications for Learning
Frequency and recency of neuron synapses increase memory	Increase frequency through practice and maintain fluency through use
Emotions strengthen memory	Appeal to and engage emotions while learning

Table 6.2 (continued overleaf)

6 https://www.youtube.com/watch?v=BEwg8TeipfQ

Recent Brain Research Finding – *cont...*	Implications for Learning – *cont...*
Learning causes changes to the physical structure of the brain	Engaging in learning increases our ability to learn throughout our lives
Memories are stored in multiple parts of the brain	Engage all senses when learning
Our brains are programmed to focus on new and unusual inputs	Learning should tap into the brain's natural curiosity and intrinsic motivation

Table 6.2 – continued

Learning styles

Learning and development is about remembering things, and how to do them. Estimates vary (see Figure 4.1 for the pyramid model) but broadly speaking it is thought that on average we actually remember around:

- 10% of what we read
- 20% of what we hear
- 30% of what we see
- 50% of what we see and hear
- 70% of what is discussed with others
- 80% of what is experienced personally
- 95% of what we teach to someone else

These are only averages, because each person prefers different techniques and ways of learning.

Learning styles group common ways that people learn. Everyone has a mix of learning styles. Some people may find that they have a dominant style of learning, with far less use of the other styles. Others may find that they use different styles in different circumstances. There is no right mix. Nor are your styles fixed. You can develop ability in less dominant styles, as well as further develop styles that you already use well.

Generally speaking there are seven learning styles:

- *Visual* (spatial) – you prefer using pictures, images, and spatial understanding.
- *Aural* (auditory-musical) – you prefer using sound and music.
- *Verbal* (linguistic) – you prefer using words, both in speech and writing.
- *Physical* (kinaesthetic) – you prefer using your body, hands and sense of touch.
- *Logical* (mathematical) – you prefer using logic, reasoning and systems.
- *Social* (interpersonal) – you prefer to learn in groups or with other people.

- *Solitary* (intrapersonal) – you prefer to work alone and use self-study.

By recognising and understanding your own learning styles, you can use techniques better suited to you. This improves the speed and quality of your learning.

Formal and informal learning

Formal learning is planned learning that derives from activities within a structured learning setting. Formal learning is enrolling on a programme of study, attending lectures, preparing coursework, and engaging in seminar/tutorial discussions.

Informal learning is learning that originates from activities external to a structured learning context, or unstructured learning within a structured learning environment.

Benefits of formal learning:

- Large numbers of employees will learn the same information and/or processes at the same time.
- If properly designed, the course content should be accurate and up to date.
- Employees learning through formal training programs come up to speed faster once they start their jobs.
- Properly designed formal training programs can include a variety of methods to appeal to all learning styles.

Benefits of informal learning:

- Creating informal learning situations can be less costly and more time efficient given technology and the social media currently available.
- Learning informally can be more personal and less intimidating for some people.
- Subject-matter experts may be more willing to share their knowledge with others this way.
- Since learning this way happens more naturally during the workday, employees may be more enthusiastic about learning new things.

The four stages of competence

The earliest origins of the 'four stages of competence' theory are uncertain and could be very old indeed. Noel Burch, a former employee of the US organisation Gordon Training International, formalised the theory in the 1970s[7]. Burch suggested that individuals are initially unaware of how little they know, or unconscious of their incompetence. As they recognise their incompetence, they consciously acquire a skill, and then consciously use it. Eventually, the skill can be operated without it being consciously thought through: the individual is said to have acquired *unconscious competence* (Figure 6.3).

7 http://www.gordontraining.com/

A learning secret: don't take notes with a laptop[8]

New research by Pam Mueller and Daniel Oppenheimer demonstrates that students who write out their notes on paper actually learn more.

Across three experiments, Mueller and Oppenheimer had students take notes in a classroom setting and then tested students on their memory for factual detail, their conceptual understanding of the material, and their ability to synthesise and generalise the information. Half of the students were instructed to take notes with a laptop, and the other half were instructed to write the notes out by hand. As in other studies, students who used laptops took more notes. In each study, however, those who wrote out their notes by hand had a stronger conceptual understanding and were more successful in applying and integrating the material than those who used took notes with their laptops.

What drives this paradoxical finding? Mueller and Oppenheimer postulate that taking notes by hand requires different types of cognitive processing than taking notes on a laptop, and these different processes have consequences for learning. Writing by hand is slower and more cumbersome than typing, and students cannot possibly write down every word in a lecture. Instead, they listen, digest, and summarise so that they can succinctly capture the essence of the information. Thus, taking notes by hand forces the brain to engage in some heavy 'mental lifting,' and these efforts foster comprehension and retention. By contrast, when typing students can easily produce a written record of the lecture without processing its meaning, as faster typing speeds allow students to transcribe a lecture word for word without devoting much thought to the content.

...

Technology offers innovative tools that are shaping educational experiences for students, often in positive and dynamic ways. The research by Mueller and Oppenheimer serves as a reminder, however, that even when technology allows us to do more in less time, it does not always foster learning. Learning involves more than the receipt and the regurgitation of information. If we want students to synthesize material, draw inferences, see new connections, evaluate evidence, and apply concepts in novel situations, we need to encourage the deep, effortful cognitive processes that underlie these abilities. When it comes to taking notes, students need fewer gigs, more brain power.

Unconscious incompetence

- The person is not aware of the existence or relevance of the skill area.
- The person is not aware that they have a particular deficiency in the area concerned.
- The person might deny the relevance or usefulness of the new skill.
- The person must become conscious of their incompetence before development of the new skill or learning can begin.
- The aim of the trainer or teacher is to move the person into the 'conscious competence' stage, by demonstrating the skill or ability and the benefit that it will bring to the person's effectiveness.

Conscious incompetence

- The person becomes aware of the existence and relevance of the skill.

8 http://www.scientificamerican.com/article/a-learning-secret-don-t-take-notes-with-a-laptop/

- The person is therefore also aware of their deficiency in this area, ideally by attempting or trying to use the skill.
- The person realises that by improving their skill or ability in this area their effectiveness will improve.
- Ideally the person has a measure of the extent of their deficiency in the relevant skill, and a measure of what level of skill is required for their own competence.
- The person ideally makes a commitment to learn and practise the new skill, and to move to the 'conscious competence' stage.

Conscious competence

- The person achieves 'conscious competence' in a skill when they can perform it reliably.
- The person will need to concentrate and think in order to perform the skill.
- The person can perform the skill without assistance.
- The person will not reliably perform the skill unless thinking about it – the skill is not yet 'second nature' or 'automatic'.
- The person should be able to demonstrate the skill to another, but is unlikely to be able to teach it well to another person.
- The person should ideally continue to practise the new skill, and if appropriate commit to becoming 'unconsciously competent' at the new skill.
- Deliberate practice is the single most effective way to move to the next stage.

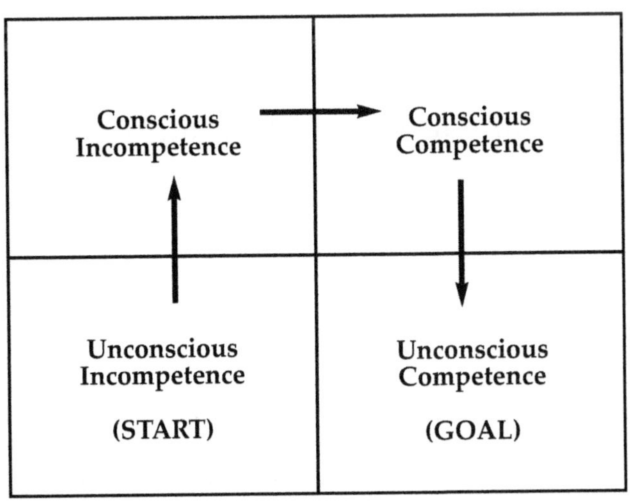

Figure 6.3

Unconscious competence

- The skill becomes so practised that it enters the unconscious parts of the brain – it becomes 'second nature'.
- Common examples are driving, sports activities, typing, manual tasks, listening and communicating.
- It becomes possible for certain skills to be performed while doing something else, for example, knitting while reading a book.
- The person might now be able to teach others in the skill concerned, although after some time of being unconsciously competent the person might actually have difficulty in explaining exactly how they do it – the skill has become largely instinctual.
- This arguably gives rise to the need for long-standing unconscious competence to be checked periodically against new standards.

Our body is constantly creating new neural stem cells, or embryonic brain cells, by a process known as neurogenesis. Here is the catch: if you don't learn something so new that you fire those new neurons, they get digested. And it's only in the phases of conscious incompetence and, a bit, of conscious competence, that you are actually learning something new.

So the advice to stick to what you are good at is terrible from the perspective of putting your hard-won new baby neurons to work. Better advice would be to start learning something new, and stick with it as long as it feels uncomfortable and you know that you haven't mastered it. As soon as you are good at it, start something new.

Several elements, including helping someone 'know what they don't know' or to recognise a blind spot, can be compared to some elements of a Johari Window (see Chapter 2), although Johari deals with self-awareness, while the four stages of competence deals with learning stages. Also, the GROW model that is used in this book relies for an important part on the same ideas.

Learning and development in the EU administration

'Live as if you were to die tomorrow. Learn as if you were to live forever.' – Mahatma Gandhi

The EU institutions depend on the expertise of their staff to achieve their goals, as EU staff are mostly knowledge workers. For staff with short-term contracts, the priority is to learn rapidly what they need to be effective. However, the biggest element of the EU staff is the permanent officials, who stay with the institutions for an average of 27 years or more. The EU needs to respond to constant change in the technological, economic, and political environment, and the resulting policy priorities of the EU. Staff cannot do the same job, in the same way, throughout their careers. With recruitment reduced, the institutions' future development depends very considerably on the learning capacity of current staff.

Learning and development is not an end in itself, it is only a means to an end. The goal of the (Commission's) strategy is therefore to ensure that staff:

- Have the knowledge and the skills they need to do their job effectively.
- Have the flexibility to adapt, to learn and to lead change.
- Work effectively together, in networks across the institutions, and with partners outside.

To enable staff to develop, it is necessary for them to have access to appropriate training and opportunities to move jobs. The EU institutions offer a wide range of opportunities for staff to develop.The Human Resources and Security DG (HR.B.3)organises language training centrally for all Commission staff. It also aims to organise general training (e.g. on HR policies, personal development and financial procedures) where this is the most cost-effective or appropriate approach.

In addition, DGs organise training locally, mainly for their own staff. In each DG or department, the 'Coordinateur en matière de Formation' (COFO), or training coordinator, is responsible for training at the DG level for the Commission. The other institutions also have their own learning and development policy (usually in coordination at interinstitutional level).

The central IT training courses are provided by DIGIT at the Digit Training Services (DTS). A team of informatics training managers organises the courses and manages the enrolments.

The Learning Centre is an assisted self-tuition centre installed in a welcoming, quiet environment conducive to study. The range of different learning aids enables everyone to find the most suitable formula.

Syslog Formation covers all needs concerning the treatment of information for the Commission's management of training. It facilitates the exchange of information between the different user groups on central and local level. The purpose of Syslog is to plan and organise training activities for the whole of the Commission staff, as well as staff of other institutions and agencies.

The **European School of Administration (EUSA)** is responsible for training in induction, certification and management. It was founded in 2005 with the aim of improving and extending the range of learning opportunities available to staff of the European civil service. By bringing staff of different institutions together the School also contributes to the spread of common values, promotes better inter-institutional understanding and cooperation, and facilitates the creation of valuable networks at various levels in the institutions. The School's training offer, which concentrates on skills and behaviours that are needed across the European civil service, is complemented by the individual institutions' own programs to meet their specific needs.

In the Commission, *internal mobility* is considered to be an important tool for staff to diversify their experience and for the acquisition of competencies within the organisation. Internal mobility is facilitated by the sheer number of policy domains and the variety of competences and tasks exercised by the Commission. It is generally accepted that officials should stay at least two years in a given post to ensure a degree of stability and to give a return on learning experience. Furthermore, a rule of five to seven years as a maximum in post applies for sensitive positions. Limiting the number of years a person can occupy a sensitive post is one way of reducing the risk that the person concerned may benefit from misuse of their discretionary powers.

In the other institutions, bodies and agencies, internal mobility possibilities are more limited because of the smaller size of these organisations, and (in agencies) the even more specialised profiles of many of the people working there. However, it is sometimes possible to move to another institution, even though the Staff Regulations explicitly favour internal mobility (Article 29).

The institutions can also support the investment staff make in learning in their own time. Where a personal initiative is relevant to the current job, or the future career, but is not essential and/or would not be cost-effective to be fully financed by the employer, staff can apply for partial reimbursement of costs. In addition, special leave can be awarded.

In its 2012 Special Report N° 10[9], the Court of Auditors made some recommendations on how to improve and further optimise this offering. As a consequence certain things will change over the coming years. For a more detailed and up-to-date overview of these possibilities you can always consult the Annual Activity Reports from DG HR and Security, and EPSO (which covers EUSA as well).

The aim of the **Erasmus for Public Administration** programme is to help young national civil servants dealing with EU affairs to learn more about the EU decision-making processes and the way the institutions function. It also offers excellent networking opportunities. This one-and-a half week study programme comprises conferences, training seminars, and visits to the institutions in Brussels, Luxembourg and Strasbourg (plenary session of the European Parliament). It also includes two-and-a-half days of 'job shadowing' in an institution of the participant's choice. Three sessions per year are organised for a maximum of 45 participants per session.

Seeing the bigger picture

Motivation is an important factor in learning and development. From Chapter 2 we learned that *purpose* is a necessary condition for motivation. Purpose is not just about earning money, it is not just about having a nine-to-five job; it means having a higher goal, or a more important objective in what you do.

Onge good way to build motivation and purpose is by learning and understanding all you can about the EU and its institutions.

You can start by reading about the EU on the web. Some examples worthwhile exploring:

- http://europa.eu/legislation_summaries/institutional_affairs/treaties/
- http://www.europarl.europa.eu/aboutparliament/en/007c895f4c/Powers-and-procedures.html

9 The Effectiveness of Staff Development in the European Commission (2012), European Court of Auditors.

The perfect Commission official's toolkit

The European Union is first and foremost a legal construction. This very much influences the Commission staff, who anchor their work to a framework of rules. Commission staff activities are framed by some basic rules/guidelines which can be found in a set of basic documents (always at hand's reach of most staff):

- The treaties – these define for staff the limits of the competences attributed to the EU and the procedures to be followed (material and procedure competences).
- The Commission's rules of procedure, implementing rules and manual of procedures that give a core set of rules for organising the internal decision-making and relations with external actors.
- The Code of Good Administrative Behaviour
- The Internal Control Standards.

At DG level we also have:

- Programming and reporting documents of the DG Commission work programme, EU budget, DG annual management plan, annual report, synthesis report.
- The DG's organisational chart.
- List of contacts (name, function, phone numbers) from the Directorate/unit.
- For staff dealing with the budget: the Financial Regulation (general and Commission) and its implementing rules.
- For staff dealing with or interested in human resources issues: the Staff Regulation and implementing rules.
- For staff dealing with policy-making
  - –The basic rules relevant to the field of activity of each official including legislative acts, delegated acts and implementing measures.
  - – Any other document (consultative documents including white papers, green papers, communications, etc).

(Source: 'The European Commission: A Practical Guide', by Manuel Szapiro)

- http://www.europedia.moussis.eu/books/Book_2/2/4/3/?all=1
- http://europa.eu/eu-law/

Of course, there are also some very good books that have been written about this topic. I will limit myself to a few titles from my own publisher, John Harper[10], who specialises in EU affairs:

- 'The European Commission – A Practical Guide' by Manuel Szapiro
- 'The European Parliament' by Richard Corbett et al.
- 'How the EU Institutions Work' edited by Erik Akse
- 'The European Council in the Era of Crises' by Jan Werts

Recent information on the institutions can also be found in their Annual Activity Reports, and on their intranet and public websites.

Furthermore, it is important that you keep informed about the EU 'hot topics'. For this, of course, the specialised press is the place to be:

- http://europa.eu/rapid
- http://euobserver.com

10 https://www.johnharperpublishing.co.uk/books/

- http://www.euractiv.com
- http://www.presseurop.eu
- http://www.politico.eu

Basic User	A1	• Can understand and use familiar everyday expressions and very basic phrases aimed at the satisfaction of needs of a concrete type • Can introduce him/herself and others and can ask and answer questions about personal details such as where he/she lives, people he/she knows and things he/she has. • Can interact in a simple way provided the other person talks slowly and clearly and is prepared to help.
	A2	• Can understand sentences and frequently used expressions related to areas of most immediate relevance (e.g. very basic personal and family information, shopping, local geography, employment). • Can communicate in simple and routine tasks requiring a simple and direct exchange of information on familiar and routine matters. • Can describe in simple terms aspects of his/her background, immediate environment and matters in areas of immediate need.
Independent User	B1	• Can understand the main points of clear standard input on familiar matters regularly encountered in work, school, leisure, etc. • Can deal with most situations likely to arise while travelling in an area where the language is spoken. • Can produce simple connected text on topics that are familiar or of personal interest. • Can describe experiences and events, dreams, hopes and ambitions and briefly give reasons and explanations for opinions and plans.
	B2	• Can understand the main ideas of complex text on both concrete and abstract topics, including technical discussions in his/her field of specialization. • Can interact with a degree of fluency and spontaneity that makes regular interaction with native speakers quite possible without strain for either party. • Can produce clear, detailed text on a wide range of subjects and explain a viewpoint on a topical issue giving the advantages and disadvantages of various options.
Proficient user	C1	• Can understand a wide range of demanding, longer texts, and recognise implicit meaning. • Can express ideas fluently and spontaneously without much obvious searching for expressions. • Can use language flexibly and effectively for social, academic and professional purposes. • Can produce clear, well-structured, detailed text on complex subjects, showing controlled use of organisational patterns, connectors and cohesive devices.
	C2	• Can understand with ease virtually everything heard or read. • Can summarise information from different spoken and written sources, reconstructing arguments and accounts in a coherent presentation. • Can express him/herself spontaneously, very fluently and precisely, differentiating finer shades of meaning even in the most complex situations.

Table 6.3: The Common European Framework for languages

Learning another language

Article 45, point 2 of the Staff Regulation stipulates:

> 'Officials shall be required to demonstrate before their first promotion after recruitment the ability to work in a third language among those referred to in Article 314 of the EC Treaty. The institutions shall adopt common rules by agreement between them for implementing this paragraph. These rules shall require access to training for officials in a third language and lay down the detailed arrangements for the assessment of officials' ability to work in a third language, in accordance with Article 7(2)(d) of Annex III.'

This effectively means that mastering three languages is considered to be 'normal' for an EU official, as it is a requirement for the first promotion. Upon recruitment, proficiency in only two languages (mother tongue plus one of the three 'working languages' – English, French, or German) is required. The EU institutions also provide a lot of facilities (classroom training, online language courses ...) to make this happen. I have known former EU colleagues – not translators or linguists – who mastered up to six different languages, so it is possible!

Mastering multiple languages is not only about hard skills; it enables a better understanding of the different cultural backgrounds of your colleagues, and hence develops your interpersonal – or soft – skills.

As a Dutch (Flemish actually) native speaker, I consider it to be particularly important to point out that Brussels is not only the capital of Europe, but also of Belgium and the Flemish Community alike. Both French and Dutch are commonly spoken languages in Brussels. So, in my opinion it makes sense that an EU official, who spends the better part of his or her life in Brussels, acquires at least the basic notions of both these languages, so that they can step outside of the 'European bubble'. This can only benefit the image of the EU and its institutions.

The **Common European Framework** divides language learners into three broad divisions that can be divided into six levels; for each level, it describes what a learner is supposed to be able to do in reading, listening, speaking and writing. These levels are described in Table 6.3. on the previous page.

Mnemonic strategies

A mnemonic (pronounced: ne-mo-nic) is any learning technique that aids information retention in the human memory. Mnemonics aim to translate information into a form that the brain can retain better than its original form. Typically the initial letter of each word gives us the mnemonic.

In Chapter 1 we discussed the 'SMART' mnemonic which stands for Specific, Measurable, Achievable, Realistic, and Time-bound. Likewise in Chapter 3 we had the IDEAL mnemonic for analysing and problem-solving and in Chapter 4 the STAR mnemonic for Situation, Task, Action, Results.

There are many types of mnemonics, and I am sure you are sometimes use them as well. Just be aware that this is a simple, but powerful technique that can improve your learning skills.

Deliberate practice

'What we hope ever to do with ease, we must learn first to do with diligence.' – Samuel Johnson

Repetition is perhaps the most intuitive principle of learning, traceable to ancient Egyptian and Chinese education. In ancient Greece, Aristotle commented on the role of repetition in learning by saying 'it is frequent repetition that produces a natural tendency' and 'the more frequently two things are experienced together, the more likely it will be that the experience or recall of one will stimulate the recall of the other'[11].

Repetition is one of the most basic learning techniques. Children use it to learn to speak. Athletes use it to perfect their athletic skills. Repetition is sometimes seen as boring, or looked down upon as an attempt to simply memorise rather than understand. However, repetition is essential, because it effectively creates the neural pathways in our brain needed for remembering and understanding new information and skills.

Deliberate practice is not the same as mere repetition, or 'drill and kill'. Simply repeating a task will not by itself improve performance. Deliberate practice involves awareness, attention, rehearsal and repetition, and leads to new knowledge or skills that can later be developed into more complex knowledge and skills. Although other factors such as intelligence and motivation affect performance, practice is necessary, but not sufficient, for acquiring expertise.

Research suggests that several conditions must be in place in order for practice activities to be most effective:

- Building on existing knowledge
- Repeated opportunities
- Encouragement
- Timely and descriptive feedback

Trial and error

'Mistakes are a fact of life. It is the response to the error that counts.' – Nikki Giovanni[12]

Trial and error is a method of learning in which various responses are tentatively tried, and some discarded, until a valid solution is reached.

Edward Thorndike[13] was the chief exponent of the theory of *connectionism* or trial and error. He conducted Stimulus – Response (S-R) theory experiments with the help of animals. Thorndike was the first to study the subject of learning systematically using standardized procedures and tools. All learning, according to Thorndike, is the construction of bonds or connections between Stimulus and Response.

If circumstances permit, learning from our mistakes is a very powerful way of learning. That is why it is advised to managers and leaders to create a 'safe' environ-

11 'Aristotle' (2004) by Sir David Ross.

12 American poet and activist (1943).

13 Edward Lee 'Ted' Thorndike (1874–1949) was an American psychologist.

Trial and error in the EU

It is rather atypical for the EU institutions to accept trial and error as a learning model. Very few, if any, of them have 'Research and Development' or 'Innovation' departments, which goes hand in hand with the concept. However, the Joint Research Centre (JRC) is the European Commission's in-house science service. It provides independent scientific and technical advice to the European Commission to support a wide range of EU policies. It has seven scientific institutes, located at six different sites in Belgium, Germany, Italy, the Netherlands, and Spain. The Directorate-General of the JRC is located in Brussels.

ment for those who work under them. A safe environment is an environment where people are not afraid to make mistakes, where they can learn and develop, and are supported rather than punished for whatever goes wrong.

Mind mapping

A *mind map*, as in Figure 6.5, is a powerful graphic method that provides a universal key to unlock the potential of your brain. It exploits the full range of cortical skills – word, image, number, logic, rhythm, colour and spatial awareness – in a single, powerful manner. In so doing, it gives you the freedom to explore all the areas of your mind.

A mind map is basically a diagram that connects information around a central topic. At the centre is your main topic, and the branches are related points. Greater levels of detail branch out to sub-points from there, and branches can be linked together. Mind maps link and group concepts together through natural associations. This helps to generate more ideas and find deeper meaning in your subject, and also prompts you to fill in more or find what you are missing. Mind mapping is a very intuitive way to organise your thoughts, because mind maps imitate the way your brain thinks.

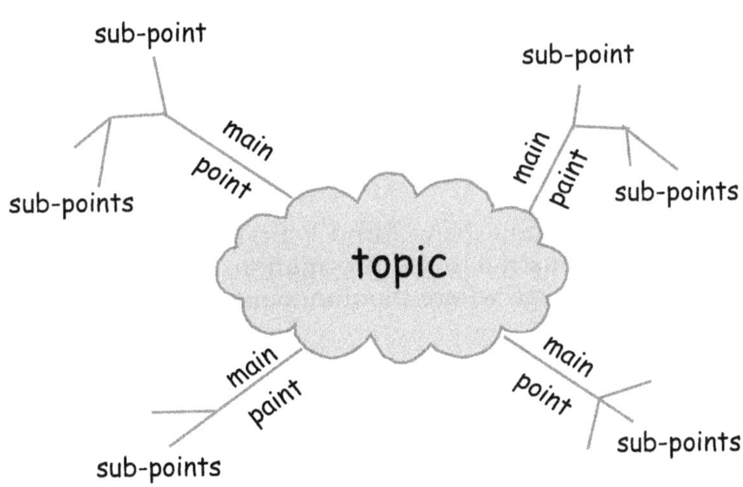

Figure 6.5

Mind maps can be used for pretty much any thinking or learning task, from studying a subject (such as a new language) to planning your career or even building better habits. They are great for teams to use as well, for brainstorming and interactive presentations.

70-20-10 model

The 70-20-10 model (Figure 6.6) is a learning and development model, usually credited to Morgan McCall and his colleagues, Lombardo and Eichinger, working at the Centre for Creative Leadership[14] (CCL). In their 1996 book, 'The Career Architect Development Planner'[15], they published the results of a survey asking nearly 200 executives to self-report on how they believed they learned. These results were that lessons learned by successful and effective managers are roughly:

- 70% from tough jobs
- 20% from people (mostly the boss)
- 10% from courses and reading

Lombardo and Eichinger gave the rationale behind the 70-20-10 Model as:

> 'Development generally begins with a realization of current or future need and the motivation to do something about it. This might come from feedback, a mistake, watching other people's reactions, failing or not being up to a task – in other words, from experience. The odds are that development will be about 70% from on-the-job experiences – working on tasks and problems; about 20% from feedback and working around good and bad examples of the need; and 10% from courses and reading.'

This model is used in the Commission's learning and development strategy, which is built around the ideas of 'lifelong learning' and 'lifewide learning'. Although the exact percentages vary from person to person, and job to job, this model points to the importance of on-the-job learning, alongside formal training.

Pervasive learning

Daniel Pink's[16] book 'A Whole New Mind'[17] first describes how our society has gone from agricultural to industrial to the information age. But then, he describes how we have moved on to a new age where the dominant value for most organisations is

14 www.ccl.org

15 'The Career Architect Development Planner' (2000) by Michael Lombardo and Robert Eichinger.

16 Daniel Pink (1964) is the author of books about business, work, and management and also former chief speechwriter for vice-president Al Gore.

17 'A Whole New Mind: Why Right-Brainers will rule the Future' (2006) by Daniel Pink.

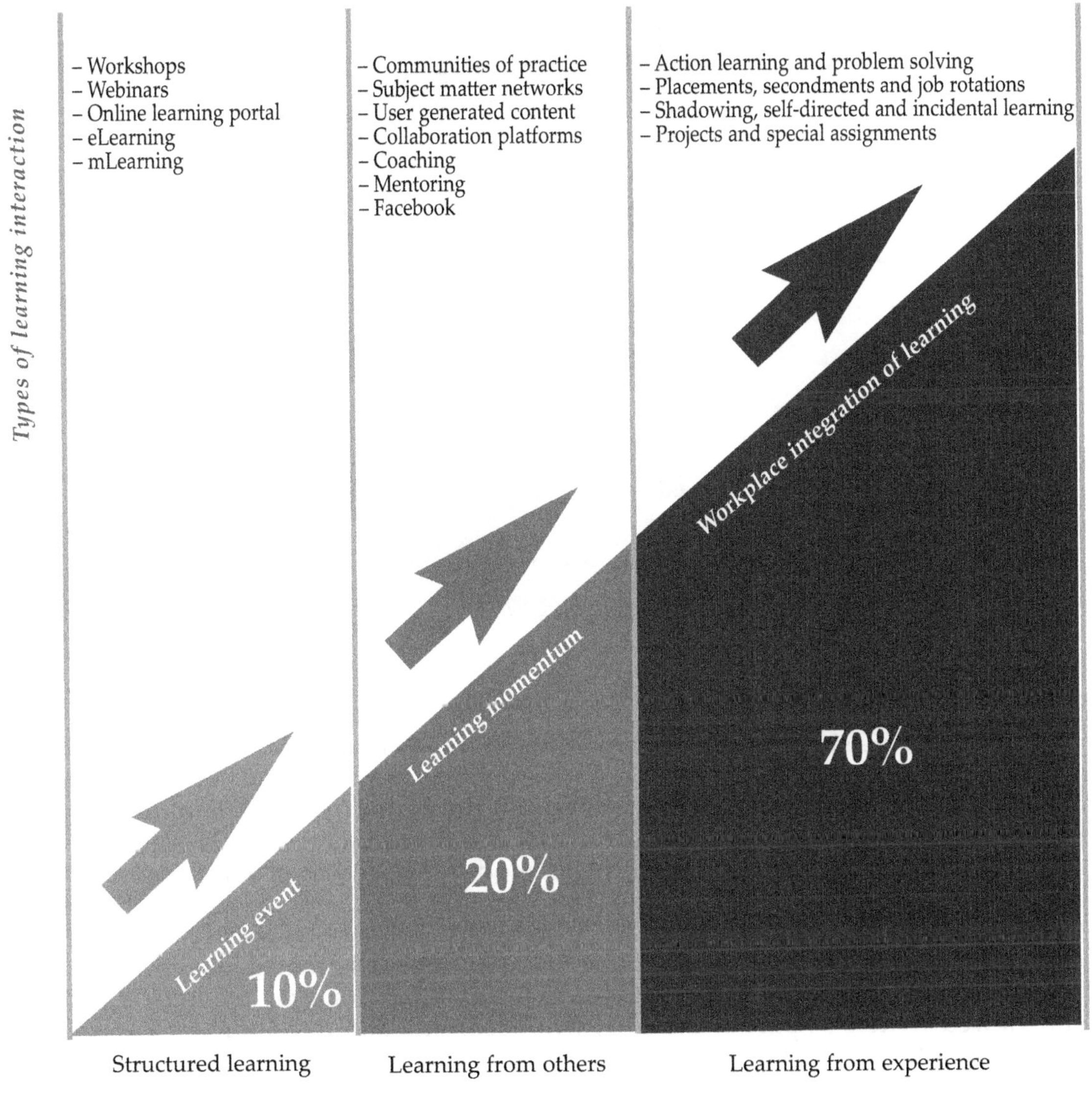

Figure 6.6: the 70-20-10 model

created by high-end knowledge workers – concept workers. For concept workers, work and learning merge.

The idea of *pervasive learning* has been around for some time and makes perfect sense as more and more of us become concept workers. In his book, 'Flat Army'[18] Dan Pontefract[19] defines pervasive learning as 'learning at the speed of need through formal, informal and social learning modalities'.

18 'Flat Army: Creating a Connected and Engaged Organisation' by Dan Pontrefact.

19 Dan Pontefract on his website describes himself as author, speaker and chief envisioner.

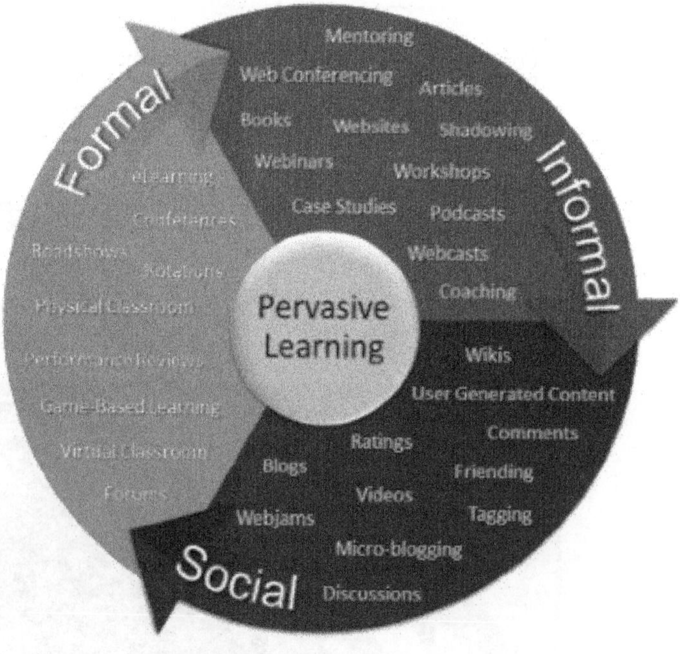

Figure 6.7: the 3-33 model

There are some similarities between Pontefract's ideas and the 70-20-10 model, but as Donald Clark[20] points out, the 70-20-10 model may not be universally applicable to all staff. Instead, Pontefract's **3-33 model** often fits better. In the 3-33 model, 33% of learning is formal, 33% is informal, and 33% is social (see Figure 6.7). What is most interesting is that the research behind this model revealed that when learners were asked to give the percentages for how they thought they learned, the numbers were very different from what the researchers actually found to be the case.

One of the other major flaws of the 70-20-10 model is that it places reading in formal learning. This error is probably due to the limited survey amongst managers who viewed writers as part of the elite, while learning and development was seen as less important.

Teaching others

'While we teach, we learn' – Seneca[21]

Most people are familiar with learning through books, or in classes, but many overlook perhaps the most comprehensive learning experience of all – *teaching*. The best test of whether or not you really understand a concept is trying to teach it to someone else. Teaching others calls for thorough understanding of the concept yourself.

20 http://www.nwlink.com/~donclark/hrd/media/70-20-10.html

21 Seneca (c. 4 BC–AD 65) was a Roman philosopher, statesman, and dramatist.

Students teaching other students work harder to understand the material, recall it more accurately and apply it more effectively. Scientists have called this 'the protégé effect.' Student teachers score higher on tests than pupils who are learning only for their own sake.

Teaching also forces you to communicate your thoughts clearly and precisely. As our society becomes ever more interconnected and interdependent, cooperation becomes more and more important. This cooperation requires communication. However, being heard is not enough; you must also be understood. Your ideas will never be more effective than your ability to make others comprehend them. Teaching helps you develop the extremely important skill of describing your ideas well enough for others to use them.

Teaching others is not limited to a simple transfer of information between individuals, be it in a formal or an informal setting. Teaching others is also coaching and mentoring them for the purpose of learning and development (Figure 6.8).

For sure, my activities, as a coach and author of books about the topic of personal development, are part of my own learning and development strategy.

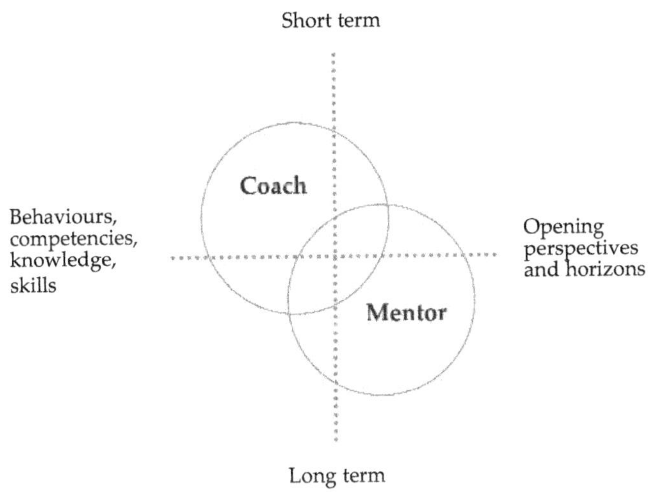

Figure 6.8

Developing your learning and development skills

Learning and development bring about changes in the way we act, think and/or feel about ourselves, about other people, and about the world around us. These changes may be permanent or temporary depending on our own perceptions of the importance and relevance of the knowledge gained.

Both learning and development are important, but they occur at different moments and rates. Learning happens via many channels – school, professional training, self-directed and life-long learning, practice, or simply through exposure to life.

Development refers to how we learn to see the world through new eyes, how we change our interpretations of experience, and how we transform our views of reality. It describes our increasing awareness, and therefore what we can integrate and influence.

Please refer to Annex 1 for further development of this competency or check out the easy-to-use app at :

http://www.johnharperpublishing.co.uk/the-ultimate-eu-career-development-toolkit/

7. Prioritising and organising

Competency definition: 'Prioritises the most important tasks, works flexibly and organises own workload efficiently.'

Prioritising and organising is more commonly known as *time management*, but what is time management? Time itself can't be managed. It is constant and it always goes forward, never backwards. Everyone has the same amount of time in an hour, a day, and a week. Therefore, time management does not mean that you are trying to manipulate time, but that you are trying to make the best use of your time.

Time management is the act of taking conscious control (*awareness and responsibility*, remember) over the amount of time you spend on specific activities. Time management is about goal setting, effective scheduling of your time, prioritising and choosing what to do and what not to do, delegating tasks, analysing and reviewing your spent time, organising your workspace, keeping your concentration and focus on your work, and motivating yourself.

You exercise time management (your prioritising and organising comnpetency) to increase your effectiveness, efficiency, and ultimately your productivity. You practise skills and use tools and techniques to aid you when accomplishing tasks, projects or are working towards goals and deadlines.

The most significant problem in today's working world is not competition, lack of skilled employees or an uncertain economy, but an *attention deficit*. Put simply, with all the noise from constant meetings, and deluges of voice mail and email, it's hard to get anyone's undivided attention anymore. In their book 'The Attention Economy'[1], authors Thomas Davenport and John Beck state that the organisations and individuals that succeed in the future will be those that focus their efforts on this problem, instead of on conventional approaches to time management. Attention, they say, is 'the new currency of business.'

Tasks

Ever since Adam and Eve were expelled from the Garden of Eden most of us have had to work for a living. But even though we have to work in exchange for a financial reward, there is nothing wrong with actually enjoying our work. After all, we spend a big slice of our waking hours at work, and spending that time in an enjoyable and productive way is part of what makes life worth living. Agreed, your boss, your colleagues, or the work you have to do are not always exciting, but 'feeling in control' of what you do – and how you do it – will at least give you some degree of job satisfaction and happiness.

The most elementary building block of work is a *task*. A task is an activity that needs to be accomplished within a defined period of time (or by a deadline) to reach work-related goals.

1 'The Attention Economy: Understanding the New Currency of Business' (2002) by Thomas H. Davenport and John C. Beck.

A task is an (abstract) three-dimensional object: input, output and time. The *input* is what you do; the efforts, knowledge, energy, focus or whatever other contribution you make to get the work done. The *output* is the result; it can be a message, a report, a presentation or any tangible or intangible deliverable of your work. The *time* is the difference between the moment you started working on the task and when your work was complete. It is important to be aware that these three dimensions are interrelated; they influence each other.

I sometimes use the metaphor of a balloon, filled with air. This is a three-dimensional object too, right? When you squeeze the balloon (thus modifying one dimension) this will influence the other two dimensions. By analogy, when you change one 'dimension' of a task this will also have an impact on the other dimensions. Say your manager changes the (expected) output; you will then be forced to either change your input or the time it takes to complete the task. If you reduce your input then either the output will have to be less or it will take you more time to complete the task (or both).

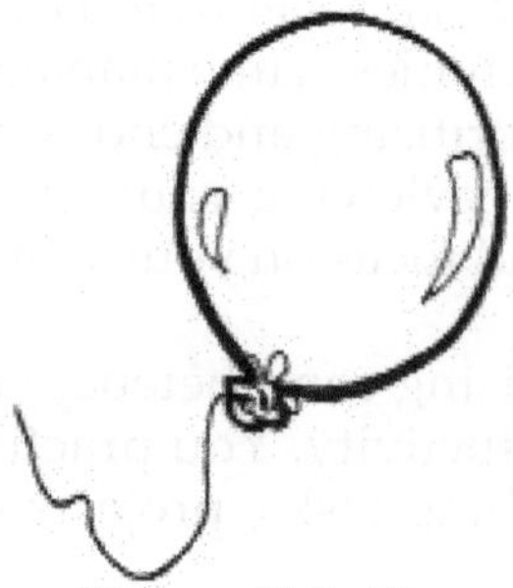

Figure 7.1: Do not squeeze too hard!

There is another nice use of this metaphor. What happens if you squeeze a balloon too hard? It will burst. Well, the same thing happens with tasks. Say the deadline (or the time allotted) is too tight: you will never manage to complete the task. If the (expected) output is too high you will never make it in time and neither will you accomplish the task if your input is too low.

Processes

According to Professor Tom Davenport[2] a process is:
'A specific ordering of work activities across time and place, with a beginning and an end, clearly defined inputs and outputs, a structure for action.'

A simple analogy would be to look at an organisation as a wheel and the individual processes as the spokes of that wheel. Having just one or two spokes loose can make a wheel roll out of balance. The longer a wheel runs out of balance, the more damaging the effect to the wheel. When the wheel becomes so unstable that its primary function fails, you would simply replace the wheel. Obviously, an organisation cannot replace itself – but your stakeholders can, and will do so if the organisation does not perform to their needs and expectations.

The purpose of a process is to transform input into output. This transformation is done through the support of resources (people, money, infrastructure, information …) and according to – formal or informal – specifications.

2 Tom Davenport is the President's Distinguished Professor in Management and Information Technology at Babson College.

A process can be broken down into several *steps* and organised in a *workflow*. Each step is performed by an actor (a person or a group of persons) with a given role in the workflow. Very often processes (also known as procedures, or operations) are implemented through an IT system.

The output of a process can be material (a product) or non-material (a service). In fact, often it is a combination of both (e.g. a paper file is the material component, while the content is the service component of a written report).

Most of the tasks we have to do are in some way part of a process: we are 'actors' with a given role, transforming input into output according to some specifications.

The nice thing about this view on matters is that it makes our life easier in terms of prioritising and organising our work. We know the input, what is expected and how much time we have to execute the task. We also have an idea of how important our tasks are. Being aware that we are part of a bigger entity is also an extrinsic motivator.

Projects

'Crash programs fail because they are based on the theory that, with nine women pregnant, you can get a baby in one month.' – Werner Von Braun

Projects have always been a part of life, ever since the first groups of humans worked together to gather, plant or hunt. Over the years, the concept of *project*

A typical process in the EU administration

A good example of a *process* within the EU administrative realm is the implementation of revenue and expenditure as governed by the EU Financial Regulation (Regulation N° 966/2012 of the European Parliament and of the Council).

Each EU institution (or body) is responsible for implementing revenue and expenditure in accordance with the principle of sound financial management and for ensuring compliance with the requirements of legality and regularity. Each EU institution (or body) has an 'Authorising Officer by Delegation' who can sub-delegate his powers by appointing other officials to oversee different budget posts, related to their functional domain of activity. Authorising Officers by (sub)delegation (in short AO) are assisted by Initiating Agents (IA), of which they are the superiors. The Verifying Agent(s) (VA) – who are independent from the AO to ensure autonomy of judgment – assist the AO in ensuring compliance with the requirements of legality and regularity by means of 'ex-ante' and 'ex-post' verification of all the files. While the AO is responsible for the financial transactions it is the Accountant (AC) who executes them (i.e. pays invoices and receives income) and keeps track of them in the accounting system. In most EU institutions and bodies this process is supported by the ABAC system, which enforces the workflow.

The 'actors' in this process are the AO, IA, VA and AC, and they all have limited access rights and permissions on the part of the budget under their control. They perform their tasks and duties in the context of the wider process, and within the time constraints as imposed by the procedure. Each step of the process has well-known inputs and outputs and the actors' tasks come down to transforming the inputs into the outputs. The (formal) specifications are laid down in the Financial Regulation (which applies to all EU institutions and bodies) and the Internal Rules (which are specific to each organisation).

management – planning and directing the activities executed by a group of people with a fixed objective and over a limited period of time – has been refined and formalised into a profession.

The Project Management Institute (PMI), a leading organisation in the development of project management principles and certification standards, defines a project as 'a temporary endeavour undertaken to create a unique product, service, or result.'

Projects and processes differ primarily in that processes are on-going and repetitive, while projects are temporary and unique.

The objectives of projects and processes are fundamentally different. The purpose of a project is to attain its objective and then terminate. Conversely, the objective of an on-going operation (a process) is to sustain the organisation. Projects are undertaken at all levels of an organisation and they can involve a single person or many thousands. Projects can involve one or many organisational units, including joint ventures and partnerships.

PRINCE2	PMBOK
Origin: UK	Origin: US
Adoption: worldwide	Adoption: worldwide
A process based methodology	A knowledge based approach
A series of management processes defining what must be done, when and how it must be done and by whom over the life of a project	Describes core practices and a wider range of techniques that can be applied to manage a project
Prescriptive	Non-prescriptive
Defines the roles of everyone involved in a project	Focuses on the project manager's role

Table 7.1: PRINCE2 and PMBOK compared

The best-known project management methodologies (or frameworks) are **PRINCE2** (Projects In a Controlled Environment) and **PMBOK** (Project Management Body of Knowledge). Table 7.1 lists the main differences:

The **PM^2 (PM square)** methodology that is used by the Commission is built on PMBOK, and is supported by four pillars:

- A project governance model (roles & responsibilities)
- A project lifecycle (project phases)
- A set of processes (project management activities)
- A set of project artefacts (templates and guidelines)

Gantt charts

Henry Gantt[3] developed one of the first project management tools, today known as *Gantt charts*. Gantt charts plot the activities necessary to complete a project on a timeline using a bar or a line, which begins and ends at a definite time (Figure 7.2). The Gantt chart also provides milestones, or markers, for assuring that a project is on track.

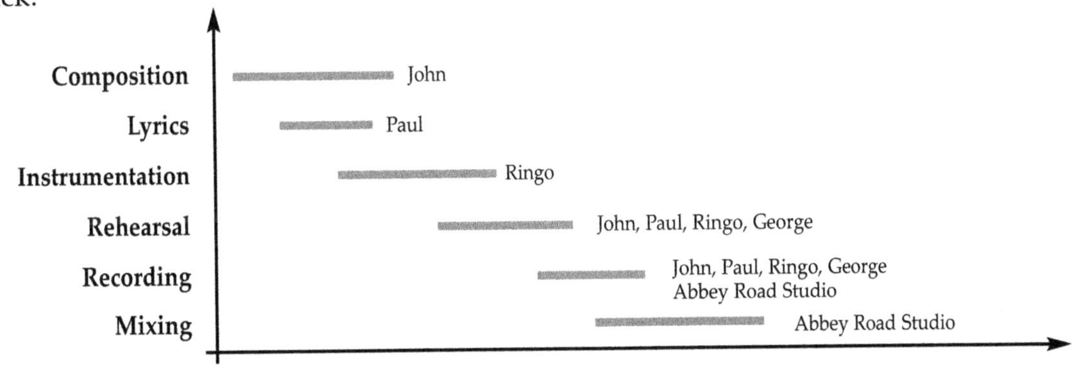

Figure 7.2: A Gantt chart

While Gantt charts have the advantage of simplicity, they can hide as much as they display. Indeed, the interrelationships between the various activities are not made explicit nor are the relationships between resources and the time to complete a task. Gantt charts can tell a manager if a program is *off* track, but they often cannot provide information about how to get it back *on* track.

N°	Activity	Resources	Estimate	Dependencies
1	Composition	John	5 weeks	0
2	Lyrics	Paul	3 weeks	0
3	Instrumentation	Ringo	6 weeks	1,2, 3
4	Rehearsal	John, Paul, Ringo, George	4 weeks	3
5	Recording	John, Paul, Ringo, George, Abbey Road Studios	4 weeks	4
6	Mixing	Abbey Road Studios	5 weeks	5

Table 7.2

PERT/CPM

The most commonly used method for documenting the relationships between tasks and determining their relative importance to the project is the **Project Evaluation and Review Technique/Critical Path Method (PERT/CPM)**. PERT was developed in 1958 to help plan and schedule the US Navy Polaris submarine project. On the other hand, the DuPont Company and the Univac division of Remington Rand

3 Henry Gantt (1861–1919) was an American mechanical engineer and management consultant.

Corporation developed CPM to provide a method for controlling maintenance in the DuPont chemical plants. Later, it was noticed that these two methods shared many similarities and their approaches were combined in one method.

PERT/CPM graphs provide a general overview of a project. They consist of activities and events. Activities are operations in the project that consume resources and take time. Events occur at a point in time and represent the beginning, the end (or both) of an activity.

Table 7.2 on the previous page shows the interdependencies among the various tasks shown in Figure 7.2.

The PERT/CPM graph looks like this (Figure 7.3).

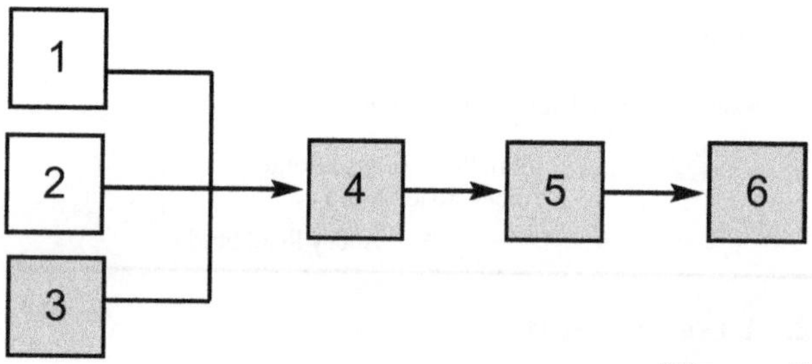

Figure 7.3

The most time-consuming path in the graph is called the critical path (this would be 3, 4, 5 and 6 in the example above). Each activity within this longest path is critical, as any delays in realising a critical activity will delay the entire project. The critical path can change during a project (as 'slippage' on a previously non-critical activity can extend the length of that path so that it becomes the longest).

Please note that the example above is extremely simplistic, for the sake of clarity. In real projects there can be hundreds – or thousands – of activities, and the diagrams are managed through a computer application, which instantly re-evaluates the critical path whenever something changes. In the EU institutions, it is mostly Microsoft Project that is used for this.

It is amongst the tasks of the project manager to constantly monitor the progress of the project and – if necessary – to reallocate resources and/or execute tasks in parallel in order to keep control of the critical path. There are some very nice tools on the market, which implement the above techniques and more. Probably the best known is Microsoft Project. So, if you are involved in project management you are strongly advised to get acquainted with these techniques.

Also in the EU administration there are many activities that can be considered as projects. To give some examples:

- The annual budget cycle (even if it is repetitive, every budget is unique)
- Organising a call for tender
- Organising a conference or public hearing
- Legislative procedures

You may have noticed that the above examples are projects that span multiple organisational entities (services, units, directorates, even institutions). This means that EU officials of all disciplines are being confronted with project work – even if they are not aware of it. The point is to understand how projects are managed and act accordingly in terms of prioritising and organising your contribution.

Symptoms of poor time management

The following list covers some of the most common symptoms of poor time management, regardless of the quantity of work you actually bring to a conclusion. If you recognise some of these symptoms in your own behaviour, there is likely some room for improvement.

- *Poorly defined goals* – Your goals help you to identify your priorities. They outline what you want to achieve, when you want to achieve it by, and why the task is important. If you do not have clearly defined goals, how are you supposed to know which tasks need to be done first?
- *Poor punctuality* – You are regularly late for your appointments or in completing your tasks. This may be due to you accepting too many tasks or your inability to assign the correct amount of time to your activities.
- *Rushing* – We all have to rush a little, from time to time, but if you find yourself constantly rushing from one appointment to another then you have an issue. You should allow sufficient time between appointments to cope with unforeseen events such as a previous meeting overrunning, or simply traffic jams.
- *Impatience* – Impatience is usually a sign of poor time management. You may accuse other people, or technology, of delaying you but the truth is that you have failed yourself by failing to manage your time properly.
- *Perfectionism* – You spend so much time trying to prepare and make sure that you perform your tasks perfectly that you either fail to start or go incredibly slowly. In reality, most of the time, 'good enough is best'.
- *Indecisiveness* – You are unable to choose an option and run with it. You spend excessive time going over the options without coming to a conclusion.
- *Saying 'Yes' to everything* – Constantly saying 'Yes' will leave you with an excessive workload. One of the quickest ways to improve your time management is to be assertive and learn to say 'No'.
- *Doing everything yourself* – It doesn't matter whether you are a Director, Head of Unit, Administrator or Assistant, there are always tasks which can be delegated, automated or outsourced. These tasks need to be identified and removed from your workload.
- *Procrastination* – Sometimes you know what needs to be done but you keep putting it off. Eventually, when you decide to complete the task, the deadline is usually approaching and you are under pressure to complete the task in time.

- *Lack of energy* – When you constantly have to work extra hard to catch up, your energy levels begin to drop and you lose motivation. It becomes harder to catch up and so you fall further behind which drains you of even more energy.

Poor time management impacts every area of your life, from work to relationships. Don't confuse being busy with being an accomplished time manager. Getting more work done does not automatically mean that you are managing your time effectively; if the extra tasks are unimportant, you are just filling your schedule. Focusing on getting the important tasks done is the key to effective time management.

Estimating time

It is important to realise that a time estimate for a task is not a single number, but a range of possibilities, a statistical entity. Everybody knows that if somebody wants to talk to you 'for a couple of minutes' it will most likely actually take 15 minutes, and if it is important it will be more like 45 minutes. On the other hand, there are no tasks with a negative duration, so the distribution of estimations is not symmetrical (Figure 7.4).

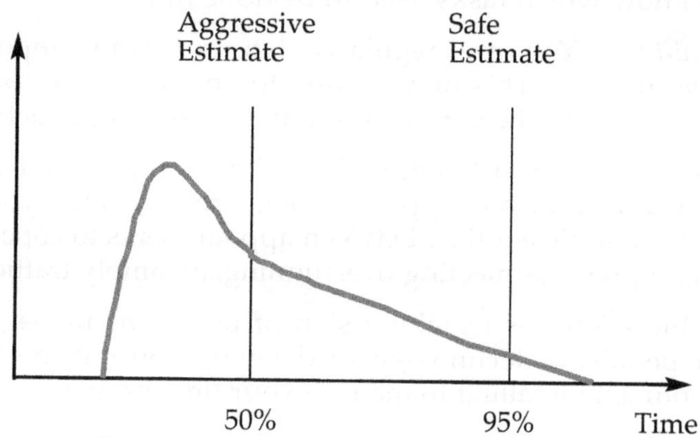

Figure 7.4

Most people have a tendency to give an estimate that they think they can make in 95% of the cases (they make a *safe* estimate). A safe estimate can easily represent twice the time of an aggressive estimate, one we think we can make in 50% of the cases.

In order to improve your own estimation of how long a given task will take it is a good idea to keep track of your own work and – based on your experience – use the actual (average) time you spent on similar tasks as the basis of your estimate. You can still decide if you want it to be safe or aggressive, depending on the importance, the urgency and circumstances you are in at that moment.

STOP

In his book 'The Inner Game of Work'[4] Tim Gallwey introduces the concept of *mobility*, which he defines as: 'the ability to move or adapt, change or be changed. It also means the ability to reach one's objectives in a fulfilling manner – to reach goals at the right time and in a way we feel good about. Therefore, mobility is not only change but fulfilment and harmony with one's progress.'

Not everything we do at work is mobility. The hard part is to remain conscious of what we are trying to achieve while busy working. The STOP tool is used to:

- **S**top
- **T**hink
- **O**rganise your thoughts, and
- **P**roceed

STOPs can be of any duration, maybe only for a few seconds. For example:

- STOP before you speak
- STOP at the beginning of each work day
- STOP at the end of each work day
- STOP at the beginning and end of any work project
- STOP to make a conscious change
- STOP to address mistakes
- STOP to correct miscommunication
- STOP to learn or coach
- STOP to rest

And a good signal that it is time for a STOP is when working just isn't fun anymore.

Multitasking

'The first law of success is concentration – to bend all the energies to one point, and to go directly to that point, looking neither to the right or to the left.' – William Mathews, 19th century

Multitasking is doing multiple things – or performing multiple tasks – 'at the same time'.

Since the 1990s, psychologists have conducted experiments on the nature and limits of multitasking. The results of these experiments suggest that multitasking is not as

4 'The Inner Game of Work: Overcoming Mental Obstacles for Maximum Performance' (2000) by Timothy Gallwey.

efficient as work performed on a single task. Because the brain cannot fully focus when multitasking, people take longer to complete tasks and are predisposed to error.

When people attempt to complete many tasks at one time, or alternate rapidly between them, the error rate goes up and it takes far longer – often double the time or more – to get the jobs done than if they were done sequentially. This is largely because the brain is compelled to restart and refocus. Ultimately you want to shift important facts from your short-term memory to your long-term memory. Research shows that this process takes about 8 seconds of focused attention on a specific item. A study by David Meyer[5] and David Kieras[6] found that in the interim between each exchange, the brain makes no progress whatsoever. Therefore, multitasking people not only perform each task less well, but also lose time in the process.

In terms of your prioritising and organising competency this essentially means that you'd be better off planning to execute your tasks in a sequential way, keeping your focus on one task at a time.

Our limited multitasking capabilities are also severely challenged by modern technology. Office computers, Voice-over-IP telephones, smartphones and tablets are all designed to give us 24/7 accessibility. Besides the potentially devastating effect on our work-life balance this technology also impedes our prioritising and organising competency.

In his book 'The Shallows: What the Internet is doing to our Brains', one of my favourite authors, Nicholas Carr[7] states: 'Once I was a scuba diver in a sea of words. Now I zip along the surface like a guy on a Jet Ski'. Carr is finding it harder to concentrate and attend to long pieces of reading and writing. He also crystallises one of the most important debates of our time: as we enjoy the internet's bounties, are we sacrificing our ability to read and think deeply?

Even though I am (originally) an IT person myself, it is my opinion that information and communication technology has not lived up to its promise of improving our productivity, especially in the white-collar arena. One of the reasons for this is the introduction of too much multitasking amongst our workers, pushing them far too often into their panic zone.

One can conclude that having a good personal strategy for mastering technology is paramount for your prioritising and organising competency.

The art of delegation

No matter how efficient and masterful you are at your job, you have the same number of hours in the day as your colleagues. There are only so many tasks you can achieve within the same time frame, so to free yourself up and lighten the load: *delegate*.

The key to successful delegation is being absolutely clear about what you are expecting for the outcome. How much direction you provide to get from point A to B will depend on the level of expertise of the person doing the task.

You can read more about the art of delegation in Chapter 10 (Leadership).

5 Professor David Meyer is the director of the University of Michigan's Brain, Cognition, and Action Laboratory.

6 David Kieras is a professor in the Electrical Engineering and Computer Science Department at the University of Michigan.

7 'The Shallows: What the Internet is doing to our Brains' (2011) by Nicholas Carr.

Goal setting

'The greater danger for most of us is not that our aim is too high and we miss it, but that it is too low and we hit it.' – Michelangelo (attributed)

Top-level athletes, successful business people and high achievers of all kinds use *goal setting*. Setting goals gives you long-term vision and short-term motivation. By setting sharp, clearly defined goals, you can measure and take pride in the achievement of those goals, and you can see progress in what might previously have seemed a long and pointless journey. You will also raise your self-confidence, as you recognise your own ability and competence in achieving the goals that you have set.

From Chapter 2 of this book you already know that 'SMART' stands for Specific, Measurable, Achievable, Realistic, and Time-bound. You will also have realised that it is important – both for your motivation and your development – to push the boundaries of your comfort zone by working in your learning zone. Now how can you achieve all this in your daily work at the office?

Edwin Locke[8] and Gary Latham spent many years researching the theory of goal setting. They identified five elements that need to be in place for us to achieve our goals: clarity, challenge, commitment, feedback, and task complexity.

Clarity – When your goals are clear, you know what you are trying to achieve. You can also measure the results accurately. That is why SMART is such a useful mnemonic. However, when a goal is vague it is not easy to measure, and it is not motivating. You may not even know you have achieved it. Write your goal down and be as detailed as possible. Then think about how you will measure your progress towards this goal.

Challenge – Is the goal outside your comfort zone? Consider how the goal makes you feel.

Commitment – Try to visualise in your mind how you will feel when the goal is achieved. Does it motivate you?

Feedback – Measure your own progress and ask for feedback from others. Schedule time to analyse your progress.

Task complexity – Is the behaviour to achieve your goal inside your learning zone? Is the task not too complex, thus pushing you into your panic zone? If so, break it into smaller, less complex sub-goals.

Prioritising

I am sure you know the feeling of getting up for work in the morning with the sense of having so much to do that you don't know where to start. There are times when everything that you have to do seems like a priority, which makes it tough to figure out where to begin.

Don't worry; there are many techniques that can be used to prioritise the tasks you have to perform. Usually, these techniques are very simple and somewhat intuitive, but they work.

8 'A Theory of Goal Setting and Task Performance' (1990) by Edwin Locke et al.

To-do list

By far the simplest technique is known as the to-do list. This is simply a list, in no particular order, of all the things you have to do, your tasks.

Don't keep your tasks on different post-it notes or in your head but at the beginning of each day or week, write on a sheet of paper what you want to get done and by when. Clearly, when making a new list you should not forget to transfer the tasks you have not finished from your previous list. You can refine this technique a bit by adding the amount of time you think it will take you (estimate) to perform every task and re-order the list in descending order (longest tasks first). You then work your way down the list assuming that the most important tasks are the ones that will take you the most time. Obviously, every time you complete a task you have to strike it from your list.

After completing your list with the associated time needed you may come to the conclusion that you won't be able to do everything in the time available. No problem! Maybe the remaining tasks are not that important after all, so you simply drop them. Maybe the remaining tasks are important but not urgent, so you simply move them to the next list. Tasks that are urgent *and* important are moved to the top of your list and you start working on these right away.

In many instances your to-do list related to the processes you participate in is 'generated' by the workflow system; the tasks will be in your 'inbox' and the deadline for execution will be clearly indicated. When you are part of a project team your project-related tasks will be given to you by the project manager, who is responsible for the overall timing and output of the project.

The 80/20 principle

Management thinker Joseph M. Juran first put the 80/20 principle into currency in the 1940s, dubbing it the *Pareto principle* (after the Italian economist Vilfredo Pareto, who in the 1890s observed that 80% of the land in Italy was owned by 20% of the population and that this distribution seemed to apply in many other cases too). The assumption is that most of the results in any situation are determined by a small number of causes.

This principle can also be applied to prioritising your tasks, based on the idea that most of the results (output) will be generated by a small proportion of your effort (input). When looking at your to-do list you simply pick those tasks that will generate the most (relevant) output and you take these as your priorities. The remaining tasks are executed when there is time left.

It is fair to say that this is true only up to a point and should not be taken as gospel in all cases. The principle cannot be applied to all kinds of work or tasks; it is not applicable across the board. For example, translators may spend time screening incoming work to find appropriate reference materials (before sending a job for freelance translation, so as to ensure a better final product), performing written or oral summaries of long texts with input from the party requesting the translation, or doing full-length translations. But they cannot say 'I'll do only summaries this week because the output will be greatest'. That is to ignore the crucial but very short one-and-a-half page letter waiting to be translated to a tight deadline.

The ABC method

The ABC method is a powerful priority setting technique that you can use every single day. This technique is so simple and effective that it can, all by itself, make you one of the most efficient and effective people in your team.

Once again, your to-do list is the starting point. Behind every item you put a letter A, B or C depending on the following criteria:

A – Very important. This is something that you must do. This is a task for which there can be serious consequences if you fail to do it.

B – A task that you should do, but it only has mild consequences. This means that someone may be unhappy or inconvenienced if you don't do it, but that's about it.

C – A task that would be nice to do, but for which there are no consequences at all.

The Eisenhower matrix

Although it was Stephen Covey who made this method popular in his book 'First Things First'[9], the concept is originally credited to US President Dwight D. Eisenhower[10]. Whenever confronted with something that needed to be done, he would ask himself two questions: First, is the task important? Second, is it urgent?

Based on this, the task would end up in one of four categories: important and urgent, important but not urgent, not important but urgent, and neither important nor urgent.

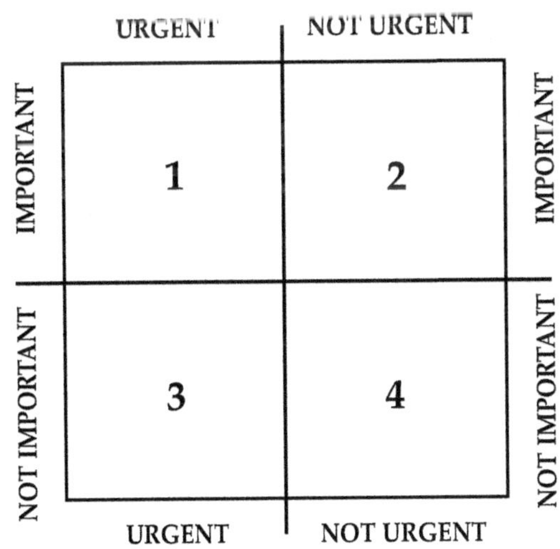

Figure 7.5

9 'First Things First' (1996) by Stephen Covey.

10 Dwight D. Eisenhower (1890–1969) was the 34th President of the United States, from 1953 until 1961 and supreme allied commander in the 1944 D-day landings in Europe.

Obviously the first priority should go to the tasks that are both important and urgent (quadrant No. 1 in the matrix in Figure 7.5). However, what is not so obvious is that tasks labelled important but not urgent get the next priority (No. 2). This is what Eisenhower's point was all about: 'What is important is seldom urgent and what is urgent is seldom important'. Tasks that are in quadrant No. 3 are typical candidates for delegation, and the ones in No. 4 can even be dropped because they are neither urgent nor important, so why bother?

Tasks performed in the context of processes or projects are almost by definition important. Their urgency depends on the time constraints of the process or the timing of the project and whether the task is on the critical path or not. Doing your planning for the coming week is for sure important, but it probably is not urgent. Phone calls from outside are probably not important (unless you are waiting for one) and many text messages or emails are not important either.

There are tools that implement the Eisenhower matrix method on your personal computer or smartphone; you can even drag-and-drop to-do lists from other people in your team into your own matrix. For most people, however, a simple paper version will do.

Timeboxing

Timeboxing is used as a time management technique whereby the schedule is divided into a number of separate time periods – or *timeboxes*. Each timebox has its own deliverables, deadline and budget. It is also used for individual use to address personal tasks in a smaller time frame in order to improve the productivity of the user.

In project management, the three constraints are time, resources, and outcome. Changing one constraint will impact the rest. Without timeboxing, projects usually work with a predefined outcome. Under these circumstances, when some deliverables cannot be completed you will either have to adjust the time constraint, or add extra resources, or do both. With the timeboxing approach the time constraint is fixed, but the outcome may be reduced. This helps to focus on the most important deliverables, which requires of course a clear prioritisation (see also the section on expectation management in Chapter 5).

Individuals can use timeboxing for personal tasks. By using a reduced scale of time (e.g. one hour instead of a full week) and well-defined deliverables, personal timeboxing is said to help control perfectionist tendencies. Personal timeboxing also helps to overcome procrastination and many people find that the time pressure created boosts their creativity and focus.

Planning tools

'In preparing for battle I have always found that plans are useless, but planning is indispensable.' – Dwight D. Eisenhower

Besides your to-do list it is a good idea to plan all your activities, whether they are process-related, project-related, related to your working conditions or your personal life.

Schedule for the unexpected

Most people have a tendency to fill their schedules to the edge with work and meetings, and then suddenly something unexpected comes up. An emergency that you have to focus on, even though you have other things to do; your boss who needs a last-minute answer, a stakeholder who suddenly demands your attention, or your kid that gets sick at school.

In those cases, you have to drop everything and deal with it. You put the other tasks off into the future, reschedule meetings, and rearrange tasks. Clearly, this can have a huge impact on your productivity.

Here's the secret: *schedule for the unexpected*. Typically, I block out an hour a day, preferably late in the afternoon. No meetings, no phone calls. That way, when something comes up, I have an hour of flexibility to address it. Of course, you might need more or less than an hour. The important thing is to take the time you need to ensure that you are not always stressing everything out. By doing this, I have learned that while the unexpected always *seems* to come up, in reality it doesn't. In those cases, you get an extra hour to work on whatever needs doing — or head home early. It's an added bonus.

In the old days most people had a 'personal organiser' – a small, usually leather-bound book – and they had it with them all the time. With the advent of the internet and smartphones these have been gradually replaced by a version 'in the cloud'. The iCalendar protocol is supported by most – if not all – platforms, which means that you can have one organiser for all your activities or tasks (both private and professional) and that you have access (read/write) from wherever you are (provided of course you have access to the internet). You can also share (parts of) your calendar with other people and even invite people for activities you plan to do. Some companies even offer 'cloud scheduling software' which makes scheduling activities with other participants even more convenient.

However, 'a fool with a tool is still a fool'. If you use these tools you have to do it right. You have to put ALL your 'A' and 'B' (or '1' and '2') tasks or activities in there and respond accordingly when you receive the alert that the 'event' is about to start. You also have to schedule some time for the other activities and for the necessary breaks; in most situations it is sufficient to leave these time slots blank. Don't put every little activity in your calendar because otherwise you will have too much overhead or feel overwhelmed by all the things you are supposed to do (and be disturbed time and again by the alerts). It is also a good idea to work with larger blocks (with a minimum of say half an hour) so that you don't have to switch your focus too often.

Attention management

In their book 'The Attention Economy'[11], Thomas H. Davenport and J. C. Beck define the concept of attention as follows: 'Attention is focused mental engagement on a particular item of information. Items come into our awareness, we attend to a particular item, and then we decide whether to act.'

11 see page139

There are different kinds of attention. *Proactive attention* is the kind of sustained focus you need to draft an important memo, lead a team meeting or come up with creative solutions to a business problem. *Active attention* is necessary when you're making smaller day-to-day decisions, writing to-do lists or attending meetings. *Inactive attention* is more suited for tasks like deleting unnecessary emails or filing paperwork.

When an item of information has our attention we store it in our short-term memory, and the more focused our attention is, the more items of information we store.

Short-term (or working) memory acts as a kind of 'scratch-pad' for temporary recall of the information which is being processed at any point in time. It holds a small amount of information for a short period of time. The short-term memory has a limited capacity. Experiments by George Miller in 1956 suggest that the number of objects an average human can hold in working memory (known as 'memory span') is between 5 and 9 (7 ± 2, which is sometimes referred to as Miller's Law). However, memory span varies widely from person to person, and modern estimates of the average are typically lower, in order of just 4 or 5 items. Moreover, our memory span is not constant during the day and it depends to a large extent on our physical state and the environment we're in.

Based on this information, here is a way to organise your workday by managing your attention span. This technique is based on the work of Graham Allcott, author of 'How to Be a Productivity Ninja'[12] The goal is to help you become more efficient at the office by figuring out when during the day you are the most or least focused. Then you match those times with tasks that require the appropriate level of attention:

- Make a list of all the tasks (big and small) that you complete in a typical day.
- Next, decide whether each task requires proactive, active or inactive attention.
- Think back over the last couple of weeks and ask yourself when you felt focused and productive. What time was that?
- With this information in mind, create a work schedule that matches the appropriate tasks to your attention level throughout the day.

Of course, you will have to make some exceptions. Even if you don't have as much flexibility as you would like, it is still useful to know what level of attention you need for a certain task. Just remember that attention management is about you dictating your time rather than having your tasks dictate to you. After all, only you know your brainpower best.

But beware! As a manager you can be faced with the underperformer who'll take solace from this and even exploit it. 'I'm not a morning person'; 'My biorhythms are at their highest at 6 pm – I do my best work then'; 'If you make me come in to work so early (9.30), you won't get anything out of me'. Try not to encourage this!

Procrastination

Procrastination is carrying out less urgent tasks in preference to more urgent ones, or doing more pleasurable things in place of less pleasurable ones, and thus putting off tasks to a later time, sometimes to the 'last minute' before the deadline. Procrastination

12 'How to be a Productivity Ninja' (2015) by Graham Allcott.

is negative behaviour in the context of effective time management. Procrastination is wasting time.

A form of procrastination is also known as the *student syndrome,* the phenomenon whereby people will only start to fully apply themselves to a task just at the last possible moment before a deadline. The student syndrome usually includes more of a plan and sincerely good intentions. In project and task estimating, a time or resource buffer is applied to the task to allow for overrun or other scheduling problems. However, with student syndrome, because tasks are started at the last moment possible, the buffer for any given task is wasted beforehand, rather than kept in reserve. In this context it is also worth citing Parkinson's Law: 'work expands so as to fill the time available for its completion'[13] I would even add: 'and then some'.

If you are honest with yourself, you probably know when you are procrastinating, but how do you fight this bad habit?

The first step is *awareness*. When you find yourself doing low-priority tasks from your to-do list while higher priority tasks are put aside, or when you are waiting for the right mood or the right time to tackle an important task, or when you say yes to unimportant tasks that others ask you to do knowing that you have other work on your plate, you are probably procrastinating.

The next thing is to ask yourself the question *why* you are procrastinating. Is it because you don't like the task, you find it unpleasant? Is it because you are simply disorganised and can't distinguish priorities? Or is it because you are afraid of doing the task, or in other words the task will push you into your panic zone?

Clear desk

Is your monitor framed with layers of post-it reminders? Is your workspace hidden under stacks of papers, or your guest chair buried under a pile of outerwear? A majority of people admit they judge co-workers by how messy they keep their work environment. Co-workers will associate a messy office with your organisational skills and assume their project or proposal will get lost in the landfill that is your desk.

Most people spend at least 30 minutes to an hour a day looking for things. In addition to saving time and money, a clear desk policy helps organisations reduce the risk of information theft, fraud, or security breaches caused by sensitive information being left unattended and exposed.

So, is a clear desk better for the workplace? As with many things in life, there is no clear-cut answer to this question. Proponents claim that people see measurable life improvements from becoming neat and tidy, and they can point to millions of euros in annual revenue as evidence of success. In contrast, many creative individuals with Nobel prizes and other prestigious awards prefer – and in fact cultivate – messy environments as an aid to their work.

Working at a clear desk seems to encourage people to do what is expected of them. But research also shows that a messy desk may confer its own benefits, promoting creative thinking and stimulating new ideas. Disorderly environments seem to inspire breaking free of tradition, which can produce fresh insights.

Once again the conclusion is that this is a matter of individual awareness and responsibility. If the clutter on your desk is too intimidating to tackle, you can set a reg-

13 'Parkinson's Law: or the Pursuit of Progress' by C. Northcote Parkinson, first published in 1958.

Is doing overtime good or bad?

Now this is an interesting question worth some debate.

Let's first have a look at the regulations ruling this matter in the EU institutions – the Staff Regulations.

EU personnel – that is people who have a permanent or temporary employment governed by the Staff Regulations – have to work an average of 40 hours per week (this used to be 38, before the 2013 reform). In most places there is a 'flexitime' regime in place, meaning that individuals can arrive at work within given time ranges, they can have a flexible lunch break, and they can leave work in the evening at the time they choose. The only 'obligations' are an average of 40 hours per week and being present (in the office or at the workplace) during the 'core' time (usually 10AM-Noon and 2PM-4PM).

In many instances telework – or working from home – is allowed, within certain limits.

These arrangements have been designed to cope with cultural differences (Greeks and Finns, for example, tend to have rather different life styles) and to allow for staff to manage their personal work-life balance (people with children have very different needs in this respect from those without).

Whereas these rules are applicable to most statutory staff there are exceptions for certain categories (management, linguists, security staff, IT people, drivers ...) who are required to adapt their working hours to the circumstances. Also, these 'general' rules may be implemented differently in the individual institutions, directorates-general or even at unit level.

For external agents, the above rules do not apply. In Belgium it is forbidden by law to have a 'formal management' relationship between internal staff (representing the customer) and external staff (representing the supplier of services or goods). Imposing working hours would be an infringement in this respect. The working hours of external agents are governed by this person's employer (which is not the customer) and these will be fixed in the contract between the customer and the supplier.

What is overtime?

If – and when – EU statutory staff work more than the average of 40 hours (typically this is settled on a monthly basis) they can 'compensate' this time by taking extra time off (with the agreement of their superior and limited to one or two half-days per month).

Only time that exceeds these limits (after compensation) is considered to be overtime. Other than for some rare exceptions, this is not compensated (financially or with extra holidays), meaning that the employee is working for free during this overtime.

So – is doing overtime good or bad?

Allow me at this point to give a consultant's answer: 'it depends'.

There is nothing wrong with overtime as long as you are personally motivated for it. By this I mean that it is your own decision – based on your assessment of the situation – and it is not your boss who randomly imposes it on you. If imposed, there have to be good and compelling reasons for this and it has to be known and scheduled beforehand.

There is nothing wrong with overtime if you do it for the right reasons. Some people 'burn hours' by just being at the office, spending their time with daydreaming, surfing the internet, socialising all day long, or drinking coffee in the cafeteria. Doing overtime while not being productive but merely to build up a compensation time later on is not good, because you are actually 'stealing' time from your employer.

There is nothing wrong with overtime if it doesn't affect your productivity. But human beings are not machines that can go on and on without resting. Our attention span is limited in time and we can only be truly productive for a certain period of time, after which our output – or the quality of our work – decreases.

There is nothing wrong with overtime if it is necessary to deliver something urgent and important to schedule.

President Eisenhower once said: 'Usually, urgent things are not important, and most important things are not urgent.' These wise words have been converted by

cont....

Is doing overtime good or bad? – *continued*

management consultants like Steven Covey into personal productivity (or time-management) methods. The basic idea is to focus first on what is really important AND urgent, then on what is important but maybe not so urgent, and postpone – or even drop – the other tasks. Don't waste your time on things that are not important, and don't be inclined to opt for overtime to carry out work that may be 'urgent' but not important.

There is nothing wrong with overtime if you don't hurt yourself by doing it. By this I mean that you are taking serious risks of running into a burn-out – or a depression – when doing overtime is your only strategy for coping with high workloads or tight deadlines. This will at a minimum affect your motivation and productivity.

There is nothing wrong with overtime if you don't hurt your colleagues by doing it. Especially when you are in a managerial position and try to 'set a good example' by burning lots of time at the office, you may be putting pressure on your colleagues to do overtime against their will (see first argument above). Those people – your typical workaholics – who are doing overtime just to please the boss are hurting their colleagues by doing so.

Finally, there is nothing wrong with overtime if you keep control over your work-life balance. Work-life balance is a very individual thing and differs widely from person to person. It is even variable over time. Don't project your personal situation on that of your colleagues. Bear in mind that a good work-life balance is essential for your resilience.

Conclusion

There is no clear-cut, black-and-white answer to this question. An important point is not to confuse overtime with the consequences of procrastination. I once had a colleague who turned weekend working into a virtue: 'I worked overtime to finish this'. In fact, she was forced into spending the weekend doing it because she did not do the job during the week when she should have (and could have). It is important for colleagues and managers alike to distinguish true overtime from false.

ular reminder on your calendar to tidy up your workspace once a week. But if you feel comfortable in your mess and if you do not breach any official policy with that, then, by all means, stick to it.

Speed reading

A word here about *speed reading*, because it has a place among the 'best practices' of prioritising and organising, and will help you to manage your time better.

Speed reading, also known as *diagonal reading*, is about skimming through reading material to gather its general meaning and purpose. You browse through the documentation and read the titles, pull-out quotes and any diagrams or bullet lists. You then go back and read the table of contents and the summary, if applicable. This sets your mind up to better understand the purpose and terminology before you delve into the text. In fact, you already practise speed reading – most likely without being aware of it – whenever you flick through a newspaper or magazine, or browse the internet, in search of stories that you're really interested in.

Most diagonal readers give the content a first pass by reading a text 'passively' – just like one would browse a magazine, look at photographs, or watch television, i.e.

they are not really paying attention to the small details, rather they are waiting for something to really pop out at them. The average person reads about 240 words per minute, whereas a diagonal reader 'scans' closer to 15 words per second or about 900 words per minute. So, there are at least three, and up to five important sections of an article that a diagonal reader will see in the approximately 10 seconds they will initially allocate to a text:

- The title or headline.
- The subtitles or subheadings within the text.
- Any bold, underlined, quoted, or otherwise highlighted text.
- Pictures, graphs, charts, or images of any nature.
- A summary of the article.

Effective speed reading takes a lot of practice to master – typically years – and it is not the purpose of this book to turn you into a proficient speed reader. There are, however, some ideas you can usefully apply when reading an everyday text:

- Don't read everything
- Don't read in order
- Don't try to understand everything

Let us now expand a bit further on these ideas.

There seems to be a strange idea (especially amongst translators, lawyers and engineers) that you have to read absolutely everything. This is just not true; you don't have to read everything! The idea behind this is that when you read, you should read with a purpose. Usually, this is the extraction of information from a piece of text. Once you have that information – you're done. There's no need to read any longer. In fact, I would say that most of the texts you will encounter are simply filler (or 'payload') – you don't need to read all of it, just the relevant parts. Also, well-written texts contain a lot of repetition. I have a rule: if I start reading a text and after a few sentences I still haven't found what I am looking for, I move on.

Another mistake is the idea that you have to read start-to-finish. There is absolutely no reason you can't start by reading the conclusion or summary, then go back to the introduction or jump around through different paragraphs or chapters. Sometimes it's worth picking what you're interested in from the table of contents or index and starting there. It's more than likely that you are reading this book in this way, so why not do it for all the documents you have to deal with?

The other common, but erroneous, idea is 'perfect' comprehension. There's no such thing. Of course, your comprehension will go down a bit when you speed read, but that is not really a problem. When you read, you should read for a purpose and for certain bits of information anyway – no one cares if you remember every single fact and figure from a text, or what the 7th word in the third sentence on page two was.

A corollary to this is that you don't need to understand absolutely everything in a piece of text. We mostly read to understand main concepts anyway. If you really must understand absolutely everything, you should be taking notes (or drawing a mind map), and you can always re-read certain sections to note down facts and figures.

A few other ideas that will help you with speed reading:

- *Summaries* are often as good as the whole text itself. If you are lucky, there will be a management summary or an introduction to the text you are reading. So, if there is, first have a look at this, as it may provide you with all the answers you need right away!
- *Eliminate distractions.* If you are surrounded by noise, even background noise like music, do everything you can to get rid of it. Isolate yourself with nothing but the text and a comfortable reading position. By eliminating potential distractions, your mind can better focus on absorbing the words on the sheets of paper or your screen.
- *Focus the right senses on reading.* Although many people are used to reading out loud or imagining a voice attached to the words, your mind may absorb the material faster by 'cutting out the middle men' and connecting them straight from the eye to the brain. Read without moving your lips. In fact, by using your finger or a pen as a guide, you can actually read and comprehend the material faster. Your finger can act as a pace-setter for your brain, going as fast as you can retain the information.
- *Read faster by using your peripheral vision* to focus on seeing the text as a whole before understanding the words individually. By using an imaginary line down the middle of the page, your mind can start to sort the text into blocks. You will start to read the pages in a diagonal fashion, rather than a linear way. This also allows you to focus on key words, rather than spending time on decorative phrases.
- *Take frequent breaks* by pacing yourself accordingly. By taking breaks, you give your mind a chance to rest and recoup since it is absorbing information much faster than it's used to. Read the text in installments, and take short breaks.
- *Don't speed read all the time.* The above speed reading tips should only be used when going through material produced by others. When you are revising your own texts, trying to make the meaning clearer, fashioning good arguments, or just weeding out spelling errors, you should NOT speed read. In that case you have to pay close attention to every word and idea to tidy up your text and make it is as good as you can.

Caveat: you need to differentiate between various reading tasks. For example, translators do speed read for scanning purposes or oral/written summarising, but they cannot translate a text they don't read in full detail. Translators do not have the luxury of deciding what parts of a text are important; that is for the desk-officer to decide.

Developing your prioritising and organising skills

Time management is not very difficult as a concept, but it's surprisingly hard to do it in practice. It requires the investment of a little time to prioritise and organise yourself. But once done, you will find that with some fine-tuning, your day, your week, and your month, fall into place in an orderly fashion, with time for everything you need to do. The distinction between urgent and important is the key to prioritising and organising your time and your workload.

Perhaps the most important thing is to stay calm and keep things in perspective. Remember that the world won't come to an end if you fail to finish your last task of the day; you can usually leave it until tomorrow, especially if you have prioritised judiciously.

Please refer to Annex 1 for further development of this competency, or check out the easy-to-use app at:

http://www.johnharperpublishing.co.uk/the-ultimate-eu-career-development-toolkit/

8. Resilience

Competency definition: 'Remains effective under a heavy workload, handles organisational frustrations positively and adapts to a changing work environment.'

'The difference between winners and losers is how they handle losing.' – Rosabeth Moss Kanter[1]

Resilience is the process of adapting well in the face of adversity, trauma, tragedy, threats or significant sources of stress. Resilience – the ability to effectively cope with losing, failing, and not getting what you want – is an important quality for anyone to cultivate in order to achieve success and well-being. To live and to work is to risk failure, and resilience helps people to bounce back from the inevitable adversities and obstructions that risk entails.

Resilience is ordinary, not extraordinary. Resilience is not a trait that people either have or do not have. It involves behaviours, thoughts and actions that can be learned and developed in anyone.

Resilience is sometimes confused with *perseverance*, but there is a difference. In short, perseverance keeps us going when we are convinced that we are on the right track, but we are just not getting enough traction to get to our destination. Resilience enables us to build a new track, fix the locomotive and start all over again when the wheels come off.

Another related concept is *grit*. Grit is a personal characteristic based on an individual's passion for a particular long-term objective, coupled with a powerful motivation to achieve that objective. This perseverance of effort promotes the overcoming of obstacles or challenges, and serves as a driving force in achievement realisation.

Developing resilience is a personal journey. People do not all react the same to traumatic and stressful events. An approach to building resilience that works for one person might not work for another.

Six signs of resilient people

- They stay happy. They don't waste time or energy on things they can't control.
- They celebrate other people's success. They don't resent that success.
- They are willing to take calculated risks.
- They move on. They don't waste time and energy feeling sorry for themselves.
- They are kind, fair, and unafraid to speak up.
- They embrace change. They welcome challenges.

1 Rosabeth Moss Kanter is a Harvard Business School professor.

Change

'There are only three certainties in life: death, taxes, and change.' – Anonymous

The EPSO definition of resilience ends: '... *and adapts to a changing work environment.*' In fact, this definition is referring to *organisational change.*

Organisational change is any modification in the people, structure or technology of an organisation:

- *People*: changes in attitudes, expectations, perceptions and behaviours.
- *Structure*: changes in job, responsibilities, departments, management structure, organisational design.
- *Technology*: changes in work, processes, equipment, methods and software.

One can readily say that organisational change is constant, but it varies in degree and direction. Organisational change produces uncertainty, but it is not completely unpredictable, and organisational change creates both threats and opportunities.

Organisational change affects employees differently. While some will welcome it, others will become worried and stressed at the mere mention of change. They will fear that any reorganisation might challenge their standing and worry how they will fit into the new structure.

Clearly, the EU institutions are subject to organisational change, and that is why being able to adapt to a changing work environment is part of the core competencies of EU staff.

Stress

Stress is the body's response to change. Stress is defined in many different ways and the things that cause stress can vary from person to person. Stress affects our performance.

There are four types of stress:

- *Acute stress* is the type of stress we experience on a day-to-day basis – for example, the stress of getting our to-do list finished or the stress of unexpected obstacles.
- When a person rarely gets relief from stress, this is called *episodic acute stress*. This type of stress usually goes on for longer periods of time with little relief.
- *Chronic stress* is characterised as long-term stress, where there is little hope for relief. These are long-term situations where the person has given up trying to find a solution.

- Not all stress is bad; some stress can actually help us to perform better and challenge us. This type of stress is called *eustress*[2].

Dr Peter Nixon, a British cardiologist, developed a diagram called the Human Function Curve (Figure 8.2) that illustrates the balance of good and bad stress.

Nixon calls any state where we are awake and reacting to stimuli an *arousal state*, such as being at work. If we compare the amount of stress to our performance, our performance actually improves when we experience eustress. However, according to this model, there is a point where chronic stress can impede our performance. In Figure 8.2 you can see in the drone zone, for example, that our performance is low. We may be bored and not have enough positive stress for us to perform at a decent level. In the C zone, in contrast, we may experience eustress, which raises our performance. However, when we reach the fatigue zone, we could be experiencing chronic stress, which impedes our performance. As you can see, performance is actually improved with a certain amount of stress, but once that stress becomes episodic or chronic, our performance deteriorates.

'Boreout'

According to Peter Werder and Philippe Rothlin[3], it is the absence of meaningful tasks, rather than the presence of stress, that is the main problem for many workers. What they call 'boreout' consists of three elements: boredom, lack of challenge, and lack of interest. These authors disagree with the common perception that a demotivated employee is lazy; instead, they argue that the employee has lost interest in work tasks. Those suffering from boreout are 'dissatisfied with their professional situation' because they are frustrated at being prevented – by institutional mechanisms or obstacles rather than their own lack of aptitude – from fulfilling their potential. Fulfilling their potential means using their skills, knowledge, and abilities to contribute to their organisation's development and/or receiving official recognition for their efforts. Such employees have given up and become resigned to their situation, experiencing boreout, which is effectively the opposite of burnout.

Here are some typical symptoms of boreout:

- Frequent private surfing on the internet combined with frequent usage of the 'Alt-Tab' shortcut.[4]
- Burning long hours at work: going as early as possible to the office and leaving as late as possible, without producing much.
- Procrastination: tasks are split up over more periods of time and are constantly interrupted or moved.
- Remaining work is taken home but not worked on.

2 Not to be confused with EU stress ;-)

3 'Boreout – Overcoming workplace demotivation' (2008) by Peter Werder and Philippe Rothlin.

4 If you know what this means you may already have a problem.

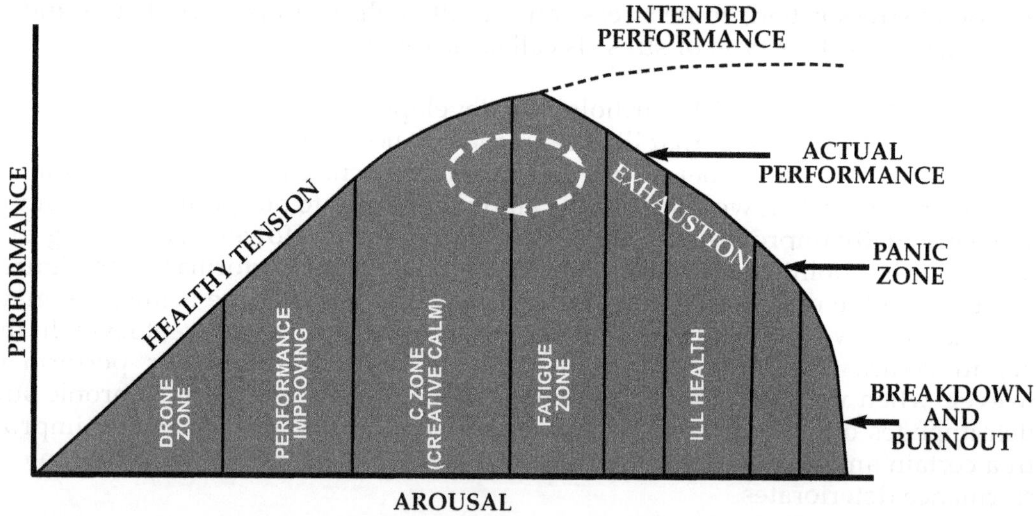

Figure 8.2

- Emphasising to colleagues and supervisors continually how busy and overburdened you are.
- Feeling unsatisfied by your working situation and constantly feeling unchallenged and bored.

The dangerous effects of boreout should not be underestimated: dissatisfaction, apathy and the loss of appetite for life – not to mention the reduction of the organisation's efficiency resulting from bored employees spending hours of company time surfing the net.

Boreout has become widespread among employees around the world, although employers have only recently begun to recognise the problem. It is my personal feeling that in the EU institutions too this could be a major problem. Not because there's not enough interesting work to be done but because of the very political nature of the organisation. EU staff mainly have an administrative or – at best – a consultative role, and the real decisions are taken by politicians, based often on non-technical arguments. Also, due to the very competitive nature of the recruitment process, only the 'best' administrators and specialists are hired, only to find themselves in positions for which they are sometimes very much overqualified. For sure, this is a phenomenon to be considered by managers, leaders, and HR professionals alike.

Comfort zone

Your *comfort zone* is any type of behaviour that keeps you at a low anxiety level. Everyday activities that you are used to doing won't make you feel anxious and uneasy, so they are part of your comfort zone.

Brené Brown[5], a research professor at the University of Houston Graduate College of Social Work, has another definition of comfort zone: 'Where our uncertainty, scarcity and vulnerability are minimized – where we believe we'll have access to enough love, food, talent, time, admiration. Where we feel we have some control.'

Although people often refer to 'getting outside your comfort zone' in terms of trying new things, anything that raises your anxiety levels can be counted as being outside that zone. Anxiety is not something we are prone to go looking for, but a little bit can be surprisingly beneficial. We often need just a hint of anxiety to push us to get our work done, or to improve our performance.

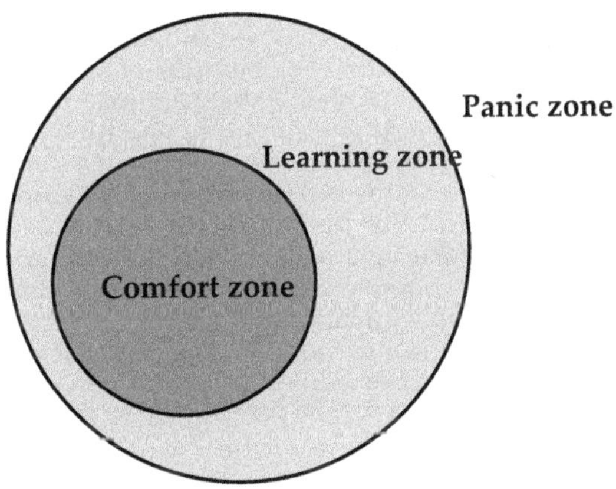

Figure 8.3

From panic zone to comfort zone

A couple of years ago, I had the opportunity to help my daughter to learn how to drive a car. I am sure you can imagine that the first time she sat behind the steering wheel, not even knowing where to put her feet on the pedals, her 'level of anxiety' was very high; she was in – or very close to – her panic zone. So, I decided not to let her start the engine for that very first time, but just to explain a couple of general principles and show her where all the controls of the car could be found, and what these were used for. Giving her a bigger challenge would have been pointless, since the level of anxiety was too high.

The next step was to just let her start the engine and move forward for a couple of metres, giving her the feeling of how to

5 'The Gifts of Imperfection' (2010) by Brené Brown.

continued

play with the pedals to achieve this. Of course, we did this on a quiet parking lot in our neighbourhood, where no other vehicles or obstacles were in the way. Needless to say that the engine stalled numerous times and the first movements of the car were more like jumping than riding, but after a while (maybe 30 attempts or so) she had the initial 'feeling' of how the car responded to her actions. And that was it. She had accepted the first – small but achievable – challenge, moving into her learning zone.

Over subsequent lessons, each time with a couple of days in between, I gradually added challenges to her portfolio – driving around in circles (first gear), starting and stopping, emergency braking – until the time had come to use the clutch. The car, especially the gearbox, suffered a lot, but I considered that this was the price to be paid for her learning experience (it was my wife's car anyway).

Then came the day that we moved away from the parking lot and went for a drive on the road. We usually practised during the weekend and in an industrial area with little or no traffic around. She first had to get a better feeling of the vehicle, especially when driving at somewhat higher speeds. Initially, the trips we made were very short and always the same; the only purpose of this was to remove the anxiety that comes with driving in an unfamiliar environment, allowing her to concentrate on the driving.

Many weekends later we went out on real roads. I live in the countryside, so I could choose roads with very moderate traffic, just to let her gradually get used to the idea that she is not alone on the road, and that other drivers may make mistakes as well. In fact, she even had a little accident during that time. It was dark and rainy and she misjudged her braking distance to a car that stopped in front of us. There was some small damage to both cars (she was driving my own car this time) but nobody was hurt. I am sure that this was a great learning experience for her …

After a number of months of messing around on country roads we finally went to a (small) city to prepare her for the driver's exam.

In fact, she failed first time round. Not because of her driving skills, but because she had misinterpreted a rather complex traffic situation (I was sitting next to her and made the same mistake). Once again, tears were flowing, but once again this was a great learning experience. Anyway, the second time she got her driver's licence and since then has driven safely thousands of kilometres in very variable circumstances. I believe she is now inside her comfort zone.

The comfort zone is often illustrated like the image in Figure 8.3, where the comfort zone extends into a learning zone, but eventually leads to a panic zone, where anxiety is too high.

How we deal with uncertainty

A lot of the anxiety that comes from leaving your comfort zone is due to uncomfortable levels of uncertainty. There is a reason that cooking dinner is no big deal when you do it all the time; you know what to expect. Driving a car for the first time, or skydiving, or starting a new job, are all activities that are full of uncertainty, and thus, anxiety. Uncertainty can make us respond more strongly to negative experiences. We are more likely to respond negatively to new things, even though we may come to like them over time.

Familiarity is comfortable and enjoyable, so it is no real surprise that new things get our guard up. From an evolutionary perspective, we see familiar things as more

likely to be safe, and so we are more drawn to what we know. Trying new things also takes energy, so we are more likely to lean on old habits than take a new risk.
Breaking out of your comfort zone
So, should you try to break out of your comfort zone? Is it actually good for you to try? The answer is 'yes' – to some degree. 'We need a place of productive discomfort,' says Daniel H. Pink[6]. 'If you are too comfortable, you are not productive. And if you are too uncomfortable, you are not productive either. We can't be too hot or too cold.'

The objective is to reach that optimal level so that our skills increase and we become comfortable with that new level of anxiety — then we are in an expanded comfort zone. And ideally, we will get more used to those feelings of 'productive discomfort' and won't be so scared about trying new things in the future.

When mixed with a feeling of success, some anxiety and self-doubt can lead to personal growth. This is why outdoor adventures like rock climbing or skydiving can be so exhilarating: they induce anxiety and unease but when completed, they give us a huge feeling of accomplishment and increase our base levels of confidence.

Flow

'Flow' is a state of complete immersion in an activity, being completely involved in an activity for its own sake. Your whole being is involved, and you are using your skills to the utmost.

In his book 'Finding Flow', Mihaly Csíkszentmihályi[7] explains that flow is likely to occur when an individual is faced with a task that has clear goals that require specific responses. Flow also happens when a person's skills are fully involved in overcoming a challenge that is just about manageable, so it acts as a magnet for learning new skills and increasing challenges. If challenges are too low, one gets back to flow by increasing them. If challenges are too great, one can return to the flow state by learning new skills. Flow can occur when workers are engaged in tasks where they are able to focus entirely on the task at hand.

In addition to making activities more enjoyable, flow can lead to improved performance. Flow can also lead to further learning and skill development because the individual must continually seek new challenges and information in order to maintain the state of flow.

Csíkszentmihályi produced a graphic (Figure 8.4) showing the relationship between the level of someone's skills and the level of challenge faced. As you can see, flow is most likely achieved when a high challenge level coincides with a high skills level.

Owen Schaffer[8] proposed seven conditions for flow to occur:

- Knowing what to do
- Knowing how to do it

6 'Drive: The Surprising Truth about What Motivates Us' (2009) by Daniel H. Pink.

7 'Finding Flow' (1998) by Mihaly Csíkszentmihályi.

8 Owen Schaffer is lead usability analyst at Human Factors International, the world's largest company specialising in user experience design.

- Knowing how well you are doing
- Knowing where to go
- High perceived challenges
- High perceived skills
- Freedom from distractions

Schaffer also published a tool, the Flow Condition Questionnaire (FCQ), to measure each of these seven flow conditions for any given task or activity.

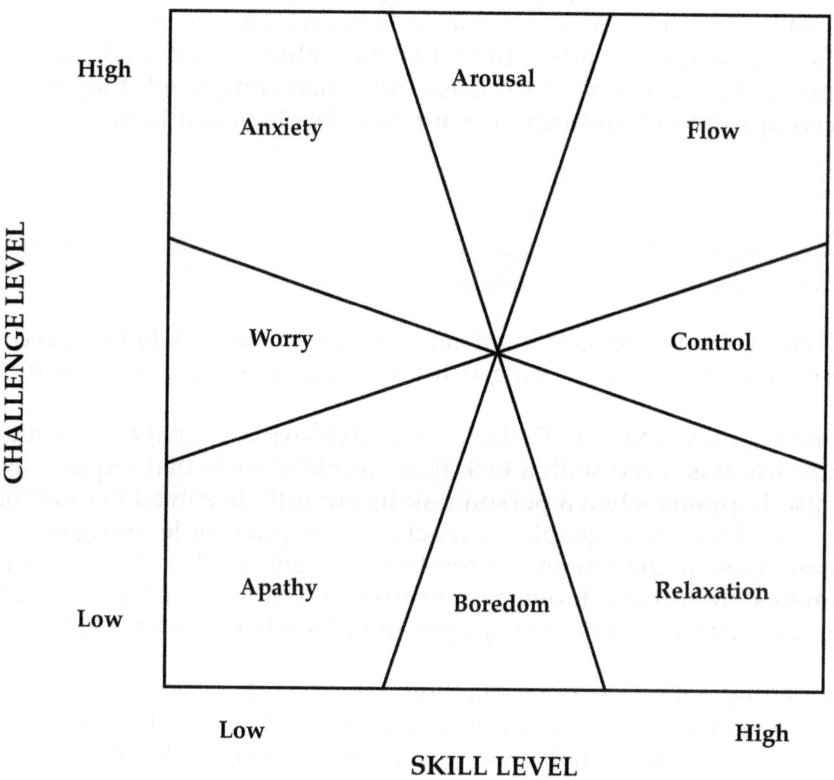

Figure 8.4

Fight or flight

The *fight or flight* response – also called the *acute stress response* – is a physiological reaction that occurs in response to a perceived harmful event, attack, or threat to survival.

When our fight or flight response is activated, sequences of nerve cell firing occur and chemicals like adrenaline, noradrenaline and cortisol are released into our bloodstream. These patterns of nerve cell firing and chemical release cause our body to undergo a series of very dramatic changes. Our respiratory rate increases. Blood is shunted away from our digestive tract and directed into our muscles and limbs, which require extra energy and fuel for running and fighting. Our pupils dilate. Our awareness intensifies. Our sight sharpens. Our impulses quicken. Our perception of pain diminishes. Our immune system mobilises with increased activation. We become prepared – physically and psychologically – for fight or flight.

When our fight or flight system is activated, we tend to perceive everything in our environment as a possible threat to our survival. By its very nature, the fight or flight system bypasses our rational mind and moves us into 'attack' mode. This state of alert causes us to see everyone and everything as a possible enemy. We may overreact to the slightest comment.

You can see how it is almost impossible to have a positive attitude to work when you are stuck in survival mode. The rational mind is disengaged. Making clear choices and recognising the consequences of those choices is not possible. We are focused on short-term survival, not the long-term consequences of our choices. When we are overwhelmed with excessive stress, our life becomes a series of short-term emergencies. We lose the ability to relax and enjoy the moment. We live from crisis to crisis, with no relief in sight. Burnout is inevitable.

General adaptation syndrome

The general adaptation syndrome (GAS) is a term used to describe the body's short-term and long-term reactions to stress; it was originally described by Hans Selye[9]. Stressors include such physical and environmental phenomena as starvation, being hit by a car, or dealing with severe weather. Additionally, people can suffer emotional or mental stressors such as the loss of a loved one, the inability to solve a problem, or having difficulties at work.

Holmes and Rahe (1967) developed a questionnaire called the Social Readjustment Rating Scale (SRRS) for identifying major stressful life events. They surveyed over 5,000 medical patients and asked them to say whether they had experienced any of a series of 43 life events in the previous two years. Each event, called a life change unit (LCU), had a different 'weight' for stress. The more events the patient added up, the higher the score, and the more likely the patient was to become ill. You can try this questionnaire for yourself at:

http://www.mindtools.com/pages/article/newTCS_82.htm.

Selye thought that the general adaptation syndrome involved two major systems of the body, the nervous system and the endocrine (or hormonal) system. He then went on to outline what he considered as three distinctive stages in the syndrome's evolution. He called these stages the alarm reaction, the stage of resistance, and the stage of exhaustion.

- *Alarm* – the first stage of the general adaptation syndrome, the alarm reaction, is the immediate reaction to a stressor. In the initial phase of stress, people exhibit a fight or flight response, which prepares the body for

9 Hans Selye (1907–1982), an Austrian-born physician who emigrated to Canada in 1939.

The General Adaptation Syndrome

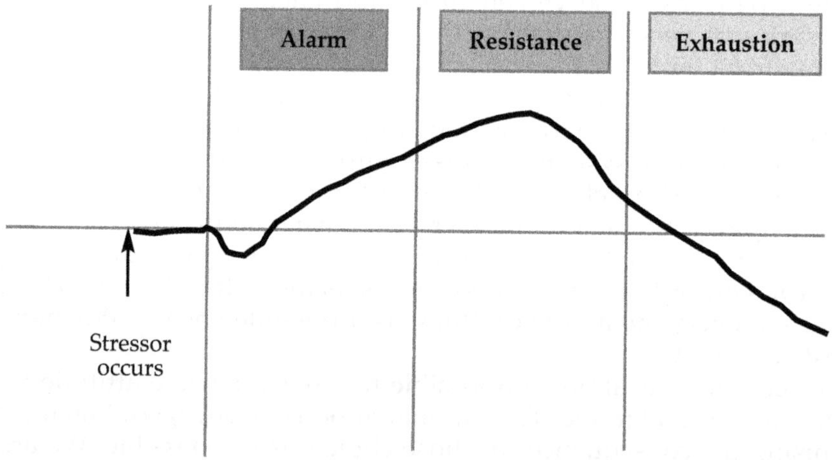

Figure 8.5

physical activity. However, this initial response can also decrease the effectiveness of the immune system, making people more susceptible to illness during this phase.

- *Resistance* – during this phase, if the stress continues, the body adapts to the stressors it is exposed to. Changes take place at many levels in order to reduce the effect of the stressor. For example, if the stressor is starvation, the person might experience a reduced desire for physical activity to conserve energy, and the absorption of nutrients from food might be maximised. Stage 2 is also named the stage of adaptation, instead of the stage of resistance.
- *Exhaustion* – in this stage, the stress has continued for some time. The body's resistance to the stress may gradually be reduced, or even collapse. Generally, this means the immune system, and the body's ability to resist disease, may be almost totally eliminated. People who experience long-term stress may succumb to heart attacks or severe infection due to their reduced immunity.

Burnout

Burnout is a state of physical, emotional or mental exhaustion combined with doubts about your competence and the value of your work. Burnout can result from various factors, including:

- Lack of control

- Lack of resources
- Unclear job expectations
- Dysfunctional workplace dynamics
- Mismatch in values
- Poor job fit
- Extremes of activity
- Lack of social support
- Work-life imbalance

The difference between stress and burnout is a matter of degree, which means that the earlier you recognise the signs, the better able you will be to avoid burnout. Here are some signals you have to pay attention to:

- *Chronic fatigue.* Lack of energy and feeling tired most days, or feeling a sense of anxiety about what lies ahead on any given day.
- *Insomnia.* Trouble falling asleep or staying asleep, or inability to sleep altogether.
- *Impaired concentration and attention.* Lack of focus and forgetfulness, or you can't get your work done and everything begins to pile up.
- *Physical symptoms.* Physical symptoms may include chest pain, heart palpitations, shortness of breath, gastrointestinal pain, dizziness, fainting, and/or headaches.
- *Increased illness.* Because your body is depleted, your immune system becomes weakened, making you more vulnerable to infections, colds, flu, and other immune-related medical problems.
- *Loss of appetite.* In the early stages, you may not feel hungry and may skip a few meals. In the latter stages, you may lose your appetite all together and begin to lose a significant amount of weight.
- *Anxiety.* Symptoms of tension, worry, and edginess. As you move closer to burnout, the anxiety may become so serious that it interferes with your ability to work productively and may cause problems in your personal life.
- *Anger.* Interpersonal tension and irritability. This may turn into angry outbursts and serious arguments at home and in the workplace.
- *Loss of enjoyment.* Not wanting to go to work or being eager to leave, or trying to avoid challenges and figure out ways to escape work all together.
- *Pessimism.* A general sense that nothing is going right or nothing matters, issues of trust with co-workers and family members and a feeling that you can't count on anyone.
- *Isolation.* In the early stages, this may seem like mild resistance to socialising; in the latter stages, you may become angry when someone

speaks to you, or you may come into work early or leave late to avoid interactions with colleagues.

- *Detachment*. Removing yourself emotionally and physically from your job and other responsibilities; you may call in sick often, stop returning calls and emails, or regularly come in late.
- *Depression*. In the early stages, you may feel mildly sad, occasionally hopeless, and you may experience feelings of guilt and worthlessness as a result. At its worst, you may feel trapped, severely depressed, and think the world would be better off without you. (If your depression has reached this point, you should seek professional help immediately.)

You can read more about this topic in 'The Truth about Burnout'[10] or – on a lighter note – in 'Fried'[11]

Paradoxically enough, top performers are most likely to experience burnout, because they are given the toughest assignments with the biggest challenges. They are the most likely to struggle with overwork, and least likely to ask for help or set limits.

Burnout is not a simple result of hard work or long hours. The cynicism, depression and lethargy of burnout can occur when you're not in control of how you carry out your job, when you're working toward goals that don't resonate with you, and when you lack social support. If you don't tailor your responsibilities to match your true vocation, or at least take a break once in a while, you could face a mountain of mental and physical health problems. Beware!

Resilience factors

For sure, the origins of our stress are often outside of ourselves, and the way our body and mind react are largely physiological and thus beyond our immediate control. However, a combination of factors can contribute to our resilience. Many studies show that the most important factor is having caring and supportive relationships within and outside the family. Relationships that create love and trust, provide role models and offer encouragement and reassurance help reinforce a person's resilience.

Besides social support, several additional factors are associated with resilience, including:

- A healthy life style.
- A positive view of yourself and confidence in your strengths and abilities.
- The capacity to make realistic plans and taking steps to carry them out.
- Skills in communication and problem solving.
- The capacity to manage strong feelings and impulses.

10 'The Truth About Burnout – How Organisations Cause Personal Stress and What to Do About it' (2000) by Christina Maslach and Michael P. Leiter.

11 'Fried – Why you Burn Out and how to Revive' (2012) by Joan Borysenko.

All of these are factors that people can develop themselves. Some, or many of the ways to build resilience in the following pages may be appropriate to consider in developing your personal strategy.

Social support

Numerous studies indicate that social support is essential for maintaining physical and psychological health. Both the detrimental consequences of poor social support, and the protecting effects of good social support have been extensively documented. Social support has been described as 'support accessible to an individual through social bonds with other individuals, groups, and the larger community – a network of family, friends, neighbours, and community members.' One might add that the possibility of being able to call on the help of a mentor or a coach could also be counted as social support. Coaches like Ian McDermott[12] recommend the 'buddy system', especially for managers, in this respect.

With respect to exactly what social support means, perhaps the psychiatrist Sidney Cobb gave one of the best definitions. He proposed that social support was a subjective sensation in which the individual feels: 'That he is cared for and loved. That he is esteemed and valued; that he belongs to a network of communication and mutual obligation.'

Theoretical models of social support specify the following two important dimensions:

- A *structural dimension,* which includes network size and frequency of social interactions.
- A *functional dimension* with emotional (such as receiving love and empathy) and instrumental (practical help such as gifts of money or assistance with child care) components.

Most research has found that the *quality* of relationships (the functional dimension) is a better predictor of good health than the *quantity* of relationships (the structural dimension), although both are important.

For EU staff, this may pose a particular problem, since the vast majority of those who work for the EU are expats. They have had to leave their homes, their relatives, colleagues and social networks behind, and may find it difficult to build a new network of social support from the ground up. I have seen brilliant people – highly skilled and motivated professionals – who could not cope with this. I remember one Spanish colleague who had left his girlfriend back home during the nine months of his probation period. He was so homesick and socially isolated that he decided to quit prematurely, giving up the prospect of life-long employment and an interesting job. I think this was probably the best decision he could make, because, if he had stayed, he was bound to run into serious trouble, deeply unhappy at work, and ultimately a burnout.

The EU institutions are well aware of this. That is why they are actively involved in the many leisure, sports and cultural clubs open to EU staff and their families, including athletics, dance, theatre, art and language exchange. I would also advise you to break out of the 'euro bubble' in and around Brussels, and join local organisations and (service) clubs. Belgians are known for their cordiality, and you will soon get genuine friends you can rely on.

12 https://www.linkedin.com/in/ianemcdermott

The benefits of reading for pleasure

'Reading is to the mind what exercise is to the body.'[13] – Richard Steele

A study[14] conducted at the University of Liverpool explored the emotional, social and psychological benefits to adults of regular reading for pleasure.

Regular readers for pleasure reported fewer feelings of stress and depression than non-readers, and stronger feelings of relaxation from reading than from watching television or engaging with social media. Reading creates a parallel world in which personal anxieties can recede, while also helping people to realise that the problems they experience are not theirs alone. A fifth of respondents said reading helped them to feel less lonely.

Those who read for pleasure also have higher levels of self-esteem and a greater ability to cope with difficult situations. Readers have expanded models and repertoires of experience, which allow them to look with new perspectives and understanding on their own lives. Readers find it easier to make decisions, to plan and prioritise, and this may be because they are more able to recognise that difficulty and setbacks are unavoidable aspects of human life.

People who read regularly feel closer to their friends and their community than lapsed or non-readers. Reading not only produces greater understanding and empathy with others; it also gives a currency for sharing experience more meaningfully than is possible in ordinary social conversation. Readers also have a stronger and more engaged awareness of social issues and of cultural diversity than non-readers.

The conclusions of the study were that readers feel happier about themselves and their lives. Reading for just 30 minutes a week produces greater life satisfaction, enhances social connectedness and sense of community spirit, and helps protect against, and even prepare for life's difficulties.

Mens sana in corpore sano

The expression *mens sana in corpore sano* – 'a sound mind in a sound body' – is widely used to express the idea that physical health is an important part of mental and psychological well being. Caring for your physical needs by eating healthy food, exercising, finding time to relax, and getting enough sleep can help you cope with stress:

- Eating healthily can help boost your brain's serotonin levels, which will combat higher cortisol associated with stress.
- Exercise and other physical activity produce endorphins – chemicals in the brain that act as natural painkillers.
- Stay well-hydrated – keeping the body hydrated helps the heart pump blood more easily through the blood vessels to the muscles and your brain.
- Sleep is a necessary human function – it allows our brains to recharge and our bodies to rest, which in turn reduces stress. Your brain needs downtime to stay sharp. If you don't get enough sleep, you'll tax your memory and start forgetting things. Stay rested so you can keep your mind alert.
- Limit your alcohol intake. Alcohol is a depressant, which means that it slows down the brain and the central nervous system's processes.

13 Sir Richard Steele (1672–1729) was an Anglo-Irish writer and politician.

14 https://epale.ec.europa.eu/en/resource-centre/content/benefits-adults-reading-pleasure

Stress and smoking

While I was still a smoker – I used to smoke cigars – I was convinced that smoking relieves stress. Studies have found, however, that in reality, smoking has the opposite effect: it causes long-term stress levels to rise, not fall.

In one study conducted at the London School of Medicine and Dentistry, researchers looked at 469 people who tried to quit smoking after being hospitalised for heart disease. At the start, the subjects had similar levels of stress and generally believed that smoking helped them to cope.

A year later, 41 per cent had managed to stay abstinent. After controlling for several factors, the scientists found that the abstainers had 'a significantly larger decrease in perceived stress,' roughly a 20 per cent drop, compared with the continuing smokers, who showed little change.

The scientists' hypothesis was that the continuing smokers were dealing with uncomfortable cravings between cigarettes multiple times a day, while the abstainers, after facing some initial withdrawal, had greater freedom from nicotine cravings and thus had eliminated a frequent and significant source of stress.

The bottom line: the calming effect of a cigarette is a myth, at least in the long term.

- Limit your caffeine intake. The effects of drinking coffee are long-lasting and exaggerate the stress response, both in terms of the body's physiological response as reflected in raised blood pressure and stress hormone levels, and also in terms of increasing a person's feeling of being stressed.

The brain is roughly 2% of one's body weight, but consumes about 20% of the oxygen. The ability to get more oxygen to the brain allows more of the brain to be accessed, and a healthy body can make this happen.

Positive thinking

'Optimism is a moral duty' – Immanuel Kant[15]

A study released in 2013 found that optimists have a better biological response to stress than pessimists. Researchers at Concordia University's Department of Psychology found that 'the stress hormone' cortisol tends to be more stable in people with a positive outlook.

Joelle Jobin[16] found that pessimists tend to have a higher stress baseline than optimists. Pessimists generally had trouble regulating their sympathetic nervous system when they go through stressful experiences. The inability to look on the bright side causes cortisol to stay constantly elevated.

Like most hormones in our bodies, 'the stress hormone' cortisol is complex with many functions. Although cortisol is linked to many health problems it is also our 'get

15 Immanuel Kant (1724–1804) was a German philosopher, a central figure of modern philosophy.

16 https://www.concordia.ca/cunews/main/releases/2013/07/23/optimists-better-at-regulating-stress.html

up and do things hormone,' according to Jobin. Just like we have 'eustress' (good stress) and 'distress' (bad stress), we need cortisol to stimulate our sympathetic nervous system and kick-start our bodies into action.

Each of us has the free will to be an optimist or a pessimist. The daily choices of mindset and behaviour that we make create biological changes throughout our bodies that have long lasting ramifications.

Albert Ellis[17] discovered in 1955 that people's beliefs strongly affected their emotional functioning. In particular certain irrational beliefs made people feel depressed, anxious or angry and led to self-defeating behaviours. Ellis created the ABC model to help us understand the meaning of our reactions to adversity:

- A is the adversity – the situation or event.
- B is our belief – our explanation of why the situation happened.
- C is the consequence – the feelings and behaviours that our belief causes.

Adversity -> Beliefs -> Consequences

The word 'belief' means a conviction of the truth, actuality, or validity of something. So a belief is a thought with an emotional component (conviction) and a factual component (truth, actuality or validity). Beliefs can be either positive or negative. Having a negative belief is not necessarily a bad thing; however, when one believes in something that is false, a negative belief tends to become what Ellis called an 'irrational' belief. Irrational beliefs are not friendly to happiness and contentment and are definitely unhelpful for getting one's basic desires for love and approval, comfort and achievement or success met.

Sometimes it's hard to identify our beliefs; we tend to be better at labelling our feelings. The B-C connections can be used in reverse to help us identify our beliefs. For example, feelings of guilt are often produced when we believe that we have violated another person's rights. B-C connections help us increase our self-awareness – an important first step to a resilient response to adversity.

In his Rational Emotive Behaviour Theory (REBT) Ellis argues that:

- Unconditional self-acceptance, other-acceptance and life-acceptance are of prime importance in achieving mental wellness.
- People and the world are fallible and people are better off accepting themselves and others, life's hassles and unfairness, as they are.
- People should consider themselves valuable just as a result of being alive and kicking, because all humans do both good and bad deeds and have both (not either/or) good and bad attributes and traits.

Clearly, all this should certainly not be an excuse to just 'cop out', i.e. take the easy way out of a sticky situation; you are responsible for your own behaviour and development after all.

17 Albert Ellis (1913–2007) was an American psychologist.

Lastly, for reading matter, I would strongly recommend the UK psychologist/author Gill Hasson, who has written an excellent and very easy to read guide to Mindfulness and another one on Emotional Intelligence. They are really well worth recommending as background reading.

Planning

'To achieve great things, two things are needed: a plan and not quite enough time.' – Leonard Bernstein[18]

We all come across periods of very high workload and tight deadlines, but some people simply don't know how to handle this. They freak out, and start running around like headless chickens. Not sufficient progress is made and, obviously, the deadlines are not met. This creates even greater stress.

Before I start with our individual behaviour during these periods of high stress, let me mention what the bestselling author on change and motivation, John Kotter, says about urgency. In his book 'A Sense of Urgency'[19] Kotter identifies the single biggest factor to successful change: creating a true sense of urgency. Urgency he says, is 'a compulsive determination to move, and win, now.'

Resilient behaviour in these situations is to keep your cool, step back a bit, and make a plan. The key to managing your stress under these circumstances is to kill the negative emotions and stay in control.

One of my coachees (a Spanish banker) gave me a great metaphor for this. He told me that the worst thing you can do when facing a dangerous snake is to freeze, because the snake will eventually kill you. Instead back away from the snake, analyse the situation, and work out how to kill the snake yourself.

Planning does not mean working longer hours, dropping holidays, or taking work home during the weekends. Now I am not saying that – from time to time – you cannot do this, but it has to fit into your plan; if burning long hours at work is your only strategy to cope with workload stress you are bound to run into a burnout.

Planning means *staying in control*, and not being controlled by your negative emotions. Planning means cutting the big problem into smaller chunks, allocating time and resources, deciding on the priorities, outsourcing, delegating or asking for help, and possibly even renegotiating the expected outcome or deadlines. Breaks and time to relax should also be part of your plan.

Create a to-do list every day with no more than 10 items numbered in order of priority. Tackle your most challenging to-do items first thing in the day when your brain is most refreshed. Review your list at the end of every day.

Learn to say 'No' – sometimes. It may be pressures from family and/or work that lead to too much stress, and sometimes it may be expectations that you have of yourself that might not be completely realistic. *If you don't set priorities for your own life, someone else will.*

18 US composer and conductor (1918–1990)

19 'A Sense of Urgency' (2008) by John P. Kotter.

Don't allow a heavy workload to frustrate you. When the pressures are coming from something over which you have no control, rather than fight against it, accept it and move on, like a true professional.

Dealing with variations in workload

Variations in workload occur in virtually every work environment; periods of heavy workload are followed by relatively calmer periods. This can be due to the inherently periodic nature of the organisation's activities (e.g. meeting agendas, budget cycle, etc.) or simply because of holiday periods.

We have already seen how good planning can help you cope with the periods of heavy workload, but effective management of your agenda can be very useful during the calmer periods as well. Here are some things you can schedule for the calmer periods at work:

- *Taking care of your backlog*. Activities that were postponed during the 'busy' period because they were not urgent – and not so important – can usefully be performed during a calmer period. Typically, dealing with unanswered emails is one of these activities.
- *Cleaning up*. Reorganising your desktop, filing documents, inventory, etc.
- *Anticipating future work*. Preparing forms, questionnaires, checklists, contact lists, etc.
- *Planning*. It is often possible to plan ahead, even when not all the necessary details are available yet.
- *Professional and personal development*. Training, workshops, seminars and conferences.
- *Networking*. Calmer periods are great opportunities to take care of your operational, personal, and strategic networks (see Chapter 9 to find out the difference).
- *Recharging your batteries*. Clear your brain by taking holidays, spending more time on the things you enjoy, etc.

Communicating and problem solving

Mental noise is the constant chatter of the mind that never stops. It is the inner conversation that goes on constantly in the mind. This mental noise is like a background noise that never ceases, from the moment of waking up to the moment of falling asleep. It is a sort of inner voice that constantly analyses everything about what you are doing, what is going on around you, and the people you meet.

The mind also repeats the same thoughts over and over again, like in a loop, like a record that got stuck. If these are positive thoughts, that's fine. However, too often, they are negative thoughts that intensify stress, worry, anger or frustration.

Clearly, thinking is a vital activity required for solving problems, analysing, comparing, studying, planning, etc. – but too often, the mind wanders where it will, occupying your attention with trivial matters and unimportant, useless thinking that wastes your time and energy.

The mind is a tool therefore that needs to be kept under control. The *mental noise theory* states that clear communication happens only when we overcome a certain degree of mental distraction. It further suggests that when people are stressed, they have greater difficulty hearing, understanding and remembering information.

Here are some important things to keep in mind when communicating under stress in the workplace:

- *Listen first.* The higher the level of stress, the more important it is to show that you are listening. People are more willing to listen to what you have to say when they believe you are listening to them in turn. In the words of Stephen Covey: 'Seek first to understand, then to be understood'.
- *Clarity, brevity and repetition.* Remember, the greater the stress, the greater the need for clarity, brevity, and repetition. To help people understand your message, provide information in small portions that are easily absorbed. Use familiar words and simple sentences, and repeat important points, to be sure that you are understood.
- *Make it personal.* Use face-to-face communication, not email, to help get your message across during times of high stress. When interacting in person, pay particular attention to body language, as this is directly linked to people's emotions.

Another human trait that often blocks communication is our tendency to focus on the negative. This is called *negative dominance theory* or negativity bias. Because of this bias, people generally attach more weight to negative statements – and remember them longer – and this tendency of concentrating on what is perceived to be negative becomes even stronger when we are stressed out. So it is important to considerably increase the ratio of positive to negative statements in times of high stress.

The more stressful our environment, the more we need to connect and communicate. In times of crisis and anxiety people need to feel listened to, and feel that they belong to the group. In these circumstances, more than ever, our communication must demonstrate compassion, conviction, truthfulness and credibility. Our presentations, conversations and documents must be brief, clear and repeat key messages. Remember that the characteristics of good communication don't change under stress; they just become more important.

Self-control

'You have power over your mind – not outside events. Realise this, and you will find strength.' – Marcus Aurelius[20]

Self-control separates us from our primitive ancestors and from the animals, thanks to our large prefrontal cortices. Rather than responding to immediate impulses, we can

20 Military leader, philosopher and Roman emperor from 161 to 180.

plan, we can evaluate alternative actions, and we can refrain from doing things we may eventually regret.

For most people, stress or boredom makes them instinctively reach for something to allay it, and this often takes the instant-gratification form of sugar, alcohol, nicotine or distractions like social media.

Train yourself to be mindful enough to know when you are entering your danger zone (i.e. feeling stressed out, tired, bored, etc.). Becoming more conscious of your mood and the likelihood of lapsing will help you to act with intention instead of habit. But it is not enough to simply try to break a bad habit; the process is much more effective when actively replacing it with a good habit. If you're addicted to nicotine, try chewing gum to address the oral fixation, but avoid substituting food for the cigarette. Remember, this isn't just a habit you're trying to kick; it's a lifestyle adjustment. Cultivate a new way of being.

Anger management involves spotting the triggers for anger as early as possible and expressing these feelings and frustrations in a cool, calm and composed way. Anger management is about unlearning ineffective coping mechanisms and re-learning more effective ways to deal with the problems and frustrations associated with anger. There are many anger management techniques that you can learn and practise by yourself. However if you experience a lot of regular anger then seeking help, usually in the form of a counsellor, can be more effective.

Dealing with change

In the workplace, change is inevitable, and dealing with change requires some mental adjustments:

- Approach change as a process; processes take time.
- Embrace change; choose to give positive meaning to changes.
- Be prepared to move with changes because they are going to happen anyway.

If you are aware of an upcoming change, such as a move or a new job, you can help to alleviate stress about the event in multiple ways:

- *Create an action plan.* By setting (SMART) goals and creating a series of steps to get from one intermediate objective to another, you will feel more in control of the situation, which should help minimise your stress.
- *One change at a time.* If you have a big change coming up, it's important that you create consistency in the rest of your life as much as possible. For example, if you're going to be changing jobs soon it may be best not to attempt to change personal habits (stop smoking for example) at the same time.
- *Rely on your social support network.*

Sometimes, change occurs without warning. Here too, there are a number of steps you can take to help you cope and adapt:

- *Relax.* Try to take time to relax every day, even if it's only for a few minutes. You can also use relaxation techniques like meditation or deep breathing as a tool for coping with stress.
- *Laugh.* Laughter can help decrease the effects of stress.
- *Seek professional support.* If stress management techniques do not work for you, then seek care from a qualified professional such as a life coach, a therapist, or social worker.

Working with your manager

'The single biggest problem in communication is the illusion that it has taken place.' – G.B. Shaw (attributed)[21]

Like most large administrations, the EU institutions are *hierarchical organisations.* A hierarchical organisation is a structure where every entity, except one, is subservient to a single other entity. Members of hierarchical organisations mainly communicate with their immediate superior and with their immediate subordinates. Structuring organisations in this way is useful because it can reduce the communication overhead by limiting information flow. However, this is also its major limitation.

Communication builds relationships, including the working relationships that allow people within an organisation to coordinate their efforts for the common good. Communication flows up, down and across the levels of an organisation. Communication flowing up the chain of command gives management valuable information about the state of affairs. Feedback, reports, suggestions and work needs all flow from subordinate to manager. Communications that flow down from one level to the next range from operational to strategic matters. Operational matters include directives, feedback, training and appraisals. Starting at the top, though, management must also provide leadership by communicating broader concerns — guiding principles, such as the organisation's vision, mission and strategic goals.

The problem is that communication is never perfect. This is because all organisations are built with people, and people aren't perfect. Our hierarchical superiors are normal human beings too, with their inherent imperfections. Perfect leaders or perfect managers do not exist; even the most highly esteemed, world-class leaders have their personal weaknesses and blind spots. Your superior may be inexperienced in their new job; they may have been promoted to their 'level of incompetence' (the Peter Principle, discussed earlier); or – at worst – they may have a hidden agenda. In any case, your interaction with management will never be without stress and anxiety.

Having worked with numerous not-so-inspiring managers in my own career, I learned that they provided me with unique opportunities for developing my own leadership skills, and learning 'what not to do' when managing people myself. However bad your manager may be, you can always develop ways to handle your

21 Anglo-Irish playwright, 1856-1950.

relationship with him or her in a better way. Rather than think of your line manager as your 'boss', think of them as a difficult 'client' – one you have to figure out how to work with if you want to get ahead, even if you'd rather not be in that situation.

In any event, it's better for you to work with the management rather than against it; here are some strategies to help you on your way:

- *Know their 'why'.* The better you understand what your manager does, and more importantly, why they do it, the better positioned you are to deliver results, manage expectations, and avoid lose-lose situations. When you know what drives your manager, you can structure your views and communicate in ways that line up with their core values, concerns and priorities.
- *Adapt your communication style.* If you have ever done a personality assessment like the MBTI, try to find out what your manager's preferences are, and how these may be different from yours. It can help you adapt your communication style and save a lot of tension.
- *Work around their weaknesses.* Exposing your manager's incompetence will only reinforce your misery and may even damage your own reputation. By doing what you can to help your manager succeed, you lay a solid foundation for more success for yourself.
- *Keep your mind focused on top performance.* Never let your manager's bad behaviour be an excuse for your own. As Gandhi wrote: 'Be the change you want to see in the world.' In this case, act like the leader you wish your manager was.
- *Have the courage to speak up.* Instead of saying nothing, suffering in silence, or complaining privately to colleagues, speak up; you at least owe your manager the opportunity to respond.

If things really don't work out, there still is the Staff Committee to complain to. The Staff Committee is a statutory committee that represents the interests of your institution's staff vis-à-vis management and assures continuous contact between management and staff.

And don't forget: nothing lasts forever. On average, we only work for the same manager for a couple of years; natural staff mobility will take care of that. In the EU institutions staff mobility is even actively encouraged, so if you are finally moving away from a bad manager, nobody will blame you for that.

Personality type and stress

Everybody has a different reaction to stress. One of the main differentiators is our personality. Table 8.1 lists some possible tactics you can apply, depending on your MBTI preferences:

Your Preferences	Your Stressors	Possible Tactics
Extraversion	• Working alone • Having to communicate mainly in writing • Lengthy work periods without interruptions • Having to reflect before taking action • Having to focus in depth on one thing • Getting feedback in writing only	• Networking with others outside your team • Asking others to voice their ideas • Paying attention to written communication • Allowing others to think about your ideas before they provide feedback
Introversion	• Working with others • Having to communicate mainly by talking • Interacting with others frequently • Having to act quickly, without reflection • Too many concurrent tasks and demands • Getting frequent and verbal feedback	• Arriving at work early, taking advantage of the quiet time • Intentionally seeking private/reflective time, taking a walk over lunchtime or the long way home • Planning private breaks to collect your thoughts • In meetings, voicing even partially thought-through perspectives
Intuition	• Having to attend to realities • Having to do things the proven way • Having to attend to details • Checking the accuracy of facts • Needing to focus on past experience • Being required to be practical	• Practise presenting information in a step-by-step manner • Providing specific examples of vital information • Honouring organisational values surrounding experience and tradition • Reading the fine print and getting the facts straight
Sensing	• Attending to own and others' insights • Having to do old things in a new way • Having to give an overview without details • Looking for the meaning of facts • Focusing on possibilities • Too many complexities	• Getting involved in projects that require long-range or future thinking • Practise brainstorming • Preparing yourself to look for patterns • Going beyond specifics, trying to discover meaning and themes
Thinking	• Using personal experience to assess situations • Adjusting to individual differences and needs • Noticing and appreciating what is positive • Focusing on processes and people • Using empathy and personal values to make decisions • Having others react to questioning as divisive	• Working on projects in which alternative causes and solutions are evaluated in personal terms • Reminding yourself that factoring in people is logical even if people aren't • Softening critical remarks, finding the positive too • Asking for others' opinions and concerns; looking for points of agreement before discussing issues

Table 8.1 (continued overleaf)

Your Preferences	Your Stressors	Possible Tactics
Feeling	• Analysing situations objectively • Setting criteria and standards • Critiquing and focusing on flaws • Being expected to use logic alone to make decisions • Asking questions that feel divisive	• Practise laying out an argument by saying 'if… then', or by considering the causes and effects • Understanding that critical feedback is often given in the spirit of improving your professionalism • Paying attention to stakeholders' concern regarding project/work • Using brief and concise language to express your wants and needs
Judging	• Waiting for structures to emerge from process • Too much flexibility around time frames and deadlines • Having to marshal energy at the last minute • Staying open to re-evaluation of tasks • Dealing with surprises	• Seeking out projects that have definite planning and milestones • Trying to wait on a decision for a few days, continuing to gather more information and paying attention to ideas that may come up • Understand that work is progressing despite differences in work styles • Making your own milestones and deadlines
Perceiving	• Having to organise their and others' plans • Working with time frames and deadlines • Others' distrust of last minute energy • Having to finish and move on • Developing contingency plans • Being required to plan ahead	• Recognising that deadlines set by the organisation may not be negotiable • Using a past decision you believe others rushed to demonstrate the advantages of slowing down to gather more information • Becoming active in projects where the process is just as important as the outcome • Keeping surprises to a minimum and reducing your options

Table 8.1 (continued)

The upside of stress

'The Upside of Stress'[22] is a book that brings together research on the relationship between resilience and mindset. Author Kelly McGonigal[23] works together science, stories, and exercises with the idea of showing you:

- How to cultivate a mindset to embrace stress.
- How stress can provide focus and energy.
- How stress can help people connect and strengthen close relationships.

22 'The Upside of Stress – Why Stress is good for You, and how to get Good at It' (2015) by Kelly McGonigal.

23 Kelly McGonigal (1977) is a health psychologist who is known for her work in the field of 'science help'

- Why your brain is built to learn from stress, and how to increase its ability to learn from challenging experiences.

McGonigal's TED talk[24] on the same subject has had millions of views.

Developing your resilience

Resilience is ordinary, not extraordinary. Resilience is not a trait that people either have or do not have. It involves behaviours, thoughts and actions that can be learned and developed in anyone.

Please refer to Annex 1 for further development of this competency, or check out the easy-to-use app at:

http://www.johnharperpublishing.co.uk/the-ultimate-eu-career-development-toolkit/

24 https://kellymcgonigal.com/

9. Working with others

Competency definition: 'Work co-operatively with others in teams and across organisational boundaries and respect differences between people.'

'It takes two flints to make a fire' – Louisa May Alcott[1]

Some things are easy to achieve by working on your own, but there will inevitably be many times when you have to work with other people to get a job done.

Working with others is the ability to effectively interact, cooperate, collaborate and manage conflicts with other people in order to complete tasks and achieve shared goals. This includes working with just one other individual, either in person or at a distance, or working in small or large groups of people, for example co-workers, managers, stakeholders, and contractors.

Wherever people work together, groups will be formed. People will belong to one or more groups, with each group having a different goal and purpose. These groups may be formal or informal. Formal groups are created to complete defined tasks, whilst informal groups are created voluntarily and are made up of individuals with common interests or roles. Informal groups are not usually recognised by the organisation but they can have significant impact upon the work of others.

Effectively working with others involves understanding and working within the group's culture, rules and values; joint planning and decision-making; negotiating and compromising; expressing one's opinions and ideas and respecting those of others, including people of differing backgrounds; and being flexible in terms of roles, including knowing when to take a leadership role and knowing when to seek a team approach.

Groups versus teams

'The nice thing about teamwork is that you always have others on your side.' – Margaret Carty

In English, the words 'group' and 'team' can sometimes be used interchangeably, but in other situations there are clear differences in meaning between them. For example, we have a football team, not a football group – or we have a special interest group, not a special interest team. While the differences may be subtle, they are indeed different, and we need to understand what those differences are.

In the business world – and by extension in public administration – there are *work groups* and *work teams*. A work group is two or more individuals who are either dependent or independent in their activities and may or may not work in the same department. A work team has members who work interdependently on a specific, common goal to produce an end result for their organisation.

1 Louisa May Alcott (1832–1888), American writer, most famously of 'Little Women'.

In work teams, the leader acts as a facilitator; the members actively participate in the discussions and influence the outcome. It is the team members who decide on the distribution of work assignments. In contrast, in work groups it is the leader who dominates and controls the group; it is very clear who is in charge, and the leader will conduct the meetings and assign work to the group members.

Usually, work teams meet more often than work groups. Work groups may meet periodically, based on the manager's style, primarily to listen to and share information. Teams, in contrast, do much more than communicate when they meet. Team meetings are opportunities for planning work, solving problems, making decisions about work, and reviewing progress. In short, meetings are vital to a team's existence.

Dependent-level work groups are the traditional work unit or department-level groups, with a supervisor who plays a strong role as the superior. Each person in a dependent-level work group has their own job and works under the close guidance of the manager. In fact, most problem solving, work assignments, and other decisions affecting the group come from the manager.

Independent-level work groups are the most common form of work groups on the business scene. Like a dependent-level work group, each person is responsible for their own main area. But unlike the dependent level, the manager tends not to function like a controlling boss. Instead, staff members work on their own assignments with just general direction and minimal supervision. Sales representatives, research scientists, accountants, lawyers, police officers, and teachers are among the professionals who tend to work in this fashion. People in those professions come together in one department because they serve a common overall function, but almost everyone in the group works fairly independently.

Members of an *interdependent-level* entity rely on each other to get the work done. Sometimes members have their own roles and at other times they share responsibilities. However, in either case, they coordinate with one another to produce an overall product or set of outcomes. When this interdependence exists, you have a team.

As you can see from the above, the situation in the European Commission – and the other EU institutions for that matter – offers a very mixed picture in terms of groups and teams, and it is not always clear from the organogram whether Sector ABC or Unit XYZ is a group or a team. Also, some entities work at a dependent level, while others are either independent or interdependent. Many groups or teams do not even show up on the organogram, and we talk of 'task forces' (i.e. teams) or – sometimes, interinstitutional – 'work groups' or 'committees' that are set up on a more or less ad hoc basis to serve a certain purpose. Clearly, it is up to the participants to find their way in this labyrinth, and interact with the other participants accordingly.

Group dynamics

One of the main sources of stress in the workplace has to do with work relationships. *Group dynamics* is a system of behaviours and psychological processes occurring within a group, or between groups. The study of group dynamics can be useful in dealing with conflicts and stress, but also in understanding decision-making behaviour.

In 1965 Bruce Tuckman[2] identified four stages of group development, adding a fifth stage in his later writings ten years later.

Stage 1: Forming

In the Forming stage, personal relations are characterised by dependence. Group members rely on safe, patterned behaviour and look to the group leader for guidance and direction. Group members have a desire for acceptance by the group and a need to know that the group is safe. Serious topics and feelings are avoided. During this stage, group members are assessing one another and the scope of the task and how to approach the task.

Stage 2: Storming

The next stage, Storming, is characterised by competition and conflict in the personal-relations dimension and organisation in the task-functions dimension. As the group members attempt to organise for the task, conflict inevitably affects personal relations. Individuals have to adjust their feelings, ideas, attitudes, and beliefs to suit the group organisation. These reflect conflicts over leadership, structure, power, and authority. Some group members will like the fact that real issues are starting to surface while others will feel uncomfortable.

Stage 3: Norming

In the Norming stage, interpersonal relations are characterised by cohesion. Group members are engaged in active recognition of all members' contributions, community building and maintenance, and solving of group issues. It is during this stage of development (assuming the group gets this far) that people begin to experience a sense of group belonging and a feeling of relief as a result of resolving interpersonal conflicts. Group members are now listening to each other better and identify themselves as part of a group. In some groups, the fact so much work was invested in reaching this stage may mean group members become reluctant to change anything.

Stage 4: Performing

Not all groups do reach the Performing stage. If group members are able to evolve to stage four, their capacity, range, and depth of personal relations expand to true interdependence. In this stage, people can work independently, in subgroups, or as a total unit with equal facility. There is support for experimentation in solving problems and an emphasis on achievement. The overall goal is productivity through problem solving and work.

Stage 5: Adjourning

Tuckman's final stage, Adjourning, involves the termination of task behaviours and disengagement from relationships. In some texts this stage is also referred to as Mourning.

Tuckman's original work simply described the way he had observed groups, whether they were conscious of it or not. Later work recognised that the real value is in identifying where a group is in the process, and helping it to move to the Performing stage. In the real world, groups are often forming and changing, and each time that happens, they can move to a different stage. A group might be happily

2 Bruce Tuckman (1938) is Professor Emeritus at Ohio State University; he carried out research in the theory of group dynamics.

Norming or Performing, but a new member might force them back into Storming. Leaders will be ready for this, and will help the group get back to Performing as quickly as possible.

There are many other models of group development, to name a few: Tubb's Systems model, Fisher's theory of decision emergence in groups, Poole's multiple sequences model, McGrath's Time, Interaction, and Performance (TIP) theory, etc.

Esprit de corps

'Esprit de corps' is a French expression (also used in English) that refers to a collective group spirit and solidarity. Esprit de corps is one of Henri Fayol's[3] 14 administrative principles. The principle states that an organisation must make every effort to maintain group cohesion. It notes that dividing your competition is a clever tactic, but dividing your own team is a serious error.

Being ex-military myself you will not be surprised that I will use an example from a military context – where people rely on each other for their own survival – to illustrate the notion of esprit de corps. In the military this notion can take extreme proportions, up to the level of being immoral or illegal. Check the following fragment of dialogue from 'A Few Good Men', a fantastic movie with Jack Nicholson as Colonel Jessep – the Commanding Officer – and Tom Cruise as a junior military lawyer, Lt. Daniel Kaffee, who defends two Marines accused of murder; they contend they were acting under orders.

Col. Jessep: You want answers?

Kaffee: I think I'm entitled to.

Col. Jessep: You want answers?

Kaffee: I want the truth!

Col. Jessep: You can't handle the truth!

[pauses]

Col. Jessep: Son, we live in a world that has walls, and those walls have to be guarded by men with guns. Who's gonna do it? You? You, Lt. Weinburg? I have a greater responsibility than you could possibly fathom. You weep for Santiago, and you curse the Marines. You have that luxury. You have the luxury of not knowing what I know. That Santiago's death, while tragic, probably saved lives. And my existence, while grotesque and incomprehensible to you, saves lives. You don't want the truth because deep down in places you don't talk about at parties, you want me on that wall, you need me on that wall. We use words like honor, code, loyalty. We use these words as the backbone of a life spent defending something. You use them as a punchline. I have neither the time nor the inclination to explain myself to a man who rises and sleeps under the blanket of the very freedom that I provide, and then questions the manner in which I provide it. I would rather you just said thank you, and went on your way, Otherwise, I suggest you pick up a weapon, and stand a post. Either way, I don't give a damn what you think you are entitled to.

Kaffee: Did you order the Code Red?[4]

Col. Jessep: I did the job I...

Kaffee: Did you order the Code Red?

Col. Jessep: You're Goddamn right I did!

Please note that I have mentioned the notion of esprit de corps in the background part of this chapter, and not in the context of 'best practice', and I did this for a good reason. Esprit de corps is a two edged-sword and there are times when esprit de corps in a small group sense can be very much against esprit de corps in a broader sense, the broader public interest or the interest of an organisation as a whole. A recent example from another field would be the rigging of markets by small groups of traders working closely together in large banks – their esprit de corps was tremendous, but they did huge damage to their organisation's reputation or even solvency.

3 Henri Fayol (1841–1925) was a French mining engineer who developed a general theory of business administration known as Fayolism.

4 'Code Red' was an illegal punishment ordered by a commanding officer but executed by someone in the unit.

Group structure

A group's structure is the internal framework that defines members' relations to one another over time. As discussed above, groups come together for many different reasons and in many different ways. However, to ensure that individuals can work together effectively, it is important that everyone should recognise and understand the roles and responsibilities of others, and how they can contribute to getting things done efficiently and well.

Roles can be defined as a tendency to behave, contribute and interrelate with others in a particular way. Roles may be assigned formally, but more often are defined through the process of role differentiation. Role differentiation is the degree to which different group members have specialised functions.

In many professional or administrative meetings there is the role of *moderator*. The moderator takes on the role of a formal or informal chair, and has to show awareness of the expected outcome (the mandate) and manage the sequence of events during the meeting by actively guiding the discussions and making sure that everyone gets a chance to contribute. Thus it is a high profile role in steering the group and achieving a successful outcome. The essential element is to periodically summarise what has been said by others thus far, and also to try to advance the discussions by closing as many open points as possible and then proposing the next step or the way forward.

A second role is that of *timekeeper*. A timekeeper monitors the process from a scheduling point of view. He or she keeps an eye on the clock and warns the group when there is a risk of time overrun. The timekeeper is not a standalone role and anyone, at any point, can remind the group of the time left and where you are in the discussion.

In many professional meetings, there is a *secretarial function* for taking notes, and drafting the minutes.

Status differentials are the relative differences in status among group members. When a group is first formed the members may all be on an equal level, but over time certain members may acquire status and authority within the group; this can create what is known as a *pecking order* within a group.

What is an optimal team size?

'Too many cooks spoil the broth' – an expression meaning that a team turns out to be inefficient if too many people take part in it, as it becomes more difficult to coordinate, communicate with all members and maintain the necessary discipline. The reason lies in the mathematics of networks. To understand the magnitude of this effect, let's look at the number of connections in a team, which is $N(N-1)/2$ (Figure 9.1):

Notice that after the low-digit numbers the equation tends towards $N^2/2$, with N representing the number of team members. The number of connections within the network grows much faster than the number of team members does. And that creates an obvious problem: human beings can only handle, or maintain, much smaller numbers of connections. In fact, the optimal size of small teams is the same as the effective range of short-term memory in our brains. Our minds seem to work best in the zone of seven, plus or minus two. On top of that, the connections are not perfect, because of the imperfection of human communication mechanisms.

Thus the ideal size of a team is around three to four people. When more people are needed, the overall efficiency of the team will decrease rapidly.

- 2 members = 1 connection
- 3 members = 3 connections
- 4 members = 6 connections
- 5 members = 10 connections
- 6 members = 15 connections
- …
- 16 members = 120 connections
- …
- 50 members = 1225 connections

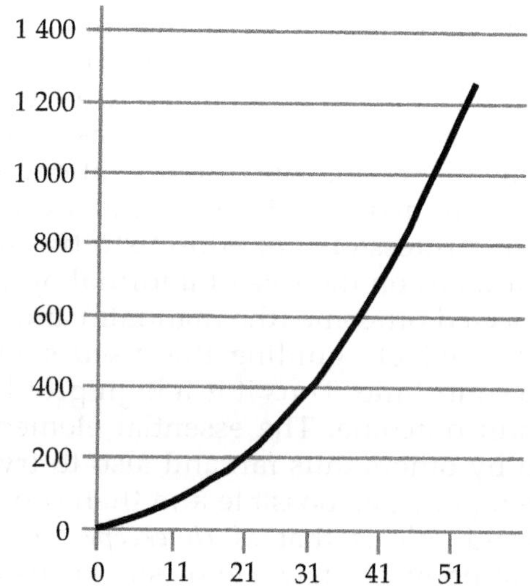

Figure 9.1

This simple observation also has far-reaching implications for the so-called *span of control* of managers and leaders. The commonly accepted definition of 'span of control' is as follows: 'the number of subordinates directly reporting to a leader or a manager.'

In hierarchical organisations of the past it was not uncommon to see average spans of 4 or even less, and the relationship was basically top-down – the manager simply telling the subordinate what to do. In fact, there were even fewer (N) connections, since the subordinates were not even supposed to communicate with each other.

In 1916, Henri Fayol[5] proposed that subordinate employees should be allowed to communicate directly with each other, but only when their superiors had agreed upon this procedure. This principle became known under the name of 'Fayol's bridge'. This can be considered as a first attempt to create a horizontal integration of related activities under a certain level of self-management.

As information technology has advanced, many organisational structures have 'flattened' and average spans have moved closer to 10, resulting in fewer middle managers having to manage more subordinates (sometimes for less money). The idea behind this is that a considerable amount of decision making can be delegated to staff at lower

5 See footnote 3.

organisational levels. This is the application of Fayol's bridge combined with the principle of employee initiative that he also proposed. In this model, supervision of staff is reduced from constant direct control to 'exception handling'; simply having access to a supervising manager is considered sufficient to satisfy the need for control in standard situations. Peter Drucker[6] referred to this principle as the *span of managerial responsibility* and underpinned the importance of self-directed, cross-functional teams.

This trend has inevitably strengthened the case for development of 'core competencies' for all staff at all levels. For a 'flatter' organisation to thrive, everybody needs to be aware and responsible – and that takes more than just professional competence in the specific technicalities of one's own tasks.

	Asynchronous[7]	**Synchronous**
Collocated[8]	• Resource sharing (printers, shared folders, DropBox) • Document Management systems	• Voting systems • Decision support
Non-collocated	• Email • News groups • Mailing lists • Web content management • Group calendars • Workflow systems • Knowledge management systems • Social media	• Chat rooms • Voice conferencing • Videoconferencing • Shared whiteboards

Table 9.1

How rituals deliver performance

All organisations have rituals – ranging from regular routines like coffee breaks, weekly team meetings and unit meetings, to major, less frequent events like annual meetings and retirement parties. It is important to understand that rituals like these are levers for improving the organisation's performance, because:

- Rituals create a shared identity
- Rituals stimulate the emotions and reduce anxiety
- Rituals reinforce desired behaviours
- Rituals bring team members' external networks into the family

Hence, as an individual, it is important to participate in your organisation's rituals, and not belittle them as a waste of time.

6 Peter Drucker (1909–2005) was an Austrian-born American management consultant, educator, and author.

7 Not occurring at the same time; the opposite of synchronous.

8 Meaning grouped together in a system or order; used in logistics.

Groupware

Whereas personal productivity tools like word processing and spreadsheets most certainly have improved each individual's information processing capabilities, they do not necessarily result in improvement in the productivity of teams as a whole. Staff can end up spending more and more time in looking for relevant information and less and less using it in a significant and productive manner.

Groupware systems typically reside on a network (private intranet or public internet). They can be typically categorised along two dimensions: time and space (Table 9.1)

Obviously, these systems have a tremendous effect on how people work together, but care has to be taken to make sure that the right tools are used for the right purpose: as we said before, 'a fool with a tool is still a fool'. Moreover, they typically impose constraints in terms of privacy and data protection, and add some significant overhead cost to streamlining the communication processes.

Personality types

'*Chassez le naturel, il revient au gallop*'[9] – French proverb

The Oxford dictionaries define personality as 'The combination of characteristics or qualities that form an individual's distinctive character' while the American Psychological Association (APA) says: 'Personality refers to individual differences in characteristic patterns of thinking, feeling and behaving.'

There are many theories on personality[10], and most are in some way based on – or related to – the work of Carl Jung[11]. There are both type and trait theories; trait personality questionnaires are useful in selection and recruitment as they can be more readily mapped to job requirements, whilst the type models are useful in personal and team development, as the type categories are helpful in understanding oneself and others.

Probably the best-known type theory is the **Myers-Briggs Personality Type Indicator (MBTI)** created by Isabel Briggs Myers and her mother, Katharine Cook Briggs. Without going into too much detail I just want to convey you that the MBTI is based on the idea that each personality type is composed of four pairs of preferences – or dichotomies (see Table 9.2):

As a result, people are 'classified' into one out of 16 'type indicators' like ISTJ or ESTP. Based on these type indicators a number of common characteristics can be described like:

> 'ISTJ - Quiet, serious, earn success by thoroughness and dependability. Practical, matter-of-fact, realistic and responsible. Decide logically what should be done and work towards it steadily, regardless of distractions. Take pleasure in making everything orderly and organised – their work, their home, their life. Value traditions and loyalty.'

(From 'Introduction to TYPE' – sixth edition)

9 As said in English: 'A leopard cannot change its spots'

10 Big Five, Enneagram, Kersey…

11 Carl Gustav Jung (1875 – 1961) was a Swiss psychiatrist and psychotherapist who founded analytical psychology.

Mussels from Brussels

This is a picture I took from my son's plate after he had enjoyed a yummy dish of Belgian mussels. What does this say about his personality?

Figure 9.2

Please note that the terms used for each dichotomy have specific technical meanings relating to the MBTI. For example, extraversion means 'outward-turning' and introversion means 'inward-turning'. These specific definitions vary somewhat from the popular usage of the words. Also, the MBTI instrument measures aptitude; it simply indicates for one preference over another. Someone reporting a high score for extraversion over introversion cannot be correctly described as *more* extraverted: they simply have a clearer . Sometimes, these 'personality types' are designated with a name, summarising in just one word the archetypical behaviour of the type.

A more detailed description can be found on the website of the Meyers and Briggs Foundation.[12]

	Subjective	**Objective**
Deductive	i**N**tuition vs **S**ensing	**P**erception vs **J**udging
Inductive	**F**eeling vs **T**hinking	**I**ntroversion vs **E**xtraversion

Table 9.2

12 http://www.myersbriggs.org/my-mbti-personality-type/mbti-basics/the-16-mbti-types.htm

It is sometimes argued that the MBTI test is unreliable because 50% of people who take the test a second time get a different result. What this really means is that most people who take the test will score near the middle on at least one dichotomy. So, on the second taking, that dichotomy could tip one way or the other over the threshold. The real problem with MBTI is not the stability issue, but that many people take the test too literally, especially when they go around classifying people and assuming that they now understand the person because they have found a category. This error is the same as assuming that all people are the same.

Many people who take the MBTI ask whether or not their psychological type can change. According to type theory, basic type preferences for perception or judgment are innate and do not change. However, it is also known that people, as a result of interacting with their environment and through life experiences, also develop behaviours, habits, and strategies that are *not* consistent with their type description.

So why is this important? For one, you may have *natural* preferences (innate tendencies) that are not fully used or have been suppressed by your education or environment. Or, you may have facets of your personality that you would like to modify so

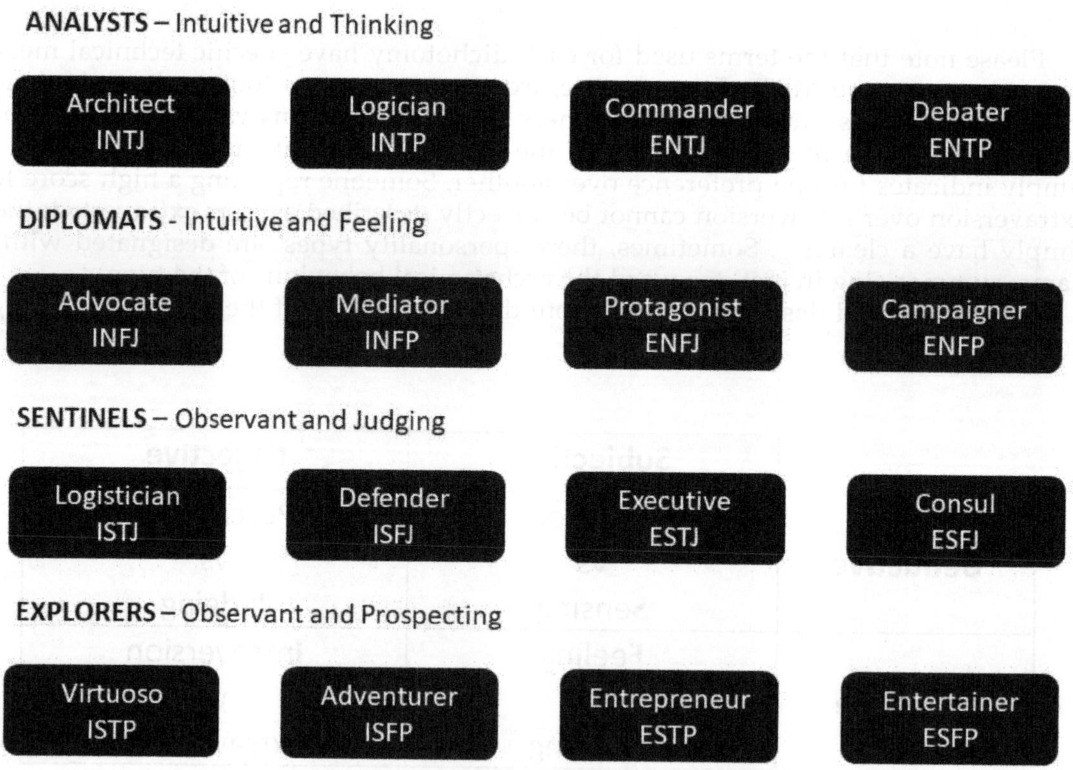

Figure 9.2

Who am I?

I am an engineer, brought up and shaped in the Cold War military environment. I started my career in the Belgian Air Force as a technical officer, responsible for an outfit of technicians dealing with the maintenance of military aircraft (Mirage V, the 'Belgian' version of the French Mirage III). When I took the MBTI for the first time the verdict was that I was an ISTJ. I invite you to read again the description of this type above (which is by the way the most frequent amongst men). In hindsight, this really corresponded to who I was, and it was a near-perfect match with the kind of person I was expected to be at that time.

In 1993, shortly after the end of the Cold War, I left the military to join a public sector organisation involved in the socio-medical field. After being an IT project manager I moved into the role of Chief Information Officer. In this role I had responsibility for all aspects relating to the IT environment supporting my employer and had to take a much more holistic view. Then, in 2000, I joined the EU administration, still in a managerial position related to IT. Around 2005 I had the opportunity to become Head of Unit for Budget and Finance and had to take management training for that. During this training I took my second MBTI test and, guess what, I had become an INTJ. INTJ's are described as 'Architects', imaginative and strategic thinkers with a plan for everything. Notice how my previous 'Sensing' preference had turned into a more 'Intuitive' one. In fact, the engineer had turned into a manager.

In 2013 I started my own business, as a coach and trainer for people who want to become EU officials. From a manager working for an employer, I had become an entrepreneur. Out of curiosity and in the context of this book, I took another MBTI test. Surprisingly, it turned out that I am an ESTJ now. ESTJ's are 'Executives', excellent administrators, skilled at managing things or people. In short, I went back to the 'Sensing' mode and switched my 'Introversion' preference to 'Extraversion', at least in my behaviour. Please note that the 'Thinking' and 'Judging' aspects of my personality have remained unchanged throughout my entire career.

How to make sense of this?

I believe that the consecutive personality types (ISTJ – INTJ – ESTJ) were – and are – pretty close to who I really was or am at these different stages of my life. I was influenced by my environment and adapted my behaviour according to what (I believed) was expected of me. In the role of an engineer I had to behave in the 'Sensing' way, while as a manager and leader I needed to rely more on my intuition. On the other hand, as an employee, I could follow my natural 'Introversion' tendency, while as an entrepreneur I have to behave in the 'Extraversion' mode. I must admit, it took me a number of years before I fully realised this necessity…

that you don't fall into the same unhelpful patterns time and again. The elegance of MBTI is that it is a dynamic system that *acknowledges and encourages* an individual to change as a part of healthy type development (even as one's basic type theoretically does not change). There is evidence that either the environment or deliberate intention can indeed bring about these changes. This is very good news indeed!

Personality tests tend to be referred to as 'questionnaires', as there are no objective 'right' or 'wrong' answers. It is more about understanding what is helpful or less helpful to achieve personal goals and aspirations. I do recommend that you take a personality questionnaire yourself. Ideally, you would have this done by a real specialist, accredited for example in the MBTI, but a good start can be to take a free online test [13]. You will be amazed about how much you will learn about yourself.

MBTI personality types are not evenly distributed throughout the population, nor are they amongst men and women. Nevertheless, it is easy to understand that the chances of having to work with people who have different personality than yours are huge. For example, in a group of six people, with each person potentially having one

13 http://www.16personalities.com/personality-types

out of 16 personality types, the number of possible combinations is 16^6, which is over 16 million!

In practical terms this means that every group of people you ever work with will be different in terms of the mix of personality types around the table. The bad news is that there is not much you can do about this; you have to work with the people that happen to be in the same group as you are. The good news, however, is that you can adapt your own behaviour in order to cope with the differences, by taking the (presumed) personality traits of the other participants into account.

I already discussed the practical tactics on how to cope with stress, based on your personality type, and I will come back on the practical application of personality type in the chapter on Leadership.

One last thing: there are no 'good' or 'bad' personality types. After all, life would be boring if we were all the same.

Working with other cultures

The world we live in is becoming more culturally diverse, and this is certainly the case when working for the EU. Nevertheless, we all carry within us patterns of thinking, feeling and acting learned throughout our lifetime. Much of this was acquired in early childhood because it is then that we are most susceptible to learning and assimilating. As soon as specific patterns of thinking, feeling and acting are established, we have to unlearn these patterns before learning something different – and unlearning is harder than learning for the first time.

The topic of cultural diversity is so important that I decided to dedicate a separate chapter to this. So, if you want to read more about this, I gladly refer you to Chapter 13.

Active listening

'Two monologues do not make a dialogue.' – Jeff Daly

A way to become a better listener is to practise *active listening*. This is where you make a conscious effort not only to hear the words that another person is saying but, more importantly, try to understand the complete message that is being sent. In order to do this you must pay attention to the other person very carefully.

There are five key elements of active listening. They all help you ensure that you hear the other person, and that the other person *knows* you are hearing what is said.

Pay attention – Give the speaker your undivided attention, and acknowledge the message by:

- Looking at the speaker directly, keeping eye contact.
- Putting aside distracting thoughts.

- Not mentally preparing a rebuttal.
- Avoiding distractions like side conversations.
- Observing the speaker's body language.

Show that you are listening – Use your own body language to convey your attention by:

- Nodding occasionally.
- Smiling and using other facial expressions (avoiding a 'poker face').
- Noting your posture and making sure it is open and inviting.
- Encouraging the speaker to continue with small verbal comments like 'yes', and 'hmm'.

Provide feedback – Our personal filters, assumptions, judgements, and beliefs can distort what we hear. As a listener, your role is to understand what is being said. This may require you to reflect what is being said by:

- Paraphrasing: 'What I'm hearing is …' and 'Sounds like you are saying …'
- Asking questions to clarify certain points: 'What do you mean when you say …?'
- Summarising the speaker's comments periodically.

Defer judgement – Interrupting is a waste of time. It frustrates the speaker and limits full understanding of the message:

- Allow the speaker to finish each point before asking questions.
- Don't interrupt with counter arguments.

Respond appropriately – Active listening is a model for respect and understanding. You are gaining information and perspective. You add nothing by attacking the speaker or otherwise putting him or her down:

- Be candid, open, and honest in your response.
- Assert your opinions respectfully.
- Treat the other person in a way that you think he or she would want to be treated.

It is a luxury to be really listened to, to be truly heard. Active listening will support your colleagues both personally and professionally, and you will improve your own productivity.

Empathy and sympathy

Empathy is the experience of understanding another person's condition from their perspective. You place yourself in their shoes and feel what they are feeling. The word 'empathy' was brought into use in 1909 by British psychologist Edward B. Titchener.

While the word's spelling borrows from an ancient Greek word, *empátheia*, which meant 'passion,' Titchener used 'empathy' for the purpose of translating a German word (*einfühlungsvermögen*) and its concept of shared feeling.

Empathy is not to be confused with *sympathy*. When you sympathise with someone, you have compassion for that person, but you don't necessarily share their feelings. Sympathy has broader applications that don't necessarily have to do with one person's feelings for another. You can sympathise with a cause, for instance, or with a point of view that resonates with you. The word 'sympathy' comes from the ancient Greek *sunpathos*, meaning 'with/together' and 'suffering.'

The capacity to sympathise and empathise is considered vital for a sense of humanity – the ability to understand one's fellow humans and their problems. People who lack this capacity are often classified as narcissistic, sociopathic, or in extreme cases, psychopathic. However, these terms are only applicable if a person consistently lacks the capacity to sympathise or empathise with others.

In general, there are many cases where people may not feel sympathetic or empathetic due to lack of knowledge or because their experiences are different; this does not imply abnormal behaviour. On the other hand, some people are overly empathetic and can eventually be overwhelmed by the negative feelings they take on from their relationships and encounters with other people.

To start using empathy – and sympathy – more effectively when working with others consider the following:

- *Examine your own attitude.* Are you more concerned with getting your way, winning, or being right? Or, is your priority to find a solution, build relationships, and accept others as they are?
- *Try to see things from the other person's point of view.* You will probably realise that they are not in fact stupid, evil, unkind, stubborn, or unreasonable; they are most likely just reacting based on the knowledge and understanding they have.
- *Acknowledge the other person's perspective.* Acknowledgement does not always equal agreement. You can 'agree to disagree'.
- *Practise active listening.*

I would also advise you to have a look at the TED talk[14] on empathy given by Daniel Goleman[15].

Preparing for a meeting

'Knowing is not enough; we must apply. Willing is not enough; we must do.' – Goethe

Meetings are critical for team development and task management. However, meetings can easily fail without adequate preparation and leadership. A large part of what

14 http://www.ted.com/talks/daniel_goleman_on_compassion?language=en

15 Daniel Goleman (1946) is an author, psychologist, and science journalist specialising in emotional intelligence.

makes a meeting successful occurs in the preparation phase. Although it may vary by committee, department or unit, there are seven key responsibilities expected of chairs or moderators before a meeting takes place:

- *Clarify purpose and aims.* The purpose of a meeting should be stated at the top of the meeting agenda. A weekly or monthly staff meeting may not require meeting aims beyond the agenda items.
- *Create an agenda.* An agenda is a structure that guides and supports the meeting. An agenda helps focus the group's work on achieving desired outcomes. Good agenda items provide focus and structure for a meeting.
- *Schedule the meeting properly.* Scheduling a meeting involves much more than just making a list of attendees. It requires identifying key people who ideally must attend and either finding times that work for them or at the very least notifying them as far in advance as possible of when the meeting will take place. Once an optimal date and time are decided on, a meeting location can be selected. Sometimes, of course, the choice of meeting location dictates the time of the meeting and how long it can go on for – and you certainly don't want to find you have to leave a meeting room before your business is finished just because someone else has booked it.
- *Post and send out the agenda.* An agenda should be sent to participants ahead of time to help them prepare to participate. Don't leave this to the last minute or you will simply irritate people.
- *Circulate supporting information.* You should always circulate supporting documentation to participants in advance of the meeting. However, deciding how much documentation to send out can present a problem. Some people won't want to look at anything prior to the meeting and some will conscientiously read everything they receive. Focus therefore on the documentation that it is *essential* people study in advance, and make it clear that that is what you are sending them.
- *Make room arrangements.* Ensure that the meeting room is set up properly. Apparently trivial details (are there enough chairs? Are there drinks, and if so enough cups/glasses?) can certainly influence people's perceptions of how professionally run a meeting is and hence of your authority in steering it. Most importantly, make sure that all participants are going to be able to see and hear each other properly.
- *Arrange for a secretary.* The secretary of the meeting takes notes on paper, laptop or on flip charts. Meeting notes should be distributed as soon after the meeting as possible. The longer the delay, the less confidence the members will have that their contribution will result in action. For groups that meet regularly, the secretary is responsible for keeping previous meeting notes and agendas in one place where they can be referenced later such as from a notebook or shared network drive, etc.

Group negotiation

Virtually all groups work under some type of constraint. The constraint may be time, it may be resources, it may be regulatory/compliance factors, or it may be technical limitations. These constraints lead to the necessity to balance conflicting demands. This then leads to the need for effective negotiations between the group members in order to optimise the project and group performance (Figure 9.3).

The **Thomas-Kilmann Conflict Mode Instrument**[16] (TKI) provides a suggested negotiation strategy for different conflict contexts. Based upon the desire to retain the relationship between team members and need to achieve a solution, different negotiation strategies are suggested.

Obviously, collaborative approaches are often desired but, unfortunately, some of those you have to deal with may see themselves as opponents and will attempt to 'win' at all costs. It is therefore a good idea to be aware of the following negotiating strategies, so you understand what is really going on:

- *Fait accompli strategy.* One side does whatever it wants and expects the other side to accept the terms and the outcome without further ado.
- *Standard practice strategy.* The claim is that what is being suggested is acceptable because it is 'standard practice'. If you are negotiating in an area that is unfamiliar to you, make sure you research any 'standard practice' claims before agreeing to them.
- *Deadline strategy.* If the other side knows your deadline, they may delay giving you a draft (and possibly throw in a few very late changes) until the last minute to gain the advantage. The closer you are to your deadline the more concessions you're likely to make.
- *Decoy strategy.* This strategy involves inflating the importance of a minor issue to mask the importance of a larger issue or a hidden agenda. If the other side concedes what they have made you believe is a major issue, but what is for them a minor one, they will then expect you to concede on one of your truly important issues.
- *Faking withdrawal strategy.* Faking an intention to withdraw from a prospective deal is another strategy to be wary of. Its purpose is to gain a concession, usually a significant one, by pretending to be unconcerned about whether the deal happens or not.
- *Limited authority strategy.* This strategy involves the other side trying to avoid making concessions by claiming they don't have the authority to make concessions on their own.
- *Salami strategy.* The salami technique is used to gain concessions piece by piece. The basic premise is this: instead of trying to grab the whole salami, cut off thin slices over time.

16 http://www.kilmanndiagnostics.com/overview-thomas-kilmann-conflict-mode-instrument-tki

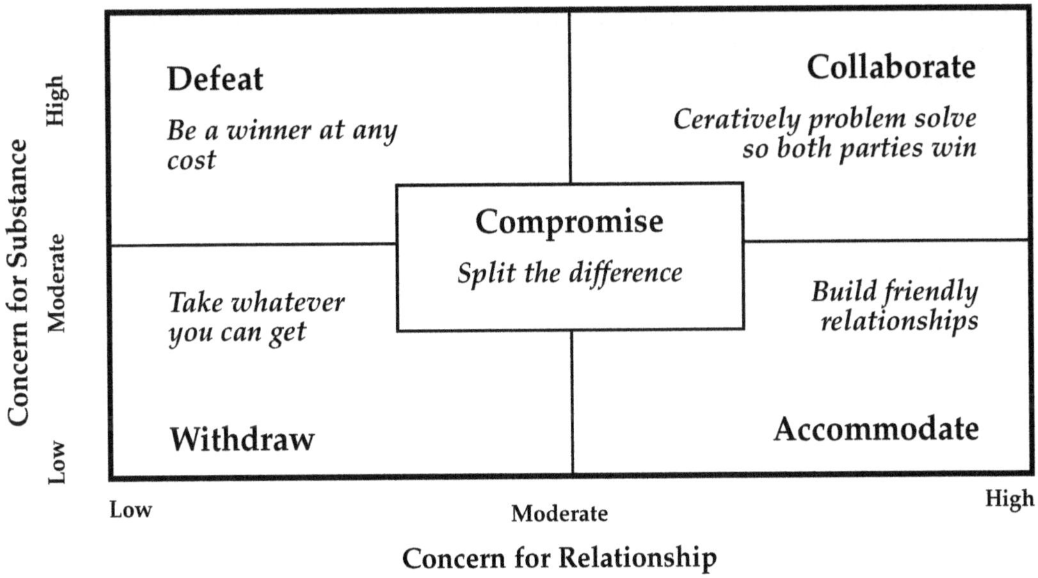

Figure 9.3

Conflict resolution

I think it is time to introduce at this point the **Goals, Roles, Processes** and **Interpersonal Relationships** (GRPI) model that was first presented by Richard Beckhard[17] in 1972. Goals, Roles, Processes and Interpersonal Relationships are four critical and interrelated aspects of teamwork. The GRPI is a four-step project-planning tool to help team leaders ensure productivity, efficiency and quality:

G – Goals: the goals of the project are agreed to by the team.

R – Roles: the roles and responsibilities of each team member are determined.

P – Processes: the actual project processes or activities are defined, estimated, and planned.

I – Interpersonal: as the project unfolds, everyone begins to work together and the interpersonal relationships are established and strengthened.

For *conflict resolution*, this model can be used in reverse order. If conflict arises in the team, you should first see if there is any interpersonal issue involved and, if there is, work on resolving that. However, you should always check the next higher level to see if the problem goes deeper into the project. Moving up a level, you need to see if there is a difference of opinion as to what the team should be doing, and how it should be

17 Richard Beckhard (1928–1999) was an American academic and pioneer in the field of organisation development.

done. If that is the problem, then resolve that issue and usually the interpersonal relationships will be re-established.

If there are *process* problems look further up to see if there are problems with the assignment of roles and responsibilities. Once those are resolved, the responsible person can then make decisions about the processes, and the interpersonal relationships will be re-established. If there are problems with the roles, check to ensure that the team is aligned to the project goals. If there is misalignment on goals, that must be resolved before you can even begin to create and execute a viable plan. Often if the issue is goal alignment, the stakeholders must be brought in to align the team members on the project objectives.

Assertiveness

Assertiveness is an attitude and a way of relating to the outside world, backed up by a set of abilities. You need to see yourself as being valuable, and this goes hand in hand with you valuing others equally, respecting their right to an opinion. Many people find it difficult to communicate honestly, directly and openly with other people. It is sometimes said about assertive behaviour that it involves being aggressive. It doesn't! Assertiveness involves clear, calm thinking and respectful negotiation where each person is entitled to their opinion. Assertiveness, properly understood and applied, ensures that you – and other people – are not hurt, used or abused.

There are only two alternatives to being assertive: being passive or being aggressive. Passive modes of communication are in reality an attempt to punish or undermine the other person: playing games, being sarcastic, or remaining silent all together. Aggression involves bottling up feelings that eventually explode, leaving no room for communication.

Assertiveness includes:

- Being clear about what you feel, what you need and how it can be achieved.
- Being able to communicate calmly without attacking another person.
- Being able to say 'no', rather than agreeing to do something just to please someone else.
- Being happy to defend your position, even if it provokes conflict.
- Being confident about handling conflict if it occurs.
- Understanding how to negotiate if two people want different outcomes.
- Being able to talk openly about yourself and being able to listen to others.
- Having confident, open body language.
- Being able to give and receive positive and negative feedback.
- Having a positive, optimistic outlook.

The nice guy syndrome

'Nice Guys have a difficult time comprehending that in general, people are not drawn to perfection in others. People are drawn to shared interests, shared problems, and an individual's life energy.' – Robert Glover

The 'nice guy syndrome' refers to a behavioural pattern of being overly nice to others. A leading authority on this topic is Dr Robert Glover, a therapist who specialises in working with men with the nice guy syndrome, and author of the best-selling self-help book for men 'No More Mr Nice Guy'[18]. According to Dr Glover, all nice guys operate on the same basic paradigm: 'If I can hide my flaws and become what I think others want me to be then I will be loved, get my needs met, and have a problem-free life.'

A nice guy's primary goal is to make other people happy. Nice guys are dependent on external validation and avoid conflict at any cost. According to Glover, nice guys are guided by the following three 'covert contracts':

- If I am a good guy, then everyone will love me and like me (and people I desire will desire me).
- If I meet other people's needs without them having to ask, then they will meet my needs without me having to ask.
- If I do everything right, then I will have a smooth, problem-free life.

These covert contracts operate at an unconscious level. They don't work for a number of reasons, but nice guys are convinced they should.

As a result of this syndrome, nice guys have mediocre careers compared with how skilled they are, no matter how hard they work, and they sabotage almost every aspect of their lives:

- They appear needy and insecure.
- They are generic and predictable.
- They end up ignoring their own needs and not taking care of themselves.
- They end up not being there for the people who really matter, because they try to please everybody.
- They are full of repressed rage and they tend to detonate at the most inappropriate times.
- They lie, hide and they try to get what they want in indirect, manipulative ways.

In conclusion: being a 'nice guy' is not a healthy or productive way of being; the concept is flawed.

Even after you realise that being a nice guy does not work, your automatic thinking will still be influenced and disempower you. You will need to consciously change your thinking and change your behaviour. Specific actions may include:

18 'No More Mr Nice Guy' (2003) by Robert Glover.

- Express yourself more, even when you may upset someone.
- Ask for what you really want and say 'no' to others.
- Take more time for yourself and take care of your own needs.
- End toxic relationships that go nowhere.

The earlier you start, the faster you will enjoy the benefits of no longer being too much of a 'nice guy'!

Parliamentary procedure

'Robert's Rules of Order'[19] is the short title of a book, originally written by United States Brig. Gen. Henry Martyn Robert in the 1870s and revised at intervals ever since, containing rules of order intended to be adopted for use by a deliberative assembly. The procedures prescribed by the book were loosely modelled on those used in the United States House of Representatives, with such adaptations as Robert saw fit for use in other assemblies.

According to Robert's Rules of Order, *parliamentary procedure* is based on the consideration of the rights of the majority, of the minority (especially a large minority greater than one-third), of individual members, of absentee members, or all of these groups taken together. It provides common rules and procedures for deliberation and debate in order to place the whole membership on the same footing and speaking the same language. The book states:

> 'The application of parliamentary law is the best method yet devised to enable assemblies of any size, with due regard for every member's opinion, to arrive at the general will on the maximum number of questions of varying complexity in a minimum amount of time and under all kinds of internal climate ranging from total harmony to hardened or impassioned division of opinion.' (*Robert's Rules of Order Newly Revised,* 11th edition: Introduction, p. liii)

In the EU, obviously, parliamentary procedure – or variants – is used throughout all the 'official' meetings that take place in the various institutions and agencies, but it is also applied in many 'internal' meetings across the board. So, if you haven't yet done so at this point in your career, it's a good idea to get acquainted with the ideas and rules governing this kind of meeting.

Brainstorming

Brainstorming is a group creativity technique by which efforts are made to achieve a solution to a specific problem by gathering a list of ideas spontaneously contributed by its members. Alex F. Osborn popularised the term in his book 'Applied Imagination'[20].

19 http://www.robertsrules.com/

20 'Applied Imagination: Principles and Procedures Creative Problem Solving' (1953) by Alex F. Osborn.

Brainstorming provides a free and open environment that encourages everyone to participate. Original ideas are welcomed and built upon, and all participants are encouraged to contribute fully, helping them develop a rich collection of creative solutions.

When used during problem solving, brainstorming brings team members' diverse experience and backgrounds into play. It increases the richness of ideas investigated, which means that you can often find better solutions to the problems that you face. It can also help you get buy-in from team members for the solution chosen – after all, they are likely to be more enthusiastic about an approach if they were involved in developing it. What's more, because brainstorming is amusing, it helps team members bond, as they solve problems in a positive, rewarding environment.

Brainstorming is popular for two reasons, one good and one bad. The good reason is that a typical brainstorming session brings people together in the creative process, and increases the social nature of the project. If the meeting is run properly, everybody feels as though they are contributing to what they will be working on in the future. More importantly, it gets people thinking and communicating with each other about topics relevant to their work.

The bad reason that brainstorming is popular is that it is an easy way for bad managers to pretend that the team is involved in the direction of the project. A team leader can be convinced that he or she knows how to cultivate and work with ideas that are not their own simply by holding a meeting.

The most important thing about a brainstorming session is what happens after it ends, because some good ideas will surface, no matter how poorly you run a brainstorming meeting. But depending on what happens after the session, those ideas may or may not impact anything.

While brainstorming can be effective, it's important to approach it with an open mind and a non-judgmental attitude. If you don't do this, people are likely to clam up and the number and quality of ideas, and morale, will suffer as a consequence.

Gamestorming

Humans are hardwired to play games. We play them for fun. We play them in our social interactions. We also play them at work, but that last one is tricky; playing games and work don't seem like a natural pairing.

The authors of 'Gamestorming'[21] have a different perspective. They contend that embracing and understanding game mechanics can generate multiple benefits in many work environments, particularly those where old hierarchical models are no longer applicable, like the creatively driven knowledge work of today's cutting edge industries.

- Overcome conflict and increase engagement with team-oriented games.
- Improve collaboration and communication in cross-disciplinary teams with visual-thinking techniques.
- Improve understanding by role-playing customer and user experiences.
- Generate better ideas and more of them, faster than ever before.

21 'Gamestorming: A Playbook for Innovators, Rulebreakers, and Changemakers' (2010) by Dave Gray, Sunny Brown and James Macanufo.

- Shorten meetings and make them more productive.
- Simulate and explore complex systems, interactions, and dynamics.
- Identify a problem's root cause, and find the paths that point toward a solution.

Visual meetings

When people work visually they have better ideas, make better decisions, and are more committed to producing results. Author David Sibbet in his book 'Visual Meetings'[22] provides many ideas to unlock creativity, collaboration, and breakthrough thinking:

- Use graphic recording, visual planning, storyboarding, idea mapping, and similar techniques.
- Give better presentations without resorting to PowerPoint.
- Consult and sell ideas with graphics and visualisation tools.
- Get beyond paper and whiteboards to tablets, iPads, and other new media platforms.
- Make all meetings more interesting and productive.
- Improve both face-to-face and virtual group work.

Six Thinking Hats

'Six Thinking Hats'[23] is a bestselling book by Edward de Bono that provides a tool for group discussion and individual thinking involving six coloured hats.

Team members learn how to separate thinking into six clear functions and roles. Each thinking role is identified with a symbolic 'thinking hat' and team members can adopt in turn the roles and thought patterns associated with each hat.

- The 'White Hat' calls for information known or needed: 'the facts, just the facts.'
- The 'Yellow Hat' symbolises brightness and optimism. Under this hat you explore the positives and probe for value and benefit.
- The 'Black Hat' is judgement – the devil's advocate, or why something may not work.
- The 'Red Hat' signifies feelings, hunches and intuition. When using this hat you can express emotions and feelings and share likes, dislikes, loves, and hates.
- The 'Green Hat' focuses on creativity: the possibilities, alternatives, and new ideas.

22 'Visual meetings: How Graphics, Sticky Notes & idea mapping can transform group productivity' (2010) by David Sibbet.

23 'Six Thinking Hats' (1985) by Edward de Bono.

- The 'Blue Hat' is used to manage the thinking process. It is the control mechanism that ensures the Six Thinking Hats guidelines are observed.

Networking

Networking is about making connections and building enduring, mutually beneficial relationships. The word 'work' is part of networking, and it is not easy work, because it involves reaching outside the borders of your comfort zone.

There are basically three forms of networking: *operational, personal* and *strategic*.

The purpose of *operational networking* is getting work done efficiently, or – in other words – building and maintaining the capacities and functions required of the groups you are part of. Your contacts are mostly internal and orientated towards your current activities. Key contacts are prescribed mostly by your tasks and the organisational structure, so it is relatively clear who is relevant. Operational networks include not only direct reports and superiors but also peers within an operational unit, other internal players with the power to block or support a project, and key outsiders such as suppliers and clients. Operational networking focuses on depth: building strong relationships.

As you move into a leadership role, your network must reorient itself externally and toward the future. In *personal networking*, enhancing personal and professional development is key; providing referrals to useful information and contacts. Contacts are mostly external and orientated towards current interests and future potential interests; this means that it is not always clear who is relevant. According to the famous *six degrees of separation principle*[24], our personal contacts are valuable to the extent that they help us reach, in as few connections as possible, the distant person who has the information we need. Personal networking focuses on breadth: reaching out to contacts that can make referrals.

Finally, for *strategic networking* the purpose is figuring out future priorities and challenges. Contacts are both internal and external and orientated towards the future. Having lateral and vertical relationships with other people outside your immediate control becomes a lifeline for figuring out how your own contributions fit into the big picture. What distinguishes a leader from a manager is the ability to figure out where to go and to enlist the people and groups necessary to get there. As they step up to the leadership transition, some managers accept their growing dependence on others and seek to transform it into mutual influence. Others dismiss such work as 'political' and, as a result, undermine their ability to advance their goals.

Building a network is less a matter of skill than of will. When first efforts do not bring quick rewards, some may simply conclude that networking isn't among their talents. But networking is not a talent; nor does it require an expansive, extroverted personality. It is a skill, one that takes practice.

24 'Six degrees of separation' is the theory that everyone and everything is six or fewer steps away, from any other

Figure 9.4

'Wikinomics'

'Throughout history corporations have organised themselves according to strict hierarchical lines of authority. Everyone was a subordinate to someone else—employees versus managers, marketers versus customers, producers versus supply chain subcontractors, companies versus the community.

There was always someone or some company in charge, controlling things, at the 'top' of the food chain. While hierarchies are not vanishing, profound changes in the nature of technology, demographics, and the global economy are giving rise to powerful new models of production based on community, collaboration, and self-organisation rather than on management and control ....

Smart companies are encouraging, rather than fighting, the heaving growth of massive online communities—many of which emerged from the fringes of the Web to attract tens of millions of participants overnight. Even ardent competitors are collaborating on path-breaking science initiatives that accelerate discovery in their industries. Indeed, as a growing number of firms see the benefits of mass collaboration, this new of way organising will eventually displace the traditional corporate structures as the economy's primary engine of wealth creation.'

(From: 'Wikinomics – How Mass Collaboration Changes Everything.'[25])

Developing your working with others skills

Making others feel important requires that you appreciate the people around you and remind them of their positive qualities. It conveys the notion that you notice their talents and abilities. It will boost their self-esteem and increase their sense of self-worth.

When people feel appreciated, they are more likely to be happier and more productive. This creates a pleasant environment that is more conductive to relationships

25 'Wikinomics: How Mass Collaboration Changes Everything' (2010) by Don Tapscott and Anthony D. Williams. person in the world.

where people enjoy working with each other and are more positive. People inherently want to know that they are valued. If you work on making them feel appreciated you will be validating your relationship with them.

Please refer to Annex 1 for further development of this competency, or check out the easy-to-use app at:

http://www.johnharperpublishing.co.uk/the-ultimate-eu-career-development-toolkit/

10. Leadership

Competency definition: 'Manage, develop and motivate people to achieve results.'

'A leader is a dealer in hope.' – Napoleon Bonaparte

The EPSO definition of leadership indicates that the EU institutions seek two – distinct but concurrent – capacities: people who are both potentially good 'managers' and also potentially good 'leaders'. Management consists of controlling a group or a set of entities to accomplish a goal. Leadership refers to an individual's ability to influence, motivate, and enable others to contribute toward organisational success. Influence and inspiration distinguish leaders from managers, not power and control. I will expand on this distinction further on in this chapter.

In EPSO competitions the leadership competency is only assessed in the case of candidates in Administrator-level (AD) competitions; Assistant-level (AST) candidates are not assessed on this competency.

How can the assessment of leadership be considered relevant to AD competitions across-the-board, given the fact that for some of the biggest competitions no previous (management) experience of any kind is required? The reason is that EPSO selects candidates to be eligible for life-long employment at the EU. Even inexperienced recruits will eventually be promoted to a position where they will have to apply their leadership competency, so it is important that people have at least a basic understanding and the proper attitude towards leadership and management, as they will need it throughout their career. ASTs subsequently seeking to become ADs will have to go through 'certification' training, during which their leadership competency will be further developed.

Established administrators who are called for the duties of Head of Unit have to take the Management Training Program[1] (MTP) in the European School of Administration (EUSA), where their leadership competency will be sharpened. External applicants for middle management positions in the EU are extensively assessed by EPSO in this particular competency.

Leadership versus management

'I have a dream.' – Martin Luther King Jr.

Leaders lead people. Managers manage tasks. There is a difference.

Managers have subordinates; they have a position of authority vested in them by the organisation. Management is transactional; it operates within the framework of a fixed set of rules. The manager tells the subordinate what to do, and the subordinate does this because they have been promised a reward (a salary, a promotion…) for doing so.

1 EUSA's objective is to provide a range of learning and development opportunities that contribute to an improvement in the performance of staff who exercise or who may exercise management responsibilities, thereby helping them and their institution achieve greater effectiveness.

Managers are paid to get things done (they are subordinates too), often within tight constraints of time, resources and results. Managers are relatively risk-averse and they will seek to avoid conflict wherever possible.

Leaders have followers, not just subordinates. Many leaders do also have subordinates, but only because they are also managers. However, when they want to lead they have to give up their formal authority because following (or being led) is a voluntary activity. This does not mean that leaders do not pay attention to tasks – in fact they are often very achievement-focused. What they do realise, however, is the importance of inspiring others to work towards their vision, or the vision of the institution.

Leaders are also relatively risk-seeking. They consider it natural to encounter problems and hurdles that must be overcome along the way. They are thus comfortable with risk and will seek routes that others avoid, seeing them as opening up potential opportunities for advantage, and will happily break rules in order to get things done. (Up to a point! Leaders have to set a good example as well, and sometimes that means very visibly obeying certain rules – such as presence during core time, seeking or passing on information correctly and at the appropriate time, etc. Some rules can be happily broken – others come at a cost).

According to John Kotter[2] management is a set of practices: planning, budgeting, staffing, controlling, problem-solving. Management makes a system function the way it was designed to function while leadership is about creating a vision and motivating people to buy into it.

	MANAGER	LEADER
Role	Transactional	Transformational
Vision	Short-term	Long-term
Values	Results	Achievements
Approach	Plans around constraints	Sets direction
Concerns	Do things right	Do the right things
Appeals	The Head	The Heart
Decisions	Makes	Facilitates
Control	Formal	Informal
Culture	Endorses	Shapes
Actions	Directs	Inspires
Risks	Minimises	Embraces
Rules	Makes	Breaks
Direction	Status quo	Challenges
Focus	Managing work	Leading people
Collaborators	Subordinates	Followers

Table 10.1: Managers and leaders compared

2 John Kotter (1947), best-selling US author and management consultant who taught at the Harvard Business School.

John and Pierre: a manager and a leader

Imagine that John is the manager of a McDonalds franchise and Pierre is the chef of a fine, French cuisine restaurant. John has to make sure that his restaurant is properly operated and complies with all McDonalds' standards, policies and strategies. John cannot choose the style of the decoration, the way food is prepared, the ingredients or even the way he hires and manages staff as everything is dictated by McDonalds. McDonalds wants to give the same experience to all its customers, worldwide. *John is a manager.*

Pierre, on the other hand, has a dream. Pierre wants to create a unique and superb customer experience. He wants to distinguish his restaurant from the crowd. His dream is to gain a Michelin Star – or even two – and he does whatever it takes to obtain this award, and to keep it for years thereafter. Besides being an excellent cook and manager Pierre has to inspire his co-workers to follow his dream. *Pierre is a leader.*

Contrasting the qualities of leaders 'versus' managers of course involves something of a paradox, given that many people have to be both. Managers still can have the responsibility for leading their team into new challenges while making sure systems and procedures operate properly. Likewise even the most out-front leaders must make sure that the systems and procedures are in place to deliver on their vision – a general who leads his troops from the front is ill-advised to forget his supply lines.

In his book 'Too Many Bosses, Too Few Leaders'[3] Rajeev Peshawaria presents the underlying dynamics of what it takes to be a great leader; it is less a 'how to' and more a 'why' exploration of what leadership is about. Leadership is a special talent that goes far beyond just being a boss, and he shows that deciding to develop that talent is a critical choice. According to Peshawaria, it is clear that *trust* is one of the keys to organisational or group performance; he therefore calls trust *the currency of leadership.*

The competency of leadership is, in fact, the combination of all the other core competencies, and then some (Figure 10.1).

An effective leader combines all the other competencies in such a way that result is greater than the sum of the constituting parts.

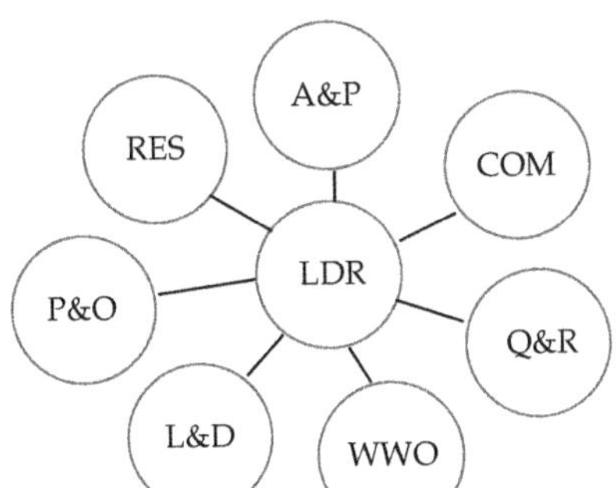

Figure 10.1

3 'Too Many Bosses, Too Few Leaders' (2012) by Rajeev Peshawaria.

Leadership styles

There are as many ways to lead people, as there are leaders.

Leaders typically have a dominant style, one they use in a wide variety of situations. However, there is no one 'best' style – leaders must adapt their style to the people being led and to the situation at hand. This is a key point. As a leader, you sometimes have to be autocratic (with some people) while 'laissez-faire' with others. Much depends on the level of independence of the individual concerned – some need a lot more hand-holding than others. It's a delicate balancing act, and one that we don't always get right. The important thing is that you shouldn't beat yourself up about getting it wrong occasionally, but just learn from the mistake.

Fortunately, a number of useful frameworks that describe the main ways that people lead have been developed. When you understand these frameworks, you can develop your own approach to leadership, and become a more effective leader as a result.

Lewin's leadership styles

Psychologist Kurt Lewin[4] developed his 'leadership styles' framework in the 1930s, and it provided the foundation of many of the approaches that followed afterwards. He argued that there are three major leadership styles:

- *Autocratic* – Also known as *authoritarian* leadership style. These leaders provide clear expectations for what needs to be done, when it should be done, and how it should be done. This style of leadership is strongly focused on both command by the leader and control of the followers. There is also a clear division between the leader and the followers. Autocratic leaders make decisions independently, with little or no input from the rest of the group. This can be appropriate when you need to make decisions quickly, when there's no need for team input, and when team agreement isn't necessary for a successful outcome. However, this style can be demoralising, and it can lead to high levels of absenteeism and staff turnover.
- *Democratic* – Also known as *participative* leadership style. These leaders make the final decisions, but include team members in the decision-making process. Democratic leaders offer guidance to group members, but they also participate in the group and allow input from other group members. As a result, team members tend to have high job satisfaction and high productivity. This is not always an effective style to use, though, when you need to make a quick decision.
- *Laissez-faire* – Also known as *delegative* leadership. Leaders give their team members a lot of freedom in how they do their work, and how they set

4 Kurt Zadek Lewin (1890–1947) was a German-American psychologist, known as one of the modern pioneers of social, organisational, and applied psychology in the United States.

their deadlines. They provide support with resources and advice if needed, but otherwise they don't get involved. This autonomy can lead to high job satisfaction, but it can be detrimental if team members don't manage their time well, or if they don't have the knowledge, skills, or self-motivation to do their work effectively.

The Blake-Mouton managerial grid

A popular framework for thinking about leadership was developed by Robert Blake and Jane Mouton[5]. They look at a leader or manager in two dimensions:

- *Concern for people* – This is the degree to which a leader considers the needs of team members, their interests, and areas of personal development when deciding how best to accomplish a task.
- *Concern for production* – This is the degree to which a leader emphasises concrete objectives, organisational efficiency and high productivity when deciding how best to accomplish a task.

Blake and Mouton defined the following five leadership or management styles, as in Figure 10.2.

- *Country Club* – This style of manager is most concerned about the needs and feelings of the members of their team. They operate on the assumption

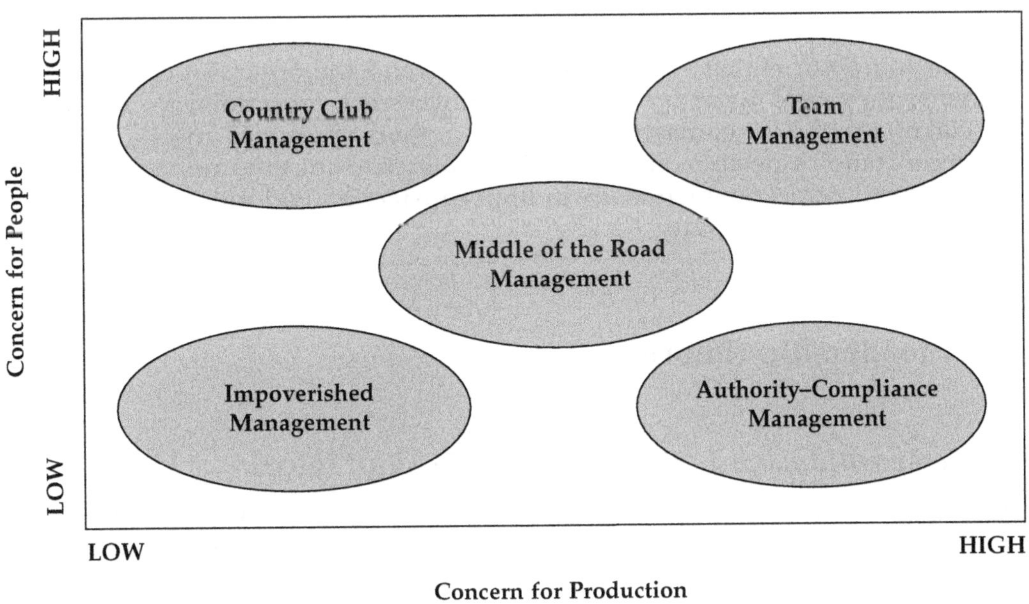

Figure 10.2

5 'The Managerial Grid III: The Key to Leadership Excellence' (1985) by Robert Blake and Jane Mouton.

that as long as team members are happy and secure then they will work hard. What tends to result is a work environment that is very relaxed and fun but where productivity suffers due to lack of direction and control.

- *Authority-Compliance* – Managers in this category believe that employees are simply a means to an end. Employee needs are always secondary to the need for efficient workplaces delivering maximum output. This type of manager is very autocratic, has strict work rules, policies, and procedures, and views punishment as the most effective means to motivate staff.
- *Impoverished* – This type of manager is mostly ineffective, failing to lead or manage at all. They have neither a high regard for creating systems for getting the job done, nor for creating a work environment that is satisfying and motivating. The result is a place of disorganisation, dissatisfaction and disharmony.
- *Middle-of-the-Road* – This style sits somewhere between the 'country club' and the 'authority-compliance' types. It may at first sight appear to be an ideal compromise. However, when you compromise, you can easily end up losing the more positive aspects of the other two styles and keeping only their disadvantages. Managers who adopt the middle-of-the-road style often settle for middle-of-the road results, too, and persuade themselves that this is the most anyone can expect.
- *Team* – According to the Blake-Mouton model, this is the summit of managerial style. These leaders give equal emphasis to the organisation's need for productivity and the needs of the people working for it. Their starting point is that staff need to understand the organisation's goals and what they need to deliver. When employees are committed to, and have a stake in the organisation's success, their personal needs and the organisation's needs coincide. This creates a team environment based on trust and respect, which leads to high satisfaction and motivation and, as a result, high productivity.

Other leadership theories

The Hersey-Blanchard 'situational leadership' theory

The Hersey-Blanchard[6] 'situational leadership' theory, or model, says that you need to use different leadership styles depending on the maturity of your team members, and defines a range of leadership styles and maturity levels. The model argues that with relatively immature individuals, you need a more directing approach, while with more mature people, you need a more participative or delegating leadership style. It has been developed in line with research over the decades since first put forward.

6 'The Management of Organizational Behavior' by Paul Hersey and Ken Blanchard was first published in 1969.

Six emotional leadership styles

Goleman, Boyatzis and McKee detailed their 'six emotional leadership styles' theory in their 2002 book, 'Primal Leadership.'[7] The theory explains the strengths and weaknesses of six leadership styles that you can use – Visionary, Coaching, Affiliative, Democratic, Pacesetting, and Commanding. It also shows how each style can affect the emotions of your team members.

Flamholtz and Randle's leadership style matrix

Flamholtz and Randle's 'leadership style matrix' aims to show the best leadership style to use, based on how capable people are of working autonomously, and how creative or 'programmable' the task is.

The matrix is divided into four quadrants – each quadrant identifies two possible leadership styles that will be effective for a given situation, ranging from 'autocratic/benevolent autocratic' to 'consensus/laissez-faire.' For instance, a person with a high level of education, skill, motivation and independence is likely to want autonomy. Someone with low motivation and skill will need – and may want – more feedback and interaction, so that he or she can complete the task successfully.

You will always find some people in the 'wrong job' who may be highly educated and skilled but are demotivated by doing a job they don't want to do or that is way below their competence levels. This, unfortunately, has become more common in the EU institutions as a result of a European Court of Justice (CoJ) ruling requiring competitions to be opened up to individuals who are vastly overqualified for the jobs involved. Many AST staff are perfect examples of this, with jobs being held by PhD holders who are more qualified than even their Directors. The result has been highly counterproductive in my view. It has also meant there are fewer job opportunities for those who need them most – the less skilled and those with just a secondary education. The CoJ judgment may have been (on the surface) an attempt at fairness in that it sought equality of input and of treatment, but it significantly failed to consider equality of outcome.

The pacesetter

Once, one of the worst members of my team was a 'pacesetter'. She had extremely high performance standards for others (which, rather ironically, she didn't achieve herself and had a blind spot about it when that was pointed out). She bad-mouthed those she considered poor performers without having access to the overall picture (which I did) and, as a result, she 'poisoned the atmosphere' as a colleague put it. I had to step in – not very successfully, unfortunately. She reacted very badly and really could not understand why I was unhappy with her behaviour. It was always everyone else's fault ...

7 'Primal Leadership' (revised edition published 2013) by Daniel Goleman et al.

Personality type and leadership

The concepts of personality type and the Myers-Briggs Personality Type Indicator (MBTI) were introduced in Chapter 9. The MBTI is based on the idea that there are basic human differences in ways of perceiving and processing information. These differences inevitably show up in the working environment.

These differences in personality type can be the root cause of many interpersonal conflicts.

People who are extravert may find that introverts are hard to read, and may even go so far as to judge them as indifferent, hard-hearted, and even arrogant. Introverts may unfairly judge extraverts as being superficial, unreliable, and dishonest.

Referring back to the MBTI classification shown in Figure 2.1 in Chapter 9, a person who values data and focuses on what is actually present (S = Sensing) will often seem too analytical and detail-oriented to a person who focuses on the big picture and uses intuition (N = Intuition).

'Thinking' (T) people can view 'Feeling' (F) people as too emotional, while 'F's' can find that 'T's' are too task-oriented and uncaring.

One of the biggest sources of conflict, however, shows up in differences between J (Judging) and P (Perceiving). A person whose style is a 'J' will be an early starter, will organise their work with attention to deadlines, and may find it offensive when others are late or indecisive. On the other hand, P-style people prefer to keep their options open, and wait until the last minute before completing or deciding. The two different personalities can drive each other crazy in a work environment.

Understanding and accepting fundamental differences in human behaviour is essential for managers and leaders alike, and self-awareness is the cornerstone for developing emotional intelligence.

The question 'What personality type makes the best leader?' often comes up. This question does not have a simple answer because all types can be effective as well as ineffective. Studies of thousands of leaders and managers worldwide have shown some profile types to be more predominant, however. This does not imply that these types make better managers, only that they are more predominant in leadership positions. There is a majority of 'Thinking' and 'Judging' preferences among leaders and managers. This is not unexpected, since the structure and values of most organisations favour logical and decisive behaviour. It may even be that 'Thinking' and 'Judging' behaviour has become the accepted description of what it means to lead and people with these preferences are seen as 'leadership material'.

Bear in mind that the most important element in the MBTI – or in any assessment tool – is the improved ability to understand oneself and those one works with[8].

Leadership in a multicultural environment

'United in Diversity' is the motto of the European Union. It signifies how Europeans have come together, to work for peace and prosperity, while at the same time being enriched by the continent's many different cultures, traditions and languages. This idea is indeed reflected in the composition of the staff of the EU institutions, as most

8 'Leadership Development: Maturity and Power' (1994) by L & N Barr.

EU employees are expats who have decided to live and work abroad – in Brussels, Luxembourg, or any of the many other locations worldwide where the EU has its activities.

In their book 'Leadership in a Diverse and Multicultural Environment'[9] authors Mary Connerly and Paul Pedersen make the case that, no matter how highly skilled, well trained, or intelligent you are, if you make the wrong or culturally inappropriate assumptions, you will not be accurate in your assessment, meaningful in your understanding, or suitable in your interactions as a leader.

It is difficult to know the cultures of others until, and unless, you have an awareness of your own culturally learned assumptions, as these control your life.

A leader has only two choices: to ignore the influence of culture or to attend to it. In either case, however, culture will continue to influence the behaviour of others, with or without the leader's intentional awareness.

Multicultural awareness provides a safe and accurate approach to managing differences across groups in our multicultural populations.

The working culture in the Commission and the other EU institutions is characterised by its diversity. Many studies have underlined the diversity of cultural, linguistic, professional, and even ideological backgrounds. This needs to be considered by all members of staff, especially by those in a leadership role. That said, the Commission has also developed its own 'in-house' culture that is a further layer to master.

More information about working in a multicultural environment can be found in chapter 13.

Communication

'The art of communication is the language of leadership.' — James Humes[10]

There's no mystery here. Regardless of whether we are talking about politics, business, the military, or sports, the best leaders are top-class communicators. Their values are clear and concrete, and what they say supports those values. It is simply impossible to become a great leader without being a great communicator.

The best communicators are great listeners and intelligent in their observations. Great communicators are skilled at sensing the moods, dynamics, attitudes, values and concerns of their audience. Not only do they read their audience well, they also possess the ability to adapt their message to the audience without missing a beat. The message is not about the messenger; it is about meeting the needs and the expectations of those you're communicating with.

'Real Leaders Don't Do PowerPoint'[11] highlights a number of very interesting ideas on how to become a more confident, commanding and compelling communicator. The author explains how real leaders speak to make a difference, to promote a vision, to change the way people think and feel and act.

9 'Leadership in a Diverse and Multicultural Environment' (2005) by Mary Connerly and Paul Pedersen.

10 James C. Humes is an author and former presidential speechwriter.

11 'Real Leaders Don't Do Powerpoint – How to Speak so People Listen' (2009) by Christopher Witt.

Motivating others

'Control leads to compliance; autonomy leads to engagement.' – Daniel H. Pink

Being able to motivate others is the most important trait of both managers and leaders. Managers may be more inclined to use what writer Daniel Pink calls *extrinsic* motivators (carrot-and-stick), while leaders will motivate their followers with the three elements of *intrinsic* motivation – *autonomy, mastery,* and *purpose.*

Autonomy is the extent to which an employee can use their own judgement in making decisions and carrying out their work. Autonomy is strongly related to 'psychological ownership', which is defined as the extent to which an employee feels as though the organisation or the job is 'theirs' – to the point that the organisation and their role in it becomes an important part of an employee's self-identity. Many studies have shown how important the feeling of ownership is for employees.

Managers and leaders can increase the autonomy of staff and co-workers and thus their motivation by:

- Involving people in making decisions that influence their work.
- Encouraging people to apply their own judgement when solving problems.
- Avoiding directive styles of management, excessive monitoring, or unnecessary approval procedures.

Mastery has everything to do with keeping people in their learning zone, by setting realistic challenges – and allowing them to make mistakes. We all want to get better at doing things. It is why learning a language or an instrument can be so frustrating at first. If you feel like you're not getting anywhere, you lose interest and you may even give up. A sense of progress, not just in our work, but in our capabilities, contributes to our inner drive.

Managers need to calibrate their expectations of what staff *ought* to do by looking realistically at what they *can* do. If the must-do tasks are too difficult, people will become worried and feel out of their depth. If the must-do tasks are too easy, they will get bored. The objective should be to give people tasks, with the necessary space and support, which stretch them in a way that fosters increasing mastery and personal growth. This requires paying more attention to how staff are approaching and feeling about their tasks, in order to avoid them losing heart in trying to cope with tasks that don't match their capabilities.

Finally, *purpose* is also related to psychological ownership through the concept of 'task identity', the extent to which a job allows someone to be involved from the beginning to the end of a project.

Managers and leaders can increase 'purpose' by:

- Communicating how employees' activities contribute to the final product so they can see the results of their work and how it fits into the 'bigger picture'.

Leadership vs. management revisited

I experienced perhaps one of the more extreme examples of the difference between leadership and management in my own career when working with outsourced staff, also known as 'body shopping'.

Body shopping is the practice of subcontracting, where one organisation buys in the technical expertise of another organisation's employees. It enables organisations to access skilled individuals or a team of professionals to work remotely or on their premises, in conjunction with its existing teams. Body shopping can help an organisation deal with the pressures of staff shortages on a short or longer-term basis, or to plug critical technology skills gaps within its own staff. For IT staff, body shopping is widely used by public administrations, especially for developing software.

In my activities as a software development manager at both the Flemish Community and the EU administration I had to deal with more than half of my staff being body shoppers; staff who were hired from external companies for the sole purpose of developing software systems. Under Belgian law it is illegal to have a 'hierarchical' relationship with external staff; there can only be a contractual relationship between the customer and the supplier – who is the real 'employer' of these resources. In practice this meant that I had the *responsibility* for the results, but not the formal *authority* over those doing the work; I had to be their *leader*, but could not be their *manager*. The 'stick-and-carrot' approach was not applicable in this context, and other – softer – motivation techniques had to be applied.

- Involving employees in more aspects of work by having them participate in the planning, reporting, and evaluation of projects rather than mere execution.
- Providing employees with the opportunity to completely finish any work they start.
- Explaining their decisions and how they have come to them.

I absolutely encourage you to read Daniel Pink's book 'Drive: The Surprising Truth About What Motivates Us'[12]. As a manager – or leader – of people you have to factor this into your own behaviour.

Starting with 'why?'

'Every organisation in the world knows WHAT they do, some organisations know HOW they do it, but very few organisations know WHY they do what they do.'

This is the main idea behind Simon Sinek's book 'Start with Why – How Great Leaders Inspire Everyone to take Action'[13]. In studying the leaders who have had the greatest influence in the world, Simon Sinek discovered that they all think, act, and communicate in the exact same way – and it's the complete opposite of what everyone

12 'Drive: The Surprising Truth about What Motivates Us' (2011) by Daniel H. Pink.

13 'Start with Why – How Great Leaders Inspire Everyone to take Action' (2009) by Simon Sinek.

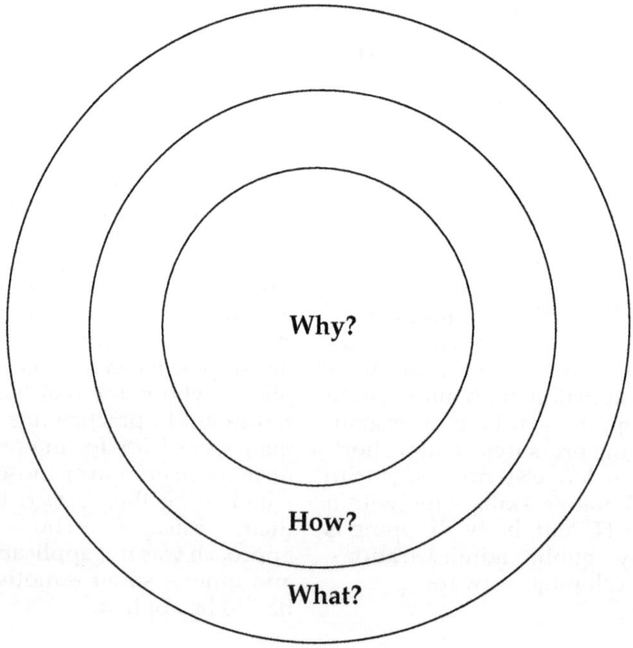

Figure 10.3

else does. People like Martin Luther King Jr., Steve Jobs, and the Wright Brothers might have little obvious in common, but they all started with the question *'why?'*

Sinek claims that there is actually a biological explanation for this; when we are communicating from the inside out we're talking directly to the limbic system. The limbic system supports a variety of functions including emotion, behaviour, motivation, and long-term memory. In fact we are addressing the person through their heart, not their mind. Allow me to suggest that you have a look at Sinek's TED talk[14] where he explains in more detail his simple but powerful model for inspirational leadership.

Coaching and mentoring

'Treat someone as he wants to be and he will become that person.' – Goethe

George Matthew Adams[15] observed that there are high spots in all of our lives and most of them have come about through support and encouragement from someone else. Whether the encouragement came informally or through a deliberate, formal program, helping us personally or professionally, we can all easily identify people who influenced and shaped our future; those were or are our coaches and mentors.

14 http://www.ted.com/talks/simon_sinek_how_great_leaders_inspire_action

15 George Matthew Adams (1878–1962) was an American newspaper columnist.

For managers and leaders it is important to realise that our subordinates and co-workers need our support and encouragement as well. In fact, the degree to which we coach, or mentor, others defines to a large extent how good – or bad – we are as managers or leaders.

It is easy to get confused about the differences between coaching and mentoring. The purpose and expected outcome of each is distinctly different although, at times, some overlap exists.

Mentoring is a pairing of a more skilled or experienced person, usually in the same field of knowledge, with a less experienced person. Ideally mentors have no line management relationship to the mentee. Mentors will often provide direction and advice and should open organisational doors for mentees. Mentors should provide a neutral sounding board, assure total confidentiality, and have no agenda other than assisting their mentees in their development and in reaching their goals. Mentoring involves helping people to develop their career, skills and expertise, drawing upon the experience of the mentor. Mentoring focuses on the 'horizontal' development (learning) of the mentee.

Coaching. While 'master-pupil' relationships have existed throughout human history, coaching as a discipline – and profession – is relatively new[16]. Its first application in a business context was pioneered in the 1980s by Sir John Whitmore[17] and Timothy Gallwey[18], author of 'The Inner Game of Work', who challenged traditional ideas by claiming that a coach's role was to remove or reduce the internal obstacles to a person's performance, without the need for much technical input from the coach. They defined coaching as: *'Unlocking a person's potential to maximise their performance.'*

In their opinion, coaching is about helping people to learn rather than teaching them. Coaches need not have first-hand experience of the coachee's line of work. Leaders and managers can use coaching techniques successfully in the management and development of team members. Coaches will ask 'powerful' questions and not offer or give advice; it is up to the coachee to find the answers. Coaching focuses on the 'vertical' development of the coachee.

Another interesting book is 'Coaching for Performance'[19], by John Whitmore. Over 500.000 copies sold! I had the pleasure of attending a three-day classroom training at Whitmore's institute, Performance Consultants International (PCI). If you ever have the opportunity, I can only recommend it.

There are many models for coaching, depending of the type of coaching, but for performance coaching the widest used model is the GROW model, which is used throughout this book as well.

16 https://www.youtube.com/watch?v=6fld90L6Hkw

17 Sir John Whitmore was chairman of Performance Consultants International, the foremost provider of coaching, leadership development and performance improvement in the workplace globally.

18 'The Inner Game of Work: Focus, Learning, Pleasure and Mobility in the Workplace' by Timothy Gallwey.

19 'Coaching for Performance – GROWing human potential and Purpose' (2009) by John Whitmore.

'Leaders eat last'

In his travels around the world since the publication of his bestseller 'Start with Why', Simon Sinek noticed that some teams were able to trust each other so deeply that they would literally put their lives on the line for each other. Other teams, no matter what incentives were offered, were doomed to infighting, fragmentation and failure. Why?

The answer became clear during a conversation with a Marine Corps general.

'Officers eat last', he said.

Sinek watched as the most junior Marines ate first while the most senior Marines took their place at the back of the line. What's symbolic in the chow hall is deadly serious on the battlefield: great leaders sacrifice their own comfort – even their own survival – for the good of those in their care.

This principle has been true since the earliest tribes of hunters and gatherers. It's not a management theory; it's biology. Our brains and bodies evolved to help us find food, shelter, mates and especially safety. We've always lived in a dangerous world, facing predators and enemies at every turn. We thrived only when we felt safe among our group.

Our biology hasn't changed in fifty thousand years, but our environment certainly has. Today's workplaces tend to be full of cynicism, paranoia and self-interest. But the best organisations foster trust and cooperation because their leaders build what Sinek calls a Circle of Safety that separates the security inside the team from the challenges outside.

The Circle of Safety leads to stable, adaptive, confident teams, where everyone feels they belong and all energies are devoted to facing the common enemy and seizing big opportunities.

As he did in 'Start with Why', Sinek illustrates his ideas with fascinating true stories from a wide range of examples, from the military to manufacturing, from government to investment banking in another book called 'Leaders Eat Last'[20].

The biology is clear: when it matters most, leaders who are willing to eat last are rewarded with deeply loyal colleagues who will stop at nothing to advance their leader's vision and their organisation's interests. It's amazing how well it works.

Leading by example

We have all experienced situations where the boss tells everyone to stay late, and then leaves early to pick up the kids from school. We probably know supervisors who criticise people for spending time on the internet and have their Facebook open all day long ...

There is hardly anything worse for the troops' morale than leaders who practise the 'Do as I say, not as I do' philosophy. No matter what the situation is, double standards always feel like betrayals. They can be very destructive. Being a poor role model is the easiest way to undermine your own authority.

Don't underestimate the fact that as a leader you are carefully watched by others. This can be for negative reasons, such as envy of your position or, more positively, because people want to follow your example – so make sure that example is a good one!

20 'Leaders eat Last: Why some teams pull together and others don't' (2014) by Simon Sinek.

Much appreciated – by 1 in 5

For a number of years my wife and I have participated in an annual activity that is organised by a dedicated and enthusiastic team of teachers at the school where my wife works. It is always a pleasant surprise to find what exactly is going to happen that day: it could be a short trip including a visit to a museum or an interesting venue; a walk in the woods; or driving around the countryside with old-timers, with a quiz thrown in. In any case, it is a full-day event with catering and transport included. These events always take place at the weekend, and the participants have to cover their own expenses.

Despite the fact that there are over 100 teachers and administrative staff, the number of participants (including husbands and wives) rarely exceeds 40. This means that only around 20 per cent – or one out of five – colleagues and partners take part in the event, and strangely – or not strangely – enough it's always the same people who do so. Moreover, during the day, people tend to stick together in smaller groups: maths and science teachers, language teachers, and administrative staff ...

Team building

When I was thinking about where to cover the subject of team building, my first idea was to put it in Chapter 9 (working with others); but then I realised that it would be better to address the *organiser* of any team building initiative – the leader or manager of the team.

Research has shown that the effectiveness of team building differs substantially from one organisation to another. The most effective team building efforts occur when members of the team are highly interdependent, highly knowledgeable, and when organisational leadership actively establishes and supports the team. Effective team building must also incorporate a link to the ultimate objective of the organisation.

These conditions imply that team building only works for real teams, and not for 'groups' of loosely associated people who happen to work for the same boss. I have heard of 'away days' for groups of 300 people (an entire Directorate) and, frankly, I don't believe in their effectiveness. The cost and effort needed to organise such an event will never be compensated by higher productivity of the group as a whole. At such large events people will stick together in small groups of 4 to 6 and spend their entire day like that, without any deeper contact with the other participants.

In addition, the level of interdependence is not high enough, and the 'ultimate objective' is too high-level and unclear to most participants. At best, people will enjoy themselves together with a few of their close colleagues during this extra day off, and they will be happy to take advantage of the free food and drink. But their productivity at work will not go up as a result. When this activity is not mandatory, but on a voluntary basis, many people will find an excuse for not participating (too much work to do, have to collect the children from school, not feeling well, etc.) simply because they don't see the point of it.

Leaders and managers should be aware of these limitations, and organise team-building events only for volunteers, not during office hours, and possibly only partially cover the expenses. Do not use team-building events to boost your own popularity, because people won't buy it.

How to give feedback

Praising good performance is easy, but what about those times when someone on your team needs a kick in the butt more than a pat on the back?

Here are some ideas to work with:

Make negative feedback uncommon. When a work environment becomes filled with criticism and complaint, people stop caring, because they feel that they will get criticised whatever they do. Also, when managers stockpile problems, waiting for the 'right moment', employees can become overwhelmed. Changes in behaviour are more easily achieved when negative feedback is administered in small doses and in real time, immediately after the fact.

It is better to give negative feedback orally. People who avoid confrontation are often tempted to use email to give negative feedback. Email is more easily misunderstood than oral feedback and it can look like you are 'building a case' against the person you are giving feedback to, by systematically documenting your (negative) feedback in writing. On the other hand, *positive feedback is best given in writing* because something put in writing usually has longer lasting impact than something dropped into a conversation.

I am, I should emphasise, talking here about one-off feedback unlikely to lead to disciplinary action (i.e. where you are expecting performance to improve). Nowadays, HR will not entertain a negative appraisal report without documentary evidence over the year to back it up – including emails. Our human resources units have actually insisted on occasion that particular individuals who performed badly should be given 'satisfactory' because of the lack of a paper trail indicating dissatisfaction. Of course in those cases the poor performer needs to know that a case is being built.

Ask powerful questions. Most of the time, people know when they are having problems and may even have good ideas about how to improve which need to be drawn out of them. Asking questions such as 'How could you have done better?' and 'What do you think you could do with improving?' involves the other person in building a shared plan. You can give better feedback if you understand how the other person perceives the situation. Asking powerful questions such as, 'Why do you approach this situation in this way?' or better 'What was your thought process?' can lead other people to discover their own solutions and their own insights.

Listen before you speak. Effective feedback begins with active listening, paying attention, stepping into the other person's shoes, appreciating his or her experience, and helping to move that person into a learning mode.

Be willing to accept feedback yourself. In fact, few things are more valuable to managers than honest feedback from their staff. Feedback from your subordinates is to be treasured rather than discouraged or ignored; after all, nobody is perfect and not even the best manager has nothing to learn.

Management coaches sometimes advise the 'sandwich approach'. In this approach you insert the negative feedback between two pieces of positive feedback. It's a common method, but the sandwich approach may have the effect of undermining both your feedback and your relationships with your direct reports. Effective leaders are transparent about the strategies they use when working with others. The sandwich approach is designed to influence others without telling them what you are doing – in other words manipulate them. People don't like to be manipulated.

And a final tip: *Be careful in the way you give feedback.* Some cultures have a very open and accepting approach to feedback, but others don't. You can cause incredible damage if you offer personal feedback to someone who is not used to it, so be delicate, and start gradually.

Feedback

'I praise loudly, I blame softly.' – Catherine the Great

Catherine the Great was the most renowned and the longest-ruling female leader of Russia, reigning from 1762 until her death in 1796 at the age of 67. She came to power following the assassination of her husband, Peter III, at the end of the Seven Years' War. During her reign, Russia was revitalised, growing larger and stronger than ever before and becoming recognised as one of the great powers of Europe.

Catherine understood that even absolute despots cannot hold power without the support of others, and if a ruler is able to maintain a position, without leadership skills, people will be led nowhere. You can occupy a throne and accomplish nothing.

Catherine's philosophy of leadership is one of the most vital skills any influencer can develop:

Praise, when given, should be generous and whole-hearted. When it is public, specific, clear, and generous, loyalty is won. Those who are praised will follow their leader practically anywhere. Others will follow as well, in hopes of earning such praise.

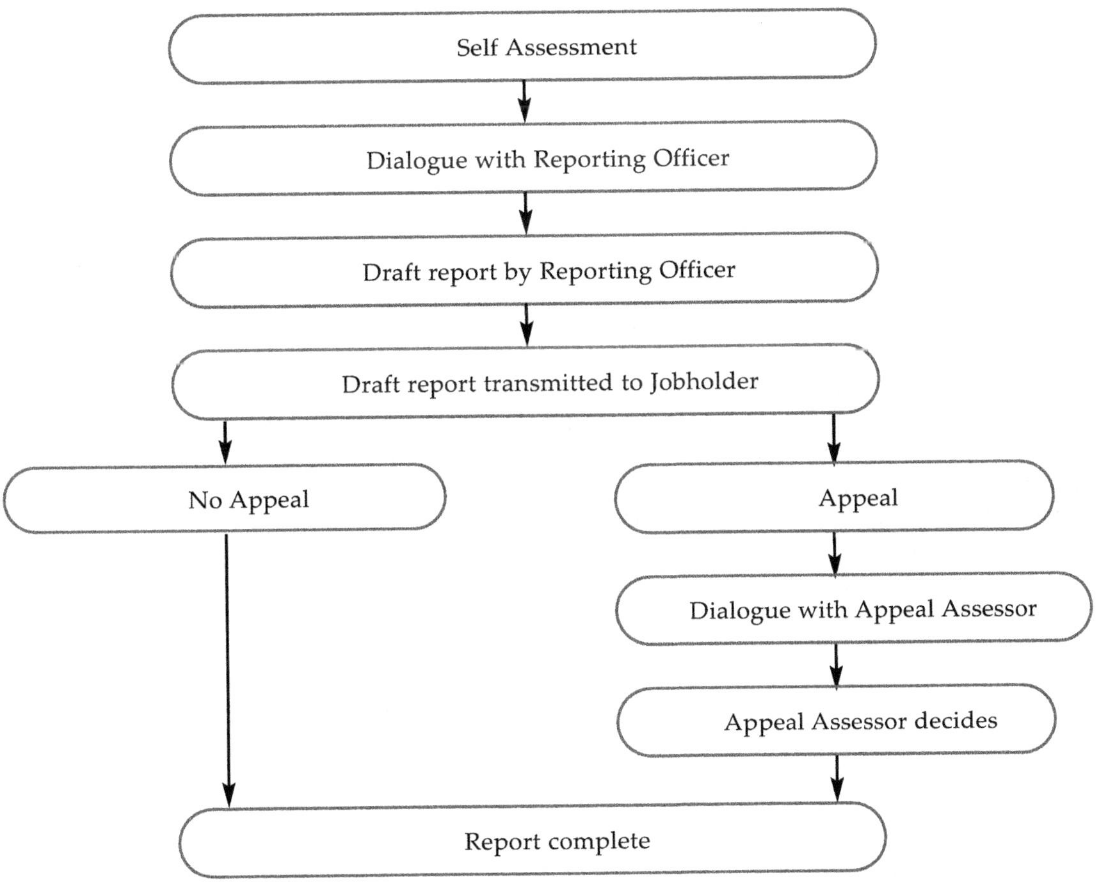

Figure 10.4: the Commission appraisal system

However, choose the target for your praise wisely. Some people love the attention – others shy away from it. I've known someone perform *less* well after public praise because they so hated being praised in public; they did their utmost to prevent it happening again – by lowering their performance. You need to know who will bask in the glow and who'd prefer not to make a big deal of things. In the latter case I talk to them in private and explain that I haven't put the spotlight on them precisely because I know they don't like it. They appreciate that better because they feel I am attuned to their needs and receptive to their feelings, including shyness. That said, I do still mention them at meetings but not in an over the top way – just a word of thanks.

Blaming softly has to be clear, direct, and specific – but private. The aim is to keep the circle of criticism as small as possible and make corrections quickly, gently, and graciously. The leader who blames softly knows that no loyalty is earned through humiliation, and that a person who can save face can develop into a valuable leader as well. We must not destroy people in the process of making them better.

Catherine the Great had a point. If we make a big deal of praise and handle criticism frankly and discreetly, we will develop the kind of leadership that can help us reach for the sky.

It is important to remember that the goal of feedback is not to tell people what to do or how to do it. That is mistaking the process for the goal. The actual goal of feedback – even negative feedback – is to improve the behaviour of the other person.

Appraisal

Appraisal is formalised feedback. The appraisal system as provided for by Article 43 of the Staff Regulations is an important opportunity to look back at the past year, and reflect on the future, both for the staff member and the so-called reporting officer.

From my own experience as a Head of Unit, and thus reporting officer for the staff under my supervision, I know that appraisal is often looked upon as a tedious, time-consuming and highly bureaucratic burden. However, you should see this as a real exercise in leadership. Through its formalised nature, and the (at least theoretical) decoupling from the yearly promotion exercise, both the staff member and the supervisor get the opportunity to have an open and honest conversation, for which otherwise over the course of the year time or courage may be lacking on both sides.

In the Commission's appraisal system (see Figure 10.4)[21], the self-assessment is the first and mandatory step in the yearly process. In fact, the self-assessment is structured into exactly the categories of the appraisal report: Efficiency, Abilities, Conduct in the service, Languages, Responsibilities, Learning, and General comment, and there is a clear mapping with the eight 'core competencies' as discussed in Chapter 1.

The self-assessment is a golden opportunity to take stock of important events during the past year. The staff member is not being asked to say if he or she is good or bad at their job, but rather to highlight their achievements and their ambitions for the future.

21 https://www.eupan.eu/wp-content/uploads/2019/02/2016_2_SK_Performance_Appraisal_in_the_EU_Member_States_and_the_European_Commission.pdf

The qualitative appraisal report brings together the information relating to the individual staff member's performance during the past year. The report should cover the main aspects of the year, including any work that may have been done outside their own unit or DG.

If the staff member thinks that their report is not a fair reflection of the dialogue, they can appeal. The appeal will be dealt with by the hierarchical superior of the reporting officer.

As a manager your job is to try to make the appraisal dialogue positive, meaningful, and helpful for staff. As reporting officer you have complete freedom to write the appraisal report, but promotion is the responsibility of senior management in a separate exercise. Senior management will discuss all staff in the DG or institution, grade by grade, to arrive at a proposal for who should be promoted, within the budget available. The goal is that all good performers should be promoted at the rates laid down in the Staff Regulation. The proposal of senior management will then be discussed with staff representatives and considered by the Joint Promotion Committee, finalised and published.

360-degree feedback

The term *360-degree feedback* refers to an appraisal and feedback system in which an employee (typically someone in a managerial or supervisory position) is evaluated by one or more supervisors, peers, and subordinates.

One of the great advantages of undergoing a 360-degree feedback evaluation is that it increases self-awareness. The feedback allows the individual to discover strengths, weaknesses and blind spots (behaviours and actions that they exhibit but are not aware of). Uncovering blind spots is key for continuous improvement and enables the employee to focus on developing skills in overlooked areas. It is – in effect – the application of the Johari window technique (see Chapter 2).

There used to be a 360-degree feedback system, for senior staff only, in the Commission, but that system has been suspended. Experience over the past years has shown that the 360-degree feedback mechanism is more suitably used as a career development tool rather than within the context of the appraisal exercise.

The European School for Administration (EUSA) uses the 360-degree mechanism for participants in training courses. This tool takes the form of a self-assessment of their competencies and feedback from colleagues that they have chosen to be consulted. A feedback report is produced automatically. The tool aims to help participants recognise, understand and manage their interpersonal behaviour and emotions effectively.

Committing to the target of 40% women in management, DG CONNECT's HR Committee on 11 May 2015 decided to give priority to a group of women, with the aim of increasing the likelihood of successful application to middle management positions. To achieve these objectives a 360-degree feedback assessment tool – an online questionnaire – has been selected. This tool helps participants to identify their strengths and areas of development. Each woman participating in the project receives feedback from different raters: their line manager, their selected peers and their team members.

The online toolkit that comes with this book gives you the opportunity to ask for 360-degree feedback, anonymously. Please do use it!

Delegation

A leader or a manager cannot – and should not – do everything by themselves; if they try, they will not be successful. Moreover, trying to do everything by yourself is a symptom of poor time management (see also the prioritising and organising chapter). Learning how to *delegate* is an indispensable skill for a leader or a manager in any organisation.

Worst is the 'control freak' type of manager who won't delegate and has staff afraid to take the smallest of decisions independently – and who then leaves the office for days or weeks at a time, leaving everything just blocked until their return.

Delegation involves giving others the authority to act on your behalf, accompanied with (a degree of) accountability for results. Effective delegation distributes the workload more evenly, helps an organisation to run more smoothly and efficiently and allows more people to become actively involved and motivated.

You *can* delegate:

- Tasks that are urgent but not important (priority 3 in the Eisenhower matrix).
- When there is a lot of work.
- When someone else has a particular skill or qualification which would suit a specific task.
- When someone expresses an interest in a task.
- When someone might benefit from the responsibility for his own development.

On the other hand *don't delegate:*

- Things you simply don't like doing.
- Your own important tasks (priority 1 and 2 in the Eisenhower matrix).
- Things that are usually your specified responsibilities.
- A task to someone who may not possess the skills necessary to do the task successfully.

I would personally not delegate the non-important/non-urgent tasks (i.e. priority 4 in the Eisenhower matrix) because this can convey the message that you don't value the person, which may cause demotivation.

Many people have difficulty delegating. Most often they would prefer to do the task themselves to make sure the 'job gets done right'. While this method can be more convenient, it can also result in the loss of followers. Sharing your authority with others can be the greatest single motivator in retaining followers and strengthening the organisation.

Managers often achieve their positions after being technical specialists themselves. They will have an opinion or view on how to 'fix' situations or problems. They believe that it's faster to tell someone what to do – or do it themselves – rather than give their subordinates an opportunity to figure it out. By always providing the answers, managers take away the opportunity for those they manage to learn and come up with alternative, and potentially better, ways of doing things.

Prioritising and organising for managers

You can't give the benefit of your advice to other people if you don't allow time to plan and do this, so you need to spend more time on priorities, preparation, and follow-up – and less time in meetings. Reducing the time you spend in meetings will give you more time to think strategically.

First, reduce the number of meeting invitations you accept.

- Ask the organiser of the meeting for the agenda so you can pass on your comments beforehand (this may on occasion force the organiser to actually produce an agenda!).
- Send someone else from your team to convey your position (this will help that person to see 'the bigger picture').
- If the meeting is only tangentially relevant to your work, excuse yourself from the meeting but request a copy of the minutes.

Second, reduce the number of meetings you schedule yourself — and reduce their length.

Opt for the least 'costly' investment of time that will still achieve your goal. Don't schedule a meeting for something that you can resolve in a phone call, and don't make a phone call for something that can be communicated in an email. If you really must schedule a meeting, challenge yourself to keep it as short as possible.

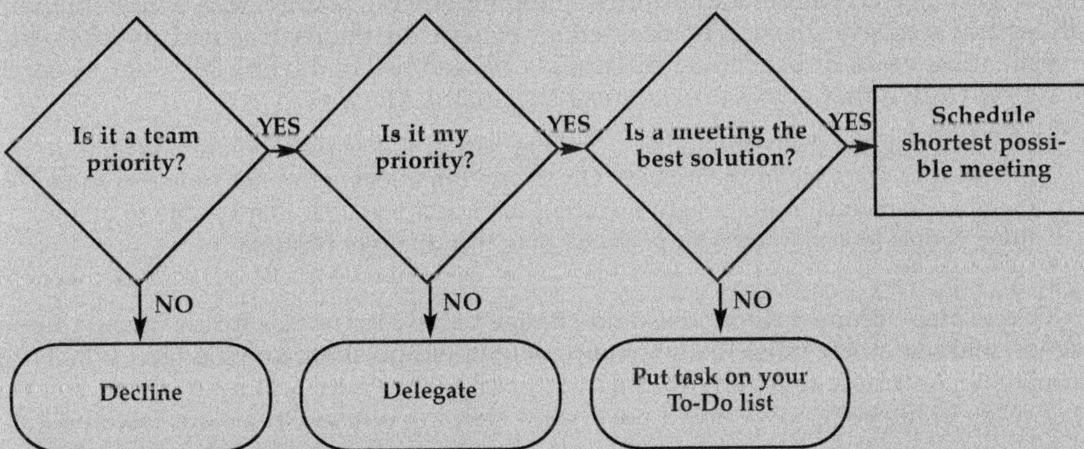

Third, start the meeting on time and aim to finish promptly to schedule.

Be on time yourself (*'l'exactitude est la politesse des rois'*[22]) and don't wait for latecomers before starting. Remember that you are burning the precious time of all those attending, so don't punish those who are on time by rewarding those who aren't.

Figure 10.5: do I need a meeting about it?

The secret to great delegation is to empower your people to make decisions when you are not around. That way, they won't rely on you to keep the wheels turning. If a manager doesn't let things get through the gate without personally reviewing them, that holds up the entire organisation.

22 'Punctuality is the politeness of kings'.

However, you should bear this important caveat in mind. *You can delegate work and authority, but not ultimate responsibility*. In the case of something going wrong, the blame is all yours if that failure occurs because you delegated a task to someone lacking the necessary skills. It is your fault since you delegated to the wrong person.

Unfortunately, the opposite scenario can also apply: a manager, such as the head of a department, can have responsibility but not authority. He or she might be held responsible for making something happen, but lacks the actual authority to enforce any directives or incentives. This is one of the major stressors that middle managers face. This is particularly an issue in the case of underperformance by a member of staff, where managers have very little in the way of tools (other than feedback) to effect a change of behaviour. Some staff take full advantage of this lack of authority (i.e. they happily chomp on every carrot they are given, knowing there is no real stick).

Give and take

'Give, and it will be given to you.' – Luke 6:38

According to organisational psychologist Adam Grant[23] there are three types of people in this world: *givers* (those who prioritise helping others), *takers* (those who help themselves) and *matchers* (those who seek equal benefit for themselves and others). After investigating years of psychological studies as well as conducting his own research, Grant concluded that givers are the most successful. He says:

> 'Givers bring out the best in others. One big part of that is seeing more potential in people than they see in themselves. Givers are often looking at the people around them as diamonds in the rough, investing in such a way that they're able to allow these people to achieve greater potential than they thought possible.'

Givers also become role models and change behaviour norms for the group, Grant argues, making others more likely to help each other and share knowledge – which can ultimately contribute to an environment of greater creativity and innovation. You can read more in his book 'Give and Take – Why Helping others Drives our Success'[24].

Leading your former peers

Becoming the manager of your former peers is a particular challenge; you need to establish your authority and credibility, without acting like the promotion has gone to your head.

Much as for any other upcoming change, you have to prepare this transition carefully. So, rather than waiting for a promotion to be announced, think first about what management style you'd like to apply, then challenge yourself to demonstrate those skills while you are still working side-by-side with your peers. That way, when you *are* promoted, there will be no surprises: people will already know what to expect, based

23 Adam Grant (1981) is an author and professor at the Wharton School of the University of Pennsylvania.

24 'Give and Take – Why Helping others Drives our Success' (2014) by Adam Grant.

Taking up the reins

I once had a rather striking experience of myself becoming the leader of my peers. One of my younger colleagues was actually the son of our boss, and everybody more or less expected that he was 'earmarked' as his father's successor. It came as a surprise when one day the boss called me into his office and announced he was going to retire. This was rather unexpected, because he was still relatively young (57); however, we all knew that he was suffering from bad health (he actually died a year later). My surprise was even greater when he told me that the board of directors had decided (on his recommendation) that I was to be his successor.

Needless to say, I expected problems with the son, but that didn't happen. He was wise enough to understand that he was too young and inexperienced to take on this role. In fact, he was even relieved, because becoming the boss would have prevented him from doing what he was really good at – being a brilliant system administrator.

With the other team members I had no problems either, because I was by far the oldest and most experienced member of the team, so I didn't face a challenge in trying to establish my credibility and authority; I already had it.

I remember this period, which lasted over four years, as one of the happiest in my entire career, and when I left to explore different horizons I happily recommended the son as my successor. I believe he is still holding this position many years later, and doing a perfect job.

on their past experience of your planning, decision-making, communication, and collaboration skills.

Here are some tips on what to do when the promotion has become a fact:

- *Address the elephant in the room.* Schedule a meeting to sit down with your new team. This doesn't necessarily have to be in a formal setting; invite them for lunch or a coffee. Even if your promotion hasn't been announced officially yet, you can bet on it that the grapevine has done its job already. Announcing the transition in a friendly atmosphere will remove the uncertainty and break the ice. Establish your authority from day one. Step decisively into the new role by letting the team know that things have changed, and that you are now their manager. Right after this first meeting, have a conversation with each individual regarding how expectations have changed; don't underestimate the power of a simple, one-on-one conversation.
- *Renegotiate your friendships.* Be honest about how your own responsibilities and priorities have changed, and ask how your friend sees theirs changing as well. Let them know they can count on you to support them in being happy and successful in their role and ask for their loyalty in return, but make it clear that there won't be any special treatment. Accept that you can no longer have close, personal friendships with your former peers. You don't need to become remote and unreachable, but you may want to attend fewer social gatherings.
- *Tread lightly at first.* You probably have loads of ideas about how to lead the team. But don't introduce any major revamps right away. You need to demonstrate your new authority without stepping on toes or damaging

relationships. You can identify a few smaller decisions you can make fairly quickly, but postpone bigger ones until you've been in the role longer and have time to gather feedback.

- *Make use of your advantages.* You are more likely to find someone you trust to give you feedback than would a complete stranger to the team. After all, you know your former colleagues very well and know who is trustworthy and who is not. Leverage this knowledge to ask for honest feedback.
- *Look beyond your team.* During this type of transition, it's easy to become overly focused on your former peers. Ask yourself how you can build credibility with new counterparts and how you can build a connection with your own new boss.

Integrity

'You are what you do, not what you say you'll do.' – C.G. Jung

Integrity means that we do not behave in ways that go against our essence; that we behave with honesty, reliability, and caring – with ourselves and with others. Doing what you say you will do is a matter of integrity.

I don't trust people who don't keep their word. Decades ago I had a boss who had clearly reached his 'level of incompetence'[25]. He said different things to different people, trying to save face with the person he was actually talking to. To his boss, the general manager, he promised one thing, while he was instructing the external consultants to do something different. The financial manager then got yet another version of his story, and as for his immediate colleagues, well, they didn't know what to think about all of this. I remember this episode as one of the most unhappy of my entire career, because I didn't trust my boss, I felt unsafe.

I lose respect for people whose word doesn't mean anything to them. If you want to feel respected by others, then you need to say 'yes' when you mean 'yes' and 'no' when you mean 'no', and not allow your fear of rejection to get in the way of being a trustworthy person.

We cannot feel worthy when we let others down. People who default on their word do not value themselves enough to act with integrity. Self-worth is the result of treating others with caring and respect.

When people have the sense that a leader is worthy of their trust they will invest time and take risks in ways they never would if their leader had a reputation built upon lack of integrity. Keep in mind that people will forgive many things where trust exists, but will rarely forgive anything where trust is absent.

25 According to the Peter Principle (see Chapter 1) 'managers rise to the level of their incompetence'.

A man for all seasons

My wife and I were recently binge watching the 'The Tudors' on Netflix. The series is based upon the reign of King Henry VIII of England. One of the key players, Sir Thomas More, refused to endorse King Henry VIII's desire to divorce his first wife, Catherine of Aragon, because she could not bear him a son. Henry VIII wanted to marry Anne Boleyn, the sister of his former mistress. I was so impressed by More, whose sense of principle was such that he chose to die rather than lose his integrity. Sir Thomas More was a man of significant personal power, deeply loved by his family and the people. I realised that it was his authenticity that gave him the strength to die rather than compromise his integrity in order to live. In his eyes, his life would not be worth living if he were not true to himself. He was, in the words of the title of a play about him 'a man for all seasons'.

Authentic leadership

'To thy own self be true.' – Polonius, in Shakespeare's 'Hamlet'

In 2003, following a series of corporate scandals in the US, Bill George[26] made the case that we needed new leaders, not just new laws, to get us out of the corporate crisis in his book 'Authentic Leadership'[27].

According to George, authentic leaders are 'self-actualized'[28] individuals who are aware of their strengths, their limitations, and their own emotions. They also show who they really are to their followers. They do not act one way in private and another in public; they don't hide their mistakes or weaknesses out of fear of looking weak. Authentic leaders lead with their hearts, not just their minds. They are not afraid to show their emotions, their vulnerability, and to connect with their employees. This does not mean that authentic leaders are 'soft.' Being open about yourself helps to break down hierarchical barriers. It is only when your staff know the person behind the façade that you start building the foundations of good leadership: trust and respect.

Besides being open and honest with their followers, authentic leaders always put the mission and the goals of the organisation ahead of their own self-interest. They do the job in pursuit of results for the organisation, not for their own power, money or ego. Authentic leaders focus on the long-term stakeholder's value. They realise that to nurture individuals and an organisation requires hard work and patience, but the approach pays large dividends over time.

26 William W. George is Professor of Management Practice at Harvard Business School.

27 'Authentic Leadership – Rediscovering the Secrets of Creating Lasting Value' (2003) by Bill George.

28 'The full realization of one's potential, and of one's true self' (Abraham Maslow).

Followership: the other side of leadership

'I must follow the people. Am I not their leader?' – Benjamin Disraeli[29]

The other side of leadership is *'followership'*. It seems reasonable that if leadership is important to performance, followership must have something to do with it too. But strangely, followership gets only a small fraction of the exposure that leadership does.

Followership is a straightforward concept. It is the ability to take direction well, to get in line behind a program, to be part of a team and to deliver on what is expected of you. One could say that it is closely related to 'delivering quality and results' as described earlier in this book. However, being a good follower is sometimes looked down on. This is a pity because the practical reality is that one does not progressively reach more responsible leadership positions without demonstrating an ability to follow and function effectively as part of a group. The fact is that in organisations everybody is *both* a leader *and* a follower depending on the circumstances. How well the followers follow is probably just as important to an organisation's success as how well the leaders lead.

Quite a number of interesting studies have been conducted on the topic of followership. To name a few which you can check out if you are interested:

- Zaleznik's follower typology: based on control and activity.
- Kelley's follower typology: five different types.
- Kellerman's follower typology: five different types.
- Chaleff's follower typology: based on type of support.

Followership will always be in the shadow of leadership. Nonetheless, while it is true that an organisation is only as good as its leaders, it is also only as good as its followers. *There are no leaders without followers.*

Developing your leadership competency

Leadership skills play a large role in your career development. Often, your technical skills can only take you so far. To help you move forward in your career, you need soft skills such as the ability to be a good leader. Few people are born to be leaders. Most of us need to practise being a good leader, and that is why leadership development is so important.

Please refer to Annex 1 for further development of this competency, or check out the easy-to-use app at:

http://www.johnharperpublishing.co.uk/the-ultimate-eu-career-development-toolkit/

29 19th century British Prime Minister.

PART III: SPECIAL CHALLENGES

11. Digital persuasion

'You are 34 times more persuasive communicating in person than on digital platforms. Yet, in today's world, you spend the majority of your time trying to influence others to say YES to you using social media, email, and messenger.' – Erin Gargan King

As the quote above notes, for better or worse digital persuasion has become the new normal.

There are of course lots of advantages to using digital communication as compared to more traditional forms of speaking (face-to-face, or on the phone) or writing (letters, paper memos). To name a few:

- *Flexibility*. Digital communication is accessible 24/7, any place, as long as you have an internet connection.
- *Levelling*. When text-based, shy people who usually don't speak up can say as much as they like without being overruled by 'loud' participants in a discussion or a meeting.
- *Documented*. Unlike in-person conversations, online discussions are lasting and can be revisited.
- *Encourage reflection*. People can think more about their contribution before they intervene.

Nevertheless, there are some disadvantages as well:

- *Text-based*. Much of digital communication is text-based, which can be challenging for those who don't like to write or have poor keyboard skills.
- *Fewer physical cues*. Without body language or facial expressions, the richness of our messages disappears, and this has a negative effect on communication.
- *Information overload*. Large volumes of digital information can be overwhelming and hard to follow, even stress-inducing.
- *Inefficient*. Digital communication often takes longer than in-person communication, often also leaving questions unanswered.

Because of its importance in today's world, I have dedicated this separate chapter to digital persuasion, complementing the chapter on the general competency of 'communication' earlier in this book. I will focus on four 'channels' that are predominantly used in the world of business and public administration: email, public speaking, digital meetings, and videoconferencing.

When and when not to use email

Today, email is by far the most used form of communication in business and public administration. Email is a very good tool to document and track conversations and activities and send files to one another or a group of people. Email can be managed from your desktop, smartphone, and tablet, even if you're on the move or don't have a permanent access to the internet.

Email is an excellent way to get your message across when:

- You need to get in touch with a person who is hard to reach or is not located in the same part of the country or world, or lives in a different time zone.
- The information you want to share is not time sensitive. For many people, keeping up with their email correspondence is a part of their job, and they only do it during regular business hours.
- You need to send someone an electronic file, such as a document, a spreadsheet, or a draft of your ideas.
- You need to distribute information to a large number of people quickly.
- You need a written record of the communication, provide some kind of proof, or review the content of an important meeting or memo.

However, nearly everyone seems to use email for every type of communication, even when not appropriate. Miscommunication can quickly occur when people have different expectations about the messages that they send and receive. People copy you in on irrelevant email threads. As a consequence, the volume of emails has increased so much today that automatic filters had to be introduced, creating the risk that important emails get filtered out.

Email is NOT an effective means of communication when:

- Your message is long and complicated or requires additional discussion that would best be accomplished face-to-face.
- The information is highly confidential. Your message could be forwarded on to other people without your knowledge. Backup copies can be easily retrieved by interested parties, even when you have deleted the message and think it is gone forever.
- Your message is emotionally charged, or the tone of the message could be easily misunderstood. If you would hesitate to say something to someone's face, do not write it in an email.

How to write better emails

The following section is partly based on a webinar *How to write better emails and be more productive at work*[1] by Andras Baneth, managing partner of EU Training[2].

First, let's have a look at the following email:

> **SUBJECT: Stakeholder conference details**
>
> Mr. Smith,
>
> I'm contacting you on behalf of EU Training regarding the upcoming 'EU careers post-COVID-19' conference.
>
> To organise a successful event, I need to know if you're going to publish a press release or after the event.
>
> As regards the approval process, I need to know if you're going to publish a press release before or after the event.
>
> To understand our approach better, I'm attaching our detailed (9-page) event guidelines so we can discuss the relevant points at our meeting.
>
> Thank you in advance,
> Andras Baneth

At first sight, this email looks OK, right? Now try to put yourself in the position of Mr. Smith, the (imaginary) recipient of this email. You should imagine that Mr. Smith is an EU official, working in DG HR, and in charge of the press relations of his DG. EU Training is a private company with no official or contractual relations with the EU institutions.

So, one morning, Mr. Smith, who is working from home that day, opens his work email and sees that there are over 100 'unread' messages waiting for his reply. The messages are ordered chronologically, the most recent messages first. Since this email was sent the day before, in the early afternoon, it is in position 75, below the 'fold' of the first page containing the 50 most recent messages…

Mr. Smith, being used to dealing with lots of emails during a working day, is a very well-organised person. He spends about two hours in the morning working on the most important and most urgent emails, leaving the less important and less urgent messages for the afternoon. Things that are not important and not urgent are simply deleted from his inbox.

1 https://www.youtube.com/watch?v=lPMn7_NRsiM

2 https://eutraining.eu/about-us#

By the time he reaches the second page of his inbox, after one hour or so, Mr. Smith sees the subject line ('Stakeholder conference details') and wonders who Andras Baneth is. He cannot decide whether this is important and urgent, so he decides to come back to it in the afternoon.

In the afternoon then, he finally opens the email, briefly reads it, and is still puzzled about what Andras wants from him. Does he want a press release? By when? And what does he have to do with the 9-page document in the attachment? Read it? Summarise it? Distil a press release from it? Confusion abounds. The email gets deleted.

A few important lessons can be drawn from this scenario.

Recipient(s)

Ensure you use the correct email address for the recipient(s) in the To: line and request a 'delivery receipt' if this is an important message.

Cc: and Bcc: ('carbon copy' and 'blind carbon copy')

In professional settings, copying someone else in on an email can help get things done, especially if the person receiving the copy is in a supervisory role. Be aware, however, that when you send a message to more than one address using the Cc: field, *all* the recipients can see *all* the addresses in the To: and Cc: fields. Some of the recipients may not appreciate this breach of their privacy. A nice little trick is to put the main recipient's supervisor in Cc when you thank them for a job well done. People usually don't boast to their supervisor about their performance themselves, so you help the recipient make a good impression (delivering quality and results).

Blind copying emails to a group of people can be helpful when you don't want everyone on the list to have each other's addresses. The only recipient addresses that will be visible to all recipients are in the To: field. If you don't want ANY of the recipients to see the list's email addresses, you can put your own address in the To: field and use Bcc: exclusively to address your message to others. Also, someone who is blind copied may hit 'reply all' and send a reply to everyone, revealing that they were included in the original message.

Only use Cc: or BCc: if the recipient is for information only; no action needed.

Subject line

Email subject lines are like newspaper headlines. They should convey the main point of your message or the reason why you are sending the email to that particular person. Therefore, be as specific as possible. If your message is time-sensitive, you might want to include a date in your subject line. In a compelling subject line, the most important information comes first. Is this FYI only, an invitation, a request for input ...? The subject line will determine if your mail will be opened or simply discarded. The best subject lines are only 5-6 words, military-style.

To avoid endless threads when introducing a new topic or idea in the conversation, change the subject line.

Greeting

Don't just start with your text, and don't just stop at the end without a polite signature. If you don't know the person well, you may be confused about how to address them or sign off. When in doubt, address someone more formally to avoid offending them. Some common ways to address your reader are:

- Dear Mr. Smith,
- Hello, Mr. Smith,
- Hi, John, (only if you know the person well)

If you don't know the name of the person you are addressing, or if the email addresses a group, try something broad:

- To whom it may concern, (do NOT use this when applying for a job)
- Dear members of the selection committee,
- Dear all,

Body

Think about your message before you write it. Don't send email in haste. First, decide on the purpose of your message and what outcome you expect from your communication. Then think about the recipient(s) and what they may need for your message to have the intended result. Keep your text as short as possible while still ensuring you get the essential points across. Some people simply don't read emails that don't fit on the screen of their smartphone.

Reflect on the tone of your message. When communicating via email, your words are not supported by gestures, voice inflections, or other cues, so it may be easier for someone to misread your tone. Cynicism and puns are often misinterpreted and may even offend the person you are writing to. Be careful with emoticons in professional emails. You can use Boomerang[3] to check the tone (Positivity, Politeness, and Subjectivity) on-the-fly, while writing. This tool will also indicate the likelihood of receiving a response to your email.

Strive for clarity and brevity in your writing. Miscommunication can occur if a message is unclear, disorganised, or too long and complex for the reader to follow. Here are some steps you can take to make sure that your message is understood:

- Briefly state your purpose for writing at the very beginning of your message.
- Be sure to provide the reader with some context. If you're asking a question, cut and paste any relevant text into the email, or in an attachment, so that the reader understands the context of your question.

3 https://www.boomeranggmail.com

- Offer alternative solutions or options when asking for an answer or a decision. In this way you make the recipient's task easier and increase your chances of getting a reply.
- Use a tool like Doodle4 when scheduling a meeting with more than two people.
- State the desired outcome at the end of your message. Ending your email with the next step can be useful, especially in work settings. Be careful with relative dates like 'tomorrow' or 'next week' and preferably add the names of the days, full date, and time with time zone.
- Format your message so that it is easy to read. Use paragraphs to separate thoughts. Use white space to separate paragraphs visually. Bullet significant details so that they are easy to pick out. Use bold, italic, or underline to highlight critical information, such as due dates.
- Proofread. Re-read messages before you hit the 'send' button. Check your grammar, spelling, capitalisation, and punctuation. If your email program doesn't support this, you can use the Grammarly[5] plug-in. Try reading your message out loud to help you catch any mistakes or bizarre phrasing that you might otherwise miss.

Closing

For your closing, something brief but friendly will do for most correspondence:

- *Thank you,*
- *Best wishes,*
- *See you tomorrow,*
- *Regards,*
- *Looking forward to your answer,*

For a very formal message, such as a job application, use the kind of closing that you might see in a business letter:

- *Sincerely,*
- *Respectfully yours,*

Always sign off with your name at the end of your message. When unsure if the reader knows who you are, you might also consider including your title and the organisation you belong to.

The improved email from the beginning of this section could look as follows:

4 https://www.doodle.com

5 https://www.grammarly.com

SUBJECT: Request for a meeting - EU Careers conference

Dear Mr. Smith,

As the event coordinator at EU Training, Europe's largest training service for EU careers, I'd like to request a virtual meeting regarding the upcoming 'EU Careers post-Covid-19' conference.

To make sure this event is a success, I'd be grateful to have your views on the following details:

- Is there any plan to issue a press release before or after the event?
- Understanding the approval process in your DG concerning who can speak 'on record.'
- The role and involvement of your Director in the event's preparation.

I'd like to find the best time to discuss the above with you and your team.

Would any day at 10 AM between 25-28 May be feasible for you?

I can set up a virtual meeting or use any platform of your choosing if that's more convenient for you. I'm also planning to invite our project manager to join the discussion to facilitate the information flow.

I look forward to your reply in the following days.

Thank you and best regards,

Andras Baneth
EU Training Managing Partner

PS - I'm attaching a 1-page extract from our event manual, which I hope will help the planning process.

How do you think Mr. Smith will respond to this email?

Digital presentations

Whether you're in a physical conference room or a virtual meeting, audience engagement is always a challenge. In physical settings, the use of presentation software has to be considered with care because the visuals tend to monopolise your audience's attention. And in a virtual setting, using visual content is probably the best solution to keep your audience on their toes.

Images and videos break down information into smaller portions, and when you choose the right visuals, they provide more clarity than longer text or spoken presentations. People also more easily associate emotions with visuals. And when no one knows what's coming next, they'll pay more attention. People understand what you're saying faster and remember it longer with visual aids. Visual aids can be a useful part of oral presentations, but do not think about them as unavoidable. Steve Jobs[6] put it even more strongly: 'People who know what they are talking about don't need PowerPoint.'

Visual aids have to be meaningful, creative, and interesting in order to help you get a message across. Visual aids are supposed to help to illustrate and strengthen your points, not be a distraction from what you are saying. The key to successful use of visual aids is that they effectively support the presentation's theme; they support its transmittal but do so without being confused, complicated, or even too entertaining.

Do's and Don'ts for digital presentations

Here are some useful tips on how to make the best possible use of digital presentations:

- *Organise your information clearly.* Focus on one message per slide. Putting more than one message on a slide causes the audience to choose which message to focus on.
- *Limit the number of slides.* A good practice is using one slide per minute.
- We read seven times faster than we speak. Therefore, if there are 7 sentences on a slide, the audience have finished reading the seventh sentence when the speaker has finished the first sentence.
- *Create slides that people can 'get' in three seconds.* Audiences can process only one stream of information at a time. They will either listen to you or look at your slides. Make sure they can quickly understand your visuals and then turn their attention back to what you are saying.
- *Don't read aloud the text on your slides.* Avoid this by not having proper sentences on your slides, but only keywords. Your slide deck is not the presentation! Too many speakers just read out loud what's on the presentation slides. Your audience could have done that themselves in the comfort of their office or at home.
- *Use dark backgrounds on your slides.* Remember that you are the presentation. When you stand next to a huge bright screen, the presentation becomes less about you and more about the slides.
- *Minimise numbers.* Though data can be helpful in illustrating a point or backing up an argument, most numbers are too complex to understand quickly. If you want to emphasize a statistic, consider using a graphic or image to convey the point.
- *Use section divider slides.* This will help break up content into memorable chunks.

6 https://en.wikipedia.org/wiki/Steve_Jobs

- *Distribute handouts at the end, not before or during the presentation.* Unless it is imperative that people follow a handout while you're presenting, wait until you're done to distribute them.

Instead of sending out presentations or meeting agendas ahead of time, you can upload them to your virtual meeting room, so participants must be present to get the information. And if you're giving feedback or constructive criticism in a meeting, you can display documents or collateral with your edits and comments.

Despite all this, there are some clear 'don'ts' when using presentation software:

- Don't put everything on your slides. Only put the essence down. It's recommended that you don't use more than seven items per slide. In 1956, George Miller of Harvard University wrote that most people could retain roughly seven items of information in their short-term memory. So, don't challenge your audience's short-term memory.

- *Remove all non-essential information.* Eliminate unnecessary words and discard superfluous slides. Once you're finished drafting your slides, imagine you're one of the people listening to your remarks while you review them. If something is irrelevant, distracting or confusing, edit ruthlessly.
- *Don't rely on your slides.* Your slides should never be the main source of information for the audience. Use them as an extension that makes your speech more engaging or credible. Remember that your audience needs to learn from you, the speaker, not from your slides. To know if you're relying too heavily on your slides or not, ask yourself this question: 'Would my presentation still make sense without the slides?' If the answer's no, then you should rethink your script.
- *Don't overcomplicate your slides.* The white space on your slides is good. When your slides become too cluttered, the audience will, at best, have a difficult time following, and at worst, give up trying to understand.
- *Don't read everything from your slides.* One of the most prevalent and damaging habits is to read the visual presentation to the audience. Not only is that redundant, but it makes even the most appealing presentation boring. The audience didn't come to read your presentation slides. They came to hear you.
- *Don't rush.* Give your audience sufficient time to read each slide, but don't delay so long as to lose their attention. Also, don't start speaking as soon as the next slide loads. Give the audience a few moments to scan the slide and get ready to hear what you have to say about it. Likewise, don't hit the next slide as soon as you finish discussing the current one. Give your audience time to digest the information.
- *Don't overuse statistics.* No one needs to be shown all the raw data that went into your presentation. They want you to synthesise that information for them. If you have a stat you think is vital to the story you are telling, try to format it in a visually interesting way like a simple chart or graph. If you

want to provide all the details, put them on your website or in your handout materials.

- *Don't overuse transitions, animations and sound.* These effects are meant to increase the impact of one idea. They can become a distraction very quickly. Most presentations are just a visual aid. If you overload them, the audience will try to read the slides and not pay attention to you.
- *Don't use hard-to-read colour combinations and fonts.* Aim for high contrast between background and text. Try not to use different colours and fonts on every single slide. Your template will help with this.
- *Don't use generic graphics that you found on Google.* Make sure your pictures are well-designed and suited for your audience. The same goes for stock photos that have been used by everyone. Chances are someone has seen or used that image as well, so instead of helping, it hurts your point.
- *Don't think the slides are the presentation.* The slides are meant to help the audience follow you and give them clues to organise the information you share. The slides are not your presentation.

Why bullet points are bad for presentations

You have probably heard this before: don't use bullet points in your presentations. This is because bullet points make information harder to remember when the lists exist along with spoken words.

In 2014, the International Journal of Business Communication published the results from *The Use of Visualisation in the Communication of Business Strategies*[7], a study designed to gather empirical evidence regarding whether the use of visualisation is superior to text in business information communication. The results of that experiment confirmed that lists of text are ineffective for presentations. Slides with visuals are more effective than slides with text. In other words, when your slides contain lists of text, your audience will struggle to pay attention to your slides, they will find it very hard to agree with your message, and they will remember less information.

Dr. Chris Atherton[8] discovered that the limits of our working memory are to blame for this. By actively processing the information instead of simultaneously reading the slides and listening to the presenter, audience members are more likely to retain the presentation's meaning. Dr Atherton recommends creating slides with minimal text to limit the cognitive load of your presentation. Besides, she also recommends using visuals to communicate complex ideas. Since the human brain area that processes visuals has a working memory capacity that is separate from the short-term memory limit of the brain's linguistic and auditory processing areas, you expand the amount of information that audience members can process by using visuals on your slides.

7 http://job.sagepub.com/content/early/2014/04/01/2329488414525444.abstract
8 https://www.slideshare.net/CJAtherton/chris-atherton-at-tcuk09

Digital presentation software

Presentation software has caused an explosion of visualisation in human communication across the world. Slides are almost a mandatory tool for communication in many organisations. People plan with them, sell with them, present with them, and share them with one another.

When most people think of using a presentation tool, they probably think of Microsoft PowerPoint. But even though PowerPoint is still a prevalent presentation tool, there are good alternatives and today's presenters have a wide choice of products that may better meet their needs.

PowerPoint

There are some obvious reasons why people use PowerPoint. First, it is often the only presentation tool they have ever used. Second, PowerPoint comes with the MS Office package. Third, it is widely supported and used. PowerPoint is known to be the standard 'go-to' software when making presentations. In fact, for many people, the word 'PowerPoint' is synonymous with 'presentation.'

PowerPoint allows users to create presentations composed of a series of slides. Since it's fully integrated with the other tools of the Microsoft Office suite, the user can import content created with Excel or Word into PowerPoint, and other media such as pictures, audio and video clips. A series of templates are used to provide the user with pre-defined layouts for different purposes. The theme of the presentation is set by defining a standard font, background colour and design.

During a PowerPoint presentation, the presenter has the freedom to define the pace by controlling the flow manually or having the slide swap at pre-set intervals, which may also be different for each slide. Individual elements, such as bullet points or videos may also appear after a specific command is issued. With pre-defined transition effects, the user can time the slides so that the presentation advances automatically.

In older versions of PowerPoint, presentations were saved only as a standard .pptx format. Newer versions allow the users to save presentations in different common formats such as odp or pdf.

Keynote

When Steve Jobs returned to Apple in 1996, he was assigned the title of iCEO (interim CEO) but considered himself to be the chief salesperson of Apple. He asked his software designers to build something he could use in his keynote speeches and gave them a long list of features. The program was first sold publicly as Keynote 1.0 in 2003, competing against Microsoft PowerPoint.

If you are a Mac user and want to create presentations that 'don't look like PowerPoints', then Keynote is for you since it comes included with most Apple devices. Most of the functionality in Keynote is similar to PowerPoint, but a simple, more intuitive interface puts essential tools front and centre, so you can easily create attractive charts, edit photos and incorporate cinematic effects.

With outline view for iPhone and iPad, you can quickly jot down your thoughts, restructure ideas, and move concepts from slide to slide. With Scribble and Apple

Pencil, your handwritten words are automatically converted to typed text. You can also use Apple Pencil on your iPad to create diagrams or illustrations that bring your slides to life. And with real time collaboration, your team can work together, whether they're on Mac, iPad, iPhone, or using a PC.

Google Slides

Google Slides, PowerPoint and Keynote have a similar interface. You won't feel completely lost going from one presentation software to the other. However, they have unique templates. While Microsoft has a decent number of templates to choose from, some of the themes are ultra-specific. This means you may not even use half the templates you're given. And while Apple's eye-catching templates are fantastic, you may only use a handful of simpler designs here too. Google Slides themes may have the upper hand here since they're already pretty universal.

Google Slides was created primarily to be an online application and works perfectly when you have a decent internet connection. Google Slides works on the web but lets you work on offline mode too. Just make sure to switch it to offline mode before going offline. Google Slides works on Android, iOS, PC, and Mac. All Slides' features remain uniform across platforms.

Google Slides can be accessed for free as a Google application and used to create presentation slides without the need for a subscription. You can also get Google Slides as part of the G Suite Business application, which comes with several additional features and has a monthly subscription.

Prezi

Prezi's presentations are non-linear, which is suitable for people who like to jump around to different ideas a lot throughout their presentation. Users or presenters can click on the background of the presentation to zoom outward to an overview. From there, another click allows for the zoom to come into any area of the presentation. That makes it easier to answer questions, explore ideas, or provide specific details without losing one's place within the overall presentation path. Prezi's unique format allows true conversational presenting, the ability to adapt your presentation on the fly to focus on your audience's interests.

Powtoon

Powtoon gives users the ability to create animations by letting them manipulate objects and images. Animated elements are combined with music, narration or videos to create movie-like presentations instead of slide-decks. Powtoon has developed two add-ins attached to PowerPoint, enabling you to integrate Powtoon with the Microsoft presentation software seamlessly. These add-ins work in both directions: to export your PowerPoint to Powtoon and to embed your Powtoon into a PowerPoint presentation. A free version with limited features is available, while its full version comes as a paid subscription offer.

Outsourcing presentation design

If you are an EU official, aesthetics may not exactly be your forte. Much like persuasive speaking, persuasive designing is an art. Experienced designers know which elements go well together and which don't in terms of colours, text styles, icons, etc. They can arrange your presentation so that it comes together and forms a unified big picture for your audience. A good designer can make your slides look unique and aesthetically pleasing, and also ensure that your message is at the forefront of your presentation.

If you don't have access to in-house designers, outsourcing your presentation design may be an option. This can also give you time to focus on other tasks rather than spending most of your time on slide design. This could be rehearsing your speech or getting control over your body language. As Peter Drucker[9] summarised it in one simple phrase: 'Do what you do best and outsource the rest.'

Outsourcing presentation design has disadvantages and challenges too. Finding the best third-party provider can be time-consuming. If you work with sensitive data, security can be an issue. And communication can be a challenge; it can be influenced by time zones, or language, or cultural barriers.

Digital meetings

Remote working – or telecommuting – presents a series of clear advantages to the individual worker. When teleworking, you can choose if you want to work from home, the local coffee shop, or even down at the beach or in the countryside. This allows you to design your ideal workspace to be more productive. This is your space, which means that you are in control. You can be more flexible with your time as well. There will always be deadlines or meetings, but outside of those time constraints, you can set your hours and plan your own schedule.

Digital meeting software

As meeting solutions become more essential, driven by the demand for better human interactions in a remote environment, there are countless options to choose from.

Gartner's Magic Quadrant (MQ) is a series of market research reports published by the IT consulting firm Gartner that rely on proprietary qualitative data analysis methods to demonstrate market trends, such as direction, maturity, and participants. In September 2020 Gartner categorised the players in this segment as 'leaders', 'challengers' and 'visionaries' as in Table 10.1.

Leaders

Cisco led the Magic Quadrant for 2020. Webex offers an entirely cloud-based content and video sharing solution. Webex Meetings is an excellent tool for meeting and collaboration as it also provides access to Cisco Webex Teams (earlier known as Cisco Spark). For joining a Webex meeting, you can use any device, be it Windows, MacOS, Ubuntu, Red Hat, Open SuSE, or Fedora.

Microsoft's Office 365 cloud solution includes Microsoft Teams, the tool quickly emerging as the world's favourite option for enterprise collaboration with remote and

9 https://www.bl.uk/people/peter-drucker

	Leaders				Challengers		Visionaries
Product	**Zoom**	**Skype***	**Teams**	**Webex**	**Google Meet****	**GoToWebinar**	**BlueJeans**
Company	Zoom	Microsoft	Microsoft	Cisco	Google	LogMeIn	Verizon
Chatting	Yes	Yes	Yes	Yes	Yes	Yes	Yes
Recording	Yes	Yes	Yes	Yes	Yes	Yes	Yes
Screen sharing	Yes	Yes	Yes	Yes	Yes	Yes	Yes
Whiteboard	Yes	No	Yes	Yes	No	Yes	Yes
End-to-End encryption	No	Yes	No	Yes	No	Yes	Yes
Mobile App	Yes	Yes	Yes	Yes	Yes	Yes	Yes
Participants (max)	1000	50	300	1000	250	3000	100
Free Trial	Yes	n/a	Yes	Yes	n/a	Yes	No

* Skype for Business has been replaced by Microsoft Teams - ** Formerly Google Hangouts

Table 10.1: Video conferencing software

dispersed teams globally. You can use Microsoft Teams apps and software across various devices, such as Windows, Linux, Ubuntu, and Mac.

Skype is quite popular for one-on-one conversations and group video calls. You can manage your Skype account through any device, be it Xbox, Alexa, mobile or PC. While Skype is free, you can initiate audio and video calls with as many as 50 people easily.

Zoom made big strides after the start of the Covid pandemic thanks to its excellent meeting and webinar solutions. Zoom also supports third-party integration with many popular third-party sites like Google Drive, Slack, HubSpot, DropBox, Hipchat, etc. Zoom works on MacOS, Windows, Red Hat, Oracle Linux, ArchLinux, and Android.

Challengers

Google's G Suite (now Workspace) solution bundles a host of useful tools into a single environment, including Google Meet. Google's deployment model focuses only on SaaS[10] , with sales and service operations that span the globe.

LogMeIn serves the Meeting environment with GoToTraining, GoToMeeting, and GoToWebinar. There's also the Join.Me option to ensure that companies have a wide selection of meeting scenarios to choose from. There are various hardware options available through partners, and LogMeIn operates entirely on the cloud, making it easy for businesses to get started.

Visionaries

Purchased by Verizon in 2020, BlueJeans provides meetings and events solutions either as standalone tools or as part of Verizon UCaaS systems. Interoperability with

10 Software as a service is a software licensing and delivery model in which software is licensed on a subscription basis and is centrally hosted.

Microsoft Teams is an option through the BlueJeans gateway. There is no free version, and the app only focuses on video conferencing. The BlueJeans app can be used in-browser or simply installed as a desktop app. The desktop app is the only one that has all the features; however, there is an app available for iOS and Android.

Audience interaction software

Audience interaction software allows presenters to interact with audiences via live polls, surveys, quizzes, or Q&A sessions. This type of software is used to bring a level of interactivity to conference sessions or speaking engagements, allowing presenters to easily capture attendees' ideas or opinions. Typical features for this kind of software are:

- Live polls
- Audience Q&A
- Live slide sharing
- Native PowerPoint integration
- Brainstorming
- Audience feedback
- Share additional documents
- Share your contact information
- Control presentation on second screen
- Audience analytics
- Collect audience emails
- Attendees' note-taking

Using audience interaction software is a new way to brainstorm ideas. You can collect and curate the best ideas from your participants, whether you're deciding on team projects or summarising the key learnings from your workshop.

Another advantage of these tools is that they remove the fear of asking questions from the shy members of your audience. You can increase the quantity and quality of questions by allowing people to ask anonymously.

Modern audience response solutions are cloud-based and enable audience members to use their personal devices simply by accessing an event-specific link in their web browser or through an event-specific mobile application. Slido[11] and Kahoot![12] are the best-known contenders, but there are many other and cheaper players in this arena.

11 https://www.sli.do/

12 https://www.kahoot.com/

Presenting from your home office

The physical environment you are in and the equipment used will make a huge difference to your ability to work at home and the impression you make during online sessions with colleagues and others. For illustration, here is a photo of my own remote coaching set up.

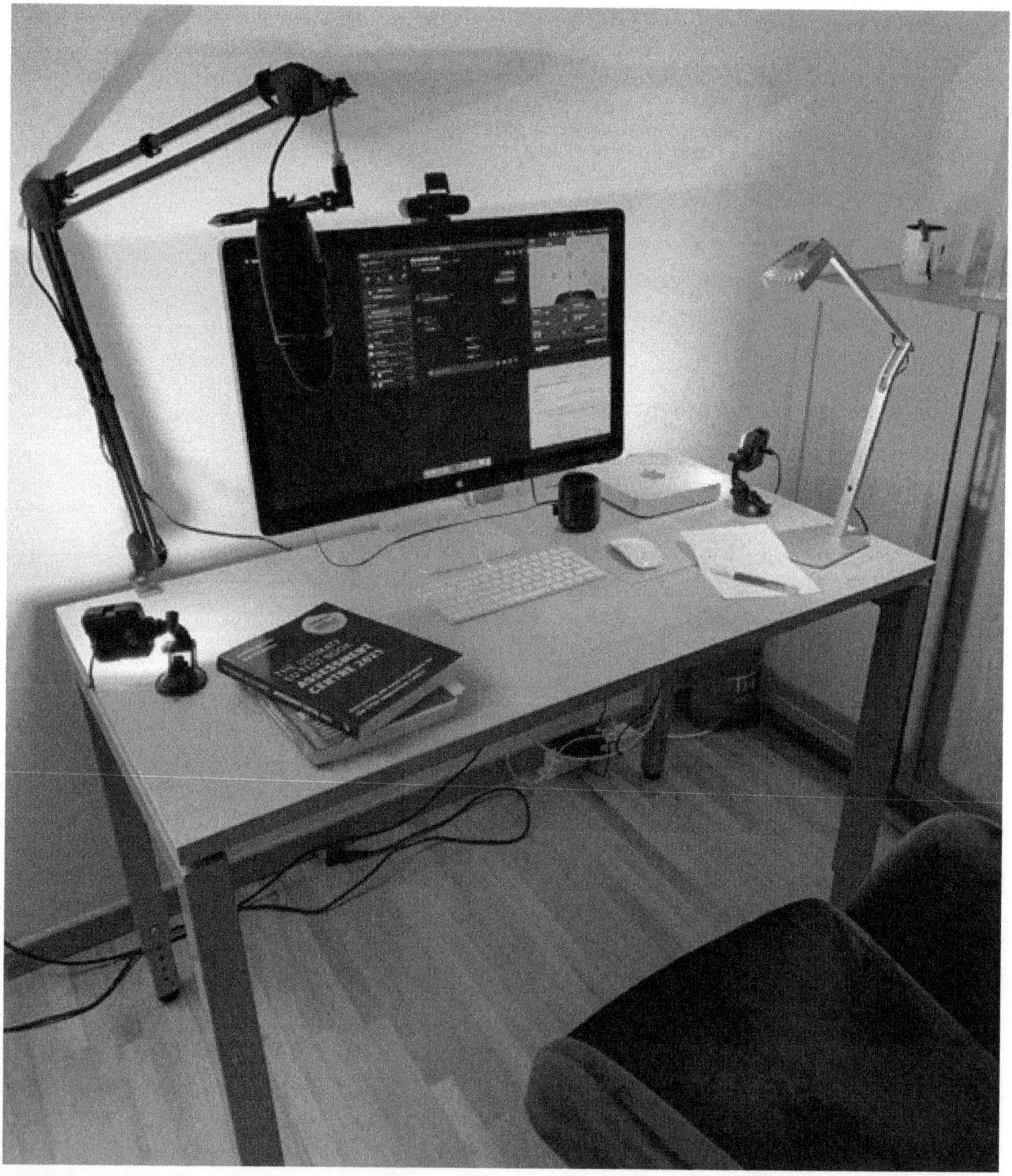

The room

Everyone's living situation is different. But wherever you set up your home office, try to find a space that offers privacy, adequate lighting, and easy access to power and internet.

Appropriate temperature control and fresh air are equally important to consider when you set up your home office. It is impossible to concentrate when working in an airless room, so make sure your working space is well-ventilated. Keep indoor humidity between 30 and 50% and room temperature between 22 and 25 °C. A study from Cornell University[13] tested different office temperatures at a large Florida insurance company and found that when temperatures were low (20 °C) employees made 44% more mistakes than at optimal room temperature of 25 °C. The problem isn't just that if you are cold you feel uncomfortable, the study points out. The problem is that you are distracted. If you are feeling cold, you are using a substantial amount of your energy to just keep warm. A lot less of your energy goes towards concentration, inspiration and focus. And a warmer environment doesn't just make us more productive, it also makes us happier.

Get natural light. A recent study[14] found that adults who get natural light sleep better (46 minutes more than those who don't get natural light). Another study[15] found that 40% of workplaces with natural light experience 3%-40% improvements in productivity. Natural light just feels better to work in as well, so make sure to position your desk and chair in a well-lit room.

Try to add some personality and warmth with decoration and green plants. Decoration and green plants won't just make your home office space feel more inviting, it will also improve productivity. Also try to avoid creating an environment that is a depressing jumble of cables and other clutter.

Furniture

A comfortable chair is the heart of a productive home office. You'll spend nearly half your day on it. Selecting the right chair can be a challenge. To find the right fit, pay attention to back, thigh and arm support.

When seated, your feet should be flat on the floor and your knees should be at a 90-degree angle. The *backrest* should provide adequate lumbar support. The backrest should be upright with a slight backwards lean of about 5 to 10 degrees. The armrests on your chair should gently support your forearms when your elbows are bent about 90 degrees. When your back is against the chair's backrest, there should be 5-7 cm of space between the back of your knees and the seat.

Consider buying a standing desk. There is a growing body of research that shows that sitting for extended periods of time is bad for your health. This explains why the new generation of workers are embracing standing desks.

A standing desk will improve your productivity, focus and heart health. Most of these desks are height adjustable. Some more expensive versions can even be converted into conventional sit-down desks on the fly.

13 https://news.cornell.edu/stories/2004/10/warm-offices-linked-fewer-typing-errors-higher-productivity

14 https://news.northwestern.edu/stories/2014/08/natural-light-in-the-office-boosts-health

15 https://www.eco-business.com/opinion/why-natural-light-matters-in-the-workplace/

You can use the ergotron workspace planner[16] to help you set up your workspace. This tool will tell you exactly where to keep your monitor, keyboard, chair and desk based on your height.

Internet connection

For remote video speaking it is essential to plan for sufficient bandwidth. You can think of bandwidth as a water-pipe that connects your house to the internet. All the internet traffic (water) that goes to and from your house must run through that pipe simultaneously and the diameter of that pipe limits you.

Most broadband connections can accommodate single-user video conferencing without any issues. However, keep in mind that multiple users at home may be using bandwidth-intensive applications including gaming, streaming, downloading software updates, etc. All this affects available bandwidth. Also note that video conferencing has much higher upstream requirements than other applications. With residential internet connections, upstream bandwidth is usually much lower than downstream bandwidth.

Check your internet speed with a specialised service like Speedtest[17]. For more accurate results, do multiple tests and do them when no one in your home network is downloading or sharing files or doing video streaming and video chats.

For videoconferencing, the best solution is to have a wired (Ethernet) connection between your router and workstation. If that is not an option, place your router high off the ground and in the centre of your house for better Wi-Fi signal strength. Install a Wi-Fi repeater if necessary.

Computer

Ideally, you should use a desktop computer. Laptops and tablets do not allow you to separate the keyboard from the monitor, forcing you to look down at the screen while typing and losing the eye contact with your audience. If you must use a laptop, perhaps consider purchasing either a separate monitor or a separate keyboard to connect to the laptop. That way your keyboard and monitor can be separate from one another, allowing you greater flexibility.

For the monitor, the basic specs you will want to look for are 1080p resolution and a 27-inch screen. If you can afford it, 1440p and 4K monitors are better, but 27 inches is a nice balance between having plenty of screen space without having your monitor dominate your desk.

Place your computer monitor directly in front of you. When looking at your monitor, the top third of the screen should be at eye level. When seated, your elbows should be bent about 90 degrees and your forearms should be directly in front of you. Your computer keyboard should be in line with your arms and wrists.

Webcam

The camera in your laptop, phone or tablet is perfectly placed … to look up your nose. To avoid unflattering angles, to keep everything in proportion and have your eyes

16 https://www.ergotron.com/tools/workspace-planner

17 https://www.speedtest.net

looking up, put something under your laptop or find a way to set your phone or tablet so the camera is at the same height as your eyes.

The best solution, of course, is to use a standard video camera for face-to-face communication online but using a webcam is normally cheaper. Webcams come in a wide variety of different models, some are wireless, and some can pan and zoom, while still others have movement sensors and night vision capabilities. There are many webcams that can provide the professional quality that make you really shine in high-definition and high-quality video. For this, a webcam with 720p resolution will do the job, but, of course, 1080p or 4K is even better. To avoid jerky video, get a webcam that can deliver at least 20 frames per second under this resolution. If you're willing to spend the money, get one that shoots up to 30 or even 60 frames per second. To counter sudden movements and lighting changes, get a webcam that has highly reactive autofocus and lighting-correction capabilities. Some computer users simply place a sticker over their webcam, but the adhesive leaves behind a film that makes the camera unusable. A webcam privacy cover protects the camera, while preventing hackers from spying on you when the camera isn't in use.

In early-generation webcams, the task of video encoding, the process by which video streams are compressed using a codec such as H.264, relied on a computer's general-purpose CPU. Since 2011, chipset makers like Intel and AMD have recognised the growing popularity of video calling and streaming applications, and they have enhanced their chipsets with hardware acceleration for video. Many of the current generation of computers have onboard hardware acceleration for video of 4K or higher using successors to H.264 such as H.265, also known as HEVC, or VP9, part of the WebRTC standard. The net result of these hardware and encoding advances is that there is no longer a need for in-camera encoding in today's computers, freeing up in-camera resources and instead focusing on delivering better image quality, for an affordable price.

With an online webcam test[18] you can easily find the technical information about your webcam and see if it works well.

Microphone

There's an old adage in the audio-visual business that good sound makes video look better. The first and most important component of an effective video meeting is audio quality. Video conferencing is about communication, so audio should always be your top priority. You don't want to be in a room with lots of echoes, background noise or ambient noise. Conduct your talks in a quiet and preferably well-furnished space to keep echoes and background noise to the absolute minimum. And remind others in your household to be quiet for the duration of your session.

The kind of microphone you use will affect the other participants' ability to hear you. Don't rely on the poor-quality internal microphone in your device – it can't help but pick up the entire room around you and mix your voice with a big dose of noise and confusing echoes. At the very least, use earbuds that have a microphone in the cable or advanced wireless earbuds with multiple noise-cancelling microphones.

Headset microphones should sit an inch or so away from your face and a few centimetres away from the corner of your lips. Clip-on microphones should sit at the upper side of the chest, about the level where shirt pockets are usually stitched.

18 https://webcamtests.com/

The best solution is to go for a separate microphone, standing in front of you, or mounted on a microphone boom with vibration blocking. You should pick a microphone with active noise cancellation and an ample frequency range (20Hz - 20kHz). If you're buying a professional studio-quality microphone, get something with a low impedance. 600 ohms (Ω) or below is best, since it compensates for long cables without compromising on audio quality. To set up a separate microphone properly, point it away from any speakers, and select the appropriate pick-up pattern (cardioid, omnidirectional, bidirectional, or stereo).

When pausing during a presentation or speech, make sure you don't stay silent for too long. Otherwise the audience might wonder if your audio has cut out or if your internet connection is erratic. Mute your audio if you don't expect to be talking for a while.

Speakers

Once again, it is not advisable to use the speakers of your device and there are better solutions than the speakers built-in into your webcam, provided you don't mind your your audience seeing you wearing a headset.

Headphones come in wired and wireless versions, but for videoconferencing the hands-free wireless option is probably the best choice. Make sure to have good noise cancellation so that you can concentrate on the voice of your correspondent.

Lighting

Never sit with your back to a window or have a bright light directly behind you. You will be backlit, meaning the audience will only see a blacked-out silhouette of you and nothing else. To be well lit, make sure you always face towards a bright yet soft light source. You can buy a LED video soft light panel, and a tripod, with adjustable brightness and colour temperature. If you are a professional speaker, this may be worth the investment because using a normal lamp may produce 'catch lights' (eye reflections).

If you wear glasses, adjust the lighting in the room to reduce glare from the lenses. Also, the reflections of your screen in the lenses may be 'hiding' your eyes. Using a dark background behind the viewing window can avoid this.

Framing

Framing refers to where you are positioned in the shot in relation to your camera. You want the camera to frame your face, neck, and shoulders. People are drawn to faces, so you don't want to lose that connection by being too far away, but you also don't want your face to take over the whole screen. Good webcams with zoom and pan functions allow you to adjust the framing.

Be mindful of headroom. This is the space between the top of your head and the top of the screen. If there is too much headroom or not enough, it will make you look awkward. Push your laptop/camera back to the desired distance where you are framed well.

When delivering a presentation, stand up. Standing up provides a higher energy level and forces you to put your body in a more presentation-like mode.

Backgrounds

Your background can either add to your professional presence or detract from it. When you have a video interview or a conference call in your office at work or a conference room, and unless your workspace is cluttered with files, empty coffee cups, and dead office plants, you don't need to worry about your background. But when you are conducting a video interview from home, or remotely plugging into a conference call, or hosting a webinar, people can't help but notice your background and the environment you are in. And because first impressions are so important, it's critical to set up an environment that reflects your personal brand.

Your background should be friendly, neat and professional. Remove clutter from behind and around you. Blurring the background is a cool trick in professional videoconferencing software to help clean up or hide background messes during calls. You may wish to have on your bookshelf books or documents enhancing your credibility. This can subconsciously send a message to the audience about your motivation and interest in the topic.

While it is preferable you find a nice spot at your place, sometimes it's impossible, so then you could use a virtual background. Much like 'real' backgrounds, virtual backgrounds should be not too simple, not too busy, and not too bright.

The holy-grail solution to generating a great virtual background is to place a 'green screen' behind you that spans your entire background. Then, your webcam or the video conference provider will create a beautiful chroma-keyed background using the green. The other option is to let the video conference provider figure it out without the benefit of a solid colour. It works, but often with the edges of your head and body shimmering like a phantom.

And before starting the event, let everyone in your household know to stay out of your space and place a 'Do not disturb!' sign on your door to avoid any 'BBC interview[19]' situations.

Eye contact

Eye contact is different in a video meeting. In-person, you would look directly at someone's eyes. In a video meeting, you maintain eye contact by looking into the camera. If you can't help looking at someone's face on the screen instead of their camera, it helps to reduce the size of your viewing window and move it to the part of the screen nearest to the camera. So at least you're looking at approximately the right place when you're looking at their face. If your webcam has zoom and pan you can sit further away from your screen/webcam and fake eye contact on a full-screen window.

Online audiences are easily distracted as you look away to refer to your notes. You can deliver a more persuasive video presentation by never looking away from them. Simply upload your script into a teleprompter that projects your script in a browser window over your videoconferencing window. Adjust the speed to the presentation style, and you can even pause the scrolling script to answer questions from the audience. Positioning the teleprompter on your screen is a crucial part of this process. The key to a smooth teleprompter experience is to create distance from the speaker and the teleprompter. This minimises eye movement and makes it look much more natural.

19 https://youtu.be/Mh4f9AYRCZY

Position and size the teleprompter window as close to your webcam as possible. Put your audience window towards the bottom of the screen and your teleprompter window towards the top and middle of your screen to minimise eye movements.

12. Teleworking

Both 'telecommuting' and 'teleworking' refer to a working arrangement where employees or contractors regularly perform their work outside the traditional on-site work environment. Initially the two terms referred to different situations:

- *Teleworking*. Any form of substitution of information technologies (such as telecommunications and/or computers) for regular work-related travel; moving the work to the workers instead of moving the workers to work.
- *Telecommuting*. Periodic work out of the principal office – one or more days per week either at home, a client's site, or in a telework centre, with the partial or total substitution of information technologies for the commute to work. The emphasis here is on the reduction or elimination of the daily commute to and from the workplace. Telecommuting is a form of teleworking.

In today's workplace, the two terms mean the same thing and are used interchangeably. They are both terms for the practice of working from home or off-site, making use of the internet, videoconferencing, email, chat and phone to perform duties that once were carried out only in an office environment.

Before 2020, teleworking was looked upon with much suspicion by the average manager in the Commission. And it was not a right but a favour that could only be granted if compatible with work demands. There were two kinds of telework, structural and occasional, and you needed your manager's permission for both. Structural telework was recurrent, for example, every Wednesday. Occasional telework was ad hoc – for example, 'I won't come to the office next Monday because I have something urgent to finish' (and not 'because I'm expecting a private Amazon delivery').

When Covid-19 hit, a relative mastery of telework's technical dimension had to be acquired quickly, and this went amazingly well. The managers had to adapt, of course, and generally speaking, staff were happy. But the main discovery was a general lack of knowledge of what modes of work have to be adopted. If telework has been progress, it has also encouraged the fragmentation of the EU civil service, like other organisations, and it has invaded the employee's private life with professional activities. Likewise, it has made it difficult to give a proper welcome to new colleagues or external stakeholders. Nevertheless, the prevailing consensus is that teleworking will stay a structural part of the 'new normal' of working for the EU.

Certainly, teleworking has a significant impact on our behaviour at work, and our general competencies are challenged in totally new ways. That is why I have dedicated a specific chapter to the 'hot topic' of teleworking in the EU administration.

Some food for thought

The real-life experience of working from home depends a lot on individual circumstances. For people living by themselves it can be a hard experience, isolating and disorienting.

For some, going to work is an escape from the unrelenting demands of children, for others it is just a chance to meet other people. Sharing a joke with work colleagues can be essential escapism from monotonous work.

For the Commission, the original idea of a European civil service with a strong 'esprit de corps' can only be undermined by remote working. It is already being undermined by having more and more staff on temporary contracts and recruited for specialist tasks rather than as all-rounders. All institutions that adopt remote working will risk over time losing any sense of corporate identification. It could be indeed that we end up with more and more people not working for any specific institution or firm but simply contracting their services to the highest bidder or working for different organisations simultaneously. That would mirror the gradual individualisation of society, and decline of group identities (trade unions, social clubs, political parties, etc.) that has been going on for several decades. Public institutions and big private sector firms could be contributing to their own eventual collapse.

Inevitably too, it would lead to the mere quantification of all work. The qualities of inspiring others, or helping others when they are struggling, or contributing a great idea around the water cooler are hard to show outside of a workplace context with genuine human interaction.

But doubtless, there will be many surprises along the way.

Pros and cons of teleworking

Costs and savings

Letting employees work from home can mean significant savings for organisations. For employers, these savings can be attributed mainly to minimised overhead costs. Organisations pay less for expensive office rentals, and they have smaller utility bills to worry about. And the purchase and maintenance of in-office workstations and equipment are reduced.

To illustrate this point, in January 2021, EU Commissioner Hahn proposed reducing the Commission's office space by 200,000 m^2, by a target date of 2030. The result of this drastic reduction will be that most EU staff won't have a fixed workspace anymore but instead will be working in 'collaborative spaces', 'open spaces', or 'hot desks'.

For employees, depending on where they live, the cost of getting to their job in a traditional setting easily equates to a couple of thousand euros per year. If you work remotely, this money stays in your bank account instead of going to the local fuel station. There are fewer lunches at restaurants, and you won't have the same wardrobe costs since you can work at home in less formal outfit.

On the other hand, telework leads to an increased risk of loss of network privacy and security. Maintaining safe and effective network protection can often be challenging enough within a closed environment, and when employees remotely access documents located on an internal network, privacy and security can be compromised. To help prevent potential security breaches, employers should provide teleworkers with company-issued equipment and prohibit administrator privileges. Soon, Commission officials will dispose of a 'homeworking package', comprising an office chair, computer screen, docking station, keyboard and mouse, identical to the equipment that is used in the Commission premises. Telephones already disappeared before Covid-19 and were replaced by a Skype for Business account (now Microsoft Teams). The other EU institutions have made similar arrangements.

As we saw in the previous chapter, setting up an optimal home office environment is a substantial undertaking and for most people the actual arrangements they have will inevitably involve compromises in terms of the space available, working conditions and the equipment used.

Productivity and business continuity

In a study[1] conducted on remote and office employees, researchers from the Stanford Graduate School of Business found that remote workers are 13% more productive than their office-based colleagues because remote workers tend to work their entire shift. The coffee break, having a smoke, or watercooler interruptions that limit productivity in the office disappear when working from home. You may have your kids wanting your attention or neighbours knocking on your door, but these interruptions are usually less frequent than co-workers wishing to talk about the football game they saw the night before or the latest office news.

Having teleworking arrangements in place also allows organisations to continue functioning despite the challenges and risks that may keep staff from reporting to the office. For example, during the coronavirus outbreak, the EU administration continued to carry forward its work on Brexit, negotiations with the US and China, the MFF and recovery package, and the pandemic itself. All this despite strict community quarantines and lockdowns being enforced in many countries.

On the other hand, it is clear that, when teleworking, employees have much greater opportunities to take care of private matters, using social media, browsing the internet, or even running a business on the side while officially working – and being paid by their employer. Fig. 12.1, based on a custom Scarborough survey in April 2020 that was linked with the Total Media Fusion sourced from Nielsen Media Impact[2], says a lot in this respect.

Teleworking requires a management style that is results-based and objective-driven and not simply counting the hours of presence in the office as it used to be in more traditional settings. Managers have to trust that their subordinates have enough respect for themselves and their co-workers to complete work assignments.

Motivation and job satisfaction

According to OWL Labs' State of Remote Work 2020 report[3], in the US, remote work has been the preferred choice of many when offered by their companies before Covid-

1 https://www.gsb.stanford.edu/insights/why-working-home-future-looking-technology

2 https://www.nielsen.com/us/en/solutions/capabilities/media-impact-national/

3 https://resources.owllabs.com/hubfs/website/sorw/2020/owl-labs_sorw-2020_report-download_FINAL_07oct2020.pdf

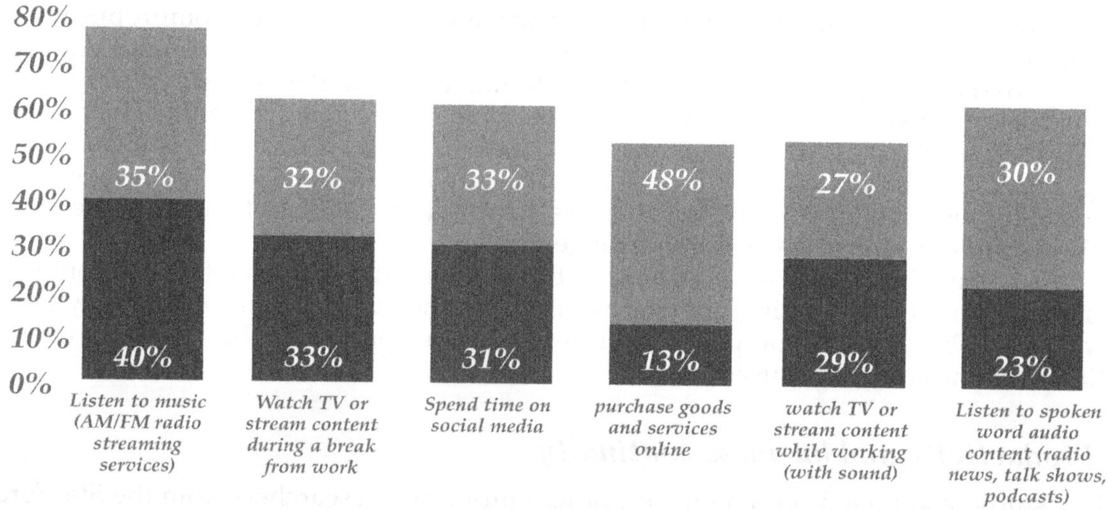

Figure 12.1: What 'work-from-homers' are doing during working hours

19. When it was an option versus a necessity, many remote workers reported feeling happier, more productive and more trusted by their managers. Now that working from home became an overnight reality for most, people realise they do prefer this way of working.

If you spend two hours per day in traffic jams or public transportation, you can easily add the equivalent of a full working day to a 40-hour week at the office. And you will arrive at work at home in a more relaxed, more productive frame of mind.

Teleworking can also increase job satisfaction. A study by Amerisleep[4] revealed that 57% of remote workers are more likely to be satisfied with their jobs. Almost 80% of the respondents also consider themselves only moderately stressed or not stressed during the workweek.

Physical and mental health

Studies report that remote workers take fewer sick days. Because they stay at home primarily, they are less exposed to germs, pollutants and allergens, and they can rest longer.

Indeed's Remote Work Survey[5] revealed that 50% of their respondents who work from home had reduced sick days. Meanwhile, 56% had fewer absences. According to Flexjobs' Work-Life-Relationship Survey[6] 86% of their employee respondents believe that having a flexible work arrangement can help reduce their stress, and 89% think it will help them take care of themselves better.

4 https://amerisleep.com/blog/remote-workers-and-rest/

5 https://www.indeed.com/lead/remote-work-survey

6 https://www.flexjobs.com/blog/post/survey-flexible-work-mental-health/

However, telework also tends to blur the lines between work and home life. When struggling to separate work from personal life, anxiety and stress creep in, which may affect an employee's mental health, ultimately leading to a 'burn out'. There is some anecdotal evidence from the Commission's HR department that the number of long-term sickness leaves has increased during the Covid pandemic.

Talent acquisition and management

According to the Global Workspace Survey 2019[7] of the International Workplace Group, 80% of US workers would choose a job that offers telecommuting benefits over one that doesn't. They might even reject a prestigious position just to have the privilege of working from home. And there are no reasons to believe that European workers, especially younger ones, are different in this respect.

In 2020, due to the Covid-19 outbreak and to conclude the competitions within a reasonable period, EPSO decided to organise remote online testing for the Assessment Centre tests. Remote online testing allows candidates to sit the tests at home, in the office, or in an EPSO accredited test centre throughout Europe and worldwide. At the time of writing this book, it seems possible that EPSO will continue and expand remote testing of all candidates for the various selection procedures (open competitions, CAST, temporary agents, ...) even when the pandemic is fully controlled.

Organisations that embrace the distributed team culture can hire remote employees more efficiently and many employers now also see remote work and flexible schedules as an influential retention factor. Thus, adopting a remote arrangement can help HR departments bridge the skills gap and find the right people for the right job at the right time.

Environmental impact

Teleworking is often considered the easiest way organisations can help reduce their carbon footprint. Indeed, teleworking can reduce greenhouse gas emissions, but the level depends entirely on context.

In a recent review paper[8], published by O'Brien and colleagues in Energy and Buildings, the authors concluded that once the scope is expanded to include home office energy use, the internet, long-term consumer choices, and other so-called rebound effects, the net savings are not necessarily significant, if not negative. (Fig. 12.2).

The researchers recommend adapting building and technologies to accommodate varying levels of occupancy and use. These ideas were taken on board in the Commission's plans for teleworking. For example, in the first quarter of 2021, DG-HR[9] DG-DIGIT[10], and DG-SCIC[11] moved to a brand-new building with workplaces for less than 70% of the people – everybody has a locker on a specific floor and workspaces have to be reserved beforehand. This concept will be gradually deployed for the entire Commission by 2030.

7 https://www.iwgplc.com/global-workspace-survey-2019

8 https://www.sciencedirect.com/science/article/abs/pii/S0378778820317710?via%3Dihub

9 Human Resources

10 Digital transformation

11 Interpretation (for its former French name Service Commun Interprétation-Conférences)

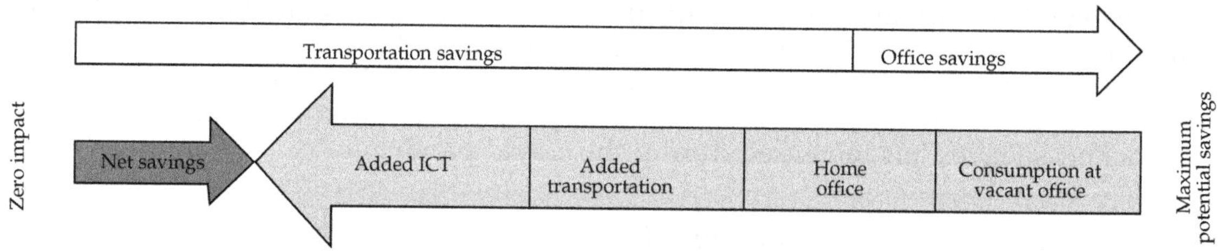

Figure 12.2: Environmental impact of teleworking

How to become a better teleworker

Below are some practical tips on how to become a better teleworker. I have organised these tips along the lines of the general competencies as discussed earlier in this book.

Analysis and problem solving

- *Be more proactive.* Being proactive means thinking and acting ahead of anticipated events. By thinking about potential issues that could arise and being aware of possible future changes, you'll be able to plan and act accordingly.
- *Brainstorm with an online whiteboard.* If you're used to using a whiteboard when brainstorming with your team, you can use an online whiteboard to do the same remotely. It gives you the benefits of visual thinking and collaboration without being in the same room as your teammates.
- *Brainstorm alone.* Brainstorming alone doesn't have to mean sitting in front of an empty screen. Walking makes you more creative, so take a walk to do

Towards a devolved EU administration?

Thus far, discussion of the merits of remote working in the EU administration has focused on the interests and needs of existing EU staff and their managers.

But what of the broader European interest?

A complaint widely heard in the member states is that 'Brussels' is a remote and faceless bureaucracy. And indeed most EU staff work either in Brussels or the smaller hub of Luxembourg. The presence on the ground of the EU administration is very small in most of the member states – perhaps a couple of hundred, mainly technical contract staff in an agency and a small number in the capital in the Parliament and Commission representations.

But if EU staff can do their jobs sitting at home, why does that have to be in Belgium or Luxembourg? Why not in an industrial town in Poland or a village in Portugal? If EU staff did not always have to relocate to (expensive) Brussels and Luxembourg, the pool of available quality candidates could expand and the EU administration could become an embedded presence in every part of the continent. That alone might not turn the tide on Euroscepticism, but it could help.

your thinking. Just be sure you have your phone on you so you can take notes as things pop into your brain.

Communication

- *Read between the lines.* Written instructions may contain cues that would otherwise be conveyed by non-verbal communication, so it is essential to read everything very carefully and not 'browse' as we tend to do in these times of over-information. Ask questions if you are not sure.
- *Communicate clearly.* Both in writing and orally, you should make an extra effort to make yourself be understood without unnecessary garnish. Check your emails and text messages twice before you hit the 'send' button. For oral communication, follow the best practices as laid out in the previous chapter.
- *Stay connected.* Many people are afraid to call or instant message colleagues who are working remotely because they don't want to bother them. Remember, they are working, not on vacation at home. Feel confident about calling or messaging a teleworking colleague at any time you would walk into their office or call them if you were working on-site. You can even keep your usual coffee break – simply plan to call or video chat with a cup in hand at the time you would typically walk to your favourite coffee corner at the office.
- *Keep the lines of communication open.* If you are working from home, be sure to check in at least once a day by email, online chat, phone or videoconferencing with your manager and co-workers. You should also set up regular face-to-face meetings with them. Relationships develop more quickly in person, and remote workers can be forgotten or overlooked for promotions or career development if they are not top of mind.
- *Show your face.* Networking is an essential part of professional life. Remote workers can have a hard time meeting other professionals in their field. As a remote worker, it is vital to put some effort into networking by actively seeking opportunities. Join discussion forums, connect with people on social media, and attend events open to the public.

Delivering quality and results

- *Make no assumptions.* People often get into hot water when they assume a co-worker, stakeholder or supervisor knows what they really expect or even what they're talking about. Don't fall into the trap of thinking someone has the same understanding of a situation, project, deadline or task that you do. You can avoid this pitfall by having a conversation in which you openly discuss what's expected, how it might be accomplished, and how success will be measured.
- *Pushing back is OK.* You have to be comfortable that the expectations are realistic and achievable. If they're not, you can – and should – push back. Being

open about what can be delivered can go a long way in instilling confidence and getting the go-ahead.

- *Set realistic goals.* Even when working from the comfort of your home, it doesn't mean that you won't have difficulties in getting things done. Don't assume you will be working during 100% of your scheduled hours. Include short breaks in your schedule, and don't be too disappointed if you're not getting everything done right on time.
- *Set daily goals.* Identify what needs to get done every day and make sure to do it. Start each day of telework by writing down what you need to achieve and then track your progress. As long as you have a plan for how to complete the list of daily tasks on your to-do list, it doesn't matter if or how you may be interrupted, as long as you get things done by the end of the day.
- *Multitasking is a myth.* There is absolutely no way for an average person to do two things simultaneously and do them both well. As soon as you choose quantity, quality will have to suffer.

Learning and development

- *Master the art of digital persuasion.* In today's world of pervasive digital communication, it is not a luxury to spend some time on mastering the 'tools of the trade,' as laid out in the previous chapter. The very least you should do is make sure you know how to use the standard tools that your employer provides. Ask for training if needed.
- *Keep yourself updated.* Make sure you attend as many training opportunities and seminars as you can, online if necessary. It is up to you to find resources and courses that will keep your skills relevant and competitive. Be proactive about learning new skills, and don't miss out on any opportunity to update your knowledge base.

Resilience

- *Separate work life from home life.* A common mistake that home workers make is working too much. That is why it is critical to set boundaries, and it is essential to impose rules for you and your family members if you're working from home. Establish 'do not disturb' guidelines, work hours, break times, and a policy on handling personal matters. The best advice is to treat your home office as if it were a real office located somewhere else.
- *Don't constantly monitor your cell phone.* Set your phone to silent or turn it off altogether when work demands your attention. The same advice can apply to checking Facebook, Twitter, LinkedIn, and other social media networks throughout the day unless that's a key part of your job.
- *Eliminate distractions.* Your partner, children, pets or a favourite hobby are only a few feet away at home. Depending on your living arrangements, you may need to hang a 'do not disturb' sign on your home office door so family

members don't interrupt you, and you might need headphones to block the noise around you.

- *Take advantage of flexible hours*. While you are supposed to follow a general work schedule, it should not be too rigid. It's perfectly normal to play outside with your children, have lunch with friends, go out for coffee, etc. Don't put too much pressure on yourself in terms of your workload. When working remotely, you can set your schedule and work at your own pace.
- *Take a few breaks*. When working from home, some people tend to stay at their desks and not take regular short breaks like they would at the office. You can quickly become too absorbed in your work and end up working non-stop for hours at a time, which can eventually lead to burnout. Take a few breaks to get out of your chair: eat a healthy snack, stretch, go for a walk, or do a mini-workout or yoga.
- *Get out of the house*. Work remotely from a coffee shop nearby. Attend a networking lunch. Go to a business happy hour. Whatever the activity, make sure you're around other people at least some of the time.
- *Skip work when you're not productive*. We have been led to believe that we must be productive during regular business hours, and we sometimes feel guilty when we aren't chained to our desks. If you aren't focused and don't feel productive, don't force it. Take some time, go for a walk, get some space, and then go back to your workplace.
- *Don't become a hermit*. You're already dealing with the absence of the usual social and physical interactions with colleagues. Disconnect from work at the end of the day. Go out with the family, play with the kids in the park, eat out if possible, go running. Don't let remote work invade your private time. Ensure a work-life balance to keep your morale up and maintain your overall health.

Prioritising and organising

- *Define your workspace*. It can be tempting to sit on the sofa with your laptop and expect to get work done. We are creatures of habit, and most of us are used to relaxing with our laptops to read the news, watch TV, play games and chat with friends and family. Establishing a workspace, even if it is your kitchen table, gives your brain a cue that it is time for work and not play. Whenever possible, don't work in the bedroom or living room; these environments should remain rest areas.
- *Set up the proper environment*. Find a space in your home that's your dedicated workspace. Ideally, the space should have a door so that you can shut out noise or interruptions. Not everyone has a comfortable, ergonomically designed office at home. However, working at home should not mean working all day from the bed or couch.

- *Establish office hours.* If you don't create a window of time for your job, you'll either work around the clock or procrastinate. Add your telecommute schedule to your email signature line.
- *Divide up your day.* Break up your workday into chunks, alternating activities like eating, doing exercise or socialising with working time. With this sort of schedule, you are not stuck behind the desk for long periods.
- *Don't let friends stop by whenever they want.* Use lunch as a time to meet with friends and if they show up at your place unexpectedly, politely tell them that it is not a good time and over the weekend would be better. You can also instruct them to call first to see if you are home.
- *Dress for work.* Just like sitting on the couch can make us feel a little too relaxed, wearing pyjamas all day makes it hard to get into work mode. Dressing casually is a benefit of working at home but 'getting ready for work' is a daily ritual that should be honoured.

Working with others

- *Stay in the loop.* Staying connected to your colleagues can be quite challenging while teleworking. Besides work-related discussions, you should always remain engaged in the institution's social life. Bonding with your peers will improve your work experience and keep your spirits up.
- *Be a team player.* The success of your project depends on everyone who takes part in it. Sharing your work with teammates and collaborating to improve your results is an essential part of a successful project. So be a team player and don't hold on to information to prove to your managers that you are the best.
- *Use chat during virtual meetings.* You can increase participation and get feedback by asking your team to enter responses into a chat during your virtual meetings.
- *Check in with co-workers and your manager several times a day.* When you're co-located with your team, you gain an incredible wealth of contextual information just by being around them. You have to try to replicate as much of that benefit as possible in a situation where you are physically separated.

Leadership

In an article titled 'The Influence of Supervisors' Leadership Style on Telecommuters'[12], Paul Madlock assessed the relative merits of task-oriented and relationship-oriented leadership styles in telecommuting. This study indicates that there exists a difference between the most effective leadership style for on-site and off-site employees. The findings were that, for telecommuters, a task-oriented leadership style is a better predictor of communication satisfaction, job satisfaction, and commitment. Madlock suggests that the reasons for this could be:

12 https://www.thefreelibrary.com/The+influence+of+supervisors%27+leadership+style+on+telecommuters.-a0294369780

- Communication between teleworkers and their managers is much more explicit. Since teleworkers do not have the conversational cues that they would in a face-to-face setting, they have to use more effort to interpret particular messages.
- Teleworkers do not expect relationship-oriented communication when talking with their supervisor because it is thought to be more difficult. Hence, they evaluate their supervisor in task terms because that is expected.
- The work that can effectively be done via technology is more task oriented; therefore, valued leadership is focused on tasks.
- Employees who are effective and comfortable with this type of work are themselves more task-oriented and, as a result, appreciate like-minded leadership.

Based on this, the following tips apply:

- *Communicate your expectations.* Communicating expectations in a clear way enhances relationships because your team is confident in their manager and can react and communicate directly in all aspects of their position. When expectations are communicated with the right amount of direction or delegation, employee ownership is further developed.
- *Be task-oriented in your communication.* Instead of relying on body language and other conversational cues, you should be very explicit and clear when expressing your expectations. The objectives should be SMART: specific, measurable, achievable, realistic, and time-based.
- *Follow up and monitor more closely.* In a typical office situation, you can be more casual and informal when supervising your subordinates; conveying the message that you trust them is mostly implicit. In a teleworking context, people expect a more direct approach.
- *Know the tools better than your subordinates.* As a leader, you should be more of an expert in teleworking tools than your collaborators so that they see that you know what you are doing. Do some extra training if necessary.
- *Lead by example.* You need to aspire to be a 'super administrator' who excels in all the general competencies and applies all the tips as laid out in this chapter.

13. 'United in Diversity'?

'The pure and simple truth is rarely pure and never simple.' – Oscar Wilde

Diversity refers to the existence of differences within a group. *Tolerance* refers to the level of acceptance people offer toward those who are different from themselves. Consider that the word 'tolerate' implies that something is painful and possibly harmful and must be endured. *Non-discrimination* is the lowest degree of tolerance as imposed by the law.

Article 1d of the Staff Regulations[1] stipulates that any discrimination based on sex, race, colour, ethnic or social origin, genetic features, language, religion or belief, political or any other opinion, membership of a national minority, property, birth, disability, age, or sexual orientation shall be prohibited. The origin of this article is found in the European Convention on Human Rights (ECHR), a post-World War II convention to protect human rights and political freedoms in Europe. All the EU member states are signatories to this convention. Nevertheless, non-discrimination was also enshrined in EU law, many decades later, in the Charter of Fundamental Rights of the European Union attached to the Treaty of Lisbon in 2009.

In the Staff Regulations, the EU pitches diversity only as 'national diversity'. Article 27 requires that EU institutions recruit staff on the broadest possible geographical basis. Article 28 states that, upon recruitment, an official should produce evidence of a thorough knowledge of one of the languages of the EU and a satisfactory knowledge of another language to the extent necessary for the performance of their duties. Finally, in Article 45, it is said that officials shall be required to demonstrate the ability to work in a third language before their first promotion after recruitment.

It has to be noted that the EU administration has done pretty well in respect of national diversity. This was the inevitable primary imperative given that the main reason behind the creation of the Union was the history of war between European nation states and the desire to prevent this in the future. But 'cultural diversity' – or multiculturalism – is today about more than just tolerating different cultures. It is respecting, empowering, and celebrating the differences. Facing today's reality of 'superdiversity' and a globalised world, the EU's limited idea of national diversity is looking somewhat dated.

The EU's capital, Brussels, is home to the world's second most diverse population. After Dubai, Brussels is the city with the highest percentage of residents born abroad. Brussels is home to approximately 70% of people of foreign origin. Roughly 32% of residents are of non-Belgian European ancestry, and 36% are of other backgrounds. Only 40% of inhabitants identify as Roman Catholic, while around 23% of Brussels inhabitants are of Islamic faith, and 30% identify as atheist. Nevertheless, you only have to walk around Brussels to see that the EU quarter is an island of whiteness. And because of the GDPR[2] it may be challenging to find statistics that would tell us how many Germans of Turkish ancestry or French whose parents came from the Maghreb

1 https://eur-lex.europa.eu/legal-content/EN/TXT/?uri=CELEX%3A01962R0031-20210101

2 General Data Protection Regulation

are working in the institutions. This issue will likely become one of increasing sensitivity, and the gloss that the EU institutions tend to put on themselves as beacons of diversity may wear a bit thin...

On the other hand, the EU is represented through some 140 EU delegations and offices[3] around the world. The EU delegations play a crucial role in presenting, explaining and implementing the EU's foreign policies. They also analyse and report on the policies and developments of their host countries and conduct negotiations per given mandates. In the EU delegations, there are over 3700 staff members. Roughly 60% of them are 'local agents' who don't have a European nationality, and for whom the Staff Regulations don't apply. Moreover, the officials and contract agents working in the delegations are subject to 'rotations' – moving to another country or a different part of the world on a regular basis. This means that they face an even more extreme exposure to cultural diversity than their colleagues working for the institutions or agencies located on European soil.

The truth is that the EU doesn't have comprehensive policies on cultural diversity, be it inside the institutions or in its role as a 'global player' on the geopolitical playing field. In this book, I can only highlight the impact – and benefits – of cultural diversity in the workplace and hand over some tools to decode how culture influences our behaviour. This is the topic of the present chapter.

Cultural diversity

11th juror (rising): 'I beg pardon, in discussing...
10th juror (interrupting and mimicking): 'I beg pardon. What are you so goddam polite about?'
11th juror (looking straight at the 10th juror): 'For the same reason you're not. It's the way I was brought up'

– Reginald Rose, 'Twelve Angry Men'

'Twelve Angry Men' is an American theatre play where twelve members of a jury have to decide on the guilt or innocence of a boy accused of murder. The quote cited is part of the confrontation between the tenth juror, a garage owner born and raised in New York, and the eleventh juror, a European-born, Austrian watchmaker.

Every person carries within him or herself patterns of thinking, feeling and acting learned over a lifetime. Much of this was acquired in early childhood because then a person is most susceptible to learning and assimilating. As soon as specific patterns of thinking, feeling and acting are established, people have to unlearn these patterns before learning something different, and unlearning is harder than learning for the first time.

In his famous book 'Cultures and Organisations', Geert Hofstede uses the analogy of the way computers are programmed. He calls such patterns of thinking, feeling and

3 https://eeas.europa.eu/headquarters/headquarters-homepage/area/geo_en

acting 'mental programs,' or, as per the book's subtitle, 'software of the mind'. Allow me to refine this metaphor. Our 'mental programming' can be compared with the operating system (OS) of our mind (you know, Microsoft Windows, MacOS, or Linux). Much like the operating system of a computer determines its basic behaviour, culture determines ours. The programs that are run on top of the OS are only 'learned' behaviour and are much easier to upgrade or replace. Also, these programs are only charged in memory when we use them, while the operating system is there all the time.

When applying this to the EU working environment, it is not difficult to understand that the mental program of, for example, a Finnish EU official who grew up in the cold and dark countryside is vastly different to the mental programming of a Spanish official originating from the light-filled, warm and vibrant city of Barcelona. Yet, both have to work side by side in Brussels or Luxembourg – to further the European vision.

Language and mother tongue make an essential part of our mental programming. We actually 'think' in our mother tongue, and you can say that you only have a good command of a foreign language when your mind is capable of skipping the mental translation of your thoughts to the words you speak (or write). As we saw in Chapter 4, there are estimated to be about 150 regional and minority languages in the European Union and there are increasing numbers of EU citizens who have been brought up speaking non-EU languages at home. Some of these languages, like Turkish or Russian or Arabic, for example, are spoken by more EU citizens than some of the national 'official' languages. Therefore, one might conclude that the current regime of 'national diversity' in respect of language requirements is insufficient to provide the full range of cultural diversity inside the EU institutions. How that diversity might be accommodated when there are already 24 official EU languages is a difficult question.

A small but significant detail illustrating this lack of multicultural awareness can be found in the EPSO selection and recruitment process. There is only one question about 'working in a multicultural environment' in the general competency-based interview under the heading of 'working with others'. Typically, for specialists, this competency is worth 10 points out of 180 and this is one out 5 anchors, meaning that its relative importance is only about 1%. Even more striking: for 'generalists' there is nothing at all in the Assessment Centre about multicultural environment. And contract or temporary staff are not assessed for their general competencies, even those hired to work in the delegations.

'The Power of Diverse Thinking'

In the Sunday Times N° 1 bestseller, 'Rebel Ideas, The Power of Diverse Thinking', Matthew Syed offered many insights as to how to harness our unique perspectives and pool our collective intelligence to tackle the challenges of our age. As this book was first published in 2019, he could not have predicted how his ideas might have helped the EU to deal with the Covid-19 pandemic, which was not exactly a success story, one might add.

Suppose the rectangle in Fig. 13.1 represents the universe of valuable ideas; that is to say, the insights, perspectives, experiences and thinking styles relevant to a particular problem or objective. With simple problems, one person might possess all the necessary information. Diversity is unnecessary. But with complex issues, no one person will have all the relevant insights. Even the most intelligent individual will only have a subset of knowledge and know-how. We can represent an intelligent person, David, with a circle. He knows a lot, but he doesn't know everything.

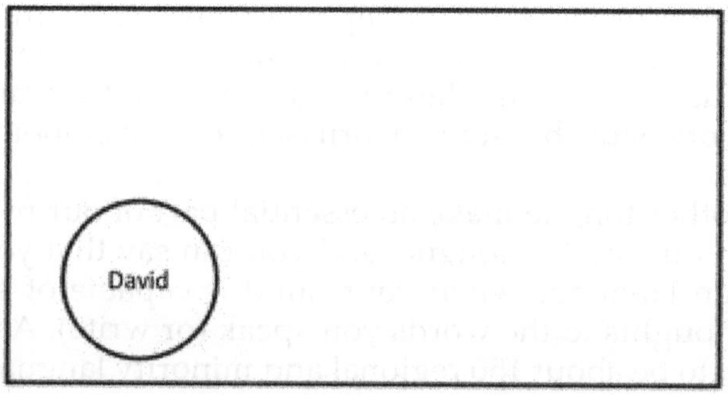

Figure 13.1: An intelligent individual

In Fig. 13.2, we can see what happens when a group of people think in the same way. Every individual is intelligent. They each have impressive knowledge. But they are also homogeneous. They know similar things and share the same perspectives. They are, so to speak, clone-like. *Homophily* is the tendency of individuals to associate and bond with similar others, as in the proverb 'birds of a feather flock together.'

Think how comforting it is to be surrounded by people who think the same way as us, who mirror our perspectives, who confirm our prejudices. It makes us feel smarter. It validates our world view. Homophily is like a hidden gravitational force, dragging human groups towards one corner of the problem space. To a large extent, because of the staff selection process, and the primary focus on national rather than other forms

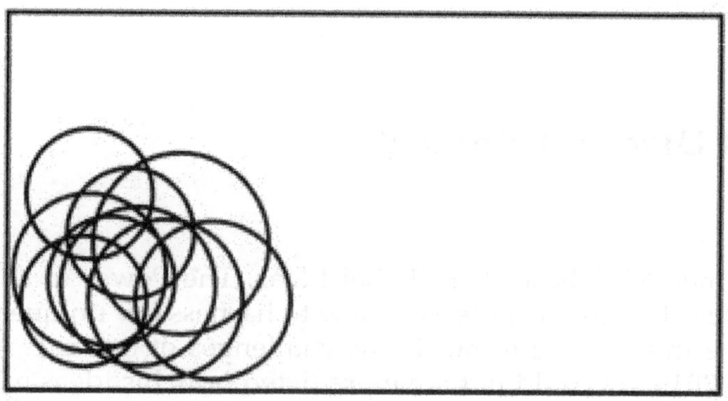

Figure 13.2: An unintelligent team (a team of clones)

The advantages of cultural diversity

Before Brexit, I once heard a perfect example of how the EU administration differs from a conventional national bureaucracy. This was from an Englishman who had previously worked in the British public administration. When the British officials discussed a problem and prepared a decision, he said, there were about ten people in the room who were all in agreement after half an hour. Everybody had the same social origins, spoke the same language, had been to the same university, had the same teachers, and had the same cultural background.

In the EU, it is quite the opposite. Participants come from different countries, have different mother tongues, and diverse cultural backgrounds. They often come from different social classes and went to different universities. The discussions usually last longer, but much more experience is fed into them, and they have more input and are more creative. This diversity usually yields a better – more balanced – result.

of diversity, the EU administration tends to be 'homophilic'[4]. Nonetheless, because of the national diversity, it is far less homophilic than most of the national administrations of the member states (see box).

Wise groups express a different dynamic. They are not clone-like. They do not parrot the same views. Instead, they are more like groups of rebels. They do not disagree for the sake of disagreeing but bring insight from different regions of the problem space. Such groups contain people with perspectives that challenge, augment, diverge and cross-pollinate. This represents the hallmark of collective intelligence: how wholes become more than the sum of their parts. In Fig. 13.3, the individuals are not smarter than those in the team of Fig. 13.2, but they possess vastly higher levels of collective intelligence. They have 'coverage'.

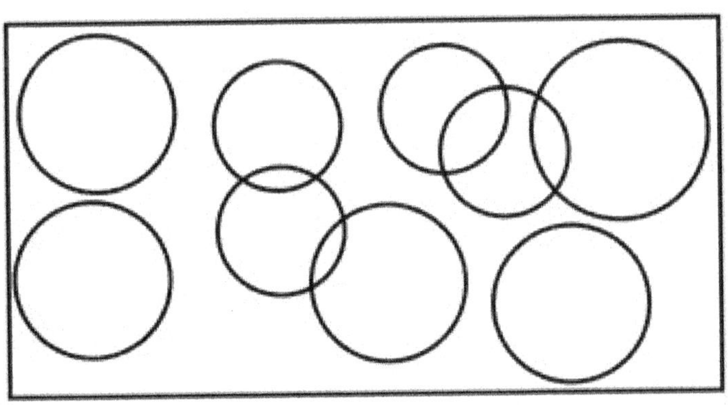

Figure 13.3: An intelligent team (a team of rebels)

4 This is not a very commonly used term but I hope you get the idea.

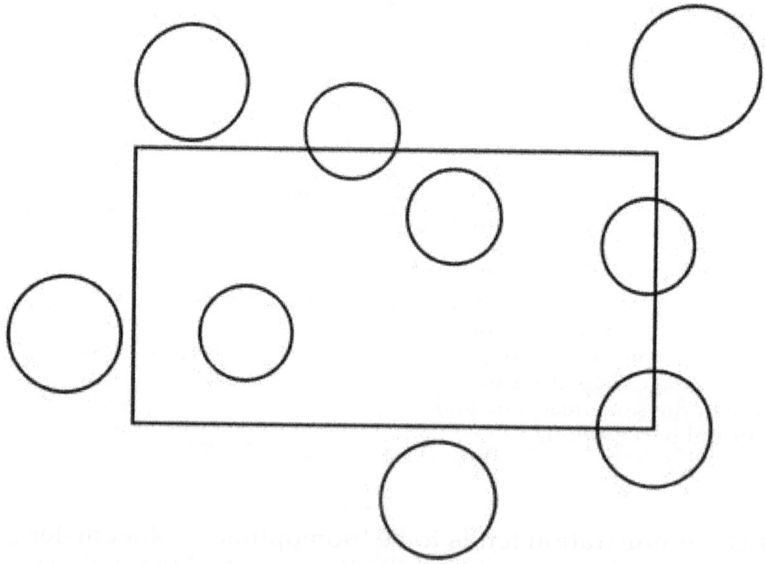

Figure 13.4: A diverse but collectively unintelligent team (rebels without a cause)

Successful teams are diverse but not arbitrarily mixed. A group of scientists designing a hadron collider is unlikely to benefit from hiring, say, a skateboarder of whatever nationality, colour, or gender. They would risk becoming a group of 'rebels without a cause' as in Fig. 13.4. Diversity contributes to collective intelligence, then, but only when it is relevant.

Today, the EU is facing challenges of unprecedented complexity: global warming, galloping science and technology, migration, growing inequality, pandemics and geopolitical instability. The question is – is the EU administration an intelligent team or a group of rebels without a cause? Are we really united in diversity? The future will tell.

'The Culture Map'

For multicultural topics, the very best and fantastic resource is Erin Meyer's 'The Culture Map'[5]. Based on her work at INSEAD, the 'Business School for the World' based in Paris, Erin Meyer provides a field-tested model for decoding how cultural differences impact international business.

Erin created an eight-scale model, with each of the scales representing a key area that managers must be aware of, showing how cultures vary along a spectrum from one extreme to its opposite. A crucial factor in understanding the meaning of the eight scales is the concept of *cultural relativity*. The point here is that, when examining how

5 https://erinmeyer.com/

people from different cultures relate to one another, what matters is not the *absolute* position of either culture on the scale but rather the *relative* position of the two cultures. It is the relative positioning that determines how people view each other (more on this below).

On her website[6], Erin Meyer has some great tools to generate different 'culture maps', depending on your needs and interests:

- *The Country Mapping Tool.* This tool allows you to click on whichever countries you are working with and receive a cultural mapping of the selected countries. With this tool you can view how two (or more) cultures fall on the eight culture map scales, comparing how each builds trust, gives feedback and makes decisions.

Cultural stereotyping

Snooty French, stiff Brits, shy Finns and humourless Germans: Europeans love their conceptions about their neighbours to be well-defined, if not necessarily true. Even if stereotypes don't teach us much about who our European neighbours really are, they do teach us a lot about how they are perceived. And sometimes our cliches about the rest of Europe have a story behind them that can reveal something about Europe's rich history - and occasionally even a grain of truth about the national character. Even if sometimes these complaints land a bit close to the bone, we talk about our fellow Europeans precisely because we are interested in them - after all, the only thing worse than being talked about is not being talked about. Just remember not to take them (too) seriously...

© https://europeisnotdead.com/european-stereotypes/

- *The Personal Profile Tool.* With this you respond to 24 questions about your personal approach to communicating, leading teams and building relationships. The results reveal your positioning on the eight behavioural scales. You can see how you compare to others of your own culture and then map your results to various countries, all on one graph.
- *The Team Mapping Tool.* Building on the Personal Profile Tool, the Team Mapping Tool allows you to compare your answers from the Personal Profile Tool with those of other members of your team along the eight dimensions introduced in The Culture Map book. You can see on one graph how you and other members have responded to those same questions and compare multiple team members' maps to the various countries you are working with.
- *The Corporate Culture Mapping Tool.* This tool enables you to map out your organisation's culture on the eight culture map scales through small group discussion. Divide your group into small teams and have them debate where the organisational culture falls on the culture map scales. Each group uses this tool to plot the positions of the organisational culture. The tool then allows you to view the maps developed by each team on one chart and create a final corporate culture map.

6 https://erinmeyer.com/tools/

Working for the EU, the use of these tools is only limited by your imagination. You could use them as an individual wanting to better understand your (cultural) position in the team (you know their nationalities, right?) – or you could convince your manager to use the team mapping tool. This could go up to the unit, directorate, directorate-general or – why not? – even the entire institution or agency levels. Working in a delegation, or an agency abroad, you could compare individual or team culture maps with the host country's culture, or, when moving to another delegation, do the mapping of the new host country in preparation of your move. Fascinating!

Collaboration across high-context and low-context cultures

Of course, we are all individuals, and no two people belonging to the same culture are guaranteed to respond in exactly the same way. However, generalisations are valid to the extent that they provide indications as to what you will most likely encounter – and how those differences might impact communication and working together.

One example is the distinction between 'high-context' and 'low-context' cultures. In some European cultures, personal bonds and informal agreements are considered far more binding than any formal contract. In others, the meticulous wording of legal documents is viewed as vital.

High-context cultures like the Mediterranean, Latin American, African, Arab, and Asian leave much of the message undetermined – to be implied through context, nonverbal cues, and between-the-lines interpretation of what is actually said. These cultures are looking for meaning and understanding in what is *not* said – in body language, in silences and pauses, and in relationships and empathy. In contrast, *low-context cultures* (most of the Germanic and English-speaking countries) expect messages to be unambiguous and detailed. These cultures place emphasis on sending and receiving accurate messages directly, and on being precise with spoken or written words.

Communicating across cultures is fraught with invisible difficulties. For example, consider a team with people from five different cultural backgrounds, say the Netherlands, Germany, Spain, Italy and France. In Erin Meyer's culture mapping Germany and the Netherlands are very much 'low-context' countries while France, Italy and Spain are 'high-context' countries.

Where do you suppose the greatest likelihood of misunderstanding will arise? Consider three options:

A. One low-context person communicating with someone from another low-context culture (for example, a Dutch person communicating with a German)
B. A high-context person communicating with a low-context person (for example, a Spaniard communicating with a Dutch person)
C. One high-context person communicating with someone from a another high-context culture (for example, a Spaniard communicating with a French person).

Many people assume that the answer is choice B – a low-context/high-context conversation. Surprisingly, the correct answer is choice C. On a multicultural team, most misunderstandings occur between people coming from two high-context cultures with entirely different roots, such as the Spaniard communicating with the French person.

Fortunately, if you are leading a multicultural team, there is no need to count the number of team members from the different ends of the Erin Meyer scale and multiply the number of members to figure out what to do. There is just one easy rule to remember: *Multicultural teams need low-context processes.*

This is why, in the EU administration, everything is put in writing, from the follow-up email after a phone call to the minutes of a meeting. Furthermore, EU officials are fond of organigrams (showing who works for whom, the hierarchical structure), job descriptions (project manager, case handler, desk officer, or 'assistant'), written objectives (who is responsible for accomplishing what), and performance appraisals (stating in writing how each person is doing).

After all, there are good reasons why the EU administration's bureaucratic approach is a workable solution. And this may even turn out to be an advantage if teleworking becomes the norm.

General competencies in a multicultural environment

Since this book is mostly about general competencies it makes sense to translate cultural behaviour and preferences into actionable tips on how to be more effective in a multicultural environment. These tips are only scratching the surface of working in a multicultural environment. If you want to get to the bottom of it, you should definitely read Erin Meyer's book.

Analysis and problem solving

- *Embrace diversity.* Consistently and effectively seek input from peers and stakeholders from diverse origins and submit your solutions for their scrutiny. Recognise that differences are a valuable asset – a resource, not a liability. We are enriched by the diversity in our work environments and networks. Multicultural brainstorming can help.
- *Apply two styles of reasoning.* Principle-first reasoning (aka *deductive reasoning*) derives conclusions or facts from general principles or concepts, while in applications-first reasoning (aka *inductive reasoning*), general conclusions are reached on a pattern of factual observations from the real world. Most people are capable of practising both types of reasoning, but our culture's educational structure heavily influences our preferred style of reasoning. So, if you are working in a team with members from a culture different from your own, the best strategy is to cycle back and forth between theoretical principles and practical examples. This may slow down the process, but the result will be better.

Delivering quality and results

- *Know your goals*. Think carefully about your larger objectives. If your goal is innovation or creativity, the more cultural diversity the better. If your goal is speed and efficiency, then monocultural is probably better than multicultural.
- *Keep in touch with your own culture*. After spending many years in the EU bubble, some people have a tendency to become colourless bureaucrats with no clear 'stereotypical' behaviour. To a certain extent this is a good thing, but the organisation also loses valuable insights covering the entire problem space. It becomes a 'team of clones'. Socialising with people from your own culture, following the news of your home country, keeping in touch with family and friends back home, can prevent this downgrade to the lowest common denominator.

Communicating

- *Know your position in the hierarchy*. Communicate with the persons at your level. If you are the boss, go through their boss with equivalent status. If you do communicate with someone at a lower hierarchical level, copy their boss. If you skip a level – up or down – get permission from the person at the intermediate level first.
- *Address people by their last name* unless they have indicated otherwise, for example by signing their email to you with their first name only. There are significant national and other cultural variations in the ease with which people move to first name terms, so err on the side of caution.
- *Choose your communication medium appropriately*. If you are working with people from a task-based culture you can readily go for email or phone and stay brief and clear. For relationship-based people phone, videoconferencing, or face-to-face is preferrable, and take your time for social talk before getting down to business.

Learning and development

- *Learn about your personal multicultural work attitude*. You can use Erin Meyer's Personal Profile tool for that. It will cost you only a few euros.
- *Read Erin Meyer's 'The Culture Map' and Matthew Syed's 'Rebel Ideas'*. You will learn a lot about cultural diversity and how to embrace it.
- *Leverage the diversity in your team*. Take your time to learn what each person has to bring to the table and actively use their specific skills, perspectives and characteristics to become more effective. Have an individual chat with each member of your team or set up a group discussion about the cultural preferences of each team member. You can use Erin Meyer's Team Mapping tool in support.

- *Learn more languages.* Even if you are not a linguist (translator, interpreter, lawyer-linguist) it pays off to get a feeling for as many EU and even non-EU languages as you can. In the process you'll gain a deeper understanding of the underlying culture and not only understand the words that are spoken but get a better connection with the native speakers of that language. The EU administration offers excellent training opportunities in this respect.

Prioritising and organising

- *Be patient.* Planning in a multicultural environment is a challenge because different cultures have different approaches to how and when to decide.
- *Resist the temptation to push for a quick decision.* Instead, focus on the quality and completeness of the analysis and the soundness of the reasoning process.

Resilience

- *Remain flexible.* Most decisions can be adjusted, revisited or discussed again if necessary.
- *Join a multinational sports club.* In Brussels and Luxembourg and major cities where the agencies or delegations are located you will find sports clubs where you can practise your favourite sport. Not only will this keep you physically and mentally fit, but you will also experience multicultural collaboration in a literally 'hands-on' way.
- *Relax internationally.* If you work in Brussels as an EU official, you will undoubtedly know Place du Luxembourg and Place Jourdan. Both squares are conveniently located in the EU quarter and are gathering places for the international crowd. On both squares you can have a drink or enjoy a meal and meet people from the EU and beyond. Place du Luxembourg is especially busy on Thursday night, and it is said that many mixed-nationality couples have first met there.

Working with others

- *Build and foster your multicultural awareness.* When traveling to another (EU) country, for business or leisure, read as much as you can about your destination, watch documentaries, and don't stay put in your hotel once you are there but visit the local attractions and taste the local cuisine. If you are on a work trip to another country, frequently your hosts will organise cultural events. Take advantage of these opportunities.
- *Mix with other cultures.* Language conversation tables offer the opportunity to practise the language you are studying with native speakers of the language. Colleagues from different parts of the organisation come together to learn in a fun and casual environment and understand each other better. Hobby and cultural clubs are another way to mix with other cultures outside the workplace.

- *Join one of the EU trade unions.* The Staff Regulations are the legal basis for the establishment of the Staff Committee as a recognised body, to represent staff vis-à-vis their employer. The Staff Committee composition is a result of elections where several staff representative organisations (trade unions and staff associations) compete for the votes of all staff every three years. These organisations are non-political and keep the pulse of all things happening in your institution, including multicultural issues.

Leadership

- *Let your team brainstorm without you.* If you are managing a group that defers to your authority so much that you are unable to get their real opinion, ask them to brainstorm without you and then report the group's ideas back to you, in writing. Removing the boss from a meeting often allows people to feel more comfortable when sharing ideas.
- *Give clear instructions.* When you call a meeting, provide the agenda beforehand and tell the participants clearly what you expect from them. In this way they can prepare and share their ideas before the meeting.
- *Moderate meetings properly.* When chairing a meeting, invite everybody to speak up. Don't let the 'table jumpers' take control of your agenda. When you invite an otherwise shy or introverted person to speak up, you may be surprised how much they have to contribute.
- *Demonstrate patience and commitment.* When the group is divided about how to move forward, suggest a vote. All members are expected to follow a decision supported by the majority, even if they disagree.
- *Follow a decision* even if your input was not considered or overruled. Often, 'good enough is best', as long as the decision is supported by the group.

PART IV: ANNEXES

Annex 1 Competencies, anchors and indicators

Note: This Annex should be read in conjunction with Chapter 2, which explains the EPSO competency framework.

You can also carry out a free self-assessment of your competencies using the online tool at https://www.johnharperpublishing.co.uk/the-ultimate-eu-career-development-toolkit/. This has a range of additional features.

Analysis and Problem Solving

Anchors

1. Analyses and prioritises situations to identify and solve problems.
2. Solutions increase efficiency and improve quality.
3. Involves others in solving problems and making decisions.
4. Factors organisational goals into decisions.
5. Makes clear, transparent and timely decisions.
6. Dealing with complexity.
7. Identifying the relevant aspects from a mass of information.
8. Proposing useful and practical solutions.
9. Gathering information from various sources and critically evaluating it.
10. Using judgement and analysis to find solutions to problems.

Indicators

	UNSATISFACTORY	IMPROVEMENT NEEDED	MEETS EXPECTATIONS	EXCEEDS EXPECTATIONS	EXCEPTIONAL
anchor	1 - Extremely Weak 2 - Very Weak	3 - Weak 4 - Fair	5 - Satisfactory 6 - Good	7 - Strong 8 - Very Strong	9 - Excellent 10 - Outstanding
1.	Has difficulty distinguishing between critical and non-critical issues. Loses focus when resolving larger issues. Misunderstands or misinterprets key elements of information.	Needs help with analysing and prioritising problems. Tends to focus on simple operational issues.	Solves urgent, high impact problems first.	Analyses and prioritises critical problems. Stays focused on critical problems until they are successfully resolved.	Analyses and prioritises critical problems accurately and quickly. Maintains a sense of urgency in solving even complex problems.

Analysis and Problem Solving Indicators – continued

	UNSATISFACTORY	IMPROVEMENT NEEDED	MEETS EXPECTATIONS	EXCEEDS EXPECTATIONS	EXCEPTIONAL
anchor	1 - Extremely Weak 2 - Very Weak	3 - Weak 4 - Fair	5 - Satisfactory 6 - Good	7 - Strong 8 - Very Strong	9 - Excellent 10 - Outstanding
2.	Rarely proposes innovative solutions. Produces 'quick fixes' that do not yield lasting or quality results.	Proposes solutions that are usually short-term. Is rarely transformative in terms of greater efficiency and/or improved quality.	Finds solutions that effectively address issues and are easily sustainable.	Finds solutions that change the workplace both in terms of increasing efficiency and enhancing the quality of products and services. Makes processes more efficient.	Finds solutions that consistently transform the workplace. Delivers products and services that improve quality significantly.
3.	Rarely collaborates with peers and stakeholders. Doesn't look for more efficient ways to do things.	Collaborates with others only when asked to. Prefers to solve problems independently.	Collaborates effectively with others to solve problems and make decisions.	Is highly collaborative in terms of seeking input to solve problems and make decisions.	Consistently and effectively seeks input from all peers and stakeholders. Is agile and decisive.
4.	Makes decisions that have minimal or no impact in terms of improving the quality of products and services, or in aligning with department goals.	Makes decisions that focus on immediate, short-term issues, losing sight of larger departmental goals and initiatives.	Keeps organisational and departmental goals in mind when solving problems and making decisions.	Makes decisions and takes actions that align with organisational and departmental goals and initiatives.	Always has 'big picture' in mind and helps others see it. Consistently aligns decisions and actions with organisational and departmental goals and initiatives.
5.	Has difficulty articulating rationale for decisions. Often defers decision-making to others.	Makes decisions that are sometimes not clear. Tends to put off decisions on more complex issues.	Makes sound decisions based on facts and experience.	Makes decisions that consistently support and facilitate desired outcomes.	Consistently makes clear, transparent, and timely decisions. Makes decisions that consistently align with organisational and departmental goals.
6.	Does not gather a sufficiently clear picture of the problems in their full complexity. Omits important facts and details from analysis.	Captures the global picture but misses a number of important details.	Understands and summarises the main issues involved.	Understands the problem and links up the elements. Takes on board all the available information and fits everything together.	Analyses and interprets the available data correctly and completely. Gives a concise and systematic overview of the situation.

Analysis and Problem Solving Indicators – continued

	UNSATISFACTORY	IMPROVEMENT NEEDED	MEETS EXPECTATIONS	EXCEEDS EXPECTATIONS	EXCEPTIONAL
anchor	1 - Extremely Weak 2 - Very Weak	3 - Weak 4 - Fair	5 - Satisfactory 6 - Good	7 - Strong 8 - Very Strong	9 - Excellent 10 - Outstanding
7.	Is overwhelmed by high volumes of information and gets lost. Focuses more on the superfluous than the essential.	Misses logical links between items of information. Is distracted by side issues.	Tackles main problems and is not distracted by secondary issues. Distinguishes between relevant and less relevant information.	Simplifies the complex without neglecting key issues or details that matter.	Differentiates clearly between the relative importance of the different issues.
8.	Proposes solutions that do not tackle main issues to be addressed. Proposes solutions that contain elements used as justification for rejecting alternative options.	Proposes solutions that are impractical because of their implications. Proposes solutions that do not take all the factors into account.	Proposes reasonable but not particularly visionary solutions. Proposes workable solutions.	Proposes solutions that deal effectively with all aspects of the problem. Proposes solutions that exceed the expectations of the stakeholders.	Consistently proposes solutions that reflect a balanced analysis and sound judgement.
9.	Does not identify inconsistencies or contradictions in available information. Bases analysis on information from only a few of the available sources.	Is more descriptive than analytical in approach.	Takes into account different sources of information available. Compares and contrasts information drawn from different sources.	Analyses problems by comparing and contrasting drawn from all available sources.	Refers to the available sources and assesses the relative significance of each one. Identifies and resolves inconsistencies or contradictions in available information.
10.	Relies more on intuition than on analysis. Ignores options that should be explored.	Makes proposals without thinking through their implications. Does not make a convincing case for their recommendations.	Explores different options in search for solutions. Considers the implications for their proposals.	Tests different options to determine which provides the optimum solution. Weights up options and anticipates possible objections to preferred choices.	Considers all the options before deciding on the best way forward. Reacts to developments as the implementation unfolds.

Prioritising and Organising

Anchors

1. Understands goals and implements plans to achieve them.
2. Mobilises the appropriate resources to achieve goals.
3. Develops and implements metrics to measure results.
4. Anticipates and solves problems.
5. Sets realistic deadlines and milestones.
6. Manages workload efficiently and effectively.
7. Prioritises tasks appropriately.
8. Links up the various elements of the work.
9. Is flexible in taking into account new aspects coming in.
10. Collaborates effectively with others.

Indicators

	UNSATISFACTORY	IMPROVEMENT NEEDED	MEETS EXPECTATIONS	EXCEEDS EXPECTATIONS	EXCEPTIONAL
anchor	1 - Extremely Weak 2 - Very Weak	3 - Weak 4 - Fair	5 - Satisfactory 6 - Good	7 - Strong 8 - Very Strong	9 - Excellent 10 - Outstanding
1.	Does not follow an orderly method of setting objectives, scoping out difficulties, detailing work, or planning for task completion. Fails to prepare in advance.	Does not have a clear picture of unit or Institution goals; lacks perspective to pull elements into a strategic view; plans often lack substance and specificity.	Creates effective plans with defined purpose and outcomes. Breaks complex tasks into process steps, prioritises activities, itemises resources and estimates costs.	Plans with unit and Institution goals in mind. Plans clearly identify roles, responsibilities and timeframes.	Creates innovative, ambitious plans, which align with unit and Institution goals and serve as reliable roadmaps to desired outcomes.
2.	Is not able to integrate multiple activities and resources into a cohesive, actionable plan.	Has difficulty marshalling and informing resources to work together to achieve desired outcomes.	Organises, informs and supports resources to achieve goals.	Informs and mobilises resources – staff, stakeholders, technical experts – to achieve shared vision, mission, and goals.	Effectively influences, informs, and mobilises resources – staff, stakeholders, technical experts – to achieve shared vision, mission, and goals.
3.	Is unwilling/unable to create or track metrics. Allows work to continue without monitoring.	Has difficulty defining and implementing appropriate metrics to measure success. Becomes ineffective when plans need to change.	Monitors progress and determines how processes may be changed to improve quality and/or efficiency. Adapts to changes in plans effectively.	Implements metrics that effectively and efficiently measure results. Recommends improvements based on results.	Develops and implements reliable, effective metrics to measure outcomes; identifies and recommends changes to improve efficiency and effectiveness.

Prioritising and Organising Indicators – continued

	UNSATISFACTORY	IMPROVEMENT NEEDED	MEETS EXPECTATIONS	EXCEEDS EXPECTATIONS	EXCEPTIONAL
anchor	1 - Extremely Weak 2 - Very Weak	3 - Weak 4 - Fair	5 - Satisfactory 6 - Good	7 - Strong 8 - Very Strong	9 - Excellent 10 - Outstanding
4.	Ignores small problems until they become significant, jeopardising deadlines and effective utilisation of resources.	Identifies problems but does not effectively address them.	Addresses problems in process or resourcing quickly and effectively.	Anticipates and adjusts for problems and roadblocks. Resolves problems in early stages.	Proactively anticipates, analyses and solves problems and motivates others to do the same.
5.	Sets unrealistic deadlines and milestones.	Sometimes sets unrealistic deadlines and milestones.	Sets realistic deadlines and milestones.	Factors in 'what if' and plans for contingencies.	Consistently sets realistic deadlines and milestones, and always has a 'Plan B'.
6.	Works inefficiently or becomes overwhelmed with workload. Procrastinates.	Neglects work-life balance. Uses overtime as only strategy to cope with heavy workload or tight deadlines. Is overly perfectionist, indecisive, or impatient with others.	Manages to get all their work done in time and to a good quality standard.	Combines good work-life balance with efficient and effective behaviour at work.	Manages own workload as well as the workload of others effectively and efficiently.
7.	Does not identify main points and gets distracted by side issues.	Leaves the task of establishing priorities to others. Does not play an active role in identifying the issues and prioritising accordingly.	Identifies some of the key issues but overlooks others. Identifies issues that are priorities for him/her but not necessarily for their co-workers.	Has a clear picture of the remit of the unit, identifies key issues and proposes priorities.	Prioritises tasks appropriately, both for himself/herself and for the unit. Differentiates clearly between matters of primary and secondary importance.
8.	Does not grasp the general picture.	Makes few if any links between separate items of information.	Has a clear understanding of his/her mandate but is less successful in grasping the overall picture and priorities.	Sees how different elements fit together.	Focuses on both the general elements and the details of the situation. Has a clear understanding of the bigger picture. Fits things together and draws conclusions.

Prioritising and Organising Indicators – continued

	UNSATISFACTORY	IMPROVEMENT NEEDED	MEETS EXPECTATIONS	EXCEEDS EXPECTATIONS	EXCEPTIONAL
anchor	1 - Extremely Weak 2 - Very Weak	3 - Weak 4 - Fair	5 - Satisfactory 6 - Good	7 - Strong 8 - Very Strong	9 - Excellent 10 - Outstanding
9.	Sticks to own views despite consensus.	Puts most of their energy into defending own views. Is not inclined to organise and prioritise on the basis of points that emerge	Understands and defends their own position and links up with new elements. Shows good use of judgement in appraisal of new elements	Sees how new input affects the state of play and reassesses the situation if necessary.	Builds new elements into the work plan to ensure a well-balanced end result.
10.	Does not collaborate with co-workers and partners. Says 'Yes' to everything. Does everything by themself.	Keeps communication to a minimum and is reticent to share thoughts and ideas.	Maintains an open and honest dialogue with co-workers and partners. Delegates when appropriate.	Encourages others to share ideas and integrates others' thoughts and opinions in own plans and priorities.	Consistently and effectively seeks and incorporates others' ideas to ensure optimal results.

Delivering Quality and Results

Anchors

1. Taking responsibility.
2. Taking initiative.
3. Overcoming obstacles.
4. Delivering quality work on time.
5. Working to a high standard of quality.
6. Manages workload efficiently and effectively.
7. Understands the value of innovation and of quality improvement.
8. Links up the various elements of the work.
9. Demonstrates efficiency and effectiveness in own work.
10. Manages and sustains change initiatives.

Indicators

	UNSATISFACTORY	IMPROVEMENT NEEDED	MEETS EXPECTATIONS	EXCEEDS EXPECTATIONS	EXCEPTIONAL
anchor	1 - Extremely Weak 2 - Very Weak	3 - Weak 4 - Fair	5 - Satisfactory 6 - Good	7 - Strong 8 - Very Strong	9 - Excellent 10 - Outstanding
1.	Finds excuses for not dealing promptly with problems and requests. Refers problems to third parties instead of tackling themself. Blames external factors for failure to deliver quality work.	Does not always take responsibility for dealing promptly with problems that arise at work. Is slow to react to developments that affect achievability of results.	Takes his/her work seriously and applies themself to tasks. Is quality-conscious and does what is necessary to achieve high standards. Reacts to urgent requests.	Tackles assignments and accepts full responsibility for the outcomes. Reacts to developments that affect achievability of objectives.	Has a highly developed sense of responsibility and accountability. Anticipates problems and has solutions already worked out in advance.
2.	Does not do more than the minimum required to complete tasks. Sticks strictly to own job description.	Is reluctant to go beyond the call of duty. Never or rarely questions procedures or ways of working in place.	Understands procedures and workflow within their department. Follows established guidelines where appropriate. Works beyond the confines of job description if necessary.	Keeps up with events and takes initiatives that have a positive impact on quality of work. Acts without waiting to be told: takes initiative.	Goes the extra mile to ensure best possible results. Takes initiatives to make procedures and workflows more efficient or effective.
3.	Is deflected or stopped by obstacles and does not find ways around them. Goes round in circles instead of narrowing-in on solutions.	Does not deal adequately with complex tasks. Takes the first solution that comes along without standing back to weigh other options.	Achieves satisfactory results when faced with obstacles or complex tasks. Deals appropriately with unexpected developments.	Systematically ensures that desired results are delivered, notwithstanding difficulties. Thinks 'out-of-the-box'.	Demonstrates resourcefulness in finding ways around difficulties. Anticipates problems and has solutions ready.
4.	Underestimates work, gets their planning wrong and runs into time trouble. Spends too long on tasks that add little or no value to the end result.	Does not always take the right decision at the right time. Is perfectionist and loses sight of time constraints.	Deals with matters in appropriate and timely manner. Strikes acceptable balance between quality and deadlines.	Takes remedial actions when quality is in danger or compromised by deadlines. Sees where corners can be cut to meet tight deadlines.	Finds ways of delivering the best possible results under difficult circumstances and tight deadlines.

Delivering quality and results Indicators – continued

	UNSATISFACTORY	IMPROVEMENT NEEDED	MEETS EXPECTATIONS	EXCEEDS EXPECTATIONS	EXCEPTIONAL
anchor	1 - Extremely Weak 2 - Very Weak	3 - Weak 4 - Fair	5 - Satisfactory 6 - Good	7 - Strong 8 - Very Strong	9 - Excellent 10 - Outstanding
5.	Settles for quick and easy solutions.	Does not always meet expectations.	Performs to expected standards and in accordance with procedures in place.	Sets themself demanding standards and does not settle for second best.	Seeks to continuously exceed expectations. Puts a large amount of personal effort and creative thought into work. Thrives in challenging situations.
6.	Works inefficiently or becomes overwhelmed with workload. Procrastinates.	Neglects work-life balance. Uses overtime as their only strategy to cope with heavy workload or tight deadlines. Is overly perfectionist, indecisive, or impatient with others.	Manages to get all their work done in time and to a good quality standard.	Combines good work-life balance with efficient and effective behaviour at work.	Manages own workload as well as the workload of others effectively and efficiently.
7.	Resists change: prefers to continue to do things as they always have been done.	Has a limited perspective and understanding of the importance of quality improvement.	Understands the value of quality improvement. Identifies weaknesses that impede processes and recommends changes.	Understands and communicates the importance of quality improvement.	Clearly defines the value and imperative for continuous improvement. Consistently offers original, inventive ideas for improving products and services.
8.	Does not grasp the general picture.	Makes few if any links between separate items of information.	Has a clear understanding of their own mandate but is less successful in grasping the overall picture and priorities.	Sees how different elements fit together.	Focuses on both the general elements and the details of the situation. Has a clear understanding of the bigger picture. Fits things together and draws conclusions.

Delivering quality and results Indicators – continued

	UNSATISFACTORY	IMPROVEMENT NEEDED	MEETS EXPECTATIONS	EXCEEDS EXPECTATIONS	EXCEPTIONAL
anchor	1 - Extremely Weak 2 - Very Weak	3 - Weak 4 - Fair	5 - Satisfactory 6 - Good	7 - Strong 8 - Very Strong	9 - Excellent 10 - Outstanding
9.	Is extremely disorganised and unable to separate 'need to do' from less important tasks. Cannot handle more than one project at a time.	Has difficulty handling more than one task or project at a time. Disorganisation often results in poor quality work.	Successfully manages several projects to achieve desired results.	Manages several projects effectively and efficiently. Results enhance productivity and quality of the department.	Models efficiency by getting more done in less time while maintaining quality of results. Effectively manages multiple projects to achieve desired outcomes.
10.	Moves to next project before ensuring successful, sustainable implementation of previous projects.	Rarely monitors change initiatives after implementation	Sustains change through clear documentation and regular monitoring.	Ensures that operational changes are successfully implemented and sustained over time.	Employs clear post-implementation strategies to ensure sustainability. Encourages continuous improvement.

Working with Others

Anchors

1. Treats others with respect.
2. Cooperates and collaborates with colleagues.
3. Includes relevant others in decision-making.
4. Working with other cultures.
5. Utilising other backgrounds, skills and motivations.
6. Shows empathy and sympathy.
7. Assertiveness.
8. Balances individual and team goals.
9. Resolves conflicts among team members.
10. Builds productive working relationships.

Indicators

	UNSATISFACTORY	IMPROVEMENT NEEDED	MEETS EXPECTATIONS	EXCEEDS EXPECTATIONS	EXCEPTIONAL
anchor	1 - Extremely Weak 2 - Very Weak	3 - Weak 4 - Fair	5 - Satisfactory 6 - Good	7 - Strong 8 - Very Strong	9 - Excellent 10 - Outstanding
1.	Exhibits behaviour that negatively impacts the morale and accomplishments of the team.	Sometimes displays behaviour inconsistent with workplace courtesy and respect.	Treats others with respect. Encourages and appreciates individual contributions.	Is respectful and welcoming. Reaches out and engages with other people.	Promotes, supports, and influences a culture of respect and courtesy among team members. Inspires collaboration by bridging gaps among diverse individuals and units.
2.	Is not a team player. Does not seek consensus and co-operation with others. Often disrupts team process, jeopardising progress toward common goals. Ignores or belittles the contribution of others.	Has difficulty collaborating with others. Often prefers to work independently. Sees little value in letting everybody have their say.	Works effectively and cooperatively with others. Shares information and knowledge with others. Encourages others to express their views. Takes account of dissenting opinions.	Is highly collaborative. Praises the contributions of others. Seeks new alliances to expand sphere of influence and enhance quality of work.	Models cooperation and teamwork. Actively involves colleagues in decision-making processes. Creates opportunities for self and others to improve working relationships and work outcomes.
3.	Makes decisions in isolation without consulting others. Leaves to others the task of liaising with other departments and external stakeholders.	Adopts a silo mentality, does not co-operate with other organisational boundaries. Takes little interest in what other parts of the organisation do. Lacks understanding of priorities and key issues for other stakeholders.	Liaises with people outside immediate working environment. Sees when assistance is needed from other departments. Has contacts elsewhere in the organisation to call for support if necessary.	Works co-operatively across organisational boundaries. Is constantly in touch with colleagues from other departments.	Includes relevant others in decision-making. Engages with people outside own team to achieve common objectives.

Working with others Indicators – continued

	UNSATISFACTORY	IMPROVEMENT NEEDED	MEETS EXPECTATIONS	EXCEEDS EXPECTATIONS	EXCEPTIONAL
anchor	1 - Extremely Weak 2 - Very Weak	3 - Weak 4 - Fair	5 - Satisfactory 6 - Good	7 - Strong 8 - Very Strong	9 - Excellent 10 - Outstanding
4.	Shows lack of cultural sensitivity. Sees cultural differences in terms of national stereotypes. Is prejudiced and biased against people from other cultures, judges them based on personal standards.	Is aware of cultural differences but makes little or no effort to adapt to them. Shows little curiosity for understanding the reasons why people behave as they do.	Is aware of cultural differences and makes an effort to adapt to them. Makes an effort to understand other people in the context of cultural differences.	Mixes with people of other nationalities. Understands the importance of non-verbal communication patterns.	Bridges gaps between cultural differences. Is receptive to other cultural approaches. Enjoys working with people from different cultural backgrounds.
5.	Fails to consider individual differences in background, skills, or motivations. Sees things in terms of black or white.	Is dismissive of ideas that are not his/her own. Holds strong views and is reluctant to see things from other angles.	Holds strong views but is willing to consider other opinions. Listens to reason. Sees the shades of grey between black and white.	Encourages people to voice their opinions and express their views.	Effectively utilises the diverse range of backgrounds, skills and motivations of others. Actively seeks input from others.
6.	Shows no concern for the emotional state of others. Does not take steps to deal with underlying tensions at work.	Misreads other people's feelings or states of mind. Steps on other people's toes. Is dismissive of ideas that are not his/her own.	Is sensitive to the feelings of other people. Assists colleagues when asked to do so.	Is diplomatic when drawing attention to errors in other people's work or understanding of a situation.	Shows a genuine concern for the emotional state of others. Speaks up for colleagues in distress.
7.	Has low self-esteem. Allows themself to be dictated to by other people. Is 'invisible' in group discussions. Plays games, is sarcastic, or remains silent.	Bottles up feelings that eventually explode, leaving no room for communication. Is not sufficiently assertive when defending his/her views.	Is clear about what he/she feels and needs and how it can be achieved. Is able to communicate calmly without attacking other people.	Is happy to defend own position, even if it provokes conflict. Is able to say 'no', rather than agreeing to do something just to please someone else.	Understands how to negotiate if two people want different outcomes. Is able to talk openly about self and able to listen to others.

Working with others Indicators – continued

	UNSATISFACTORY	IMPROVEMENT NEEDED	MEETS EXPECTATIONS	EXCEEDS EXPECTATIONS	EXCEPTIONAL
anchor	1 - Extremely Weak 2 - Very Weak	3 - Weak 4 - Fair	5 - Satisfactory 6 - Good	7 - Strong 8 - Very Strong	9 - Excellent 10 - Outstanding
8.	Is unwilling to work outside comfort zone to support team goals.	Resists new challenges. Seems uninterested in building skills and knowledge.	Demonstrates flexibility and willingness to step out of comfort zone to support team and goals.	Is always willing to try something new. Balances individual and team goals.	Consistently goes beyond direct responsibilities to achieve team and department goals. Welcomes new challenges.
9.	Often avoids conflict. Is not prepared or willing to resolve conflict.	Is unable to resolve or constructively manage conflicts.	Works effectively with others to resolve conflict.	Manages conflict competently and efficiently. When possible, looks for and proposes middle ground solutions.	Skillfully and proactively addresses conflict. Seeks and achieves 'win-win' resolutions.
10.	Shows lack of interest in and respect for peers and partners.	Has difficulty building strong, mutually beneficial working relationships.	Builds and maintains effective working relationships with peers and partners.	Successfully builds productive, mutually beneficial relationships to solve problems and achieve common goals.	Leads colleagues to inspired cooperation and teamwork in support of department and organisational goals.

Communicating

Anchors

1. Demonstrates effective written communication skills.
2. Adapts written communication to the level of the audience.
3. Writes clearly, in a visually appealing manner.
4. Explains ideas clearly, simplifies the complex.
5. Methodical, structured and precise in speech.
6. Adapts verbal communication to the level of the audience.
7. Communicates clearly and knowledgeably.
8. Shares information with others.
9. Seeks input from others.
10. Protects private and confidential information.

Indicators

	UNSATISFACTORY	IMPROVEMENT NEEDED	MEETS EXPECTATIONS	EXCEEDS EXPECTATIONS	EXCEPTIONAL
anchor	1 - Extremely Weak 2 - Very Weak	3 - Weak 4 - Fair	5 - Satisfactory 6 - Good	7 - Strong 8 - Very Strong	9 - Excellent 10 - Outstanding
1.	Creates documents that are poorly written, unstructured, grammatically incorrect, or contain too many spelling errors. Uses incomplete sentences or bad punctuation.	Creates documents that are disorganised or contain many grammar or spelling errors. Uses sentences, that are too long, too verbose, or overly complex.	Keeps sentences and paragraphs short and concise. Leaves out words that do not contribute to the main focus of the communication. Writes documents that are syntactically and semantically correct.	Creates documents that are consistently clear and persuasive.	Writes documents that are always complete, concise, clear, concrete, correct, considerate and courteous.
2.	Creates documents that are either overly simplistic or too complex and therefore not adapted to the audience.	Creates documents that are somewhat disorganised and/or not appropriate for the audience. Uses slang, jargon, acronyms, or unexplained concepts or ideas.	Focuses on the needs of the audience. Uses simple language, without overusing clichés, jargon, and expressions or trying to impress with difficult words.	Creates documents that are concise and comprehensive and convey all the ideas that need to be addressed.	Writes documents that consistently address all the needs of specific individuals and groups within the audience.
3.	Creates visually unappealing documents; large blocks of continuous text without punctuation or white space.	Makes inappropriate use of colour coding, text formatting, capitalisation, etc. Uses no illustrations or visual elements.	Creates visually appealing documents with appropriate use of white space, indentations and graphical elements.	Makes appropriate use of colour coding, text formatting and capitalisation, enhancing the underlying structure and ideas.	Writes visually engaging documents, illustrated with tables and graphs enhancing the messages to be conveyed.
4.	Does not finish sentences or stops mid-sentence and expects the audience to second-guess and draw conclusions. Gets blocked and has difficulty in finding the right words to express themself. Speaks too fast and is difficult to follow. Has bad articulation or truncates their words.	Does not always clearly structure ideas; has difficulty in articulating his/her thoughts. Is hesitant and transmits uncertainty with body language or tone of voice. Does not engage spontaneously with	Speaks clearly, connects with his/her audience and gets messages across with relative ease. Engages spontaneously with his/her audience.	Explains issues and ideas clearly and succinctly. Strikes a good balance between detail and the need for clarity.	Explains even complex issues and ideas clearly and succinctly, simplifies the complex. Convinces sceptics and opponents of his/her points of view.

Communicating Indicators – continued

	UNSATISFACTORY	IMPROVEMENT NEEDED	MEETS EXPECTATIONS	EXCEEDS EXPECTATIONS	EXCEPTIONAL
anchor	1 - Extremely Weak 2 - Very Weak	3 - Weak 4 - Fair	5 - Satisfactory 6 - Good	7 - Strong 8 - Very Strong	9 - Excellent 10 - Outstanding
5.	Speaks in an unstructured fashion, jumps from one point to another, does not get to the point, or does not achieve flowing delivery of ideas. Makes contributions that are often unclear or inaccurate. Gives minimalist or no answers to questions.	Gets lost in complexity and does not succeed in making points clearly. Dwells too much on detail and does not get to the point. Is rather vague or evasive when answering questions.	Speaks clearly, persuasively, and concisely. Focuses on the needs of specific individuals and groups. Keeps to a logical order when explaining things. Copes well with questions and provides relevant information.	Uses verbal communication that is consistently clear, persuasive, and adapted to the audience. Goes straight to the point when answering questions. Illustrates answers to questions with appropriate and relevant examples.	Is methodical, precise and structured in speech, is articulate and makes good use of language and gesture. Anticipates information needs and gives full and complete answers to questions.
6.	Has difficulty tailoring communication to the needs of others; communicates 'too much,' 'too little,' or 'too late.'	Does not always keep the audience in mind.	Tailors information to audience and individual needs.	Effectively adjusts the level of detail and tone to the audience.	Effectively adapts verbal communication to audience; effectively distinguishes between 'need to know' and 'nice to know.'
7.	Appears distracted or uninterested; frequently interrupts others. Does not listen to what others say.	Interrupts others to express own point of view. Has difficulty getting to the point. Uses facts that are not always accurate or relevant.	Appears knowledgeable and concise. Actively listens to and synthesises perspectives of others.	Appears credible and reliable. Actively listens to and integrates diverse contributions.	Speaks with conviction and authority. Listens to, synthesises, and integrates others' ideas.
8.	Does not share information in a timely manner, creating problems for colleagues and stakeholders.	Has difficulty distinguishing between critical and non-critical information.	Gives others the information they need in a timely manner.	Shares accurate, timely information with the right people in the right format.	Displays openness and transparency in sharing information with partners and stakeholders.

Communicating -Indicators – continued

	UNSATISFACTORY	IMPROVEMENT NEEDED	MEETS EXPECTATIONS	EXCEEDS EXPECTATIONS	EXCEPTIONAL
anchor	1 - Extremely Weak 2 - Very Weak	3 - Weak 4 - Fair	5 - Satisfactory 6 - Good	7 - Strong 8 - Very Strong	9 - Excellent 10 - Outstanding
9.	Avoids contact with co-workers and partners. Is monosyllabic in conversation.	Keeps communication to a minimum. Is reluctant to share thoughts and ideas.	Maintains an open and honest dialogue with co-workers and partners.	Encourages others to share ideas and integrates others' thoughts and opinions.	Consistently and effectively seeks and incorporates others' ideas to ensure optimal results.
10.	Discloses and uses private and confidential information inappropriately, putting the organisation or other individuals at risk.	Does not consistently follow the organisation's confidentiality or privacy practices. Sometimes shares private or confidential information with unauthorised or inappropriate individuals.	Consistently follows confidentiality and privacy policies and practices. Only discloses confidential information to authorised individuals.	Understands and implements confidentiality and privacy policies.	Clearly understands and follows confidentiality and privacy policies and practices. Actively develops practices to protect confidential and private information.

Resilience

Anchors

1. Social support.
2. Healthy mind in healthy body.
3. Positive thinking.
4. Communicating and problem solving.
5. Coping with heavy workload and tight deadlines.
6. Adjusting to peaks and troughs in workload.
7. Handling failures and setbacks.
8. Working with management.
9. Facing changes.
10. Self-control.

Indicators

	UNSATISFACTORY	IMPROVEMENT NEEDED	MEETS EXPECTATIONS	EXCEEDS EXPECTATIONS	EXCEPTIONAL
anchor	1 - Extremely Weak 2 - Very Weak	3 - Weak 4 - Fair	5 - Satisfactory 6 - Good	7 - Strong 8 - Very Strong	9 - Excellent 10 - Outstanding
1.	Is socially isolated. Has few or no social contacts with colleagues, friends or family.	Has an operational network, but no personal or strategic network to rely upon. Neglects work-life balance.	Has both an operational and a personal network to rely upon.	Has good operational, personal and strategic network.	Has very good operational and personal network, combined with an excellent strategic network.
2.	Has an unhealthy lifestyle. Uses too much alcohol, caffeine or other drugs. Is a heavy smoker.	Does not do enough physical activity. Is overweight, or has high blood pressure. Gets insufficient sleep or rest.	Takes care of physical and mental health. Eats mostly healthy food, does sufficient physical activity, gets enough rest and sleep.	Has a good mental and physical condition.	Is mentally and physically in top condition.
3.	Maintains a negative, pessimistic outlook. Concentrates on negative only.	Has low self-esteem. Lacks trust in colleagues and co-workers.	Is aware of own worth and value, but also of own shortcomings and room for development. Remains in positive mood, despite setbacks.	Maintains an optimistic, positive outlook. Works on self-development.	Always looks at the bright side of life. Continuously works on self-improvement.
4.	Does not listen to what other people have to say. Is unaware of other people's feelings and emotions.	Is unable to express own feelings and views in a convincing way.	Is assertive, not passive or aggressive.	Listens to, understands, and integrates others' feelings and views in the bigger picture.	Is a 'giver' not a 'taker'.
5.	Works inefficiently or becomes overwhelmed with workload. Is not capable of adapting to high work pressure. Becomes stressed or panics when under pressure. Displays negative emotions to others inappropriately. Shows complacency.	Uses overtime as only strategy to cope with heavy workload or tight deadlines. Sometimes lacks planning and prioritising skills. Is overly perfectionist, indecisive, or impatient with others.	Generally copes with high levels of work and tight deadlines. Manages to get all his/her work done in time and to a good quality standard. Keeps cool under pressure, works more intensively and longer hours when pressure is on.	Combines good work-life balance with efficient and effective behaviour at work. Has strategies for coping with large volumes of work.	Manages own workload as well as the workload of others effectively and efficiently. Remains calm under pressure. Sees where corners can be cut to meet tight deadlines without sacrificing quality of work.

Resilience Indicators – continued

	UNSATISFACTORY	IMPROVEMENT NEEDED	MEETS EXPECTATIONS	EXCEEDS EXPECTATIONS	EXCEPTIONAL
anchor	1 - Extremely Weak 2 - Very Weak	3 - Weak 4 - Fair	5 - Satisfactory 6 - Good	7 - Strong 8 - Very Strong	9 - Excellent 10 - Outstanding
6.	Considers calmer periods as opportunities for complete inactivity, thus wasting time.	Limits himself to catching up on the backlog, deploys no extra activities otherwise.	Takes care of professional and personal development during the calmer periods at work. Expands own operational network.	Anticipates busy periods and prepares for them. Expands own personal and strategic networks.	Makes optimal use of calmer periods to further develop own performance. Prepares mentally and physically for busier periods to come.
7.	Regards unsuccessful endeavours as personal failures. Loses self-confidence and self-esteem after a failure or setback.	Responds defensively to criticism. Refuses to learn from failures and setbacks. Tends to blame the environment for own failures.	Responds confidently and non-defensively to criticism. Accepts that not everything in life works out fine. Acknowledges own mistakes, and learns from them. Moves on after setbacks and missed opportunities.	Considers failures and setbacks as learning opportunities. Turns setbacks and failures to his/her advantage.	Handles failures and interprets setbacks professionally, not personally. Anticipates failure and has a backup strategy. Has clear strategies for coping with failure.
8.	Is frustrated by the management, has little tendency to work with it constructively. Intolerant of ambiguity in work content or organisational situation. Externalises frustrations with management.	Does not always alert management to problems. Does not always take steps to establish with management the conditions for smooth working relations. Does not succeed in bringing sceptical superiors to his/her way of thinking.	Tolerates ambiguity in work content or organisational situation. Copes with demands by management and understands their role. Alerts management to problems. Has open and cooperative attitude towards management.	Actively seeks feedback from management and builds on it. Works autonomously but knows when to involve the management. Has gained the confidence of management and is a point of reference.	Understands and works with management, not against it. Actively manages expectations from management. Endeavours to become involved in decisions related to his/her work.

Resilience Indicators – continued

	UNSATISFACTORY	IMPROVEMENT NEEDED	MEETS EXPECTATIONS	EXCEEDS EXPECTATIONS	EXCEPTIONAL
anchor	1 - Extremely Weak 2 - Very Weak	3 - Weak 4 - Fair	5 - Satisfactory 6 - Good	7 - Strong 8 - Very Strong	9 - Excellent 10 - Outstanding
9	Resists organisational change, and sticks to old habits and traditional ways of working. Reacts negatively to change. Feels threatened by change or reorganisation.	Is suspicious of change and its implications. Has difficulty adapting to new working environments. Is discouraged by organisational change.	Adapts to new ways of working and broader organisational changes. Sees organisational change as part of life.	Sees change and reorganisation as an opportunity for improvement. Adjusts quickly to unexpected changes.	Embraces change. Proposes more efficient ways of doing things. Sees organisational change as a positive challenge.
10.	Lacks inner discipline. Shows over-indulgence.	Is sometimes caught up by excitement.	Is mindful. Focuses on task and is not distracted by things around. Manages to get rid of bad habits.	Keeps negative emotions under control at all time. Replaces bad habits by good ones.	Is able to control emotions, behaviour and desires in the face of external demands.

Leadership

Anchors

1. Explains ideas clearly, simplifies the complex.
2. Adapts communication to the level of the audience.
3. Communicates clearly and knowledgeably.
4. Shares information with others.
5. Seeks input from others.
6. Understands and supports organisational goals.
7. Helps others perform at their best.
8. Self-aware and open to feedback.
9. Leads by example.
10. Delegates effectively.

Indicators

	UNSATISFACTORY	IMPROVEMENT NEEDED	MEETS EXPECTATIONS	EXCEEDS EXPECTATIONS	EXCEPTIONAL
anchor	1 - Extremely Weak 2 - Very Weak	3 - Weak 4 - Fair	5 - Satisfactory 6 - Good	7 - Strong 8 - Very Strong	9 - Excellent 10 - Outstanding
1.	Has difficulty in finding the right words to express themself.	Does not always clearly structure their ideas; has difficulty in articulating thoughts and vision. Is hesitant and transmits uncertainty with body language or tone of	Speaks and writes clearly, connects with their audience and gets messages across with relative ease. Engages spontaneously with their audience.	Explains vision and ideas clearly and succinctly. Strikes a good balance between detail and the need for clarity.	Explains even complex issues and ideas clearly and succinctly, simplifies the complex. Convinces sceptics and opponents of his/her points of view.
2.	Has difficulty tailoring communication to the needs of others; communicates 'too much,' 'too little,' or 'too late.'	Does not always keep the audience in mind.	Tailors information to audience and individual needs.	Effectively adjusts the level of detail and tone to the audience.	Effectively adapts communication to audience; effectively distinguishes between 'need to know' and 'nice to know'.
3	Appears distracted or uninterested. Does not listen to what others say.	Interrupts others to express own point of view. Has difficulty getting to the point. Uses facts that are not always accurate or relevant.	Appears knowledgeable and enthusiastic. Actively listens to and synthesises perspectives of others.	Appears credible and reliable. Actively listens to and integrates diverse contributions.	Speaks with conviction and authority. Listens to, synthesises, and integrates others' ideas.
4.	Does not share information in a timely manner, creating problems for colleagues and stakeholders. Shies away from delivering tough messages.	Tends to 'hold on' to information; has difficulty distinguishing between critical and non-critical information.	Gives others the information they need in a timely manner.	Shares accurate, timely information with the right people in the right format.	Displays openness and transparency in sharing information with others. Is prepared to deliver tough messages when necessary.
5.	Avoids contact with co-workers and partners.	Keeps communication to a minimum; is reluctant to share thoughts and ideas.	Maintains an open and honest dialogue with co-workers and partners.	Encourages others to share ideas and integrates others' thoughts and opinions.	Consistently and effectively seeks and incorporates others' ideas to ensure optimal results.

Leadership Indicators – continued

	UNSATISFACTORY	IMPROVEMENT NEEDED	MEETS EXPECTATIONS	EXCEEDS EXPECTATIONS	EXCEPTIONAL
anchor	1 - Extremely Weak 2 - Very Weak	3 - Weak 4 - Fair	5 - Satisfactory 6 - Good	7 - Strong 8 - Very Strong	9 - Excellent 10 - Outstanding
6.	Resists change. Maintains focus on immediate, routine tasks. Work efforts do not align with unit and department goals.	Contributions and work efforts often do not reflect an understanding of unit and department goals.	Effectively aligns work efforts with organisational and department goals.	Understands and supports the need to align work with organisational initiatives and goals.	Encourages and leads changes that enhance organisational and workforce effectiveness.
7.	Hinders sharing of knowledge and/or expertise, focused largely on own development. Fails to spot or nurture future talent. Fails to create development opportunities for others.	Does not openly share expertise or information with others. Spots future talent but fails to nurture it.	Assists others in developing skills and knowledge. Helps people to resolve problems and overcome obstacles.	Consistently and actively assists others in expanding and developing skills and knowledge. Coaches and/or mentors others. Creates targeted development opportunities for others.	Inspires and helps others to evelop skills and competencies to perform at their best. Spots and nurtures potential future talent.
8.	Is not motivated to learn and grow, believes that others are responsible for their development.	Often resists to feedback on performance. Rarely asks for help or feedback.	Is self-aware and open to feedback from others. Displays integrity.	Very self-aware; asks others for feedback in an effort to improve skills and knowledge.	Demonstrates a high degree of self-awareness; asks others for feedback on performance; is a continuous learner. Is authentic in everything he/she does or says.
9.	Demotivates others. Betrays lack of conviction in chances of success.	Keeps too low a profile to make a leadership impact. Does not react when developments require assertive action. Is inconsistent in supporting staff to achieve defined goals.	Is enthusiastic about their work and transmits enthusiasm to others. Encourages and supports staff to achieve performance and development goals.	Sets a good example in terms of enthusiasm and commitment. Encourages and engages staff to make optimal use of skills and knowledge. Makes themself visible and accessible to colleagues.	Leads and motivates by example. Inspires staff to perform at their best. Shows drive and determination to succeed.

Leadership Indicators – continued

	UNSATISFACTORY	IMPROVEMENT NEEDED	MEETS EXPECTATIONS	EXCEEDS EXPECTATIONS	EXCEPTIONAL
anchor	1 - Extremely Weak 2 - Very Weak	3 - Weak 4 - Fair	5 - Satisfactory 6 - Good	7 - Strong 8 - Very Strong	9 - Excellent 10 - Outstanding
10	Does not delegate; does most of the work by themself. Assigns work inappropriately. Does not keep development and performance goals in mind. Has unrealistic expectations and perception of staff skills and knowledge.	Doesn't effectively match work assignments to staff talent and proficiencies. Does little to monitor team progress or provide follow-up.	Plans ahead and organises work. Thoughtfully delegates work to develop staff and achieve goals. Monitors team progress and provides follow-up.	Effectively links work assignments to achieve individual and unit performance goals.	Effectively delegates work to develop skills and knowledge. Ensures optimal outcomes, aligns work with individual, unit, and organisational goals.

Learning and Development

Anchors

1. Explains ideas clearly, simplifies the complex.
2. Actively developing and applying new knowledge, skills, and competencies.
3. Personal development.
4. Asking for advice and assistance.
5. Seeing own role within the organisation.
6. Seeing the "bigger picture".
7. Learning other languages.
8. Learning strategy.
9. Active listening.
10. Teaching others.

Indicators

	UNSATISFACTORY	IMPROVEMENT NEEDED	MEETS EXPECTATIONS	EXCEEDS EXPECTATIONS	EXCEPTIONAL
anchor	1 - Extremely Weak 2 - Very Weak	3 - Weak 4 - Fair	5 - Satisfactory 6 - Good	7 - Strong 8 - Very Strong	9 - Excellent 10 - Outstanding
1.	Has difficulty in finding the right words to express themself.	Does not always clearly structure ideas; has difficulty in articulating thoughts and vision.	Speaks and writes clearly, simplifies the complex.	Explains vision and ideas clearly and succinctly. Strikes a good balance between detail and the need for clarity.	Explains even complex issues and ideas clearly and succinctly, simplifies the complex.
2.	Allows knowledge levels to remain constant and/or outdated. Shows little interest in developing new skills or acquiring new knowledge.	Remains fixed in personal ways of working, does not try to develop. Takes a long time to learn new information.	Takes new information on board quickly. Learns from observation. Adapts to new ways of doing things.	Volunteers for new and challenging tasks. Is resourceful when it comes to familiarising themself with the latest developments in their field.	Takes active steps to improve own knowledge and development. Develops new skills on his/her own initiative.
3.	Stays in their comfort zone and settles for routine. Does little to overcome their weaknesses.	Sees personal development in exclusively professional terms. Does little to develop their strengths.	Knows own strengths and weaknesses. Identifies personal failings and tries to overcome them. Sets personal goals.	Sets themself inspiring challenges. Sets and achieves personal goals.	Works actively on developing personal strengths and overcoming their weaknesses. Improves knowledge and skills out of personal interest and natural curiosity.
4.	Does not take opportunities to ask for personal feedback from others. Fails to learn from mistakes, continues to make them. Does not accept constructive feedback.	Does not learn from experience. Avoids new challenges and learning opportunities. Makes limited use of the experience of colleagues.	Seeks personal feedback on performance from others. Learns from mistakes and avoids repeating them. Responds positively to negative feedback and learns from it.	Rethinks and adjusts their approach to take account of feedback received. Learns from input and suggestions from colleagues.	Actively seeks feedback from others to improve own performance. Pools knowledge and expertise.

Learning and Development Indicators – continued

	UNSATISFACTORY	IMPROVEMENT NEEDED	MEETS EXPECTATIONS	EXCEEDS EXPECTATIONS	EXCEPTIONAL
anchor	1 - Extremely Weak 2 - Very Weak	3 - Weak 4 - Fair	5 - Satisfactory 6 - Good	7 - Strong 8 - Very Strong	9 - Excellent 10 - Outstanding
5.	Focuses exclusively on own tasks and role. Has limited vision of developments elsewhere. Lacks understanding of how own work contributes to the objectives of the organisation.	Does not always respect the boundaries between his/her responsibilities and those of colleagues.	Knows what their department does and where it fits in. Understands the objectives of the organisation and contributes towards their achievement.	Takes initiatives to improve organisation-wide procedures and workflows.	Projects a positive image of their organisation to the outside world.
6.	Makes no effort to interact with other departments or organisations. Lacks vision of what happens upstream and downstream of own department.	Gives little thought to wider organisational objectives.	Understands how his/her department contributes to the achievement of wider organisational goals. Interacts extensively with other departments and organisations.	Uses knowledge of wider organisational processes to improve collaboration with other organisations.	Sees the 'bigger picture' and contributes actively. Is aware of the wider 'political' context, and his/her own contribution.
7.	Besides own mother tongue, is only a basic user (A1, A2) for one of the three working languages.	Besides own mother tongue, is only an independent user (B1, B2) for one of the three working languages.	Is a proficient user (C1) of at least three languages, including their mother tongue, one of the working languages, and another official EU language.	Is a proficient user (C1, C2) of the three working languages, or of more than three official EU languages.	Is a proficient user (C1, C2) of at least three official EU languages, and an independent user (B1, B2) of at least one non-EU language.
8.	Is not aware of their own learning style.	Does not apply their own preferred learning style systematically.	Knows and applies own preferred learning style.	Has a clear learning strategy, and applies it successfully.	Uses different learning styles in different circumstances

Learning and Development Indicators – continued

	UNSATISFACTORY	IMPROVEMENT NEEDED	MEETS EXPECTATIONS	EXCEEDS EXPECTATIONS	EXCEPTIONAL
anchor	1 - Extremely Weak 2 - Very Weak	3 - Weak 4 - Fair	5 - Satisfactory 6 - Good	7 - Strong 8 - Very Strong	9 - Excellent 10 - Outstanding
9.	Appears distracted or uninterested. Frequently interrupts others. Does not listen to what others say.	Interrupts others to express own point of view.	Listens to and learns from other people's ideas and contributions.	Actively listens to and learns from other people's ideas and contributions.	Listens to, synthesises, and integrates others' ideas into own understanding
10.	Keeps own knowledge and understanding to themself. Considers colleagues as competitors.	Teaches others only when explicitly asked to do so.	Considers teaching others as part of his/her job description.	Mentors or coaches others when asked to.	Actively mentors or coaches others. Sees coaching and mentoring as part of his/her job description.

Annex 2 Glossary

360-degree feedback

The term 360-degree feedback refers to an appraisal and feedback system in which an employee (typically someone in a managerial or supervisory position) is evaluated by one or more supervisors, peers, and subordinates.

70-20-10 model

The 70-20-10 model is a learning and development model, usually credited to Morgan McCall and his colleagues, Lombardo and Eichinger, working at the Centre for Creative Leadership (CCL).

80/20 principle

This principle can be applied to prioritising your tasks, based on the idea that most of the results (output) will be generated by a small amount of your effort (input).

ABC method

The ABC method is a powerful priority-setting technique. Behind every item you put the letter A, B or C depending on the following criteria: A – Very important. This is something that you must do. This is a task for which there can be serious consequences if you fail to do it; B – A task that you should do, but it only has mild consequences. This means that someone may be unhappy or inconvenienced if you don't do it, but that's about it; C – A task that would be nice to do, but for which there are no consequences at all.

Ability

A component of a competency to do a certain kind of work at a certain level.

Accountability

What are you going to do? By when will you do it? How will I know? It does NOT include blame or judgment!

Acronym

An acronym is an abbreviation used as a word, typically created from the first letters of the key words in a term or concept: an example in this book is STAR (Situation, Task, Actions, Results). Acronyms can be very useful shorthand, but only if they are understood by the person you are addressing.

Active listening

This is a communication technique used in counselling, training and conflict resolution. It requires the listener to feed back what they hear to the speaker, by way of re-stating or paraphrasing what they have heard in their own words, to confirm what they have heard and moreover, to confirm the understanding of both parties (Wikipedia).

Analysing and problem solving

General competency: Identify the critical facts in complex issues and develop creative and practical solutions.

Anchor

See behavioural anchors.

Appraisal

See performance appraisal.

Assertiveness

Assertiveness is an attitude and a way of relating to the outside world, backed up by a set of abilities.

Assessment

A way to understand a person's goals and where they are at physically, mentally and spiritually. Assessments may measure strengths and skills or may identify areas for improvement.

Authentic leadership

Authentic leadership is an approach to leadership that emphasizes building the leader's legitimacy through honest relationships with followers who value their input, and which are built on an ethical foundation (Wikipedia).

Autonomy

Some people need to have a lot of freedom in what they do, whereas others need more guidance. But there is an optimal level of how much freedom you need to have to be satisfied in your job.

Behavioural anchors

Behavioural anchors are specific, easy-to-apply examples of behaviours that demonstrate a given competency. To give a practical example: a behavioural anchor is something that may be used to define the level someone has reached on a particular competency from 1 to 10.

Body language

Body language is a kind of nonverbal communication, where thoughts, intentions, or feelings are expressed by physical behaviours, such as facial expressions, body posture, gestures, eye movement, touch and the use of space (Wikipedia).

Boreout

Boreout consists of three elements: boredom, lack of challenge, and lack of interest.

Brainstorming

Brainstorming is a group creativity technique by which efforts are made to find a conclusion for a specific problem by gathering a list of ideas spontaneously contributed by its members.

Burnout

Burnout is a state of physical, emotional or mental exhaustion combined with doubts about your competence and the value of your work.

Career development

The management of careers by individuals and organisations (e.g., through job moves and promotions).

Career guidance

Career guidance aims to help staff manage their careers (e.g., by providing advice on how to make best use of their skills in line with their aspirations).

Certification

Procedure allowing officials from the Assistant (AST) function group to become members of the Administrator (AD) function group following successful completion of training and examinations.

CLEAR

Challenging, Legal, Environmentally sound, Agreed, Recorded.

Coach

A person who offers support, advice, skills and tough love. A coach plays a vital role in the spiritual, mental and physical development of the coachee.

Coaching

Coaching is unlocking a person's potential to maximise their performance. Coaching is helping people to learn rather than teaching them. Coaches need not have first-hand experience of the line of work of the person being coached and coaching focuses on their 'vertical' development.

Cognitive

Having to do with internal mental processes. Cognitive processes are those which allow people to perceive objects and events, think, remember and solve problems. They are separate from emotional processes and are handled differently by the brain.

Comfort zone

Your comfort zone is any type of behaviour that keeps you at a low anxiety level.

Communicating

General competency: Communicate clearly and precisely both orally and in writing.

Competency

A competency is a set of defined behaviours that provide a structured guide enabling the identification, evaluation and development of the behaviours in individual employees.

Competency framework

The competency framework used by the European Personnel Selection Office is the result of a comprehensive job analysis undertaken in 2009 for all entry grades of EU officials across the institutions.

Competency passport

A competency passport gives an overview of a person's general competencies, usually in a graphical format.

Continuous (or continual) Improvement

A continuous improvement process is an unending effort to improve products, services, or processes.

Core competencies

Core competencies are general competencies common to all European Union institutions and therefore suitable for use in open competitions and appraisal procedures.

Creative thinking

Creative thinking involves a relaxed, open, and playful approach. 'Thinking outside the box' is a metaphor that means to think differently, unconventionally, or from a new perspective; it refers to creative thinking.

Critical thinking

Critical thinking is the process we use to reflect on, assess, and judge the assumption underlying our own and others' ideas and efforts.

Delegation

Delegation is giving others the authority to act on your behalf, accompanied with accountability for results.

Deliberate practice

Deliberate practice involves awareness, attention, rehearsal and repetition, and leads to new knowledge or skills that can later be developed into more complex knowledge and skills.

Delivering quality and results

General competency: Take personal responsibility and initiative for delivering work to a high standard of quality within set procedures.

Development

The growth or enhancement of abilities, skills and self-awareness.

Efficiency

Efficiency is about doing things in an optimal way, for example doing it the fastest or in the least expensive way.

Effectiveness

Effectiveness is about doing the right task, completing activities and achieving goals.

Eisenhower Matrix

Although it was Stephen Covey who made this method popular in his book 'First Things First', the concept is originally credited to US President Dwight D. Eisenhower. Whenever confronted with something that needed to be done, he would ask himself two questions: First, is the task important? Second, is it urgent? Based on this, the task would end up in one of four categories: important and urgent, important but not urgent, not important but urgent, and neither important nor urgent.

Emotional intelligence

The ability to identify, use, understand, and manage emotions in positive ways to relieve stress, communicate effectively, empathise with others, overcome challenges, and defuse conflict.

Empathy

Empathy is the experience of understanding another person's condition from their perspective.

ENFJ

One of the 16 Myers-Briggs Personality Type Indicators (MBTI). Warm, empathetic, responsive, and responsible. Highly attuned to the emotions, needs, and motivations of others. Find potential in everyone, want to help others fulfil their potential. May act as catalysts for individual and group growth. Loyal, responsive to praise and criticism. Sociable, facilitate others in a group, and provide inspiring leadership. (Excerpted from 'Introduction to Type' by Isabel Briggs Myers published by CPP. Inc.)

ENFP

One of the 16 Myers-Briggs Personality Type Indicators (MBTI). Warmly enthusiastic and imaginative. See life as full of possibilities. Make connections between events and information very quickly, and confidently proceed based on the patterns they see. Want a lot of affirmation from others, and readily give appreciation and support. Spontaneous and flexible, often rely on their ability to improvise and their verbal fluency. (Excerpted from 'Introduction to Type' by Isabel Briggs Myers published by CPP. Inc.)

ENTJ

One of the 16 Myers-Briggs Personality Type Indicators (MBTI). Frank, decisive, assume leadership readily. Quickly see illogical and inefficient procedures and policies, develop and implement comprehensive systems to solve organizational problems. Enjoy long-term planning and goal setting. Usually well informed, well read, enjoy expanding their knowledge and passing it on to others. Forceful in presenting their ideas. (Excerpted from 'Introduction to Type' by Isabel Briggs Myers published by CPP. Inc.)

ENTP

One of the 16 Myers-Briggs Personality Type Indicators (MBTI). Quick, ingenious, stimulating, alert, and outspoken. Resourceful in solving new and challenging problems. Adept at generating conceptual possibilities and then analyzing them strategically. Good at reading other people. Bored by routine, will seldom do the same thing the same way, apt to turn to one new interest after another. (Excerpted from 'Introduction to Type' by Isabel Briggs Myers published by CPP. Inc.)

EPSO

European Personnel Selection Office: EPSO organises and conducts selection procedures on behalf of the European Union Institutions. The decisions to recruit successful candidates are taken by each Institution.

ESFJ

One of the 16 Myers-Briggs Personality Type Indicators (MBTI). Warm-hearted, conscientious, and cooperative. Want harmony in their environment, work with determination to establish it. Like to work with others to complete tasks accurately and on time. Loyal, follow through even in small matters. Notice what others need in their day-by-day lives and try to provide it. Want to be appreciated for who they are and for what they contribute. (Excerpted from 'Introduction to Type' by Isabel Briggs Myers published by CPP. Inc.)

ESFP

One of the 16 Myers-Briggs Personality Type Indicators (MBTI). Outgoing, friendly, and accepting. Exuberant lovers of life, people, and material comforts. Enjoy working with others to make things happen. Bring common sense and a realistic approach to their work and make work fun. Flexible and spontaneous, adapt readily to new people and environments. Learn best by trying a new skill with other people.

ESTJ

One of the 16 Myers-Briggs Personality Type Indicators (MBTI). Practical, realistic and matter-of-fact. Decisive, quickly move to implement decisions. Organize projects and people to get things done, focus on getting results in the most efficient way possible. Take care of routine details. Have a clear set of logical standards, systematically follow them and want others to also. Forceful in implementing their plans. (Excerpted from 'Introduction to Type' by Isabel Briggs Myers published by CPP. Inc.)

ESTP

One of the 16 Myers-Briggs Personality Type Indicators (MBTI). Flexible and tolerant, they take a pragmatic approach focused on immediate results. Theories and conceptual explanations bore them; they want to act energetically to solve the problem. Focus on the here-and-now, spontaneous, enjoy each moment that they can be active with others. Enjoy material comforts and style. Learn best through doing. (Excerpted from 'Introduction to Type' by Isabel Briggs Myers published by CPP. Inc.)

Ethics and Integrity

In the European Commission, Ethics and Integrity is now a compulsory one-day course, classified under the heading 'internal procedures' and not under any of the general competencies. The focus is on six key principles: independence, impartiality, objectivity, loyalty, responsibility and circumspection.

Ethos, pathos and logos

For Aristotle, the goal of argumentative speaking or writing is to persuade your audience that your ideas are valid, or more valid than someone else's. He divided the means of persuasion, into three categories: ethos, pathos and logos.

Expectancy theory

Vroom's expectancy theory suggests that behaviour results from conscious choices among alternatives whose purpose is to maximise pleasure and minimise pain.

Fight-or-Flight

The fight-or-flight response, also called the acute stress response, is a physiological reaction that occurs in response to a perceived harmful event, attack, or threat to survival.

Fishbone diagram

A fishbone, or Ishikawa, diagram identifies the possible causes for an effect or problem.

Flow

Flow is a state of complete immersion in an activity, being completely involved in an activity for its own sake.

Formal Learning

Intentional learning that is organised in terms of objectives (e.g. instructor-led training or structured e-learning). Formal learning is planned learning that derives from activities within a structured learning setting. Formal learning is enrolling on a programme of study, attending lectures, preparing coursework, and engaging in seminar/tutorial discussions.

Four stages of competence

Individuals are initially unaware of how little they know, or unconscious of their incompetence. As they recognize their incompetence, they consciously acquire a skill, and then consciously use it. Eventually, the skill can be operated without it being consciously thought through: the individual is said to have acquired unconscious competence.

Gantt chart

Gantt charts plot the activities necessary to complete a project on a timeline using a bar or a line, which begins and ends at a definite time. The Gantt chart also provides milestones, or markers, for assuring that a project is on track.

Gender equality

Equality between women and men is one of the European Union's founding values. It goes back to 1957 when the principle of equal pay for equal work became part of the Treaty of Rome.

General Adaptation Syndrome (GAS)

A term used to describe the body's short-term and long-term reactions to stress; it was originally described by Hans Selye.

General competencies

General competencies are competencies – or behaviour – that are expected from all employees regardless of their position or function in the organisation.

Generational thinking

Labelling people according to their birth years. Baby Boomers, born between 1946 and 1964, are competitive and loyal to their employer. Gen Xers, born between 1965 and 1977, are more likely to be skeptical and independent-minded. Gen Ys, also known as Millennials, were born in 1978 or later, and like teamwork, feedback and technology. Finally, there is Gen Z. Born after 1995, they grew up in a highly sophisticated media and computer environment and will be more Internet savvy and expert than their Gen Y ancestors. This sort of generalisation is highly controversial.

Glossophobia

Fear of public speaking.

Goal setting

Goals keep you focused and on track towards what you are aiming to become. Goals are not the same as action; they are the desired result of action.

Groupthink

The term groupthink was first described in 1972 by social psychologist Irving Janis. It is a phenomenon that occurs when a group makes incorrect decisions because group pressures lead to a deterioration of 'mental efficiency, reality testing, and moral judgment'.

GROW

The GROW model is a simple, but powerful method for goal setting and problem solving. It was developed in the United Kingdom, mainly by Sir John Whitmore and is used extensively in corporate coaching. The acronym stands for: Goals – Reality – Options (or Obstacles) – and Will (or Way Forward).

GRPI

Goals, Roles, Processes and Interpersonal Relationships are four critical and interrelated aspects of teamwork. The GRPI is a four-step project-planning tool to help team leaders ensure productivity, efficiency and quality.

Hard skills

Hard skills are teachable abilities or skills that are easy to quantify. Examples of hard skills include proficiency in a foreign language, a degree or certificate, typing speed, machine operation, computer programming, etc.

Herzberg's hygiene and motivational factors

According to Herzberg, so-called 'hygiene factors' must be present (without them there is dissatisfaction) before motivators stimulate an employee. He used the term job enrichment to describe the process of redesigning work to build motivators.

IDEAL

Acronym for Identify the problem, Define the problem, Examine the options, Act on a plan, Look at the consequences.

Indicators

Indicators – or behaviour – can be associated with multiple anchors. A behavioural anchor is something that is used to define the level someone has reached on a particular competency, for example on a scale from 1 to 10. In this sense it is very similar to an indicator, but indicators tend to be simple 'positive' and 'negative' poles, whereas the anchors define all points in between.

Informal learning

Informal learning is learning that originates from activities external to a structured learning context, or unstructured learning within a structured learning environment. (e.g., coaching, on-the-job learning, sharing experiences with colleagues). See also formal learning.

Information overload

Information overload (also known as infobesity or infoxication) refers to the difficulty a person can have in understanding an issue and making decisions that can be caused by having too much information.

INFJ

One of the 16 Myers-Briggs Personality Type Indicators (MBTI). Seek meaning and connection in ideas, relationships, and material possessions. Want to understand what motivates people and are insightful about others. Conscientious and committed to their firm values. Develop a clear vision about how best to serve the common good. Organized and decisive in implementing their vision. (Excerpted from 'Introduction to Type' by Isabel Briggs Myers published by CPP. Inc.)

INFP

One of the 16 Myers-Briggs Personality Type Indicators (MBTI). Idealistic, loyal to their values and to people who are important to them. Want an external life that is congruent with their values. Curious, quick to see possibilities, can be catalysts for implementing ideas. Seek to understand people and to help them fulfil their potential. Adaptable, flexible, and accepting unless a value is threatened. (Excerpted from 'Introduction to Type' by Isabel Briggs Myers published by CPP. Inc.)

INTJ

One of the 16 Myers-Briggs Personality Type Indicators (MBTI). Have original minds and great drive for implementing their ideas and achieving their goals. Quickly see patterns in external events and develop long-range explanatory perspectives. When committed, organize a job and carry it through. Sceptical and independent, have high standards of competence and performance for themselves and others. (Excerpted from 'Introduction to Type' by Isabel Briggs Myers published by CPP. Inc.)

INTP

One of the 16 Myers-Briggs Personality Type Indicators (MBTI). Seek to develop logical explanations for everything that interests them. Theoretical and abstract, interested more in ideas than in social interaction. Quiet, contained, flexible, and adaptable. Have unusual ability to focus in depth to solve problems in their area of interest. Sceptical, sometimes critical, always analytical. (Excerpted from 'Introduction to Type' by Isabel Briggs Myers published by CPP. Inc.)

IQ (Intelligence Quotient)

The definition of intelligence is somewhat controversial amongst psychologists, but by far the most widely used in practical settings is the psychometric approach, trying to capture the complex concept into a single score known as the Intelligence Quotient, or IQ.

ISFJ

One of the 16 Myers-Briggs Personality Type Indicators (MBTI). Quiet, friendly, responsible and conscientious. Committed and steady in meeting their obligations. Thorough, painstaking and accurate. Loyal, considerate, notice and remember specifics about people who are important to them, concerned with how others feel. Strive to create an orderly and harmonious environment at work and at home. (Excerpted from 'Introduction to Type' by Isabel Briggs Myers published by CPP. Inc.)

ISFP

One of the 16 Myers-Briggs Personality Type Indicators (MBTI). Quiet, friendly, sensitive, and kind. Enjoy the present moment, what's going on around them. Like to have their own space and to work within their own time frame. Loyal and committed to their values and to people who are important to them. Dislike disagreements and conflicts and do not force their opinions or values on others. (Excerpted from 'Introduction to Type' by Isabel Briggs Myers published by CPP. Inc.)

ISTJ

One of the 16 Myers-Briggs Personality Type Indicators (MBTI). Quiet, serious, earn success by thoroughness and dependability. Practical, matter-of-fact, realistic, and responsible. Decide logically what should be done and work toward it steadily, regardless of distractions. Take pleasure in making everything orderly and organized – their work, their home, their life. Value traditions and loyalty. (Excerpted from 'Introduction to Type' by Isabel Briggs Myers published by CPP. Inc.)

ISTP

One of the 16 Myers-Briggs Personality Type Indicators (MBTI). Tolerant and flexible, quiet observers until a problem appears, then act quickly to find workable solutions. Analyse what makes things work and readily get through large amounts of data to isolate the core of practical problems. Interested in cause and effect, organise facts using logical principles, and value efficiency. (Excerpted from 'Introduction to Type' by Isabel Briggs Myers published by CPP. Inc.)

Interpersonal skills

See soft skills.

Johari Window

The Johari Window was invented by Joseph Luft and Harrington Ingham in the 1950s as a model for mapping personality awareness.

Kaizen

Kaizen is the Chinese/Japanese term for 'continuous improvement'.

KISS

KISS is an acronym for 'Keep it simple, stupid', a design principle adopted by the US Navy in the 1960s. Applied to human communication, the KISS principle means keeping conversation as simple as possible, to find a common denominator between those involved and reduce the possibility of confusion.

Lateral thinking

Lateral thinking deliberately distances itself from standard perceptions of creativity as either 'vertical' logic (the classic method for problem-solving, i.e., working out the solution step-by-step from the given data) or 'horizontal' imagination (having many ideas but being unconcerned with the detailed implementation of them). The term was coined by Dr. Edward de Bono.

Leadership

General competency: Manage, develop and motivate people to achieve results.

Learning and development

General competency: Develop and improve personal skills and knowledge of the organisation and its environment. The process of acquiring or improving knowledge and skills.

Lifelong learning

The process of continually striving to learn and understand new information and practices. Offers a way for individuals to grow continually and keep up to date.

Maslov's hierarchy of needs

Ethics, ideas and behaviour differ from country to country and from culture to culture, but all humans have similar needs. Abraham Maslow used the terms 'physiological', 'safety', 'belongingness' and 'love', 'esteem', 'self-actualisation', and 'self-transcendence' to describe the patterns of human motivation. Maslow's theory indicates that the most basic level of needs must be met before the individual will strongly desire the secondary or higher-level needs.

Mens sana in corpore sano

The expression *mens sana in corpore sano* – 'a sound mind in a sound body' – is widely used to express the idea that physical health is an important part of mental and psychological well being.

Mentoring

Mentoring is a pairing of a more skilled or experienced person, usually in the same field of knowledge, with a less experienced person. Ideally mentors have no line management relationship to the mentee. Mentors will often provide direction and advice and should open organisational doors for mentees. Mentors can provide a neutral sounding board, assure total confidentiality, and have no agenda other than assisting their mentees in their development and to reach their goals. Mentoring involves helping people to develop their career, skills and expertise, often drawing upon the experiences of the mentor. Mentoring is focused on the 'horizontal' development (learning) of the mentee.

Mind mapping

A mind map is a powerful graphic method that provides a universal key to unlock the potential of your brain.

Motivation

Motivation is the force that drives us to achieve our goals. As described by Daniel Pink, 'Motivation 1.0, 2.0, and 3.0' refer to the motivational 'operating systems' – sets of assumptions and protocols about how the world works and how humans behave – that run beneath our laws, economic arrangements, and business practices. Motivation 1.0 presumed that humans were biological creatures, struggling for survival. Motivation 2.0 presumed that humans also responded to rewards and punishments in their environment. Motivation 3.0, the upgrade we now need, presumes that humans also have a third drive – to learn, to create, and to make a better world.

Multitasking

Multitasking is doing multiple things – performing multiple tasks – at the same time.

Myers-Briggs Type Indicators (MBTI)

These indicators are based on the idea that each personality type is composed of four pairs of preferences – or dichotomies – thus resulting in 16 different personality types.

Networking

Networking is about making connections and building enduring, mutually beneficial relationships.

Nice guy syndrome

This refers to a behavioural pattern of being overly nice to others.

Outsourcing

Outsourcing is where a business or other organisation, like a public sector body, contracts a third party to provide services or do work that previously would have been undertaken in-house by the organisation's own staff.

People skills

See soft skills.

Performance appraisal

A systematic and periodic process that assesses an employee's job performance and productivity in relation to pre-established criteria and organisational objectives, as well as identifying the potential for future improvement.

Performance development

Performance development is a broad term that includes performance management and employee development. It describes both assessing and managing the work that needs to be done and providing opportunities for professional growth and development.

Personal growth

The act of developing physically, mentally, emotionally or spiritually. Measured by an increase in self-awareness, happiness and ability to respond to challenges encountered in daily life.

Personality

There are many theories on personality, and most are in some way based on – or related to – the work of Carl Jung. There are both type and trait theories; trait personality questionnaires are useful in selection and recruitment as they can be more readily mapped to job requirements, whilst the type models are useful in personal and team development, as the type categories are helpful in understanding oneself and others.

PERT/CPM

PERT/CPM graphs provide a general overview of a project. They consist of activities and events. Activities are operations in the project that consume resources and take time. Events occur at a point in time and represent the beginning, the end (or both) of an activity.

Pervasive learning

Learning at the 'speed of need' through formal, informal and social learning modalities (Dan Pontefract).

PMBOK

A Guide to the Project Management Body of Knowledge (PMBOK Guide) is a book that presents a set of standard terminology and guidelines (a body of knowledge) for project management.

PRINCE2

Acronym for PRojects IN Controlled Environments, version 2. A project management methodology.

Prioritising and Organising

General competency: Prioritise the most important tasks, work flexibly and organise own workload efficiently.

Problem analysis

Problem analysis is about gaining more information about a problem and increasing understanding. This phase is all about fact finding and analysis, building a more comprehensive picture of both the goal(s) and the barrier(s).

Problem identification

Problem identification involves detecting and recognising that there is a problem, identifying the nature of the problem or, in other words, defining the problem. Identifying a very clearly defined and specific problem is the first critical step to successful problem solving.

Process

A specific ordering of work activities across time and place, with a beginning and an end, clearly defined inputs and outputs, a structure for action (Thomas Davenport).

Procrastination

Procrastination is carrying out less urgent tasks in preference to more urgent ones or doing more pleasurable things in place of less pleasurable ones, and thus putting off tasks to a later time, sometimes to the 'last minute' before the deadline.

Productivity

Productivity is an average measure of efficiency. It can be expressed as the ratio of output to inputs used, i.e., output per unit of input.

Professional competencies

Professional competencies are skills, knowledge and attributes that are valued by the other professionals that are connected to your profession; professional competencies may also be referred to as 'technical competencies'.

PURE

Acronym for Positive, Understood, Relevant, Ethical.

QA

Quality Assurance.

Resilience

General competency: Remain effective under a heavy workload, handle organisational frustrations positively and adapt to a changing work environment. Resilience is the process of adapting well in the face of adversity, trauma, tragedy, threats or significant sources of stress.

Root cause analysis

A root cause analysis is a systematic way of uncovering the 'roots' – or underlying causes of an identified problem, or the symptom of a problem.

SFC

Solution Focused Coaching – a coaching model, alternative to the GROW model.

SMART

SMART is a goal-setting tool. The acronym stands for Specific – Measurable – Attainable (or Achievable) – Relevant (or alternatively Realistic) – and Time-framed.

Six Thinking Hats

'Six Thinking Hats' is a self-help book by Edward de Bono that describes a tool for group discussion and individual thinking involving six coloured hats. Six Thinking Hats and the associated idea of parallel thinking – a process where focus is split in specific directions – provide a means for groups to plan thinking processes in a detailed and cohesive way, and in doing so to think together more effectively.

Socratic method

The Socratic method is a method of disciplined questioning that can be used to pursue thought in many directions and for many purposes, including: to explore complex ideas, to get to the truth of things, to open up issues and problems.

Soft skills

Also known as 'people skills' or 'interpersonal skills,' soft skills refers to the way you relate to and interact with other people, to the way you behave.

STAR

STAR is the acronym for Situation, Task, Actions, Results. It is a very efficient way of telling a story, particularly useful in behavioural interviews.

STOP

STOP is an acronym for Stop – Think – Organise – Proceed.

Stress

Stress is the body's response to change. Stress is defined in many different ways and the things that cause stress can vary from person to person. Stress affects our performance.

Team

A team is a small group of people who regularly meet – physically or online – to discuss shared agendas, causes, or interests. Each team is unique and draws on the backgrounds and abilities of its members. Depending on the situation, teams can have a different name: task force, work group, study group, commission, committee, or anything of the like.

Technical competencies

See professional competencies.

Telecommuting

Periodic work out of the principal office, one or more days per week, either at home, a client's site, or in a telework centre; the partial or total substitution of information technologies for the commute to work. Telecommuting is a form of teleworking.

Teleworking

Any form of substitution of information technologies (such as telecommunications and or computers) for regular work-related travel; moving the work to the workers instead of moving the workers to work.

Theory X and Theory Y

Douglas McGregor developed a view of humanity with his Theory X and Theory Y. These are two opposing perceptions about human behaviour at work.

Timeboxing

Timeboxing is a time management technique whereby the schedule is divided into a number of separate time periods, or timeboxes. Each timebox has its own deliverables, deadline and budget.

Time management

Time management is managing the amount of time you spend on specific activities, to increase your efficiency and productivity.

Trial and error

Trial and error is a method of learning in which various responses are tentatively tried, and some discarded, until a valid solution is reached.

Total Quality Management (TQM)

TQM consists of organization-wide efforts to install and make permanent a climate in which an organisation continuously improves its ability to deliver high-quality products and services to customers (Wikipedia).

Type I behaviour

Type I behaviour is a way of thinking and an approach to life built around intrinsic, rather than extrinsic, motivators. It is powered by our innate need to direct our own lives, to learn and create new things, and to better ourselves and our world (Daniel Pink).

Type X Behaviour

Type X behaviour is fuelled more by extrinsic desires than intrinsic ones and is concerned less with the inherent satisfaction provided by an activity and more with the external rewards to which the activity leads (Daniel Pink).

Understanding

Appreciation of 'why'. For example, elementary school children memorise knowledge of the 'times table'. They can tell you that '2 x 2 = 4' because they have amassed that knowledge (being included in the times table). But when asked what is '123 x 456', they cannot respond correctly because that entry is not in their times table. To correctly answer such a question requires understanding.

Values

The stated beliefs, standards, ethics and morals of an individual or organisation. They drive behaviour and how individuals perceive themselves and their place in the world. Can be used as a positive motivator for self-improvement.

Wisdom

Evaluated understanding. Wisdom deals with the future because it incorporates vision and design.

Working with others

General competency: Work co-operatively with others in teams and across organisational boundaries and respect differences between people.

Work-life balance

The equilibrium between how much time a person spends at work and how much time they spend at home, with family and friends. A good equilibrium supports long-term health and happiness.

Annex 3 Bibliography

'Applied Imagination: Principles and Procedures of Creative Problem Solving' (1953) by Alex F. Osborn (ISBN: 9780930222734)

'A Sense of Urgency' (2008) by John P. Kotter (ISBN: 9781423369356)

'A theory of goal setting and task performance' (1990) by Edwin Locke et al. (ISBN 9780139131387)

'Authentic Leadership – Rediscovering the Secrets of Creating Lasting Value' (2003) by Bill George (ISBN: 9780787969134)

'A Whole New Mind: Why Right-Brainers will rule the Future' (2006) by Daniel Pink (ISBN: 9781594481710)

'Brief: Make a Bigger Impact by Saying Less' (2014) by Joseph McCormack (ISBN: 9781118704967)

'Boreout – Overcoming workplace demotivation' (2008) by Peter Werder and Philippe Rothlin (ISBN: 9780749453398)

'Ces gestes qui vous trahissent' (2011) by Joseph Messinger (ISBN: 9782290035016)

'Coaching for Performance – GROWing human potential and Purpose' (2009) by Sir John Whitmore (ISBN: 9781857885354)

'Cultures and Organisations – Software of the Mind' (2010) by Geert Hofstede, Gert Jan Hofstede and Michael Minkov (ISBN: 9780071664189)

'Der Europäische Landbote: die Wut der Bürger und der Friede Europas' by Robert Menasse (ISBN: 9783552056169)

'Drive: The Surprising Truth About What Motivates Us' (2011) by Daniel H. Pink (ISBN 9781594484803)

'Effective Business Communications' (1997) by Herta A. Murphy et al. (ISBN: 9780070443983)

'Emotional Intelligence: Why It Can Matter More Than IQ' (1995) by Daniel Goleman (ISBN: 9780553383713)

'Finding Flow' (1998) by Mihaly Csíkszentmihályi (ISBN 9780465024117)

'Find Your Focus Zone' (2011) by Lucy Jo Palladino (ISBN: 9781416532019)

'First Things First' (1996) by Stephen Covey (ISBN 9780684802039)

'Flat Army: Creating a Connected and Engaged Organisation' by Dan Pontefract (ASIN: B00BY3OT2W)

'Fried – Why you Burn Out and how to Revive' (2012) by Joan Borysenko (ISBN: 9781401925512)

'Gamestorming: A Playbook for Innovators, Rulebreakers, and Changemakers' (2010) by Dave Gray, Sunny Brown and James Macanufo (ISBN: 9780596804176)

'Give and Take – Why Helping others Drives our Success' (2014) by Adam Grant (ISBN: 9780143124986)

'Growing Pains' (2007) by Flamholtz and Randle (ISBN 9780787986162)

'HBR Guide to Persuasive Presentations' (2012) by Nancy Duarte (ISBN: 9781422187104)

'Hot, Flat, and Crowded' (2009) by Thomas L. Friedman (ISBN: 9780141036663)

'How the EU Institutions Work' (2020) edited by Erik Akse (ISBN: 9781838089801)

'How to be a Productive Ninja' (2015) by Graham Allcott (ISBN: 9781848316836)

'How to win Friends and Influence People' (1998) by Dale Carnegie (ISBN: 9780671027032)

'Kaizen: The Key to Japan's Competitive Success' (1986) by Masaaki Imai (ISBN: 9780075543329)

'Leaders eat Last: Why some teams pull together and others don't' (2014) by Simon Sinek (ISBN: 9781591845324)

'Leadership Development: Maturity and Power' (1994) by Barr, L., & Barr, N. (ISBN: 9780890159453)

'Leadership in a Diverse and Multicultural Environment' (2005) by Mary Connerly and Paul Pedersen (ISBN: 9780761988601)

'Management of Organisational Behaviour' by Paul Hersey et al. (ISBN 9788120335455)

'Metaphors we live by' (1980) by George Lakoff and Mark Johnson (ISBN: 9780226468013)

'No More Mr Nice Guy' (2003) by Robert Glover (ISBN: 9780762415335)

'Our Iceberg is Melting' (2006) by John Kotter (ISBN: 9780230014206)

'Parkinson's Law: Or the Pursuit of Progress' (2002) by C. Northcote Parkinson (ISBN 9780141186856)

'Prendre la parole en public' (2009) by Bernard Blein (ISBN : 9782035843562)

'Primal Leadership' (2013) by Daniel Goleman et all (ISBN 9781422168035)

'Quiet: The Power of Introverts in a World that can't stop Talking' (2013) by Susan Cain (ISBN: 9780141029191)

'Real Leaders Don't Do Powerpoint – How to Speak so People Listen' (2009) by Christopher Witt (ISBN: 9780749942601)

'Rebel Ideas – The Power of Diverse Thinking' (2019) by Matthew Syed (ISBN: 9781473613942)

'Solution Focused Coaching in Practice: Essential Coaching Skills and Knowledge.' (2012) by O'Connell, B., Palmer, S., & Williams, H. (ASIN: B00ZT0WXVK)

'Start with Why – How Great Leaders Inspire Everyone to take Action' (2009) by Simon Sinek (ISBN: 9781591846444)

'Six Thinking Hats' (1999) by Edward de Bono (ISBN: 9780316178310)

'Targeting Success' (2011) by Lorii Myers (ISBN 9780986790003)

'The Art of Conversation' (1936) by Milton Wright (ASIN: B000H1DGTE)

'The Art of Conversation – A guided Tour of a Neglected Pleasure' (2009) by Catherine Blyth (ISBN: 9781592404971)

'The Attention Economy: Understanding the New Currency of Business' (2002) by Thomas H. Davenport and John C. Beck (ISBN: 9781578518715)

'The Career Architect Development Planner' (2000) by Michael Lombardo and Robert Eichinger (ISBN: 9780965571241)

'The Culture Map' (2014) by Erin Meyer (ISBN: 9781610392501)

'The European Commission – A Practical Guide' (2013) by Manuel Szapiro (ISBN: 9780957150133)

'The European Parliament' (2016) by Richard Corbett et al. (ISBN: 9780993454950)

'The Gen Z Effect – The Six Forces Shaping the Future of Business' (2014) by Tom Koulopoulos and Dan Keldsen (ISBN: 9781629560311)

'The Gifts of Imperfection' (2010) by Brené Brown (ISBN: 9781592858491)

'The Human Condition' (1998) by Hannah Arendt (ISBN: 9780226025988)

'The Human Side of Enterprise' (1960) by Douglas McGregor (ISBN: 9780070450929)

'The Inner Game of Work: Overcoming Mental Obstacles for Maximum Performance' (2000) by Timothy Gallwey (ISBN: 9781842030158)

'The Managerial Grid III: The Key to Leadership Excellence' (1985) by Blake, R., Mouton, J. (ISBN: 9780872014701)

'The Passage to Europe' (2013) by Luuk van Middelaar (ISBN: 9780300195408)

'The Peter Principle: Why Things Always go Wrong' (2011) by Laurence J. Peter and Raymond Hull (ISBN: 9780062092069)

'The Shallows: What the Internet is doing to our Brains' (2011) by Nicholas Carr (ISBN: 9780393339758)

'The Thinker's Guide to the Art of Socratic Questioning' (2007) by Richard Paul and Linda Elder (ASIN: B0065RPUGG)

'The Truth About Burnout – How Organisations Cause Personal Stress and What to Do About it' (2000) by Christina Maslach and Michael P. Leiter (ISBN: 9781118692134)

'The Ultimate EU Test Book - Assessment Centre 2021' (2021) by Andras Baneth and Jan De Sutter (ISBN: 9781838089825)

'The Upside of Stress – Why Stress is good for You, and how to get Good at It' (2015) by Kelly McGonigal (ISBN: 9781583335611)

'The Use of Lateral Thinking' (1967) by Edward de Bono (ISBN: 9780140137880)

'The World is Flat' (2011) by Thomas L. Friedman (ISBN: 9783125737990)

'Thinkertoys – A Handbook of Creative Thinking Techniques' (2006) by Michael Michalko (ISBN: 9781580087735)

'Thinking, fast and slow' (2012) by Daniel Kahneman (ISBN: 9780141033570)

'Thinking for a Living' (2005) by Thomas H. Davenport (ISBN: 9781591394235)

'Too Many Bosses, Too Few Leaders' (2012) by Rajeev Peshawaria (ISBN: 9781451646672)

'Victims of Groupthink: A psychological Study of foreign-policy decisions and fiascoes' (1972) by Irving Janis (ISBN: 9780395140444)

'Visual meetings: How Graphics, Sticky Notes & idea mapping can transform group productivity' (2010) by David Sibbet (ISBN: 9780470601785)

'Who moved my Cheese?' (1999) by Spencer Johnson (ISBN: 9780091816971)

'Wikinomics: How Mass Collaboration Changes Everything' (2010) by Don Tapscott and Anthony D. Williams (ISBN: 9781591843672)

'Working for the EU: How to get in' (2018) by Johannes de Berlaymont (ISBN: 9781999959531)

'Working with Emotional Intelligence' (1998) by Daniel Goleman (ISBN: 9780553378580)